Guide to
Risk Management
And
Internal Financial
Control

Contents

About the Author

He is a senior finance professional with over 35 Years of rich industry experience in overall business and finance function. He is a Chartered Accountant with CS and CMA qualifications and holds a diploma in IFRS from UK.

He possesses expertise in CFO solutions and his key skillsets include implementation of international best practices in finance, corporate governance, Merger & Acquisitions including financial due diligence, business valuation, business restructuring & strategic planning, project management in ERP, systems and process Audit, change management through business process re-engineering, Enterprise Risk Management and IFRS.

He has extensive knowledge and experience in industries like industrial gases, engineering polymers, agro chemicals, FMCG and dairy products, health care and manpower services among others.
He has handled many high profile leadership positions like CFO / VP / Director Finance assignments in global MNCs (BOC Gases, DuPont, and Kelly Services) and large Indian conglomerates (Mother Dairy group, Max India). Currently he is associated with an international non-profit organization specialising in healthcare.

He provides leadership in assignments related to management consulting, corporate governance and CFO solutions. He also teaches IFRS with a well-known International Institute and his students span across reputed Transnationals.

He is also an established author and his books include contemporary business and finance topics like International Financial Reporting Standards (IFRS), Indian Accounting Standards (Ind AS), Financial Reporting under Corporate Restructuring, Financial Reporting under consolidation of subsidiaries, associates and joint ventures and Business Valuation published by reputed publishers.

LINKED IN PROFILE: in.linkedin.com/pub/biswajeet-chatterjee/2/5a9/b6/

Address:
121/105 Silver Oaks Apartments
DLF Phase I
Gurgaon 122002.
HARYANA
Mobile: 9810119275

Preface to the book

Risk and internal control are two sides of the same coin. In any organization, operations and management entails risk taking. It is in the interest of the policies of the organization to ensure that risks are identified and managed with proper control mechanism.

In Chapter 1 we have tried to explain what is risk and how do we handle risk management. We have touched upon the concept of COSO framework of Enterprise Risk Management, and explained what is controlled environment, risk assessment, control activities, information and communications and monitoring activities.

In Chapter 2, we have provided a quick glimpse and refresher on corporate governance and its critical role as a prologue to the whole concept of enterprise risk management.

In Chapter 3 and 4 we have highlighted what is financial reporting and how internal financial control takes control over financial reporting.

In Chapter 5 till Chapter 17, we have tried to provide a practical orientation of COSO framework and its application in each of the functional elements of financial statements starting from Shareholders funds to recording to reporting process.

In Chapter 18, we tried to come up with a snap shot of internal financial control over financial reporting with respect to branches.

In Chapter 19, we have summarised various illustrations of specimen audit reports in accordance with the guideline provided by the Institute of Chartered Accountants of India.

While considerable care has been taken to ensure that the contents of the book are accurate, a few errors and omissions might have crept in, for which I seek with all humility to my readers to bear with me.

I would like dedicate this book to my loving parents without whose constant inspiration this would not have been possible.

I would also like to thank my wife who stood by my side to ensure that the book saw the light of day.

B D Chatterjee

121/105 Silver Oaks Apartments
DLF Phase I
Gurgaon 122002
Email: bdchatterjee105@gmail.com

Chapter 1: Risk Management

1.1. What is risk?

According to Dowd (2005), Risk refers to the chance of financial losses due to random changes in underlying risk factors.

A risk is a random event that may possibly occur and, if it did occur, would have a negative impact on the goals of the organization. It is the probability of incurring loss due to unexpected and unfavourable movement of certain parameters.

Risk is composed of three elements — the scenario, its probability of occurrence, and the size of its impact if it did occur (either a fixed value or a distribution). Risk is thus measured by volatility.

An opportunity is also a random variable which is the other side of the coin! But it has a positive impact on the goals of the organization.

In the corporate world, accepting risks is necessary to obtain a competitive advantage and generate profit. Introducing new product or expanding production facilities involves both return and risk. When a company is exposed to an event that can cause a shortfall in a targeted financial measure or value, this is financial risk.

1.2. Types of risk

Types of risk are categorised below.

a) Political risk:	Political risk is defined as "the possibility of a multinational company being significantly affected by political events in a host country or a change in the political relationships between a host country and one or more other countries". Political risk is the unwanted consequences of political activities that will have effect on the value of the firm.
b) Country risk:	The country risk is defined as exposure to a loss in offshore lending, caused by events in a particular country, events which are, at least to some extent, under control of the Government but definitely not under the control of a private enterprise or individual. Country risk is a broad concept encompassing sovereign, political as well as other forms of risks like economic, social and external risks.
c) Economic risk:	Economic risk is concerned with the general economic climate within the country. Some of the factors which reflect the economic climate of a country are: (a) level of affluence enjoyed by the country. (b) the growth rate of income. (c) the nation's propensity to save/invest. (d) the stability of prices (inflation). (e) characteristics of the labour force. (f) level of sophistication of the financial system. (g) level of foreign debt outstanding. (h) major income earners (exports) and their sensitivity to overall global economic changes. (i) extent of dependence on major export items.

	(j) trends in balance of payments.
	(k) level of imports
	(l) level of reserve and credit standing, and
	(m) fluctuations of exchange rate and controls on foreign exchange.
d) Social risk	Social risk refers to the possibilities of loss due to factors such as religious fanaticism, ethnic polarization, dissatisfaction among the people as a result of wide disparity in income distribution, or regionalism. These sociological problems eventually lead to riot and revolutions resulting in loss of lives and property. An economy plagued by riots and revolutions will undoubtedly face problems in repaying its debts.
e) External risk	The external risk component of country risk arises due to situations outside the country. For instance, if the borrower nation is situated beside a country which is at war, the country risk ratios of the prospective borrower will be higher than what will be the case if its neighbour is at peace. This difference in the risk rating is attributable to external risk.
f) Exchange risk	The liability of the borrower of the foreign currency financing remains in the currency in which the borrower obtains loan, hence at the time of repayment the rupee liability is determined on the basis of the exchange rate prevailing on the date of repayment. The exchange rate fluctuates widely with the passage of time, so the borrower is subject to exposure to exchange rate fluctuations on the outstanding principal of the foreign currency financing. Further if the borrowing is made at a floating rate of interest, there can be substantial variations in the rate of interest with the passage of time, depends on the variations in the LIBOR.
g) Business risk	A company's business risk is determined by how it invest its funds i.e., the type of projects which it undertakes, while financial risk is determined by how it finances these investments. A company's competitive position, the industries in which it operates, the company's market share, the rate of growth of the market and the stage of maturity all influence business risk. Business risk relates to volatility of revenues and profits of a particular company due to its market conditions, product mix, input availability, competitive market condition, labour supply etc
h) Financial risk	Financial risk is primarily influenced by the level of financial gearing, interest cover, operating leverage, and cash flow adequacy. The financial risk depends on the method of financing adopted by the company. Financial risk is associated with the capital structure of a firm. A firm with no debt financing has no financial risk.
i) Systematic risk	Systematic risk refers to that part of total risk which causes the movement in individual stock price due to changes in general stock market index. Systematic risk arises out of external and uncontrollable factors. The price of individual security reflects the fluctuations and changes of general market. Systematic risk refers to that portion of variation in return caused by factors that affect the price of all securities

j) Unsystematic risk	Unsystematic risk is that portion of total risk which results from known and controllable factors. Unsystematic risk refers to that portion of the risk which is caused due to factors unique or related to a firm or industry. The unsystematic risk is the change in the price of stocks due to the factors which are particular to the stock. For example, if excise duty or customs duty on viscose fibre increases, the price of stocks of synthetic yarn industry declines. The unsystematic risk can be eliminated or reduced by diversification of portfolio
k) Market risk	The market risk arises due to changes in demand and supply, expectations of the investors, information flow, investor's risk perception etc. Variations in price sparked off due to real social, political and economic events are referred to as market risk.
l) Interest rate risk	The return on investment depends on the market rate of interest, which changes from time to time. The cost of corporate debt depends on the interest rates prevailing, maturity periods, creditworthiness of the borrowers, monetary and credit policy of the central bank, riskiness of the investments, expectations of the investors etc. The uncertainty of future market values and the size of future incomes, caused by fluctuations in the general level of interest are known as 'interest rate risk'.
m) Purchasing power risk	Uncertainty of purchasing power is referred to as risk due to inflation. If investment is considered as consumption sacrificed, then a person, purchasing securities, foregoes the opportunity to buy some goods or services for so long as he continues to hold the securities. In case, the prices of goods and services, increases during this period, the investor actually loses purchasing power.
n) Default risk	The default risk arises due to the default in meeting the financial obligations as and when due for payment. The non-payment of interest and principal amounts in time will increase the risk of insolvency and bankruptcy costs. The default risk or insolvency risk will cause a sudden dip in company's stock prices.
o) Liquidity risk	It is that portion of an asset's total variability of return which results from price discounts given or sales commissions paid in order to sell the asset without delay. It is a situation wherein it may not be possible to sell the asset. Assets are disposed off at great inconvenience and cost in terms of money and time. Any asset that can be bought or sold quickly is said to be liquid. Failure to realize with minimum discount to its value of an asset is called liquidity risk.
p) Callability risk	It is that portion of security's total variability of returns that derives from the possibility that the issue may be called or redeemed before maturity. Callability risk commands a risk premium that comes in the form of a slightly higher average rate of return. This additional return should increase as the risk increases.
q) Convertibility risk	It is that portion of the total variability of return from a convertible bond or a convertible preferred stock that reflects the possibility that the investment

	may be converted into the issuer's common stock at a time or under terms harmful to the investor's best interests.
r) Currency risk	These are associated with international investments not denominated in the home currency of the portfolio manager's beneficiaries. These risks involve the international payment of cash.
s) Industry risk	It is that portion of an investment's total variability of return caused by events that affect the products and firms that make upon industry, the stage of the industry's life cycle, international tariffs and/or quotas on the product produced by an industry.

1.3. Risk Universe

The diagrammatic representation below provides the Risk Universe. Risk Universe spreads around the normal management cycle Business Management, operations, information, financial, governance cycle along with the external environment. Risk Universe clearly defines the range and possibilities of risk and lays the foundation to risk management process.

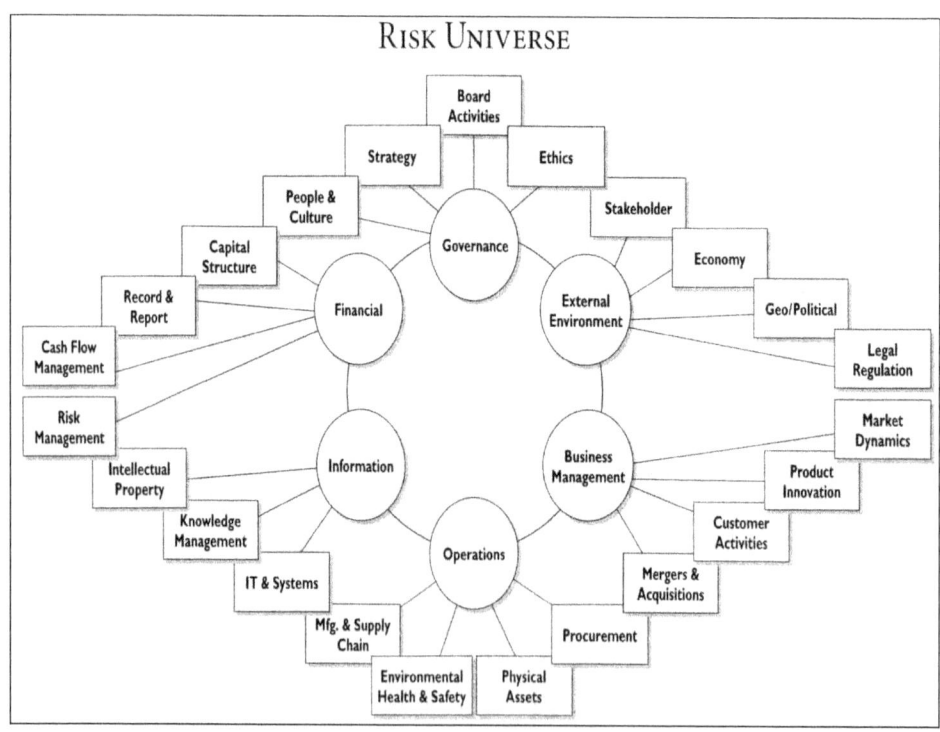

1.4. Risk Management

Risk management is the process of measuring or assessing risk and developing strategies to manage it. Risk management is a systematic approach in identifying, analyzing and controlling areas or events with a potential for causing unwanted change. It is through risk management that risks to any specific program are assessed and systematically managed to reduce risk to an acceptable level. Risk management is the act or practice of controlling risk. It includes risk planning, assessing risk areas, developing risk handling options, monitoring risks to determine how risks have changed and documenting overall risk management program.

1.4.1. Objectives of risk management

The objectives of risk management are as under:

(a)Anticipating the uncertainty and the degree of uncertainty of the events not happening the way they are planned.

(b) Channelizing events to happen the way they are planned.

(c) Setting right, at the earliest opportunity, deviations from plans, whenever they occur.

(d) Ensuring that the objective of the planned event is achieved by alternative means, when the means chosen proves wrong, and

(e) In case the expected event is frustrated, making the damage minimal.

1.4.2. Risk Management process

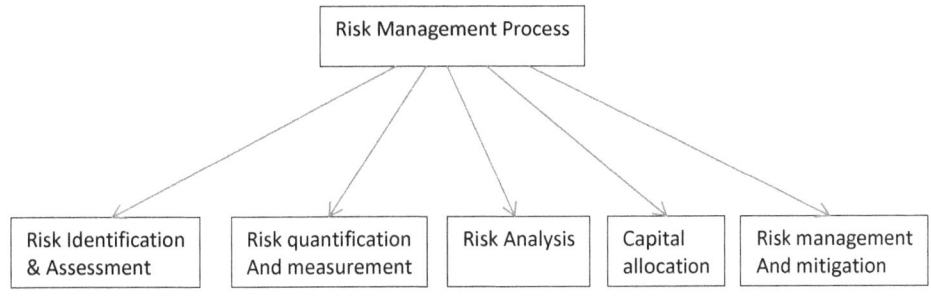

The steps are as under:

Step 1: Risk Identification and Assessment	This step involves event identification and data collection process. The institution has to put in place a system of capturing information either through key risk drivers (KRIs) or through a rating system. Once risks are identified, combine like risks according to the following key areas impacted by the risks — people, mission, physical assets, financial assets, and customer/stakeholder trust.
Step 2: Risk Quantification and Measurement	The next step is to Quantify and Measure risks-this means Rate risks according to probability and impact. Various standard tools are used by financial institutions to measure risk and understand their impact in terms of capital or its importance to the organization through a scoring technique.
Step 3: Risk Analysis, Monitor and Reporting	The next step is risk analysis, monitoring and reporting. This will help one to get the big picture and decided on the approach to risk management.

Step 4: Capital Allocation	Risk Analysis, Monitoring & Reporting sends information to the top management of the organization to take strategic decisions. Capital allocation plays key role in management decision making.
Step 5: Risk Management and Mitigation	After the above step, the last step is to make strategic decisions to manage the risk in order to mitigate the risk.

1.5. Risk Analytics – Risk mapping, risk retention and risk mitigation

Risk analytics is a procedure to identify threats & vulnerabilities, analyze them to ascertain the exposures, and highlight how the impact can be eliminated or reduced. In other words, risk analytics refers to the uncertainty of forecasted future cash flows streams, variance of portfolio/stock returns, statistical analysis to determine the probability of a project's success or failure, and possible future economic states. Risk analysts often work in tandem with forecasting professionals to minimize future negative unforseen effects.

1.5.1. Risk mapping

Risk mapping is the first step in operational risk measurement, since it requires identifying all potential risks to which the organisation is exposed and then pointing out those on which attention and monitoring would be warranted.

A risk map is a graphical depiction of a select number of a company's risks designed to (1) illustrate the *impact or significance* of risk on one axis, and (2) the *likelihood or frequency* on the other axis. Many types and variations of risk maps exist.

This risk map depicts likelihood or frequency on the vertical axis, and impact or significance on the horizontal axis. In this configuration, similar to that of a mathematical distribution curve, likelihood increases as one moves up the vertical axis, and impact increases from left to right.

The points on the profile represent risks that have been categorized into four *impact* categories and six *likelihood* categories. The categories simplify the prioritization process by forcing placement of each risk into a particular box showing its position relative to the others.

A specimen risk map or risk categorisation matrix called Holcim's risk matrix is highlighted below for easy reference.

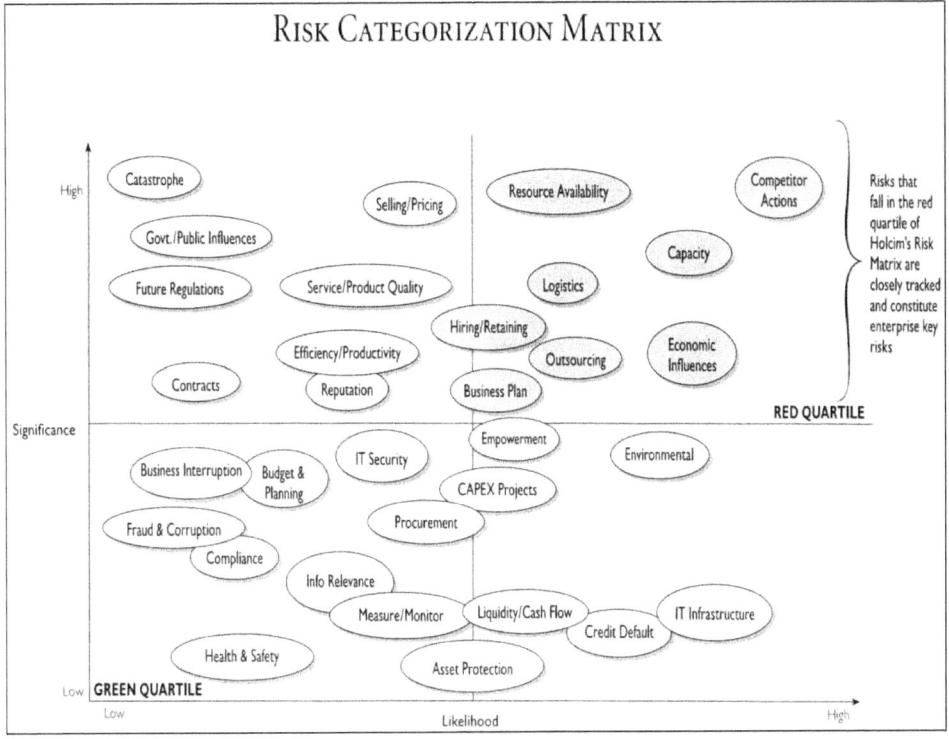

RISK CATEGORIZATION MATRIX

As mentioned in the Chart above, risks falling in red quartile of the risk matrix constitute key risks and are closely tracked.

1.5.2. Benefits of Risk mapping

- Promotes awareness of significant risks through priority ranking, facilitating the efficient planning of resources.
- Enables the delivery of solutions and services across the entire risk management value chain.
- Serves as a powerful aid to strategic business planning.
- Aids the development of an action plan for the effective management of significant risks.
- Assigns clear responsibilities to individuals for the management of particular risk areas.
- Provides an opportunity to leverage risk management as a competitive advantage.
- Facilitates the development of a strategic approach to insurance programme design.
- Supports the design of the client's risk financing and insurance programmes, through the development of effective/optimal retention levels and scope of coverage etc.

1.5.3. Key Risk Indicator

Key risk indicators come out as the result of the mapping process and should be used to provide anticipatory signals that can be useful for both operational risk prevention and measurement. In particular, they should provide early warning signals to anticipate the most critical operational events, and they may also be partly derived from the experience of audit departments defining

potential risk scores for different business units as a tool for defining priorities in their audit action plan.

1.6. Risk retention

This denotes acceptance of the loss or benefit arising out of a risk when it takes place. In short, it is also termed as self-insurance. This strategy is viable when the risks are small enough to be transferred at a cost that may be higher than the loss arising out of the risk itself. On the other hand, the risk can be so big that it cannot be transferred or insured. Such risks will have to be phased out when the eventuality occurs.

The reasons for risk retention can be cited as follows:

(1) While risk in a business is taken to increase its return, risk retention relates to such risks which have no relation to return but are part of an individual's life or organization or a company operational risk can be cited as such a risk that is inherent and needs to be accepted for retention.

(2) Sometimes, such risks are so small that they are ignored and/or phased out when they surface.

(3) This method is also useful when the probability of occurrence is very low and a reserve built within the system over a period can take care of such losses arising out of risk retention. This is normally resorted to in businesses against credit risks that are inherent due to marketing on credit basis.

(4) In some cases, the subject, who is susceptible to risk, also becomes fully aware of the nature of risk. In these situations, there is a certain amount of preparedness in the system due to risk retention

1.7. Risk mitigation

Risk reduction or optimization aims at reduction in the severity of laws or the probability that laws may not be passed. While risks can be helpful or harmful, optimization leads to a balance between negative risk and the advantages of the operation.

Risk reduction can also be termed as mitigation that would include all measures taken to reduce the effect of the hazard itself as well as the vulnerable conditions leading to the hazard. Risk reduction also includes steps to mitigate physical, economic, and social vulnerability.

The mitigation carried out is such that there should be an ultimate reduction in the loss due to a hazard. Sometimes certain steps taken to mitigate a hazard may turn out to be more damaging, as in the case of certain fire suppression systems. The cost of such steps is so prohibitive that the losses cannot be reduced intrinsically. Outsourcing can be considered an act of risk reduction if the vendor has the expertise and a higher capability in mitigating risk. For example, demolition of an old, risky, high-rise building could be outsourced to an expert vendor who could implode the building without causing any damage to the environment or people.

Risk mitigation also implies a certain extent of preparedness on the part of the risk bearer because he is aware of the risk. This helps identify the parameters that lead to the disaster and mitigate parameters ahead of the eventuality, thus reducing the risk. Studies based on HAZOP are known to help factories develop sufficient preparedness in case of a hazard or explosion. It is sometimes known as 'failsafe' activity.

1.7.1 Mitigation strategy

The plans recognize the fact that effective community involvement and public awareness can largely minimize the impact or disasters. The community-based mitigation strategy strengthens and

stabilizes the efforts of the administration. The focus is on community capacity building including formation of Community Emergency Response Teams (CERT).

Mitigation strategy also focuses on micro-risk assessment and vulnerability analysis including hazard mapping, applied research and technology transfer to improve the quality of forecast and disseminate warnings quickly. It also highlights the need for a disaster management legislation and relief and rehabilitation policy that would define specific roles and responsibilities as well as set-up permanent administrative structures and institutional mechanisms for disaster management. The importance of land use planning and regulations for sustainable development, which include development and implementation of building codes, serve as a guideline to managing disaster. Structural and non-structural measures, given in the mitigation strategy document, are used to avoid damages during disasters.

1.7.2. Case study: Risk mitigation strategy: Unilever group
Principal risk factors

Our business is subject to risks and uncertainties. On the following pages we have identified the risks that we regard as the most relevant to our business. These are the risks that we see as most material to Unilever's business and performance at this time. There may be other risks that could emerge in the future. We have also commented below on certain mitigating actions that we believe help us to manage these risks. However, we may not be successful in deploying some or all of these mitigating actions. If the circumstances in these risks occur or are not successfully mitigated, our cash flow, operating results, financial position, business and reputation could be materially adversely affected. In addition, risks and uncertainties could cause actual results to vary from those described, which may include forward-looking statements, or could impact on our ability to meet our targets or be detrimental to our profitability or reputation.

Description of risk	What are we doing to manage the risk
1.BRAND PREFERENCE As a branded goods business, Unilever's success depends on the value and relevance of our brands and products to consumers across the world and on our ability to innovate and remain competitive. Consumer tastes, preferences and behaviours are constantly changing and Unilever's ability to anticipate and respond to these changes and to continue to differentiate our brands and products is vital to our business. We are dependent on creating innovative products that continue to meet the needs of our consumers. If we are unable to innovate effectively, Unilever's sales or margins could be materially adversely affected.	We continuously monitor external market trends and collate consumer, customer and shopper insight in order to develop category and brand strategies. Our strategy focuses on investing in markets and segments which we identify as attractive because we have already built, or are confident that we can build, competitive advantage. Our Research and Development function actively searches for ways in which to translate the trends in consumer preference and taste into new technologies for incorporation into future products. Our innovation management process deploys tools, technologies and resources to convert category strategies into projects and category plans, develop products and relevant brand communication and successfully roll out new products to our consumers.
2.PORTFOLIO MANAGEMENT	Our Compass strategy and our business plans are designed to ensure that resources are prioritised

Unilever's strategic investment choices will affect the long-term growth and profits of our business. Unilever's growth and profitability are determined by our portfolio of categories, geographies and channels and how these evolve over time. If Unilever does not make optimal strategic investment decisions then opportunities for growth and improved margin could be missed.	towards those categories and markets having the greatest long-term potential for Unilever. Our acquisition activity is driven by our portfolio strategy with a clear, defined evaluation process.
3.SUSTAINABILITY The success of our business depends on finding sustainable solutions to support long-term growth. Unilever's Vision to double the size of our business while reducing our environmental footprint and increasing our positive social impact will require more sustainable ways of doing business. This means reducing our environmental footprint while increasing the positive social benefits of Unilever's activities. We are dependent on the efforts of partners and various certification bodies to achieve our sustainability goals. There can be no assurance that sustainable business solutions will be developed and failure to do so could limit Unilever's growth and profit potential and damage our corporate reputation.	The Unilever Sustainable Living Plan sets clear long-term commitments to improve health and well-being, reduce environmental impact and enhance livelihoods. Underpinning these are targets in areas such as hygiene, nutrition, sustainable sourcing, fairness in the workplace, opportunities for women and inclusive business as well as greenhouse gas emissions, water and waste. These targets and more sustainable ways of operating are being integrated into Unilever's day-to-day business. Progress towards the Unilever Sustainable Living Plan is monitored by the Unilever Leadership Executive and the Boards. The Unilever Sustainable Living Plan Council, comprising six external specialists in sustainability, guides and critiques the development of our strategy.
4.CUSTOMER RELATIONSHIPS Successful customer relationships are vital to our business and continued growth. Maintaining strong relationships with our customers is necessary for our brands to be well presented to our consumers and available for purchase at all times. The strength of our customer relationships also affects our ability to obtain pricing and secure favourable trade terms. Unilever may not be able to maintain strong relationships with customers and failure to do so could negatively impact the terms of business with the affected customers and reduce the availability of our products to consumers.	We build and maintain trading relationships across a broad spectrum of channels ranging from centrally managed multinational customers through to small traders accessed via distributors in many developing countries. We develop joint business plans with our key customers that include detailed investment plans and customer service objectives and we regularly monitor progress. We have developed capabilities for customer sales and outlet design which enable us to find new ways to improve customer performance and enhance our customer relationships.
5.TALENT	Resource committees have been established and implemented throughout our business. These committees have responsibility for identifying

A skilled workforce is essential for the continued success of our business.
Our ability to attract, develop and retain the right number of appropriately qualified people is critical if we are to compete and grow effectively.
This is especially true in our key emerging markets where there can be a high level of competition for a limited talent pool. The loss of management or other key personnel or the inability to identify, attract and retain qualified personnel could make it difficult to manage the business and could adversely affect operations and financial results.

future skills and capability needs, developing career paths and identifying the key talent and leaders of the future.
We have an integrated management development process which includes regular performance reviews underpinned by a common set of leadership behaviours, skills and competencies.
We have targeted programmes to attract and retain top talent and we actively monitor our performance in retaining talent within Unilever.

6.SUPPLY CHAIN
Our business depends on purchasing materials, efficient manufacturing and the timely distribution of products to our customers.
Our supply chain network is exposed to potentially adverse events such as physical disruptions, environmental and industrial accidents or bankruptcy of a key supplier which could impact our ability to deliver orders to our customers.
The cost of our products can be significantly affected by the cost of the underlying commodities and materials from which they are made. Fluctuations in these costs cannot always be passed on to the consumer through pricing.

We have contingency plans designed to enable us to secure alternative key material supplies at short notice, to transfer or share production between manufacturing sites and to use substitute materials in our product formulations and recipes.
These contingency plans also extend to an ability to intervene directly to support a key supplier should it for any reason find itself in difficulty or be at risk of negatively affecting a Unilever product.
We have policies and procedures designed to ensure the health and safety of our employees and the products in our facilities, and to deal with major incidents or crises including business continuity and disaster recovery.
Commodity price risk is actively managed through forward buying of traded commodities and other hedging mechanisms. Trends are monitored and modelled regularly and integrated into our forecasting process.

7. SAFE AND HIGH QUALITY PRODUCTS
The quality and safety of our products are of paramount importance for our brands and our reputation.
The risk that raw materials are accidentally or maliciously contaminated throughout the supply chain or that other product defects occur due to human error, equipment failure or other factors cannot be excluded.

Our product quality processes and controls are comprehensive, from product design to customer shelf. They are verified annually, and regularly monitored through performance indicators that drive continuous improvement activities. Our key suppliers are externally certified and the quality of material received is regularly monitored to ensure that it meets the rigorous quality standards that our products demand.
In the event of an incident relating to the safety of our consumers or the quality of our products,

<table>
<tr><td></td><td>incident management teams are activated in the affected markets under the direction of our product quality, science, and communications experts, to ensure timely and effective market place action.</td></tr>
<tr><td>

8.SYSTEMS AND INFORMATION

Unilever's operations are increasingly dependent on IT systems and the management of information.

We interact electronically with customers, suppliers and consumers in ways which place ever greater emphasis on the need for secure and reliable IT systems and infrastructure and careful management of the information that is in our possession.

Disruption of our IT systems could inhibit our business operations in a number of ways, including disruption to sales, production and cash flows, ultimately impacting our results.

There is also a threat from unauthorised access and misuse of sensitive information. Unilever's information systems could be subject to unauthorised access or the mistaken disclosure of information which disrupts Unilever's business and/or leads to loss of assets.

</td><td>

Hardware that runs and manages core operating data is fully backed up with separate contingency systems to provide real time back-up operations should they ever be required.

We maintain a global system for the control and reporting of access to our critical IT systems. This is supported by an annual programme of testing of access controls.

We have policies covering the protection of both business and personal information, as well as the use of IT systems and applications by our employees. Our employees are trained to understand these requirements.

We have standardised ways of hosting information on our public websites and have systems in place to monitor compliance with appropriate privacy laws and regulations, and with our own policies.

</td></tr>
<tr><td>

9.BUSINESS TRANSFORMATION

Successful execution of business transformation projects is key to delivering their intended business benefits and avoiding disruption to other business activities.

Unilever is continually engaged in major change projects, including acquisitions and disposals and outsourcing, to drive continuous improvement in our business and to strengthen our portfolio and capabilities.

Failure to execute such transactions or change projects successfully, or performance issues with third party outsourced providers on which we are dependent, could result in under-delivery of the expected benefits. Furthermore, disruption may be caused in other parts of the business.

</td><td>

All acquisitions, disposals and global restructuring projects are sponsored by a member of the Unilever Leadership Executive. Regular progress updates are provided to the Unilever Leadership Executive.

Sound project disciplines are used in all merger, acquisitions, restructuring and outsourcing projects and these projects are resourced by dedicated and appropriately qualified personnel. The performance of third party outsourced providers is kept under constant review, with potential disruption limited to the time and cost required to install alternative providers.

Unilever also monitors the volume of change programmes under way in an effort to stagger the impact on current operations and to ensure minimal disruption.

</td></tr>
<tr><td>

10. EXTERNAL ECONOMIC AND POLITICAL RISKS AND NATURAL DISASTERS

</td><td></td></tr>
<tr><td></td><td>The breadth of Unilever's portfolio and our</td></tr>
</table>

Unilever operates across the globe and is exposed to a range of external economic and political risks and natural disasters that may affect the execution of our strategy or the running of our operations.

Adverse economic conditions may result in reduced consumer demand for our products, and may affect one or more countries within a region, or may extend globally.

Government actions such as fiscal stimulus, changes to taxation and price controls can impact on the growth and profitability of our local operations.

Social and political upheavals and natural disasters can disrupt sales and operations.

In 2014, more than half of Unilever's turnover came from emerging markets including Brazil, India, Indonesia, Turkey, South Africa, China, Mexico and Russia. These markets offer greater growth opportunities but also expose Unilever to economic, political and social volatility in these markets.

geographic reach help to mitigate our exposure to any particular localised risk to an extent. Our flexible business model allows us to adapt our portfolio and respond quickly to develop new offerings that suit consumers' and customers' changing needs during economic downturns.

We regularly update our forecast of business results and cash flows and, where necessary, rebalance investment priorities.

We have continuity planning designed to deal with crisis management in the event of political and social events and natural disasters.

We believe that many years of exposure to emerging markets have given us experience operating and developing our business successfully during periods of economic, political or social change.

11.TREASURY AND PENSIONS

Unilever is exposed to a variety of external financial risks in relation to Treasury and Pensions.

Changes to the relative value of currencies can fluctuate widely and could have a significant impact on business results. Further, because Unilever consolidates its financial statements in euros it is subject to exchange risks associated with the translation of the underlying net assets and earnings of its foreign subsidiaries.

We are also subject to the imposition of exchange controls by individual countries which could limit our ability to import materials paid in foreign currency or to remit dividends to the parent company.

Currency rates, along with demand cycles, can also result in significant swings in the prices of the raw materials needed to produce our goods.

Unilever may face liquidity risk, i.e. difficulty in meeting its obligations, associated with its financial liabilities. A material and sustained shortfall in our cash flow could undermine Unilever's credit rating, impair investor confidence and also restrict Unilever's ability to raise funds.

Currency exposures are managed within prescribed limits and by the use of forward foreign exchange contracts. Further, operating companies borrow in local currency except where inhibited by local regulations, lack of local liquidity or local market conditions. We also hedge some of our exposures through the use of foreign currency borrowing or forward exchange contracts.

Our interest rate management approach aims to achieve an optimal balance between fixed and floating rate interest exposures on expected net debt.

We seek to manage our liquidity requirements by maintaining access to global debt markets through short-term and long-term debt programmes. In addition, we have high committed credit facilities for general corporate purposes.

Group treasury regularly monitors exposure to our banks, tightening counter-party limits where appropriate. Unilever actively manages its banking exposures on a daily basis.

We regularly assess and monitor counter-party risk in our customers and take appropriate action to manage our exposures.

Our pension investment standards require us to

We are exposed to market interest rate fluctuations on our floating rate debt. Increases in benchmark interest rates could increase the interest cost of our floating rate debt and increase the cost of future borrowings.

In times of financial market volatility, we are also potentially exposed to counter-party risks with banks, suppliers and customers.

Certain businesses have defined benefit pension plans, most now closed to new employees, which are exposed to movements in interest rates, fluctuating values of underlying investments and increased life expectancy. Changes in any or all of these inputs could potentially increase the cost to Unilever of funding the schemes and therefore have an adverse impact on profitability and cash flow.

invest across a range of equities, bonds, property, alternative assets and cash such that the failure of any single investment will not have a material impact on the overall value of assets. The majority of our assets, including those held in our 'pooled' investment vehicle, Univest, are managed by external fund managers and are regularly monitored by pension trustees and central pensions and investment teams.

Further information on financial instruments and capital and treasury risk management is included in note 16 on pages 114 to 119.

12.ETHICAL

Acting in an ethical manner, consistent with the expectations of customers, consumers and other stakeholders, is essential for the protection of the reputation of Unilever and its brands.

Unilever's brands and reputation are valuable assets and the way in which we operate, contribute to society and engage with the world around us is always under scrutiny both internally and externally. Despite the commitment of Unilever to ethical business and the steps we take to adhere to this commitment, there remains a risk that activities or events cause us to fall short of our desired standard, resulting in damage to Unilever's corporate reputation and business results.

Our Code of Business Principles and our Code Policies govern the behaviour of our employees, suppliers, distributors and other third parties who work with us.

Our processes for identifying and resolving breaches of our Code of Business Principles and our Code Policies are clearly defined and regularly communicated throughout Unilever. Data relating to such breaches is reviewed by the Unilever Leadership Executive and by relevant Board committees and helps to determine the allocation of resources for future policy development, process improvement, training and awareness initiatives.

13.LEGAL AND REGULATORY

Compliance with laws and regulations is an essential part of Unilever's business operations.

Unilever is subject to local, regional and global laws and regulations in such diverse areas as product safety, product claims, trademarks, copyright, patents, competition, employee health and safety, the environment, corporate governance, listing and disclosure, employment and taxes.

Unilever is committed to complying with the laws and regulations of the countries in which we operate. In specialist areas the relevant teams at global, regional or local levels are responsible for setting detailed standards and ensuring that all employees are aware of and comply with regulations and laws specific and relevant to their roles.

Our legal and regulatory specialists are heavily involved in monitoring and reviewing our

Failure to comply with laws and regulations could expose Unilever to civil and/or criminal actions leading to damages, fines and criminal sanctions against us and/or our employees with possible consequences for our corporate reputation. Changes to laws and regulations could have a material impact on the cost of doing business. Tax, in particular, is a complex area where laws and their interpretation are changing regularly, leading to the risk of unexpected tax exposure.	practices to provide reasonable assurance that we remain aware of and in line with all relevant laws and legal obligations. We have a Tax Risk Framework in place which sets out the controls established to assess and monitor tax risk for direct and indirect taxes.

(Source: Unilever Group: Annual Report 2014)

1.7.3. CASE STUDY: ENTERPRISE RISK MANAGEMENT: RELIANCE INDUSTRIES LIMITED

1. INTRODUCTION

Reliance actively stimulates entrepreneurship throughout the organisation and encourages its people to identify and seize opportunities. The current economic environment in combination with significant growth ambitions of the Reliance Group carries with it an evolving set of risks. Reliance recognises that these risks need to be managed to protect its customers, employees, shareholders and other stakeholders to achieve its business objectives and enable sustainable growth. Risk and opportunity management is therefore a key element of the overall Reliance strategy. This section provides an overview of the key strategic risks, the Reliance risk and control framework and its approach to risk management.

2. CREATING VALUE THROUGH RISK MANAGEMENT

Reliance operates in diverse industries and global markets and therefore requires a balanced approach to risk management. The Company's risk management framework encompasses internal control in an integrated manner and is tailored to the specific Reliance segments, businesses and functions. It takes into account various factors such as the size and nature of the inherent risks and the regulatory environment of the individual business segment or operating company. This framework undergoes continuous improvements to allow Reliance management to optimise its management of risk exposures while taking advantage of business opportunities.

3. RELIANCE'S VIEW ON RISK

3.1 RISK APPETITE

Reliance's risk appetite is linked to its strategic approach and is based on the stance it has taken across four areas:

- **Strategic and Commercial**: Reliance manages strategic risk in the pursuit of profitable growth in both mature and emerging markets. Given the volatile markets and economic climate in which it operates, the adaptability of its people, its service offering and its infrastructure are key.
- **Safety and Operations**: Reliance is committed to conduct all its activities in such a manner as to avoid harm to employees and the community. Reliance strive to deliver safe, reliable and compliant operations.
- **Compliance and Control**: Compliance with laws and regulations is fundamental to maintaining its license to operate in the various industries that it operates in. Reliance also believes that accurate and reliable information provides a competitive advantage and is key to effective management of its business. It therefore accepts minimal risk in relation to reporting risks.
- **Financial**: Reliance manages financial risk to maintain a prudent financing strategy, even when undertaking major investment and therefore taking controlled risks in this area.

3.2 RISK FACTORS

Reliance emphasises on those risks that threaten the achievement of business objectives of the Group over the short to medium-term. As part of its annual planning process, Reliance review the principal risks and uncertainties to the group. It identifies those as having a high priority for particular oversight by the board and its various committees. An overview of these risks is provided hereafter, including the actions taken to mitigate these risks and any related opportunities:

I. STRATEGIC AND COMMERCIAL RISKS

a. Commodity Prices and markets

Reliance's financial performance is subject to the fluctuating prices of crude oil and gas and downstream petroleum products. Prices of oil and gas products are affected by supply and demand, both globally and regionally. Factors that influence fluctuations in crude prices and crude availability include operational issues, natural disasters, political instability, economic conditions and Government pricing policy of petroleum products among others.

Mitigation: Since Reliance operates an integrated hydrocarbon business, some of these risks can be offset by gains in other parts of the Group. To mitigate the risks resulting from non-availability of crude and feedstock, Reliance has a diversified crude sourcing strategy from multiple geographies (Asia, the Middle East, West Africa, Latin/ South America and North Africa) under both short-term and long-term arrangements. In addition, Reliance has put in place commodity risk management policies which provide the framework for decision making with respect to exposures from commodity trading positions.

b. Major Project Execution Risk

Reliance's future growth plans depend upon successful delivery of major capital projects. Major capital projects include the Jamnagar expansion project (cracker, gasification etc.), which is designed to deliver a step change in energy costs and increase the production capacity of ethylene and other downstream products at the complex, as well as the launch of a pan India telecom infrastructure to provide 4G LTE TDD high speed wireless internet and mobile communication services. Delivery of these major projects is key to Reliance's future financial performance. Managing the risks related to the delivery of these and other major capital projects is key to enhancing Reliance's longterm shareholder value.

Mitigation: Project risk management is embedded in the way Reliance delivers projects. These includes a specialised project delivery function with experienced project management professionals, project risk modelling on a project-by-project basis, partnering with experienced vendors to execute complex projects and ongoing review and escalation of issues that undermine project success.

II. SAFETY AND OPERATIONAL RISKS

a. Evolving Health, Safety and Environmental (HSE) risks

Reliance is exposed to a wide spectrum of HSE risks, given the diversity and complexity of the industries, it operates in. The exploration and production of oil and gas, transportation of the hydrocarbons and their further refining and processing is regulated by various HSE related regulations across the geographies where Reliance operates. A major HSE incident, such as fire, oil spill, security breach can result in loss of life, environmental degradation and overall disruption in business activities.

Mitigation: Reliance follows an HSE policy that 'Safety of persons overrides all production targets', which incentivises all employees to strive for excellence in safety management for the benefit of its employees, customers and the communities. Reliance has set itself the goal of 'zero injuries and incidents'. A separate Safety and Operational Risk (S&OR) function provides oversight on HSE exposures and periodically conducts HSE audits to get assurance on the HSE management framework protocols and regulatory compliances.

b. Physical Security and Natural Calamity risks

Hostile acts such as terrorism or piracy could harm the Company's people and disrupt its operations. Some of Reliance's sites are also subject to natural calamities such as floods, cyclones, lighting and earthquakes. If the company does not respond, or is perceived to not respond, in an appropriate manner to either an external or internal crisis, its business and operations could be severely disrupted. Inability to restore or replace critical capacity to an agreed level within an agreed time frame would prolong the impact of any disruption and could severely affect Reliance's business and operations.

Mitigation: Reliance monitor for emerging threats and vulnerabilities to manage its physical security. The Company's central security function provides guidance and support to a network of security heads at the various sites who advise and conduct assurance with respect to the management of security risks affecting its people and operations. To respond to natural calamities Reliance maintains disaster recovery, crisis and business continuity management plans to respond to a disruption or an incident.

c. Cybersecurity risk

At Reliance, the use of information and telecommunication technologies is increasing, resulting in greater security threats to its digital infrastructure. A breach of its digital security or disruptions to its digital infrastructure, due to intentional actions, such as cyberattacks or human error could lead to serious impacts to its businesses. These impacts may include injury to staff, loss of control, impact on continuity or damage to assets and services, harm to the environment, the loss of sensitive data or information, legal and regulatory breaches and reputational damage.

Mitigation: Reliance continues to strengthen its responses to cybersecurity threats through proactive and reactive risk mitigations. These include, proactive activities to continuously improve its cybersecurity policies, standards, technical safeguard, ongoing monitoring of new and existing threats and IT security awareness initiatives. Its reactive responses to cybersecurity threats, which include IT disaster recovery, emergency response and business continuity management capabilities to enable the reduction of the impacts of a cybersecurity event.

III. COMPLIANCE AND CONTROL RISKS

Regulatory compliance risks

The evolution of the global regulatory environment has resulted into increased regulatory scrutiny that has raised the minimum standards to be maintained by Reliance. This signifies the alignment of corporate performance objectives, while ensuring compliance with regulatory requirements.

Mitigation: Reliance recognises that regulatory requirements can at times be challenging. A comprehensive compliance management framework has been deployed which is designed to:

- Understand changes to regulatory standards in a timely manner to strengthen decision making processes and integrate these in the business strategy of each of the industries in which it operates;
- Drive business performance through the convergence of risk, compliance processes and controls mechanisms to ensure continued operational efficiency and effectiveness.

IV. FINANCIAL RISKS

Treasury risks

Treasury risks include, among others, exposure to movements in interest rates and foreign exchange rates. Reliance also maintains sufficient liquidity, so that it is able to meet its financial commitments on due dates and is not forced to obtain funds at higher interest rates. It has access to markets worldwide and it uses a range of products and currencies to ensure that its funding is efficient and well diversified across markets and investor types.

Interest Rate risk

Reliance borrows funds from domestic and international markets to meet its long-term and short-term funding requirements. It is subject to risks arising from fluctuations in interest rates. **Mitigation:** The interest rate risk is managed through financial instruments available to convert

floating rate liabilities into fixed rate liabilities or vice versa, and is aimed at reducing the cost of borrowings.

Foreign Exchange risk

Reliance prepares its financial statements in Indian Rupee (INR), but most of the payables and receivables of hydrocarbon business are in US Dollars, minimising the cash flow risk on account of fluctuations in foreign exchange rates. Reliance avails long-term foreign currency liabilities (primarily in USD, EURO and JPY) to fund its capital investments.

Reliance also avails short-term foreign currency liabilities to fund its working capital.

Mitigation: Foreign exchange risk is tracked and managed within the risk management framework. Short-term foreign currency asset – liability mismatch is continuously monitored and hedged. The foreign exchange market is highly regulated and Reliance ensures compliance with all the regulations.

4. HOW RELIANCE MANAGES RISK

Reliance manages, monitors and reports on the principal risks and uncertainties that can impact its ability to achieve its strategic objectives. The Company has established the Reliance Management System (RMS) as part of its transformation agenda. RMS incorporates an integrated framework for managing risks and internal controls. The internal financial controls have been documented, embedded and digitised in the business processes. Internal controls are regularly tested for design and operating effectiveness. Reliance's management systems, organisational structures, processes, standards, code of conduct and behaviours together form the RMS that governs how Reliance conducts its business and manage associated risks.

Reliance has introduced several improvements to integrate Risk Management, Internal Control and Assurance processes based on the three lines of defence principle to drive a common integrated view of risks, optimal risk mitigation responses and efficient management of risk monitoring and assurance activities. This integration is enabled by common methodologies and processes supported by a single Group wide IT platform.

Reliance's risk management framework is designed to be a simple, consistent and clear framework for managing and reporting risks from the Group's operations to the Board. The framework and related processes seek to avoid incidents and maximise business outcomes by allowing management to:

- Understand the risk environment and assess the specific risks and potential exposure for Reliance.
- Determine how to deal best with these risks to manage overall potential exposure.
- Manage the identified risks in appropriate ways.
- Monitor and seek assurance of the effectiveness of the management of these risks and intervene for improvement where necessary.
- Report up the management chain to the board on a periodic basis about how risks are being managed, monitored, assured and the improvements that are being made.

GROUP RISK MANAGEMENT FRAMEWORK The Group Risk Management Framework is designed to help ensure risk management is an integral part of the way that Reliance works everywhere to enable risks to be identified, assessed and managed appropriately. The Group Risk Management Framework comprises 3 levels:

- **Oversight and Governance** - Reliance's Board, along with executive and functional leadership have articulated an absolute commitment of the Group to effective risk management and provides oversight to identify and understand significant risks. They also put in place systems of risk management, compliance and control to mitigate these risks. Dedicated Executive sub-committees review and monitor group risks throughout the year with the respective risk owners to drive a risk management culture.

Reliance's Group Risk team analyses the Group's risk profile and maintains the Group Risk

Management Framework. Its Group Audit team provides independent assurance to the Board, through its Committees, over whether the Group's system of risk management and internal control is adequately designed and operating effectively to respond appropriately to the risks that are significant to Reliance.

- **Business and Strategic Risk Management** - Through Business Risk and Assurance Committees (BRAC), Reliance businesses and functions integrate risk into key business processes such as strategy, planning, performance management, resource and capital allocation and project appraisal. The BRAC's do this by collating risk data, assessing risk management activities, reviewing near misses and incidents through root cause analysis followed by implementation of required improvements.
- **Day-to-day Risk Management** - Management and staff at Reliance's facilities, assets and functions identify and manage risk, promoting safe, compliant and reliable operations. For example, Reliance's Group-wide Operating Management System (OMS) integrates Reliance requirements on health, safety, security, environment, social responsibility, operational reliability and related issues. These Reliance requirements, along with business needs and the applicable legal and regulatory requirements, underpin the practical plans developed to help reduce risk and deliver strong, sustainable performance.

(Source: Reliance Industries Ltd Annual Report 2015-16)

1.8 Enterprise Risk Management

The Enterprise Risk Management (ERM) is defined as "a process, affected by an entity's board of directors, management and other personnel, applied in strategy setting and across the enterprise, designed to identify potential events that may affect the entity, and manage risk to be within its risk appetite, to provide reasonable assurance regarding the achievement of entity objectives".

Once the definition is glanularised, it would be as under:

Enterprise Risk Management is:	(a) A process, ongoing and following through an entity.
	(b) Effected by people at every level of an organization.
	(c) Applied in strategy-setting.
	(d) Applied across the enterprise, at every level and unit, and includes taking an entity-level portfolio view of risk.
	(e) Designed to identify potential events affecting the entity and manage risk within its risk appetite.
	(f) Able to provide reasonable assurance to an entity's management and board.
	(g) Geared to the achievement of objectives in one or more separate but overlapping categories.

ERM is about designing and implementing capabilities for managing the risks that matter. The greater the gaps in the current state and the desired future state of the organizations risk management capabilities, the greater the need for ERM infrastructure to facilitate the advancement of risk management capabilities overtime. ERM is about establishing the oversight, control and discipline to drive continuous improvement of an entity's risk management capabilities in a changing operating environment.

ERM deals with risk and opportunities affecting value creation or preservation. ERM is a comprehensive and integrated approach to addressing corporate risk. ERM enables management to effectively deal with uncertainty and associated risk and opportunity, enhancing the capacity to build value. In ERM, a risk is defined as a possible event or circumstance that can have negative

influences on the enterprise in question. Its impact can be on the very existence, the resources (human and capital), the products and services, or the customers of the enterprise, as well as external impacts on society, markets or the environment.

1.8.1. Rationale for implementation of ERM

ERM needs to be implemented for the following reasons:	(a) Reduce unacceptable performance variability.
	(b) Align and integrate varying views of risk management.
	(c) Build confidence of investment community and stakeholders.
	(d) Enhance corporate governance.
	(e) Successfully respond to a changing business environment.
	(f) Align strategy and corporate culture.

Traditional risk management approaches are focused on protecting the tangible assets reported on a company's Balance Sheet and the related contractual rights and obligations. The emphasis of ERM, however, is on enhancing business strategy. The scope and application of ERM is much broader than protecting physical and financial assets. With an ERM approach, the scope of risk management is enterprise-wide and the application of risk management is targeted to enhancing as well as protecting the unique combination of tangible and intangible assets comprising the organization's business model.

1.8.2. COSO ERM Framework

The ERM framework by the Commission of Sponsoring Organizations of the Treadway Commission (COSO) provides a more disciplined and consistent standard against which to implement and assess a company's ERM program.

ERM provides a more holistic approach that enables the alignment of the organization's strategies and operational and compliance processes across the entire company for managing all the key business risks and opportunities with the goal of maximizing value for the entire enterprise.

ERM is a process-based approach where the various components interact as part of an on-going, iterative process. COSO represents these relationships in a three dimensional cube as shown below:

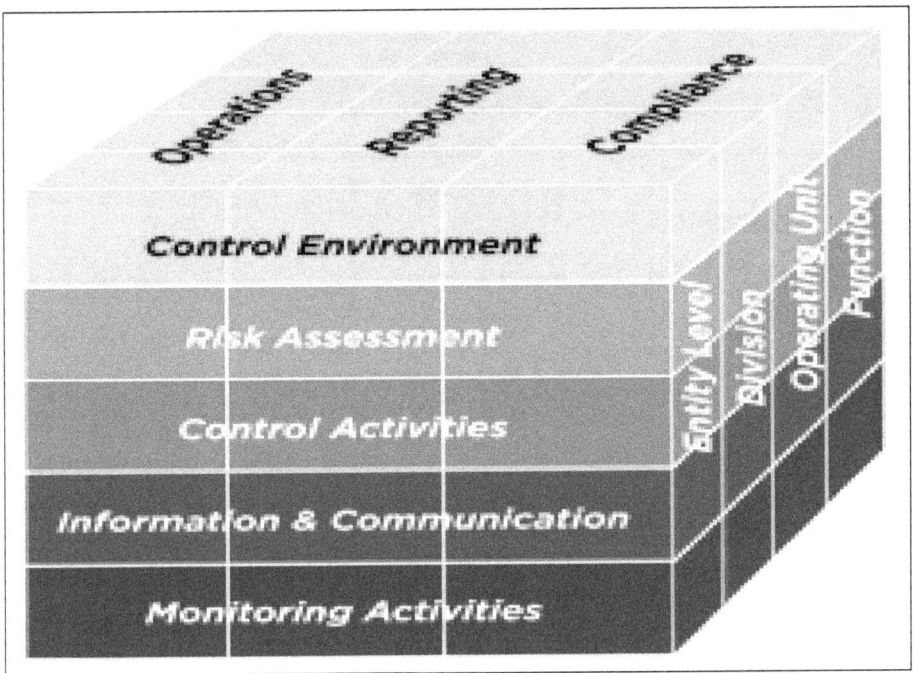

As shown above five integrated components are as under:

1.8.2.1. Control environment

It creates a set of standards, processes, and structures that provide the basis for carrying out internal control.

The control environment comprises the *integrity* and *ethical* values of an organization, as well as:
a) Management's philosophy and operating style
b) Organizational structure
c) How management assigns authority and responsibility (both along functional and administrative reporting lines)
d) The competence of the entity's people.
e) Personnel development (including training and support)

The Control Environment should ensure controls are in place, covering areas such as:	<ul><li>Clear lines of responsibility and authority</li><li>Procurement policy</li><li>Three way match in vendor payments</li><li>Code of Ethics</li><li>Whistleblower policies</li><li>Hiring practices</li><li>Training programs</li></ul>

These processes need to be continuously monitored and updated

One example of control environment for financial reporting is as under:

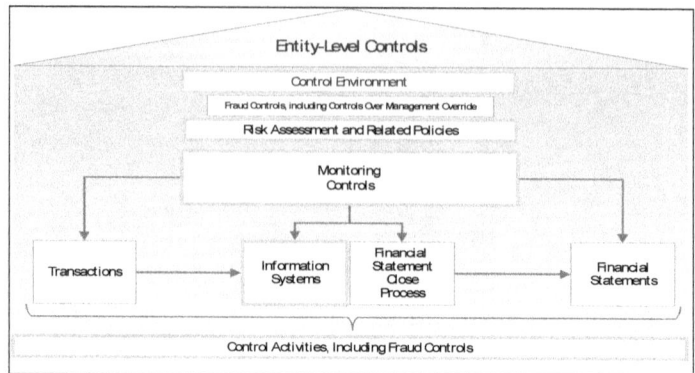

In order for the control environment to be effective, it must be documented. The first step in ensuring proper internal control is to ensure business processes are properly identified and documented.

Types of documentation that can be used include	• Process Narratives • Organizational charts • Flowcharts • Questionnaires • Memorandums • Checklists

1.8.2.2. Risk Assessment

A Risk is the possibility that an event will occur and adversely affect the achievement of objectives. Risks can be introduced by changes – for instance, new leaders and managers, new markets and products, growth, and emerging technologies.

a) Risk is categorised along 4 key risk areas:

Strategic	– including Political risk, talent and succession planning risk, and risk from dependencies on other organizations
Financial	– including risk of audit findings and other things that would undermine reporting integrity
Compliance	– including Fraud and non-compliance with fair employment practices
Operational	– including the risk that Programs fail to meet their objectives, natural disasters, and lack of technology availability

At this stage we need to understand the difference between risk management and risk assessment. This is as under:

Risk Management	Risk Assessment
A **process** applied in a strategic setting and across the entity, designed to identify and *manage* risks to stay within a **risk appetite or tolerance level**, to provide reasonable assurance about achieving entity goals and objectives.	An **element of internal control** *within* the risk management process that enables management to identify and assess key risks to achieving its objectives; this assessment **forms the basis on which control activities are determined.**

b) Risk assessment should occur at business process level and entity level as well and the primary risk assessment factors are as under:

Risk Assessment factors	Risks
1. Materiality of the amounts	<ul><li>Large value / transaction</li><li>High volume of transactions</li><li>Significant impact on key ratios or disclosures</li></ul>
2. Complexity of the process	<ul><li>Limited internal skills</li><li>Multiple data handoffs</li><li>Highly technical in nature</li></ul>
3. History of accounting adjustments	<ul><li>Accounting errors</li><li>Valuation adjustments, etc.</li></ul>
4. Propensity for change in	<ul><li>Business processes or controls</li><li>Related accounting</li></ul>

c) Considerations to assess risks are:

Internal considerations	External considerations
1. Use of qualitative/quantitative methods 2. Change in management responsibilities 3. Weak or unresponsive tone at the top 4. Human capital – quality of personnel hired/retained 5. Employee sabotage 6. System security weaknesses 7. Rapid growth 8. Changes in processes or access to assets	1. Technological advancements (more tools available, as well as existing tools we are using are outdated) 2. Changing/evolving client/constituent needs or expectations 3. Changing legislative requirements and new laws/regulations 4. Decentralized organization operations 5. Natural disasters 6. Impact of program, political, and economic changes

d) Steps in Risk Mapping
A specimen risk map is shown as under:

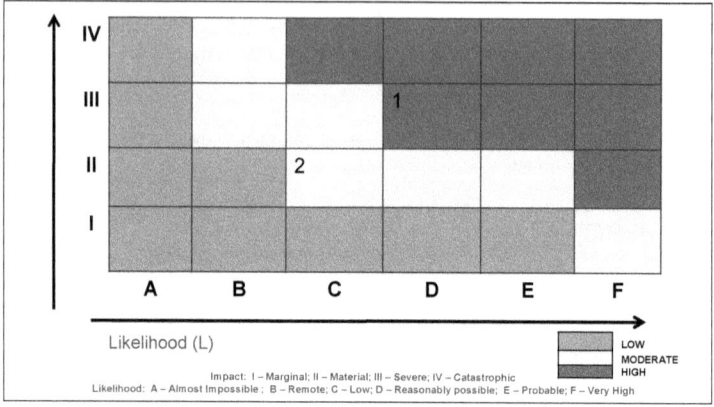

In the risk map above the x axis shows Likelihood, where:
  A-Almost impossible
  B-Remote
  C-Low
  D-Reasonably possible
  E-Probable
  F-Very High
Y axis shows Impact:
  I-Marginal
  II-Significant
  III-Severe
  IV-Catastrophic

Once we have assessed risk, we can consider the organization's risk tolerance and risk appetite related to the risk response. If the likelihood is low and the impact is marginal, then that falls within the green area on this chart, and management may decide that resources should be directed elsewhere, for more pressing needs. However, if a risk has a likelihood of reasonably possible and an anticipated impact of severe, then that falls within the red area on this chart, and management may decide to direct resources towards the mitigation of this risk.

e) Once a risk assessment is completed, and the impact and likelihood are determined, we can then determine which strategy to choose to deal with the risk.
The first is *avoidance*, which means that the process in question would not be pursued. This would be a likely option to choose if the risk likelihood was found to be very high, and the impact to be catastrophic, in other words, risks that fall within the red area of the risk tolerance map we just looked at.
The second strategy is *mitigation*, where we would improve controls to reduce the likelihood and impact of the process. This is where many control activities will be done.
The third strategy is *transfer*, where responsibility is shifted to an external party.

Another strategy is *acceptance*, where the organization simply accepts the risk. This would make sense if the risk likelihood was found to be remote, and the impact to be marginal. In general, we should accept risks only if in green area of the risk tolerance map.

The final strategy listed is *creation*, where risk activities are strategically sought to maximize opportunities. These types of decisions should lie with senior management only.

1.8.2.3. Control activities

Control Activities are the actions established through policies and procedures that help ensure management's directives to mitigate risks are carried out. These activities are performed at all levels of the entity.

Control activities are exactly what they sound like – the *activity* part of the internal control framework. While the control environment and risk assessment set the stage for good controls, the control activities are where the meat of the control work is done.

Examples of control activities include:

- Approvals & Authorizations
- Embedded verifications
- Reconciliations
- Independent Reviews
- Asset security
- Segregation of duties

Control activities are categorised as under:

Preventive controls	*Prevent* the occurrence of a negative event in a proactive manner. Examples • Approval required for purchases greater than Rs.5,000 • Passwords required for access to ERP system • Petty cash that must be held in a lockbox • Security and surveillance systems in high-risk areas, and • Pre-numbered invoices and cheques
Detective controls	*Detect* the occurrence of a negative event *after* the fact in a reactive manner. Examples • Supervisor review & approval • Reports that are run showing user activity • Reconciliation of petty cash • Annual Physical inventory counts, and • Review of missing and voided checks
Manual controls	Require action to be taken by employees. Examples include • Obtaining a supervisor's approval for overtime • Reconciling bank accounts, and • Matching receiving to Purchase Orders
Automated controls	These are Built into the network infrastructure and software applications. Examples include • Passwords • Data entry validation checks, and

	• Batch controls

18.2.4. Information and communication

This component is pretty straightforward but is also very important in ensuring a cohesive, sustainable framework. Accurate, timely information is necessary to properly carry out internal control responsibilities in support of the achievement of an organization's objectives. And communication is the continual, iterative process of providing, sharing, and obtaining that necessary information.

Management and employees must be able to obtain information from both internal and external sources as necessary, and communication paths must be viable to both internal and external parties. Information should be timely, accessible, and allow for successful control actions.

The things to communicate:	• Initiatives
	• Goals
	• Changes
	• Opportunities
	• Feedback
	• Questions
	• Answers
	• Policies
	• Procedures
	• Standards
	• Expectations

18.2.5. Monitoring activities

Monitoring activities are evaluations used to ascertain whether components of internal control are *present* and *functioning*. These evaluations can be split into two categories:

1. **Ongoing** evaluations are built into business processes and provide timely information on the underlying controls.

2. **Separate** evaluations are conducted periodically and vary in scope and frequency based on prior assessments of risk, the effectiveness of *ongoing* evaluations, and other management considerations such as resource prioritization. Separate evaluations include Internal Audit activities.

In other words, when we monitor an activity, we are assessing the performance of an internal control system over a period of time, helping to validate that the internal control system is operating as expected. Any findings that result from monitoring activities should be evaluated against relevant criteria, for example, how long has the control been compromised, and how high are the risks? Any *deficiencies* that are found, which are more pernicious to the control system than findings, should be communicated to the Board and Senior Management.

It confirms that the findings of audits and other reviews are promptly resolved so that internal controls are not compromised.

Monitoring should be directed at both internal and external risks to the organization.

Monitoring also consists of supervisory review and sign off to help ensure proper checks and balances.

1.8.2.6. Testing control processes

Testing control processes would encompass the following steps:	<ul><li>**Identify**<ul><li>transactions to be tested</li><li>key controls</li><li>applicable standards to test the transactions (i.e., criteria to judge compliance effectiveness)</li></ul></li><li>**Determine**<ul><li>appropriate type of testing</li><li>extent of testing</li></ul></li><li>**Create** test plan</li><li>**Conduct** tests for effectiveness</li><li>**Document** testing and results</li><li>**Assess** test results</li><li>**Communicate** findings, recommendations</li></ul>

1.8.2.7. Monitoring / Validating controls

a) **Deficiency in Design** – A critical control is not properly designed, i.e., even if the control operates as designed, the control objective is not always met.

When validating control design (determining effectiveness):

- Consider various factors (*how* control is performed, *who* performs the control, *what* data/reports used in performing control, *what* physical evidence is produced from the control)
- Work off of process narratives, flowcharts, and any other relevant material obtained and/or completed in the documentation stage
- Be aware that application controls are either programmed control procedures (e.g., edits, matching, reconciliation routines) or computer processes (e.g., calculations, on-line entries, automatic system interfaces).

b) **Deficiency in Operation** – A properly designed control does not operate as intended, or the person performing the control does not possess the necessary authority or qualification to perform the control effectively.

- Testing operating effectiveness includes, in part:
  - Reviewing supporting documentation for proper authorization,
  - Reviewing the results of periodic reconciliations, and
  - Reviewing policies and procedures to determine if they are being followed.
- Use appropriate sampling techniques as necessary.

c) **Documentation** should be maintained for:

- The evaluation of internal control at the entity and process levels
- What testing has been performed
- Identified deficiencies

Documentation must contain sufficient information to:

- Identify who performed the work and when
- Enable understanding of the nature, timing, extent, and results of the procedures performed
- Enable understanding of the evidence obtained
- Support the conclusions reached

1.8.2.8. Limitations of internal control

We need to keep in mind that even an effective, well-designed system of internal control can experience a failure.

Limitations may result from:

- The lack of suitability of established objectives
- The reality that human judgment in decision making can be faulty and subject to bias
- Breakdowns that can occur because of human failures such as simple errors
- The ability of management to override internal controls
- The ability of management, other personnel, and/or third parties to circumvent controls through collusion
- External events beyond the organisation control

Again, internal control provides **reasonable**, not absolute, assurance of achieving objectives. The point of internal controls is to prevent what is preventable, not to prevent *every*thing. Remember one of the key components of internal control is risk assessment.

1.8.2.9. Identification of key controls

Basic steps are as under:

Determining Where Controls are Needed	We need to document the process: 1. Pick a method that suits the process: Flowchart or Narrative 2. Identify process owner and activity owners 3. Identify the key inputs, activities, outputs, and risk points 4. Identify policies that impact the process 5. Identify standards that may specify mandatory controls

Identifying Key Control Activities	• Identify and document all controls associated with key processes
	• Identify the characteristics of controls that, when functioning as intended, would provide the evaluator with a 'level of comfort to conclude that the control is effective with respect to a given risk
	• Consider control effectiveness by focusing on:
	    • Directness and clarity of the control technique
	    • Frequency with which the control technique is applied
	    • Experience of personnel performing the control
	    • Procedures followed when a control identifies an exception condition

Understanding Control Design	For internal controls over **financial reporting**, consider the following questions: 1. Will the control techniques help achieve the control objectives? 2. Will the controls mitigate risk to an acceptable level? 3. How do the related control objectives prevent or detect a potential misstatement? 4. How do potential misstatements affect the related financial report line item? *Good controls are:* • Focused • Integrated • Accurate • Simple • Accepted • Cost Effective

1.8.2.10. Common basic internal control principles are as under:

a)Establish Delegation of Authority	Across organisation hierarchy and value chain
b)Assign Accountability	Assign each task to only one person and make him accountable
c)Segregate Duties	Don't make one employee responsible for all parts of a process, preferably in the lines of segregation of custody, recording and approval functions
d)Restrict Access	Don't provide access to systems, information, assets, etc. unless needed to complete assigned responsibilities ; except for the power user / system administrator, no single user can have access to the entire system
e)Document Procedures and Transactions	Prepare documents to show that activities have occurred ; Develop audit trail of each activity
f) Independently verify	Check others' work, introduce maker, checker and approver concept

Hence in conclusion COSO ERM framework cube represents the following:

- **Five interrelated components** of Internal Control
    1. Control Environment
    2. Risk Assessment
    3. Control Activities
    4. Information and Communication
    5. Monitoring
- Along **3 main objectives**
    1. Operations
    2. Reporting
    3. Compliance
- Across the **organization, down to the process** functions

Specimen parameters used for measurement of risk for a specific process are highlighted as under:

1. Serial Number
2. Mega process
3. Process
4. Activity
5. Risk description
6. Control objective
7. Control environment – to be certified by the process owner
8. Risk category
      Fraud risk – yes / no

      Risk category – high / medium / low

9. Internal financial control over financial reporting – yes / no
10. Prevention / detection of frauds – yes / no
11. Policies and procedures – yes / no
12. Key Control – yes / no
13. Control category

13.1. Completeness

13.2. Existence

13.3. Accuracy

13.4. Valuation

13.5. Rights / obligation

13.6. Presentation

13.7. Manual / Automatic

13.8. Preventive / detective

14. Frequency of measurement

15. Document if any

16. Responsibility

16.1. Prepared by

16.2. Checked by

17. System solution – ERP – Yes/no

18. Whethe covered under SOP – Yes / no

19. Process design gap – Yes / no

Chapter 2: Corporate Governance

2.1. What is corporate governance?

According to Investopedia.com, Corporate governance is the system of rules, practices and processes by which a company is directed and controlled.
Corporate governance essentially involves balancing the interests of the many stakeholders in a company - these include its shareholders, management, customers, suppliers, financiers, government and the community.

Since corporate governance also provides the framework for attaining a company's objectives, it encompasses practically every sphere of management, from action plans and internal controls to performance measurement and corporate disclosures"

Before we discuss the efficacy of Corporate Governance, let us take a minute to recount what happened with *Enron* and *World com*.

As we all know, *Enron* was a U.S. energy-trading and utilities company which became the seventh largest corporation in the United States. At that time little did the world know that the enterprise housed one of the biggest accounting frauds in history. Enron's executives employed creative accounting practices that falsely inflated the company's revenues. Once the fraud came to light, the company quickly unravelled and filed for bankruptcy declaration on Dec. 2001. Enron shares traded at $85 before the fraud was discovered, but plummeted to $0.30 in the sell-off after the fraud was revealed.

Formerly known as *WorldCom*, now known as MCI, this U.S.-based telecommunications company was at one time the second-largest long distance phone company in the U.S.
Today, it is perhaps best known for a massive accounting scandal that led to the company filing for bankruptcy protection in 2002. WorldCom executives effectively fudged the company's accounting numbers, inflating the company's assets by around $12 billion dollars. The swift bankruptcy that followed led to massive losses for investors.

2.2. Need for Corporate Governance

a) **Boardroom failures**: Boards of Directors, specifically Audit Committees, are charged with establishing oversight mechanisms for financial reporting in U.S. corporations on behalf of investors. These scandals identified Board members who either did not exercise their responsibilities or did not have the expertise to understand the complexities of the businesses. In many cases, Audit Committee members were not truly independent of management.

b) **Banking practices**: Lending to a firm sends signals to investors regarding the firm's risk. In the case of Enron, several major banks provided large loans to the company without understanding, or while ignoring, the risks of the company. Investors of these banks and their clients were hurt by such bad loans, resulting in large settlement payments by the banks. Others interpreted the willingness of banks to lend money to the company as an indication of its health and integrity, and were led to invest in Enron as a result. These investors were hurt as well. In Indian conditions large NPAs being carried as baggage by the banks / financial institutions

c) **Conflicts of interest with auditors**: Prior to implementation of Corporate Governance norms, auditing firms, the primary financial "watchdogs" for investors, were self-regulated. They also performed significant non-audit or consulting work for the companies they

audited. Many of these consulting agreements were far more lucrative than the auditing engagement. This presented at least the appearance of a conflict of interest. For example, challenging the company's accounting approach might damage a client relationship, conceivably placing a significant consulting arrangement at risk, damaging the auditing firm's bottom line.

d) **Insider trading** – Not charged with enough penalties, some board members allegedly carried on with insider trading which led unjust enrichment. We have illustrious cases to highlight this.

e) **Securities analysts' conflicts of interest**: The roles of securities analysts, who make buy and sell recommendations on company stocks and bonds, and investment bankers, who help provide companies loans or handle mergers and acquisitions, provide opportunities for conflicts. Similar to the auditor conflict, issuing a buy or sell recommendation on a stock while providing lucrative investment banking services creates at least the appearance of a conflict of interest.

f) **Internet bubble**: Investors had been stung in 2000 by the sharp declines in technology stocks and to a lesser extent, by declines in the overall market. Certain mutual fund managers were alleged to have advocated the purchasing of particular technology stocks, while quietly selling them. The losses sustained also helped create a frustration and anger among investors.

g) **Executive compensation**: Stock option and bonus practices, combined with volatility in stock prices for even small earnings "misses," resulted in pressures to manage earnings. Stock options were not treated as compensation expense by companies, encouraging this form of compensation. With a large stock-based bonus at risk, managers were pressured to meet their targets.

2.3. Corporate Governance in the US

Naturally with the advent of these corporate crimes, corporate governance took centre stage and laid to the introduction of the *Sarbanes-Oxley Act* in the U.S. This Act was ushered in to restore public confidence in companies and markets after accounting fraud bankrupted high-profile companies.

To protect the shareholders from these corporate crimes, *Sarbanes Oxley Act 2002*, came up with some fundamental changes in every aspect of corporate governance such as:

a) internal control
b) auditors independence
c) conflict of interest
d) corporate responsibility
e) enhanced financial disclosures
f) enhanced quantum of penalties for defaulters.

2.3.1. Implementation of Sarbanes Oxley Guidelines in US

a) Section 302: Disclosure controls
This section is mostly related to disclosure of controls and processes as distinct from financial reporting.

Under Sarbanes–Oxley, two separate sections came into effect—one civil and the other criminal. Section 302 of the Act mandates a set of internal procedures designed to ensure accurate financial disclosure. The signing officers must certify that they are "responsible for establishing and maintaining internal controls and "have designed such internal controls to ensure that material information relating to the enterprise and its consolidated subsidiaries is made known to such officers by others within those entities. The officers must "have evaluated the effectiveness of the entity's internal controls as of a date within 90 days prior to the report" and "have presented in the report their conclusions about the effectiveness of their internal controls based on their evaluation as of that date."

External auditors are required to issue an opinion on whether effective internal control over financial reporting was maintained in all material respects by management. This is in addition to the financial statement opinion regarding the accuracy of the financial statements. The requirement to issue a third opinion regarding management's assessment was removed in 2007.

b) Section 303: Improper influence on conduct of audits

a. *Rules To Prohibit*. It shall be unlawful, in contravention of such rules or regulations as the Commission shall prescribe as necessary and appropriate in the public interest or for the protection of investors, for any officer or director of an issuer, or any other person acting under the direction thereof, to take any action to fraudulently influence, coerce, manipulate, or mislead any independent public or certified accountant engaged in the performance of an audit of the financial statements of that issuer for the purpose of rendering such financial statements materially misleading.

b. *Enforcement*. In any civil proceeding, the Commission shall have exclusive authority to enforce this section and any rule or regulation issued under this section.

c. *No Pre-emption of Other Law*. The provisions of subsection (a) shall be in addition to, and shall not supersede or pre-empt, any other provision of law or any rule or regulation issued thereunder.

d. *Deadline for Rulemaking*. The Commission shall—

i). propose the rules or regulations required by this section, not later than 90 days after the date of enactment of this Act; and

ii). issue final rules or regulations required by this section, not later than 270 days after that date of enactment

c) Section 401: Disclosures in periodic reports (Off-balance sheet items)

The bankruptcy of Enron drew attention to off-balance sheet instruments that were used fraudulently. During 2010, the court examiner's review of the Lehman Brothers bankruptcy also brought these instruments back into focus, as Lehman had used an instrument called "Repo 105" to allegedly move assets and debt off-balance sheet to make its financial position look more favorable to investors. Sarbanes-Oxley required the disclosure of all material off-balance sheet items. It also required an SEC study and report to better understand the extent of usage of such instruments and whether accounting principles adequately addressed these instruments; the SEC report was issued June 15, 2005. Interim guidance was issued in May 2006, which was later finalized. Critics argued the SEC did not take adequate steps to regulate and monitor this activity.

d) Section 404: Assessment of internal control

The most contentious aspect of SOX is Section 404, which requires management and the external auditor to report on the adequacy of the company's internal control on financial reporting (ICFR). This is the most costly aspect of the legislation for companies to implement, as documenting and testing important financial manual and automated controls requires enormous effort

Under Section 404 of the Act, management is required to produce an "internal control report" as part of each annual Exchange Act report. The report must affirm "the responsibility of management for establishing and maintaining an adequate internal control structure and procedures for financial

reporting." The report must also "contain an assessment, as of the end of the most recent fiscal year of the Company, of the effectiveness of the internal control structure and procedures of the issuer for financial reporting." To do this, managers are generally adopting an internal control framework such as that described in COSO.

The SEC also released its interpretive guidance on June 27, 2007. It is generally consistent with the PCAOB's guidance, but intended to provide guidance for management.

Both management and the external auditor are responsible for performing their assessment in the context of a top-down risk assessment, which requires management to base both the scope of its assessment and evidence gathered on risk. This gives management wider discretion in its assessment approach.

The above standards together require management to:	<ul><li>Assess both the design and operating effectiveness of selected internal controls related to significant accounts and relevant assertions, in the context of material misstatement risks;</li><li>Understand the flow of transactions, including IT aspects, in sufficient detail to identify points at which a misstatement could arise;</li><li>Evaluate company-level (entity-level) controls, which correspond to the components of the COSO framework;</li><li>Perform a fraud risk assessment;</li><li>Evaluate controls designed to prevent or detect fraud, including management override of controls;</li><li>Evaluate controls over the period-end financial reporting process;</li><li>Scale the assessment based on the size and complexity of the company;</li><li>Rely on management's work based on factors such as competency, objectivity, and risk;</li><li>Conclude on the adequacy of internal control over financial reporting.</li></ul>

e) Section 404 and smaller public companies

The cost of complying with SOX 404 impacts smaller companies disproportionately, as there is a significant fixed cost involved in completing the assessment. For example, during 2004 U.S. companies with revenues exceeding $5 billion spent 0.06% of revenue on SOX compliance, while companies with less than $100 million in revenue spent 2.55%.

f) Section 802: Criminal penalties for influencing US Agency investigation/proper administration

In accordance with this section, whoever knowingly alters, destroys, mutilates, conceals, covers up, falsifies, or makes a false entry in any record, document, or tangible object with the intent to impede, obstruct, or influence the investigation or proper administration of any matter within the jurisdiction of any department or agency of the United States or any case filed, or in relation to or contemplation of any such matter or case, shall be fined, imprisoned not more than 20 years, or both.

g) Section 906: Criminal Penalties for CEO/CFO financial statement certification

(a) *Certification of Periodic Financial Reports* — Each periodic report containing financial statements filed by an issuer with the Securities Exchange Commission pursuant to section 13(a) or 15(d) of the Securities Exchange Act of 1934 shall be accompanied by a written statement by the chief executive officer and chief financial officer (or equivalent thereof) of the issuer.

(b) Content— The statement required under subsection (a) shall certify that the periodic report containing the financial statements fully complies with the requirements of section 13(a) or 15(d) of the Securities Exchange Act of [1] 1934 and that information contained in the periodic report fairly presents, in all material respects, the financial condition and results of operations of the issuer.

(c) Criminal Penalties.— Whoever— (1) certifies any statement as set forth in subsections (a) and (b) of this section knowing that the periodic report accompanying the statement does not comport with all the requirements set forth in this section shall be fined not more than $1,000,000 or imprisoned not more than 10 years, or both; or

(2) willfully certifies any statement as set forth in subsections (a) and (b) of this section knowing that the periodic report accompanying the statement does not comport with all the requirements set forth in this section shall be fined not more than $5,000,000, or imprisoned not more than 20 years, or both.

h) Section 1107: Criminal penalties for retaliation against whistle-blowers

According to this section, whoever knowingly, with the intent to retaliate, takes any action harmful to any person, including interference with the lawful employment or livelihood of any person, for providing to a law enforcement officer any truthful information relating to the commission or possible commission of any federal offense, shall be fined under this title, imprisoned not more than 10 years, or both.

On implementation of SOX Act, the focus of the companies is to have a high level of corporate governance. These days, it is not enough for a company to merely be profitable; it also needs to demonstrate good corporate citizenship through environmental awareness, ethical behavior and sound corporate governance practices.

2.4. Cadbury committee recommendations in UK:

A committee under the chairmanship of Sir Adrian Cadbury, was constituted in 1992 by the London Stock Exchange on the financial aspects of Corporate Governance, known as the Cadbury committee.

The terms of reference of the Committee were as under:	a) The responsibilities of executive and non-executive directors for reviewing and reporting on performance to shareholders and other financially interested parties; and the frequency, clarity and form in which information should be provided; b) the case for audit committees of the board, including their composition and role; c) the principal responsibilities of auditors and the extent and value of the audit; d) the links between shareholders, boards and auditors e) any other relevant matters.

According to Cadbury Committee recommendations, Corporate governance is the system by which companies are directed and controlled. Boards of directors are responsible for the governance of their companies. The shareholders' role in governance is to appoint the directors and the auditors and to satisfy themselves that appropriate governance structure in place.

The responsibilities of the board include	a) setting the company's strategic aims, b) providing the leadership to put them into effect, c) supervising the management of the business and reporting to shareholders on their stewardship.

The board's actions are subject to laws, regulations and the shareholders in general meeting.

2.4.1. Summary of recommendations of the committee is enumerated as under:

1. Compliance with code of best practice	The boards of all listed companies should comply with the Code of Best Practice set out below.
2. Statement of compliance	Listed companies should make a statement about their compliance with the Code in the report and accounts and give reasons for any areas of non-compliance
3. Statements of compliance to be reviewed by the auditors	Companies' statements of compliance should be reviewed by the auditors before publication. The review should cover only those parts of the compliance statement which relate to provisions of the Code where compliance can be objectively verified. The Auditing Practices Board should consider guidance for auditors accordingly.
4. Encouragement to Corporate Governance	**All parties concerned with corporate governance should encourage** and use their influence to ensure compliance with the Code
5. Interim reporting	Companies should expand their interim reports to include balance sheet information. interim reports should be reviewed by the auditors and the Auditing Practices Board should develop appropriate guidance. The Accounting Standards Board in conjunction with the Stock Exchange should clarify the accounting rules which companies should follow in preparing interim reports. The inclusion of cash flow information should be considered by the Committee's successor body.
6. Enhancing effectiveness of audit:	a) Directors should report on the effectiveness of their system of internal control, and the auditors should report on their statement. The accountancy profession together with representatives of preparers of accounts should draw up criteria for assessing effective systems of internal control and guidance for companies and auditors. b) Directors should state in the report and accounts that the business is a going concern, with supporting assumptions or qualifications as necessary, and the auditors should report on this statement. c) The Government should consider introducing legislation to extend to the auditors of all companies the statutory protection already available to auditors in the regulated sector (banks, building societies,

	insurance, and investment business) so that they can report reasonable suspicion of fraud freely to the appropriate investigatory authorities. **d)** The accountancy profession together with the legal profession and representatives of preparers of accounts should consider further the question of illegal acts other than fraud. **e)** The accounting profession should continue its efforts to improve its standards and procedures so as to strengthen the standing and independence of auditors.

2.4.2. Code of best practices

a) The Board of Directors	a) The board should meet regularly, retain full and effective control over the company and monitor the executive management. b) There should be clear division of responsibilities at the head of a company, which will ensure a balance of power and authority, such that no one individual has unfettered powers of decision. Where the chairman is also the chief executive, it is essential that there should be a strong and independent element on the board, with a recognised senior member. c) The board should include non-executive directors of sufficient calibre and number for their views to carry significant weight in the board's decisions. d) The board should have a formal schedule of matters specifically reserved to it for decision to ensure that the direction and control of the company is firmly in its hands. e) There should be an agreed procedure for directors in the furtherance of their duties to take independent professional advice if necessary, at the company's expense. f) All directors should have access to the advice and services of the company secretary, who is responsible to the board for ensuring that board procedures are followed and that applicable rules and regulations are complied with. Any question of the removal of the company secretary should be a matter for the board as a whole.
b) Non-Executive Directors	a) Non-executive directors should bring an independent judgement to bear on issues of strategy, performance, resources, including key appointments, and standards of conduct. b) The majority should be independent of management and free from any business or other relationship which could materially interfere with the exercise of their independent judgement apart from their fees and shareholding. Their fees should reflect the time which they commit to the company. c) Non-executive directors should be appointed for specified terms and reappointment should not be automatic. d) Non-executive directors should be selected through a formal process and both this process and their appointment should be a matter for the board as a whole.

c) Executive Directors	a) Directors' service contracts should not exceed three years without shareholders' approval. b) There should be full and clear disclosure of directors' total emoluments and those of the chairman and highest-paid director, including pension contributions and stock options. Separate figures should be provided for salary and performance-relate elements and the basis on which performance is measured should be explained. c) Remuneration of executive directors should be based on recommendations of a remuneration committee made up wholly or mainly of non-executive directors.
d) Reporting and Controls	a) It is the responsibility of the Board to present a balanced and understandable assessment of the company's position. b) The Board should ensure that an objective and professional relationship is maintained with the auditors. c) The board should establish an audit committee of at least three non-executive directors with written terms of reference which clearly reflects its authorities and duties. d) The directors should explain their responsibility for preparing the accounts next to a statement by the auditors about their reporting responsibilities. e) The directors should report on the effectiveness of the company's system of internal control. f) The directors should report that the business is a going concern, with supporting assumptions or qualifications as necessary.

2.4.3. Statement of Director's responsibility for preparing Accounts

Committee recommends that a brief statement of directors' responsibility for preparing the accounts should appear in the report and accounts.

The purpose of such a statement is to make clear that responsibility for preparing the accounts rests with the board of directors, and to remove any misconception that the auditors are responsible for the accounts. The directors' statement should be placed immediately before the auditors' report which in future will include a separate statement (currently being developed by the Auditing Practices Board) on the responsibility of the auditors for expressing an opinion on the accounts. Positioning the two statements alongside each other in this way will achieve maximum clarity about respective responsibilities.

The statement would cover the following points:	a) the legal requirement for directors to prepare financial statements for each financial year which give a true and fair view of the state of affairs of the company (or group) as at the end of the financial year and of the profit and loss for that period; b) the responsibility of the directors for maintaining adequate accounting records, for safeguarding the assets of the company (or group), and for preventing and detecting fraud and other irregularities; c) confirmation that suitable accounting policies consistently applied and supported by reasonable and prudent judgements and estimates, have been used in the preparation of the financial statements; d) confirmation that applicable accounting standards have been followed, subject to any material departures disclosed and explained in the notes to the accounts.

2.4.4. Audit Committees

All listed companies which have not already done so should establish an audit committee, and places great emphasis on the importance of properly constituted audit committees in raising standards of corporate governance.

The report provides guidance on specific terms of reference of Audit Committee, which are enumerated as under:

Constitution	1.The Board hereby resolves to establish a Committee of the Board to be known as the Audit Committee.
Membership	2. The Committee shall be appointed by the Board from amongst the Non-Executive Directors of the Company and shall consist of not less than three members. A quorum shall be two members. 3 The Chairman of the Committee shall be appointed by the Board.
Attendance at meetings	4 The Finance Director, the Head of Internal Audit, and a representative of the external auditors shall normally attend meetings. Other Board members shall also have the right of attendance. However, at least once a year the Committee shall meet with the external auditors without executive Board members present. 5 The Company Secretary shall be the Secretary, of the Committee.
Frequency of meetings	6. Meetings shall be held not less than twice a year. The external auditors may request a meeting if they consider that one is necessary.
Authority	7.The Committee is authorised by the Board to investigate any activity within its terms of reference. It is authorised to seek any information it requires from any employee and all employees are directed to co-operate with any request made by the Committee 8. The Committee is authorised by the Board to obtain outside legal or other independent professional advice and to secure the attendance of outsiders with relevant experience and expertise if it considers this necessary.

Duties	9. Duties are:
	a) to consider the appointment of the external auditor, the audit fees, and any questions of resignation or dismissal;
	b)to discuss with the external auditor before the audit commences the nature and scope of the audit, and ensure co-ordination where more than one audit firm is involved;
	c)to review the half-year and annual financial statements before submission to the Board, focusing particularly on:
	    (i) any changes in accounting policies and practices
	    (ii) major judgemental areas
	    (iii) significant adjustments resulting from the audit
	    (iv) the going concern assumption
	    (v) compliance with accounting standards
	    (vi) compliance with stock exchange and legal requirements.
	d)to discuss problems and reservations arising from the interim and final audits, and any matters the auditor may wish to discuss (in the absence of management where necessary);
	e)to review the external auditor's management letter and management's response;
	f)to review the Company's statement on internal control systems prior

	to endorsement by the Board; g)(where an internal audit function exists) to review the internal audit programme, ensure co-ordination between the internal and external auditors, and ensure that the internal audit function is adequately resourced and has appropriate standing within the Company; (h) to consider the major findings of internal investigations and management response (i) to consider other topics, as defined by the board.
Reporting procedure	10. The Secretary shall circulate the minutes of meetings of the Committee to all members of the Board.

2.5. Benefits of robust Corporate Governance

Corporate Governance is needed to create corporate culture of transparency, accountability and disclosure. It enhances corporate performance, investor trust, accessibility to global market, financing from institutions, enterprise valuation, enterprise risk management and inculcates accountability. Detailed objectives of good corporate governance are as under:

Improves corporate performance	• Assist quality of decision making • Develop robust corporate strategy • Usher in effective execution capabilities
Enhances accountability	• Effective governance process highlights and enhances accountability of Board of directors towards shareholders and • Assists in improvement in branding of the enterprise
Enhances investor trust	• Encourages investors to make investment • Encourage promotion of investors' interest through effective disclosures
Better access to global markets	• Owing to transparency in reporting, it attracts investment from global investors • Bring about better efficiencies in the financial sector
Combat corruption	• Implement robust internal control and audit processes • Enables prevention of fraud and malpractices owing to strong processes and best practices • Accurate and effective disclosure of accounting and auditing processes across operations
Funding from institutions	• Proper disclosures and sound internal control processes bring about investor confidence and results in further investment from banks and financial institutions
Enhances enterprise valuation	• Robust processes and controls results in enhancement of enterprise valuation going forward
Improved enterprise risk management	• Effective governance process develops a firewall against possible risks, and • Bring about effective enterprise risk mitigation system

2.6. Corporate Governance in India

The high profile corporate governance failure scams like the stock market scam, the UTI scam, Ketan Parikh scam, Satyam scam, which was severely criticized by the shareholders, called for a need to make corporate governance in India effective and transparent as it greatly affects the development of the country.

The Organisation for Economic Cooperation and Development (OECD), which, in 1999, published its *Principles of Corporate Governance* gives a very comprehensive definition of corporate governance, as under:

"a set of relationships between a company's management, its board, its shareholders and other stakeholders. Corporate governance also provides the structure through which the objectives of the company are set, and the means of attaining those objectives and monitoring performance are determined. Good corporate governance should provide proper incentives for the board and management to pursue objectives that are in the interests of the company and shareholders, and should facilitate effective monitoring, thereby encouraging firms to use recourses more efficiently."
Generally, Corporate Governance refers to practices by which organisations are controlled, directed and governed. The fundamental concern of Corporate Governance is to ensure the conditions whereby organisation's directors and managers act in the interest of the organisation and its stakeholders and to ensure the means by which managers are held accountable to capital providers for the use of assets. To achieve the objectives of ensuring fair corporate governance, the Government of India has put in place a statutory framework.

Kumar Mangalam Birla Committee constituted by SEBI has observed that *"Strong corporate governance is indispensable to resilient and vibrant capital markets and is an important instrument of investor protection. It is the blood that fills the veins of transparent corporate disclosure and high quality accounting practices. It is the muscle that moves a viable and accessible financial reporting structure"*

N.R. Narayana Murthy Committee on Corporate Governance constituted by SEBI has observed that *" Corporate Governance is the acceptance by management of the inalienable rights of shareholders as the true owners of the corporation and of their own role as trustees on behalf of the shareholders. It is about commitment to values, about ethical business conduct and about making a distinction between personal and corporate funds in the management of a company"*

The Institute of Company Secretaries of India has defined Corporate Governance as *" Corporate Governance is the application of best management practices, compliance of law in true letter and spirit and adherence to ethical standards for effective management and distribution of wealth and discharge of social responsibility for sustainable development of all stakeholders"*

2.7. Dr. J J Irani Expert Committee on Corporate Governance

This committee was constituted in 2004 by the Government of India for proposing revisions in the Companies Act 1956. The recommendation summary of this Committee is enumerated below:

Board composition	The law needs to provide minimum number of directors for various classes of companies and there need not be any limit on the maximum number of directors Apart from procedures of appointments, no age limit of directors need be specified in the Act
Appointment and	Every company should have at least one resident Indian director

resignation of directors	No Central Government approval required for appointment of non-resident managerial personnel The Company should be responsible to inform the Registrar of Companies regarding appointment /resignation / death of directors
Independent Directors	Law needs to recognise Independent Directors Statutes should expressly indicate the qualifications, manner of appointment, role and liability of independent directors along with criteria of independence The Rules need to prescribe the proportion of representation of Independent Directors on the Board depending on size and type of companies
Remuneration of Directors	Remuneration of directors should not be decided by Government but should be left to the company. However, this should be transparent, based on principles that ensure fairness, reasonableness and accountability and should be properly disclosed. No limits need to be prescribed. In case of inadequacy of profits also the company to be allowed to pay remuneration recommended by remuneration committee (wherever applicable) and with the approval of shareholders
Committees	Certain committees to be constituted with participation of independent directors. Participation of independent director should be mandated for certain categories of companies. In other cases constitution of such committees should be at the option of the company The statute should specify the composition of audit committee, stakeholders relationship committee and remuneration committee along with obligation on the part of the company to consult them in certain matters
Disqualification of Director	Failure to attend board meetings for a continuous period of one year to be made a ground for vacation of office regardless of whether or not leave of absence was granted to such director Specific provisions need to be made to regulate the process of resignation by a director
Board meetings	In the case of companies where independent directors are prescribed, notice of seven days has been recommended for Board meetings with provisions for holding emergency meetings at a shorter notice Consent of shareholders by way of special resolution should be mandatory for certain important matters Board meetings by electronic means to be allowed
Annual General meetings	Use of postal ballot during meetings of members to be allowed to be more widely used by companies The statute needs to provide for voting through electronic mode. AGMs may be held at a place other than the registered office in India, provided at least 10% members in number reside at such place Small companies to be given an option to dispense with holding of AGM. Demand for poll to be limited with due regard for minority interests.
Appointment of Managing Director/ Whole time Director	Managing Director/ Whole time Director/Executive Director should be in the whole time employment of only one company at a time. Provisions relating to options for appointment of directors through proportionate representation to be continued.

	Limit of paid up capital under section 269 for mandatory appointment of MD / WTD/ ED to be enhanced to Rs.10 crores
Key Management Personnel	Every company should appoint a Chief Executive Officer, Chief Finance Officer and Company Secretary as the Key Managerial Personnel whose appointment and removal shall be by the Board of Directors Exemptions may be provided for small companies, who may obtain such services from qualified professionals in practice.

2.8. Regulatory framework on corporate governance in India

The Indian statutory framework has been structured in line with the international best practices of corporate governance. Broadly speaking, the corporate governance mechanism for companies in India is enumerated in the following regulations and guidelines:

1. **The Companies Act, 2013** *inter alia* contains provisions relating to board constitution, board meetings, board processes, independent directors, general meetings, audit committees, related party transactions, disclosure requirements in financial statements, etc.

2. **Securities and Exchange Board of India (SEBI) Guidelines:** SEBI is a regulatory authority having jurisdiction over listed companies and which issues regulations, rules and guidelines to companies to ensure protection of investors.

3. **Standard Listing Agreement of Stock Exchanges:** For companies whose shares are listed on the stock exchanges.

4. **Accounting Standards issued by the Institute of Chartered Accountants of India (ICAI):** ICAI is an autonomous body, which issues accounting standards providing guidelines for disclosures of financial information. Section 129 of the New Companies Act *inter alia* provides that the financial statements shall give a true and fair view of the state of affairs of the company or companies, comply with the accounting standards notified under section 133 of the New Companies Act. It is further provided that items contained in such financial statements shall be in accordance with the accounting standards.

5. **Companies (Indian Accounting Standards) Rules 2015 converged with International Financial Reporting Standards (IFRS) notified by Government of India - Ministry of Corporate Affairs.**

6. **Companies (Indian Accounting Standards)(Amendment)Rules 2016 and Companies (Accounting Standards)(Amendment)Rules 2016** have been notified by the Ministry of Corporate Affairs as a process of ushering in IFRS in Indian shores.

7. **Secretarial Standards issued by the Institute of Company Secretaries of India (ICSI):** ICSI is an autonomous body, which issues secretarial standards in terms of the provisions of the New Companies Act. So far, the ICSI has issued Secretarial Standard on "Meetings of the Board of Directors" (SS-1) and Secretarial Standards on "General Meetings" (SS-2). These Secretarial Standards have come into force w.e.f. July 1, 2015. Section 118(10) of the New Companies Act provide that *every company* (other than one person company) shall observe Secretarial Standards specified as such by the ICSI with respect to general and board meetings.

TABLE 1: Comparison of latest SEBI Guidelines with Clause 49 and Companies Act 2013 and Rules 2014

Particulars	Regulation 16 to 27 (as amended SEBI Regulation Sept 2015)	Clause 49 (as amended from 1st Oct 2014)	Companies Act, 2013 & Rules, 2014
1.Composition of Board	*Regulation 17.* The composition of board of directors of the listed entity shall be as follows: (1)(a) board of directors shall have an optimum combination of executive and non-executive directors with at least one woman director and not less than fifty per cent. of the board of directors shall comprise of non-executive directors; (b) where the chairperson of the board of directors is a non-executive director, at least one-third of the board of directors shall comprise of independent directors and where the listed entity does not have a regular non-executive chairperson, at least half of the board of directors shall comprise of independent directors: Provided that where the regular non-executive chairperson is a promoter of the listed entity or is related to any promoter or person occupying management positions at the level of board of director or at one level below the board of directors, at least half of the board of directors of the listed entity shall consist of independent directors.	*Clause 49 (II)* 1. The Board of Directors of the company shall have an optimum combination of executive and non-executive directors with at least one woman director and not less than fifty percent of the Board of Directors comprising non-executive directors. 2. Where the Chairman of the Board is a non-executive director, at least one-third of the Board should comprise independent directors and in case the company does not have a regular non-executive Chairman, at least half of the Board should comprise independent directors. Provided that where the regular non-executive Chairman is a promoter of the company or is related to any promoter or person occupying management positions at the Board level or at one level below the Board, at least one-half of the Board of the company shall consist of independent directors.	*According to Section 149 (1),* every company shall have a Board of Directors consisting of individuals as directors and shall have – a) Minimum number of *three directors* in the case of a public company, *two directors* in the case of a private company and *one director* in the case pf a One Person Company and b) A maximum of *fifteen directors* The Act provides that the company may appoint more than *fifteen directors* but would require prior approval of shareholders through a special resolution. The 2013 Act provides that *majority of members of Audit Committee* including its Chairperson shall be persons with *ability to read and understand the financial statements.* The 2013 Act provides for appointment of at least *one woman director* on the Board for such class or classes of companies as may be prescribed. A transitional period of one year has been prescribed to companies for the compliance with this provision. The 2013 Act provides that a company should have at least *one director who has stayed in India* for a total period of not less than hundred and eighty two days in the previous calendar year. The 2013 Act introduces a new category of a company, One Person Company ("OPC"), which

			should have at least one director. For the first time, duties of the directors are defined under the 2013 Act.
2. Duties and responsibilities of Board	**Regulation 3** The board of directors of the listed entity shall have the following responsibilities: *(i) Disclosure of information:* (1) Members of board of directors and key managerial personnel shall disclose to the board of directors whether they, directly, indirectly, or on behalf of third parties, have a material interest in any transaction or matter directly affecting the listed entity. (2) The board of directors and senior management shall conduct themselves so as to meet the expectations of operational transparency to stakeholders while at the same time maintaining confidentiality of information in order to foster a culture of good decision-making. *(ii) Key functions of the board of directors-* (1) Reviewing and guiding corporate strategy, major plans of action, risk policy, annual budgets and business plans, setting performance objectives, monitoring implementation and corporate performance, and overseeing major capital expenditures, acquisitions and divestments. (2) Monitoring the effectiveness of the listed entity's governance practices and making changes as needed. (3) Selecting,	**Clause 49D** **Responsibilities of the Board** **1. Disclosure of Information** a. Members of the Board and key executives should be required to disclose to the board whether they, directly, indirectly or on behalf of third parties, have a material interest in any transaction or matter directly affecting the company. b. The Board and top management should conduct themselves so as to meet the expectations of operational transparency to stakeholders while at the same time maintaining confidentiality of information in order to foster a culture for good decision-making. **2. Key functions of the Board** The board should fulfill certain key functions, including: a. Reviewing and guiding corporate strategy, major plans of action, risk policy, annual budgets and business plans; setting performance objectives; monitoring implementation and corporate performance; and overseeing major capital expenditures, acquisitions and divestments. b. Monitoring the effectiveness of the company's governance practices and making changes as needed. c. Selecting, compensating, monitoring and, when necessary, replacing key executives and overseeing succession planning. d. Aligning key executive and board remuneration with the longer term interests of the company and its shareholders. e. Ensuring a transparent board nomination process with the diversity of thought, experience, knowledge, perspective and	**Section 166(1),** subject to provisions of the Act of 2013, a director shall act in accordance with the articles of the company. (2)A director of a company shall act in good faith in order to promote the objects of the company for the benefit of its members as a whole, and in the best interests of the company, its employees, the shareholders, the community and for the protection of the environment (3)A director of a company shall exercise his duties with due and reasonable care, skill and diligence and shall exercise independent judgement, (4)A director of a company shall not involve in a situation in which he may have a direct or indirect interest that conflicts, or possibly may conflict, with the interest of the company, (5)A director of a company shall not achieve or attempt to achieve any undue gain or advantage either to himself or to his relatives, partners or associates and if such director is found guilty of making any undue gain, he shall be liable to pay an amount equal to that gain to the company. (6)A director of a company shall not assign his office and any assignment so made shall be void. (7)If a director of the company contravenes the provisions of this section such director will be punishable with fine which shall not be less than one lakh rupees but which may extend to five lakh rupees.

compensating, monitoring and, when necessary, replacing key managerial personnel and overseeing succession planning. (4) Aligning key managerial personnel and remuneration of board of directors with the longer term interests of the listed entity and its shareholders. (5) Ensuring a transparent nomination process to the board of directors with the diversity of thought, experience, knowledge, perspective and gender in the board of directors. (6) Monitoring and managing potential conflicts of interest of management, members of the board of directors and shareholders, including misuse of corporate assets and abuse in related party transactions. (7) Ensuring the integrity of the listed entity's accounting and financial reporting systems, including the independent audit, and that appropriate systems of control are in place, in particular, systems for risk management, financial and operational control, and compliance with the law and relevant standards. (8) Overseeing the process of disclosure and communications. (9) Monitoring and reviewing board of director's evaluation framework. *(iii) Other responsibilities*: (1) The board of directors shall provide strategic guidance to the listed entity, ensure effective monitoring of the management and shall be accountable to the listed entity and the shareholders.	gender in the Board. f. Monitoring and managing potential conflicts of interest of management, board members and shareholders, including misuse of corporate assets and abuse in related party transactions. g. Ensuring the integrity of the company's accounting and financial reporting systems, including the independent audit, and that appropriate systems of control are in place, in particular, systems for risk management, financial and operational control, and compliance with the law and relevant standards. h. Overseeing the process of disclosure and communications. i. Monitoring and reviewing Board Evaluation framework. **3. Other responsibilities** a. The Board should provide the strategic guidance to the company, ensure effective monitoring of the management and should be accountable to the company and the shareholders. b. The Board should set a corporate culture and the values by which executives throughout a group will behave. c. Board members should act on a fully informed basis, in good faith, with due diligence and care, and in the best interest of the company and the shareholders. d. The Board should encourage continuing directors training to ensure that the Board members are kept up to date. e. Where Board decisions may affect different shareholder groups differently, the Board should treat all shareholders fairly. f. The Board should apply high ethical standards. It should take into account the interests of stakeholders. g. The Board should be able to exercise objective independent judgement on corporate affairs.	

	(2) The board of directors shall set a corporate culture and the values by which executives throughout a group shall behave. (3) Members of the board of directors shall act on a fully informed basis, in good faith, with due diligence and care, and in the best interest of the listed entity and the shareholders. (4) The board of directors shall encourage continuing directors training to ensure that the members of board of directors are kept up to date. (5) Where decisions of the board of directors may affect different shareholder groups differently, the board of directors shall treat all shareholders fairly. (6) The board of directors shall maintain high ethical standards and shall take into account the interests of stakeholders. (7) The board of directors shall exercise objective independent judgement on corporate affairs. (8) The board of directors shall consider assigning a sufficient number of non-executive members of the board of directors capable of exercising independent judgement to tasks where there is a potential for conflict of interest. (9) The board of directors shall ensure that, while rightly encouraging positive thinking, these do not result in over-optimism that either leads to significant risks not being recognised or exposes the listed entity to excessive risk. (10)The board of directors shall have ability to 'step back' to assist executive	h. Boards should consider assigning a sufficient number of non-executive Board members capable of exercising independent judgement to tasks where there is a potential for conflict of interest. i. The Board should ensure that, while rightly encouraging positive thinking, these do not result in over-optimism that either leads to significant risks not being recognised or exposes the company to excessive risk. j. The Board should have ability to 'step back' to assist executive management by challenging the assumptions underlying: strategy, strategic initiatives (such as acquisitions), risk appetite, exposures and the key areas of the company's focus. k. When committees of the board are established, their mandate, composition and working procedures should be well defined and disclosed by the board. l. Board members should be able to commit themselves effectively to their responsibilities. m. In order to fulfil their responsibilities, board members should have access to accurate, relevant and timely information. n. The Board and senior management should facilitate the Independent Directors to perform their role effectively as a Board member and also a member of a committee	

	management by challenging the assumptions underlying: strategy, strategic initiatives (such as acquisitions), risk appetite, exposures and the key areas of the listed entity's focus. (11)When committees of the board of directors are established, their mandate, composition and working procedures shall be well defined and disclosed by the board of directors. (12) Members of the board of directors shall be able to commit themselves effectively to their responsibilities. (13)In order to fulfil their responsibilities, members of the board of directors shall have access to accurate, relevant and timely information. (14)The board of directors and senior management shall facilitate the independent directors to perform their role effectively as a member of the board of directors and also a member of a committee of board of directors.		
3.Modified definition of Independent Directors	Regulation 16 (b) An Independent Director means a non-executive director, other than a nominee director of the listed entity: (i) who, in the opinion of the board of directors, is a person of integrity and possesses relevant expertise and experience; (ii) who is or was not a promoter of the listed entity or its holding, subsidiary or associate company; (iii) who is not related to promoters or directors in	Clause 49(II) (B) 1. For the purpose of the clause A, the expression 'independent director' shall mean a non-executive director, other than a nominee director of the company: a. who, in the opinion of the Board, is a person of integrity and possesses relevant expertise and experience; b. (i) who is or was not a promoter of the company or its holding, subsidiary or associate company; (ii) who is not related to promoters or directors in the company, its holding, subsidiary or associate company;	Section 149(6) of the Companies Act, 2013 An independent director in relation to a company means a director other than a managing director or a whole-time director or a nominee director, who: (a)in the opinion of the Board is a person of integrity and possesses relevant expertise and experience; (b)(i) who is or was not a promoter of the company or its holding, subsidiary or associate company (ii) who is not related to promoters or directors in the

	the listed entity, its holding, subsidiary or associate company; (iv) who, apart from receiving director's remuneration, has or had no material pecuniary relationship with the listed entity, its holding, subsidiary or associate company, or their promoters, or directors, during the two immediately preceding financial years or during the current financial year; (v) none of whose relatives has or had pecuniary relationship or transaction with the listed entity, its holding, subsidiary or associate company, or their promoters, or directors, amounting to two per cent. or more of its gross turnover or total income or fifty lakh rupees or such higher amount as may be prescribed from time to time, whichever is lower, during the two immediately preceding financial years or during the current financial year; (vi) who, neither himself, nor whose relative(s) — (A) holds or has held the position of a key managerial personnel or is or has been an employee of the listed entity or its holding, subsidiary or associate company in any of the three financial years immediately preceding the financial year in which he is proposed to be appointed; (B) is or has been an employee or proprietor or a partner, in any of the three financial years immediately preceding the financial year in which he is proposed to be appointed, of — (1) a firm of auditors or	c. apart from receiving director's remuneration, has or had no pecuniary relationship with the company, its holding, subsidiary or associate company, or their promoters, or directors, during the two immediately preceding financial years or during the current financial year; d. none of whose relatives has or had pecuniary relationship or transaction with the company, its holding, subsidiary or associate company, or their promoters, or directors, amounting to two per cent. or more of its gross turnover or total income or fifty lakh rupees or such higher amount as may be prescribed, whichever is lower, during the two immediately preceding financial years or during the current financial year; e. who, neither himself nor any of his relatives — (i) holds or has held the position of a key managerial personnel or is or has been employee of the company or its holding, subsidiary or associate company in any of the three financial years immediately preceding the financial year in which he is proposed to be appointed; (ii) is or has been an employee or proprietor or a partner, in any of the three financial years immediately preceding the financial year in which he is proposed to be appointed, of — (A) a firm of auditors or company secretaries in practice or cost auditors of the company or its holding, subsidiary or associate company; or (B) any legal or a consulting firm that has or had any transaction with the company, its holding, subsidiary or associate company amounting to ten per cent or more of the gross turnover of such	company or its holding, subsidiary or associate company. (c) who has or had no pecuniary relationship with the company, its holding, subsidiary or associate company or their promoters, or directors of the company during the current financial year or during the two immediately preceding financial years. (d) none of whose relatives has or had pecuniary relationship or transaction with the company, its holding, subsidiary or associate company or their promoters or directors of the company amounting to two percent or more of the gross turnover or total income or Rs 50 lakh or such higher amount as may be prescribed, whichever is lower in the current financial year or during the two immediately preceding years. (e) who neither himself nor any of his relatives, • is not a Key Management Personnel or whose relative is not a Key Management Personnel , of the company or its holding/ subsidiary/associate in the last three financial years immediately preceding the financial year in which he is proposed to be appointed. • has not been an employee or partner in a firm of auditors or company secretaries or cost auditors of the company/its holding/subsidiary/associate company or in a legal/consulting firm that has or had any transaction with the company /its holding /subsidiary/associate

company secretaries in practice or cost auditors of the listed entity or its holding, subsidiary or associate company; or (2) any legal or a consulting firm that has or had any transaction with the listed entity, its holding, subsidiary or associate company amounting to ten per cent or more of the gross turnover of such firm; (C) holds together with his relatives two per cent or more of the total voting power of the listed entity; or (D) is a chief executive or director, by whatever name called, of any non-profit organisation that receives twenty-five per cent or more of its receipts or corpus from the listed entity, any of its promoters, directors or its holding, subsidiary or associate company or that holds two per cent or more of the total voting power of the listed entity; (E) is a material supplier, service provider or customer or a lessor or lessee of the listed entity; (vii) who is not less than 21 years of age.	firm; (iii) holds together with his relatives two per cent or more of the total voting power of the company; or (iv) is a Chief Executive or director, by whatever name called, of any non-profit organisation that receives twenty-five per cent or more of its receipts from the company, any of its promoters, directors or its holding, subsidiary or associate company or that holds two per cent or more of the total voting power of the company; (v) is a material supplier, service provider or customer or a lessor or lessee of the company; f. who is not less than 21 years of age.	company amounting to ten percent or more of the gross turnover of such firm. • does not hold more than two percent (individually or with his relatives) of the total voting power. • is not Chief Executive Officer or director of non-profit organization, receiving twenty five percent or more of its receipts from the company/its promoters/directors/ its holding/subsidiary/ associate company or holds more than two percent of the voting power. (f) who possesses such other qualifications as may be prescribed as per rule 5 of the Companies (Appointment and Qualification of Directors) Rules 2014. Listed companies shall have at least one-third of the total number of directors as IDs and the CG may prescribe the minimum number of IDs for any class of public companies.
4. Qualification of Independent Directors	*Regulation 16 (b)* does not specify qualification of IDs but specifies that a person who, in the opinion of the board of directors, is a person of integrity and possesses relevant expertise and experience	The qualifications of IDs are not specified in the amended clause 49 of the listing agreement.	*Companies (Appointment and Qualification of Directors) Rules, 2014* An independent director shall possess appropriate skills, experience and knowledge in one or more fields of finance, law, management, sales, marketing, administration, research, corporate governance, technical operations or other disciplines related to the company's business.
5. Whistle-Blower mechanism	*Regulation 22: Vigil mechanism:* 1) The listed entity shall	*Clause 49 (II) (F)* The company shall establish a vigil mechanism for directors and employees to	*Section 177(9)* Every listed company and other classes of companies to establish a Vigil

	formulate a vigil mechanism for directors and employees to report genuine concerns. (2) The vigil mechanism shall provide for adequate safeguards against victimization of director(s) or employee(s) or any other person who avail the mechanism and also provide for direct access to the chairperson of the audit committee in appropriate or exceptional cases.	report concerns about unethical behaviour, actuator suspected fraud or violation of the company's code of conduct or ethics policy. This mechanism should also provide for adequate safeguards against victimization of director(s) / employee(s) who avail of the mechanism and also provide for direct access to the Chairman of the Audit Committee in exceptional cases. The details of establishment of such mechanism shall be disclosed by the company on its website and in the Board's report.	mechanism for directors and employees to report genuine concern. It provide adequate safeguards against victimization of employees and directors who avail of the Vigil mechanism and also provide for direct access to the chairperson of the Audit committee or the director nominated to play the role of audit committee, as the case may be, in exceptional cases. Once established, the existence of the mechanism may be appropriately communicated within the organization. The details of establishment of Vigil mechanism shall be disclosed by the company in the website, if any, and in the Board's Report.
6. Prohibited Stock options for Independent Directors	**Regulation 17(d)** Independent directors shall not be entitled to any stock option.	**Clause 49(II)(C)** IDs shall not be entitled to any stock options.	**Section 197(7)** IDs shall not entitled to any stock option.
7. Separate meeting of Independent Directors	**Regulation 25(3)** The independent directors of the listed entity shall hold at least one meeting in a year, without the presence of non-independent directors and members of the management and all the independent directors shall strive to be present at such meeting.	**Clause49 (II) (B) (6)** The IDs of the company shall hold at least one meeting in a year, without the attendance of non-independent directors and members of management. All the independent directors of the company shall strive to be present at such meeting.	**Section 149** read with Schedule IV IDs of the company shall hold at least one meeting in a year, without the attendance of non-independent directors and members of management. All the independent directors of the company shall strive to be present at such meeting.
8. Training of Independent Directors	**Regulation 25(7)** The listed entity shall familiarise the independent directors through various programmes about the listed entity, including the following: (a) nature of the industry in which the listed entity operates; (b) business model of the listed entity; (c) roles, rights, responsibilities of independent directors; and (d) any other relevant information.	**Clause 49(II)(B)** The company shall provide suitable training to independent directors to familiarize them with the company, their roles, rights, responsibilities in the company, nature of the industry in which the company operates, business model of the company, etc. The details of such training imparted shall be disclosed in the Annual Report.	**The Companies Act 2013** did not specify any training of Independent Directors and Board of Directors.

9. Liability of Independent Directors	*Regulation 25(5)* An independent director shall be held liable, only in respect of such acts of omission or commission by the listed entity which had occurred with his knowledge, attributable through processes of board of directors, and with his consent or connivance or where he had not acted diligently with respect to the provisions contained in these regulations.	*Clause 49(II)(E)* An IDs shall be held liable, only in respect of such acts of omission or commission by a company which had occurred with his knowledge, attributable through Board processes, and with his consent or connivance or where he had not acted diligently with respect of the provisions contained in the Listing Agreement.	*Section 149(12)* An IDs, a non-executive director not being promoter or KMP, shall be held liable, only in respect of such acts of omission or commission by a company which had occurred with his knowledge, attributable through Board processes, and with his consent or connivance or where he had not acted diligently.
10. Stakeholder Relationship Committee	*Regulation 20:* (1) The listed entity shall constitute a Stakeholders Relationship Committee to specifically look into the mechanism of redressal of grievances of shareholders, debenture holders and other security holders. (2) The chairperson of this committee shall be a non-executive director. (3) The board of directors shall decide other members of this committee. (4) The role of the Stakeholders Relationship Committee shall be as specified as in Part D of the Schedule II according to which, the Committee shall consider and resolve the grievances of the security holders of the listed entity including complaints related to transfer of shares, non-receipt of annual report and non-receipt of declared dividends..	*Clause 49(VIII)(E)* A committee under the Chairmanship of a non-executive director and such other members as may be decided by the Board of the company shall be formed to specifically look into the redressal of grievances of shareholders, debenture holders and other security holders. This Committee shall be designated as 'Stakeholders Relationship Committee' and shall consider and resolve the grievances of the security holders of the company including complaints related to transfer of shares, non-receipt of balance sheet, non-receipt of declared dividends.	*Section- 178(5)* The Board of Directors of a company which consists of more than *one thousand shareholders, debenture holders, deposit-holders and any other security holders at any time during a financial year* shall constitute a Stakeholders Relationship Committee consisting of a *chairperson* who shall be *a non-executive director* and such other members as may be decided by the Board. The SRC shall consider and resolve the grievances of security holders of the company.
11. Nomination and Remuneration Committee	*Regulation 19(1).* The board of directors shall constitute the nomination and remuneration committee as follows: (a) the committee shall comprise of at least three directors ;	*Clause 49(VIII) (C)* All pecuniary relationship or transactions of the non-executive directors vis-à-vis the company shall be disclosed in the Annual Report. In addition to the disclosures required under the Companies Act, 2013, the following	*Sec.197(12) and Companies (Appointment and Remuneration of Managerial Personnel) Rules, 2014*: Every listed company shall disclose in the Board's report- (i) the ratio of the remuneration of each director to the median

(b) all directors of the committee shall be non-executive directors; and (c) at least fifty percent of the directors shall be independent directors. (2) The Chairperson of the nomination and remuneration committee shall be an independent director: Provided that the chairperson of the listed entity, whether executive or non-executive, may be appointed as a member of the Nomination and Remuneration Committee and shall not chair such Committee. (3) The Chairperson of the nomination and remuneration committee may be present at the annual general meeting, to answer the shareholders' queries; however, it shall be up to the chairperson to decide who shall answer the queries. (4) The role of the nomination and remuneration committee shall be as specified as in Part D of the Schedule II which are as under: (1) formulation of the criteria for determining qualifications, positive attributes and independence of a director and recommend to the board of directors a policy relating to, the remuneration of the directors, key managerial personnel and other employees; (2) formulation of criteria for evaluation of performance of independent directors and the board of directors; (3) devising a policy on diversity of board of directors; (4) identifying persons who	disclosures on the remuneration of directors shall be made in the section on the corporate governance of the Annual Report: a. All elements of remuneration package of individual directors summarized under major groups, such as salary, benefits, bonuses, stock options, pension etc. b. Details of fixed component and performance linked incentives, along with the performance criteria. c. Service contracts, notice period, severance fees. d. Stock option details, if any - and whether issued at a discount as well as the period over which accrued and over which exercisable. The company shall publish its criteria of making payments to non-executive directors in its annual report. Alternatively, this may be put up on the company's website and reference drawn thereto in the annual report. The company shall disclose the number of shares and convertible instruments held by non-executive directors in the annual report. Non-executive directors shall be required to disclose their shareholding (both own or held by / for other persons on a beneficial basis) in the listed company in which they are proposed to be appointed as directors, prior to their appointment. These details should be disclosed in the notice to the general meeting called for appointment of such director.	remuneration of the employees of the company for the financial year; (ii) the percentage increase in remuneration of each director, CFO, CEO, CS or Manager, if any, in the financial year; (iii) the percentage increase in the median remuneration of employees in the financial year; (iv) the number of permanent employees on the rolls of company; (v) the explanation on the relationship between average increase in remuneration and company performance; (vi) comparison of the remuneration of the KMP against the performance of the company; (vii) variations in the market capitalisation of the company, price earnings ratio as at the closing date of the current financial year and previous financial year and percentage increase over decrease in the market quotations of the shares of the company in comparison to the rate at which the company came out with the last public offer in case of listed companies, and in case of unlisted companies, the variations in the net worth of the company as at the close of the current financial year and previous financial year; (viii) average percentile increase already made in the salaries of employees other than the managerial personnel in the last financial year and its comparison with the percentile increase in the managerial remuneration and justification thereof and point out if there are any exceptional circumstances for increase in the managerial remuneration; (ix) the key parameters for any variable component of remuneration availed by the directors; (x) the ratio of the remuneration of the highest paid director to that of the employees who are not

	are qualified to become directors and who may be appointed in senior management in accordance with the criteria laid down, and recommend to the board of directors their appointment and removal. (5) whether to extend or continue the term of appointment of the independent director, on the basis of the report of performance evaluation of independent directors.		directors but receive remuneration in excess of the highest paid director during the year; and (xi) affirmation that the remuneration is as per the remuneration policy of the company.
12. Risk Management Committee	**Regulation 21** (1)The board of directors shall constitute a Risk Management Committee. (2) The majority of members of Risk Management Committee shall consist of members of the board of directors. (3) The Chairperson of the Risk management committee shall be a member of the board of directors and senior executives of the listed entity may be members of the committee. (4) The board of directors shall define the role and responsibility of the Risk Management Committee and may delegate monitoring and reviewing of the risk management plan to the committee and such other functions as it may deem fit. (5) The provisions of this regulation shall be applicable to top 100 listed entities, determined on the basis of market capitalisation, as at the end of the immediate previous financial year.	**Clause 49(VI). Risk Management** A. The company shall lay down procedures to inform Board members about the risk assessment and minimization procedures. B. The Board shall be responsible for framing, implementing and monitoring the risk management plan for the company. C. The company shall also constitute a Risk Management Committee. The Board shall define the roles and responsibilities of the Risk Management Committee and may delegate monitoring and reviewing of the risk management plan to the committee and such other functions as it may deem fit.	
13.Audit Committee	**Regulation 18(1).** *Every listed entity shall constitute a qualified and*	**Clause 49(III)** A. A qualified and independent audit committee shall be set up,	**Section 177(1) of the Act of 2013**, audit committees made mandatory for listed companies

independent audit committee in accordance with the terms of reference, subject to the following: (1)(a) The audit committee shall have minimum three directors as members. (b) Two-thirds of the members of audit committee shall be independent directors. (c) All members of audit committee shall be financially literate and at least one member shall have accounting or related financial management expertise. Explanation (1).- For the purpose of this regulation, "financially literate" shall mean the ability to read and understand basic financial statements i.e. balance sheet, profit and loss account, and statement of cash flows. Explanation (2).- For the purpose of this regulation , a member shall be considered to have accounting or related financial management expertise if he or she possesses experience in finance or accounting, or requisite professional certification in accounting, or any other comparable experience or background which results in the individual's financial sophistication, including being or having been a chief executive officer, chief financial officer or other senior officer with financial oversight responsibilities. (d) The chairperson of the audit committee shall be an independent director and he shall be present at Annual general meeting to answer shareholder queries. (e) The Company Secretary	giving the terms of reference subject to the following: 1. The audit committee shall have minimum three directors as members. Two-thirds of the members of audit committee shall be independent directors. 2. All members of audit committee shall be financially literate and at least one member shall have accounting or related financial management expertise. **B.Meeting of Audit Committee.** The Audit Committee should meet at least four times in a year and not more than four months shall elapse between two meetings. The quorum shall be either two members or one third of the members of the audit committee whichever is greater, but there should be a minimum of two independent members present. **C.Powers of Audit Committee** The Audit Committee shall have powers, which should include the following: 1. To investigate any activity within its terms of reference. 2. To seek information from any employee. 3. To obtain outside legal or other professional advice. 4. To secure attendance of outsiders with relevant expertise, if it considers necessary. **D.Role of Audit Committee** The role of the Audit Committee shall include the following: 1.Oversight of the company's financial reporting process and the disclosure of its financial information to ensure that the financial statement is correct, sufficient and credible; 2.Recommendation for appointment, remuneration and terms of appointment of auditors of the company; 3.Approval of payment to statutory auditors for any other services rendered by the statutory auditors; 4.Reviewing, with the management, the annual	and other prescribed classes of companies. The 2013 Act provides that audit committee should consist of minimum of *three directors* with Independent Directors forming majority. Section 177(2). Further, the chairperson and the majority of the members of the audit committee should have the ability to read and understand the financial statements (referred as "financially literate" under the Listing Agreement). *The role of the audit committee includes the following activities as per the 2013 Act: Section 177(4):* i) the recommendation for appointment, remuneration and terms of appointment of auditors of the company; ii) review and monitor the auditor's independence and performance, and effectiveness of audit process; iii) examination of the financial statement and the auditors' report thereon; iv) approval or any subsequent modification of transactions of the company with related parties; v) scrutiny of inter-corporate loans and investments; vi) valuation of undertakings or assets of the company, wherever necessary; vii) evaluation of internal financial controls and risk management systems; viii) monitoring the end use of funds raised through public offers and related matters.

shall act as the secretary to the audit committee.
(f) The audit committee at its discretion shall invite the finance director or head of the finance function, head of internal audit and a representative of the statutory auditor and any other such executives to be present at the meetings of the committee:
Provided that occasionally the audit committee may meet without the presence of any executives of the listed entity.
(2) The listed entity shall conduct the meetings of the audit committee in the following manner:
(a) The audit committee shall meet at least four times in a year and not more than one hundred and twenty days shall elapse between two meetings.
(b) The quorum for audit committee meeting shall either be two members or one third of the members of the audit committee, whichever is greater, with at least two independent directors.
(c) The audit committee shall have powers to investigate any activity within its terms of reference, seek information from any employee, obtain outside legal or other professional advice and secure attendance of outsiders with relevant expertise, if it considers necessary.
(3) The role of the audit committee and the information to be reviewed by the audit committee shall be as specified in Part C of Schedule II.

financial statements and auditor's report thereon before submission to the board for approval, with particular reference to:
a. Matters required to be included in the Director's Responsibility Statement to be included in the Board's report in terms of clause (c) of sub-section 3 of section 134 of the Companies Act, 2013
b. Changes, if any, in accounting policies and practices and reasons for the same
c. Major accounting entries involving estimates based on the exercise of judgment by management
d. Significant adjustments made in the financial statements arising out of audit findings
e. Compliance with listing and other legal requirements relating to financial statements
f. Disclosure of any related party transactions g. Qualifications in the draft audit report
5.Reviewing, with the management, the quarterly financial statements before submission to the board for approval;
6.Reviewing, with the management, the statement of uses / application of funds raised through an issue (public issue, rights issue, preferential issue, etc.), the statement of funds utilized for purposes other than those stated in the offer document / prospectus / notice and the report submitted by the monitoring agency monitoring the utilisation of proceeds of a public or rights issue, and making appropriate recommendations to the Board to take up steps in this matter;
7. Review and monitor the auditor's independence and performance, and effectiveness of audit process;
8.Approval or any subsequent modification of transactions of the company with related parties;

| | | 9.Scrutiny of inter-corporate loans and investments; 10. Valuation of undertakings or assets of the company, wherever it is necessary; 11. Evaluation of internal financial controls and risk management systems; 12. Reviewing, with the management, performance of statutory and internal auditors, adequacy of the internal control systems; 13. Reviewing the adequacy of internal audit function, if any, including the structure of the internal audit department, staffing and seniority of the official heading the department, reporting structure coverage and frequency of internal audit; 14. Discussion with internal auditors of any significant findings and follow up there on; 15. Reviewing the findings of any internal investigations by the internal auditors into matters where there is suspected fraud or irregularity or a failure of internal control systems of a material nature and reporting the matter to the board; 16. Discussion with statutory auditors before the audit commences, about the nature and scope of audit as well as post-audit discussion to ascertain any area of concern; 17. To look into the reasons for substantial defaults in the payment to the depositors, debenture holders, shareholders (in case of non-payment of declared dividends) and creditors; 18. To review the functioning of the Whistle Blower mechanism; 19. Approval of appointment of CFO (i.e., the whole-time Finance Director or any other person heading the finance function or discharging that function) after assessing the qualifications, experience and background, etc. of the candidate; | |

		20. Carrying out any other function as is mentioned in the terms of reference of the Audit Committee. **E.Review of information by Audit Committee** The Audit Committee shall mandatorily review the following information: 1. Management discussion and analysis of financial condition and results of operations; 2. Statement of significant related party transactions (as defined by the Audit Committee), submitted by management; 3. Management letters / letters of internal control weaknesses issued by the statutory auditors; 4. Internal audit reports relating to internal control weaknesses; and 5. The appointment, removal and terms of remuneration of the Chief internal auditor shall be subject to review by the Audit Committee.	
14.Disclosures in Annual Report including Board report	*Regulation 18* (1) the listed entity shall submit the *annual report to* the stock exchange within twenty one working days of it being approved and adopted in the annual general meeting as per the provisions of the Companies Act, 2013. (2) The *annual report* shall contain the following: (a) *audited financial statements* i.e. balance sheets, profit and loss accounts etc; (b) *consolidated financial statements* audited by its statutory auditors; (c) *cash flow statement* presented only under the indirect method as prescribed in Accounting Standard-3 or Indian Accounting Standard 7, as applicable, specified in Section 133 of the	*Clause 49* **A. Related Party Transactions** 1. Details of all material transactions with related parties shall be disclosed quarterly along with the compliance report on corporate governance. 2. The company shall disclose the policy on dealing with Related Party Transactions on its website and also in the Annual Report. **B. Disclosure of Accounting Treatment** Where in the preparation of financial statements, a treatment different from that prescribed in an Accounting Standard has been followed, the fact shall be disclosed in the financial statements, together with the management's explanation as to why it believes such alternative treatment is more representative of the true	*According to Section 134(3),* the Board of Directors report to be laid before a company in general meeting, shall include the following: (a) the extract of the annual return as provided under sub-section (3) of section 92 (b) number of meetings of the Board (c) Directors responsibility statement (d)a statement on declaration given by independent directors under section 149(6) (e)in case of a company covered under sub-section (1) of section 178, company's policy on director's appointment and remuneration including criteria for determining qualifications, positive attributes, independence of a director and other matters provided under sub-section (3) of section 178. (f) explanations or comments by the Board on every

Companies Act, 2013 read with relevant rules framed thereunder or as specified by the Institute of Chartered Accountants of India, whichever is applicable;
(d) directors report;
(e) *management discussion and analysis report* - either as a part of directors report or addition thereto;
(f) *business responsibility report* (refer 4 below)
(3) The annual report shall contain any other disclosures specified in Companies Act, 2013 along with other requirements as specified in Schedule V of these regulations.
A. Related Party Disclosure:
1. The listed entity shall make disclosures in compliance with the Accounting Standard on "Related Party Disclosures".
B. Management Discussion and Analysis:
1.Within existing company's competitive position:
(a) Industry structure and developments.
(b) Opportunities and Threats.
(c) Segment–wise or product-wise performance.
(d) Outlook
(e) Risks and concerns.
(f) Internal control systems and their adequacy.
(g) Discussion on financial performance with respect to operational performance.
(h) Material developments in Human Resources / Industrial Relations front, including number of people employed.
2.Adherence to accounting standards
Where in the preparation of financial statements, a

and fair view of the underlying business transaction in the Corporate Governance Report.

C. Remuneration of Directors
1. All pecuniary relationship or transactions of the non-executive directors vis-à-vis the company shall be disclosed in the Annual Report.

2. In addition to the disclosures required under the Companies Act, 2013, the following disclosures on the remuneration of directors shall be made in the section on the corporate governance of the Annual Report:

a. All elements of remuneration package of individual directors summarized under major groups, such as salary, benefits, bonuses, stock options, pension etc.

b. Details of fixed component and performance linked incentives, along with the performance criteria.

c. Service contracts, notice period, severance fees.

d. Stock option details, if any - and whether issued at a discount as well as the period over which accrued and over which exercisable.
3. The company shall publish its criteria of making payments to non-executive directors in its annual report. Alternatively, this may be put up on the company's website and reference drawn thereto in the annual report.

4. The company shall disclose the number of shares and convertible instruments held by non-executive directors in the annual report.

5. Non-executive directors shall be required to disclose their shareholding (both own or held

qualification, reservation or adverse remark or disclaimer made:
(i) by the auditor in his report and
(ii) by the company secretary in practice in his secretarial audit report,
(g) particulars of loans, guarantees or investments under section 186
(h) particulars of contracts or arrangements with related parties referred to sub-section (1) of section 188 in the prescribed form
(i) the state of the company's affairs
(j) the amount, if any, which it proposes to carry to any reserves
(k) the amount, if any, which it recommends should be paid by way of dividend,
(l) material changes and commitments, if any, affecting the financial position of the company which have occurred between the end of the financial year of the company to which the financial statements relate and the date of the report
(m)the conservation of energy, technology absorption, foreign exchange earnings and outgo, in such manner as may be prescribed (see Rule 8 and Form no. AOC 2 of the Companies (Accounts) Rules 2014
(n)a statement indicating development and implementation of a risk management policy for the company including identification therein of elements of risk, if any, which in the opinion of the Board may threaten the existence of the company
(o) the details about the policy developed and implemented by the company on corporate social responsibility initiatives taken during the year,
(p)in case of a listed company

treatment different from that prescribed in an Accounting Standard has been followed, the fact shall be disclosed in the financial statements, together with the management's explanation as to why it believes such alternative treatment is more representative of the true and fair view of the underlying business transaction.

C. Corporate Governance Report: The following disclosures shall be made in the section on the corporate governance of the annual report:

a) a brief statement on code of corporate governance

b) *Board of directors*

(a) composition and category of directors (e.g. promoter, executive, non-executive, independent non-executive, nominee director - institution represented and whether as lender or as equity investor);

(b) attendance of each director at the meeting of the board of directors and the last annual general meeting;

(c) number of other board of directors or committees in which a directors is a member or chairperson;

(d) number of meetings of the board of directors held and dates on which held;

(e) disclosure of relationships between directors inter-se;

(f) number of shares and convertible instruments held by nonexecutive directors;

(g) web link where details of familiarisation programmes imparted to independent directors is disclosed.

by / for other persons on a beneficial basis) in the listed company in which they are proposed to be appointed as directors, prior to their appointment. These details should be disclosed in the notice to the general meeting called for appointment of such director

D. Management

1. As part of the directors' report or as an addition thereto, a Management Discussion and Analysis report should form part of the Annual Report to the shareholders. This Management Discussion & Analysis should include discussion on the following matters within the limits set by the company's competitive position:

a. Industry structure and developments.

b. Opportunities and Threats.

c. Segment–wise or product-wise performance.

d. Outlook

e. Risks and concerns.

f. Internal control systems and their adequacy.

g. Discussion on financial performance with respect to operational performance.

h. Material developments in Human Resources / Industrial Relations front, including number of people employed.

2. Senior management shall make disclosures to the board relating to all material financial and commercial transactions, where they have personal interest, that may have a potential conflict with the interest of the company at large (for e.g. dealing in company shares, commercial dealings with bodies, which have shareholding of management and their relatives etc.)

Explanation: For this purpose, the term "senior management" shall mean personnel of the company who are members of

and every other public company having such paid-up share capital as may be prescribed, a statement indicating the manner in which formal annual valuation has been made by the Board of its own performance and that of its committees and individual directors,

(q) such other matters as may be prescribed.

c)Audit committee (a) brief description of terms of reference; (b) composition, name of members and chairperson; (c) meetings and attendance during the year **d)Nomination & Remuneration committee** (a) brief description of terms of reference; (b) composition, name of members and chairperson; (c) meeting and attendance during the year; (d) performance evaluation criteria for independent directors. **e)Directors remuneration** (a) all pecuniary relationship or transactions of the non-executive directors vis-à-vis the listed entity shall be disclosed in the annual report; (b) criteria of making payments to non-executive directors. alternatively, this may be disseminated on the listed entity's website and reference drawn thereto in the annual report; (c) disclosures with respect to remuneration: in addition to disclosures required under the Companies Act, 2013, the following disclosures shall be made: (i) all elements of remuneration package of individual directors summarized under major groups, such as salary, benefits, bonuses, stock options, pension etc; (ii) details of fixed component and performance linked incentives, along with the performance criteria; (iii) service contracts, notice period, severance fees; (iv) stock option details, if any and whether issued at	its core management team excluding the Board of Directors). This would also include all members of management one level below the executive directors including all functional heads. 3. The Code of Conduct for the Board of Directors and the senior management shall be disclosed on the website of the company. **E. Shareholders** 1. In case of the appointment of a new director or re-appointment of a director the shareholders must be provided with the following information: a. A brief resume of the director; b. Nature of his expertise in specific functional areas; c. Names of companies in which the person also holds the directorship and the membership of Committees of the Board; and d. Shareholding of non-executive directors as stated in Clause 49 (IV) (E) (v) above 2. Disclosure of relationships between directors inter-se shall be made in the Annual Report, notice of appointment of a director, prospectus and letter of offer for issuances and any related filings made to the stock exchanges where the company is listed. 3. Quarterly results and presentations made by the company to analysts shall be put on company's web-site, or shall be sent in such a form so as to enable the stock exchange on which the company is listed to put it on its own web-site. 4. A committee under the Chairmanship of a non-executive director and such other members as may be decided by the Board of the company shall be formed to specifically look	

a discount as well as the period over which accrued and over which exercisable.

f)Shareholders' grievance committee
(a) name of non-executive director heading the committee;
(b) name and designation of compliance officer;
(c) number of shareholders' complaints received so far;
(d) number not solved to the satisfaction of shareholders;
(e) number of pending complaints.

g)General meeting
(a) location and time, where last three annual general meetings held;
(b) whether any special resolutions passed in the previous three annual general meetings;
(c) whether any special resolution passed last year through postal ballot – details of voting pattern;
(d) person who conducted the postal ballot exercise;
(e) whether any special resolution is proposed to be conducted through postal ballot;
(f) procedure for postal ballot.

h)Means of communication
(a) quarterly results;
(b) newspapers wherein results normally published;
(c) any website, where displayed;
(d) whether it also displays official news releases; and
(e) presentations made to institutional investors or to the analysts.

i)General shareholder information
(a) annual general meeting - date, time and venue;
(b) financial year;
(c) dividend payment date;
(d) the name and address

into the redressal of grievances of shareholders, debenture holders and other security holders. This Committee shall be designated as 'Stakeholders Relationship Committee' and shall consider and resolve the grievances of the security holders of the company including complaints related to transfer of shares, non-receipt of balance sheet, non-receipt of declared dividends.

5. To expedite the process of share transfers, the Board of the company shall delegate the power of share transfer to an officer or a committee or to the registrar and share transfer agents. The delegated authority shall attend to share transfer formalities at least once in a fortnight.

F. Disclosure of resignation of directors
1. The company shall disclose the letter of resignation along with the detailed reasons of resignation provided by the director of the company on its website not later than one working day from the date of receipt of the letter of resignation.

2. The company shall also forward a copy of the letter of resignation along with the detailed reasons of resignation to the stock exchanges not later than one working day from the date of receipt of resignation for dissemination through its website.

G. Disclosure of formal letter of appointment
1. The letter of appointment of the independent director along with the detailed profile shall be disclosed on the websites of the company and the Stock Exchanges not later than one working day from the date of such appointment.

of each stock exchange(s) at which the listed entity's securities are listed and a confirmation about payment of annual listing fee to each of such stock exchange(s); (e) stock code; (f) market price data- high, low during each month in last financial year; (g) performance in comparison to broad-based indices such as BSE sensex, CRISIL Index etc; (h) in case the securities are suspended from trading, the directors report shall explain the reason thereof; (i) registrar to an issue and share transfer agents; (j) share transfer system; (k) distribution of shareholding; (l) dematerialization of shares and liquidity; (m) outstanding global depository receipts or american depository receipts or warrants or any convertible instruments, conversion date and likely impact on equity; (n) commodity price risk or foreign exchange risk and hedging activities; (o) plant locations; (p) address for correspondence. *j)Other disclosures* (a) disclosures on materially significant related party transactions that may have potential conflict with the interests of listed entity at large; (b) details of non-compliance by the listed entity, penalties, strictures imposed on the listed entity by stock exchange(s) or the board or any statutory authority, on any matter related to capital markets, during the last three years;	**H. Disclosures in Annual report** 1. The details of training imparted to Independent Directors shall be disclosed in the Annual Report. 2. The details of establishment of vigil mechanism shall be disclosed by the company on its website and in the Board's report. 3. The company shall disclose the remuneration policy and the evaluation criteria in its Annual Report.

	(c) details of establishment of vigil mechanism, whistle blower policy, and affirmation that no personnel has been denied access to the audit committee; (d) details of compliance with mandatory requirements and adoption of the non-mandatory requirements; (e) web link where policy for determining 'material' subsidiaries is disclosed; (f) web link where policy on dealing with related party transactions; (g) disclosure of commodity price risks and commodity hedging activities.		
15. Directors Business Responsibility report	(f) for the top hundred listed entities based on market capitalization (calculated as on March 31 of every financial year), *business responsibility report* describing the initiatives taken by them from an environmental, social and governance perspective, in the format as specified by the Board from time to time: Provided that listed entities other than top 100 listed companies based on market capitalization and listed entities which have listed their specified securities on SME Exchange, may include these business responsibility reports on a voluntary basis in the format as specified.	Included above	According to Section 134(5) of the Act 2013, Directors Responsibility Statement shall state the following: (a) in the preparation of annual accounts, the applicable accounting standards had been followed along with proper explanation relating to material departures (b)the directors had selected such accounting policies and applied them consistently and made judgements and estimates that are reasonable and prudent so as to give a true and fair view of the state of affairs of the company at the end of the financial year and of the profit and loss of the company for that period, (c) the directors had taken proper and sufficient care for the maintenance of adequate accounting records in accordance with the provisions of this Act for safeguarding the assets of the company and for preventing and detecting fraud and other irregularities (d) the directors had prepared the annual accounts on a going concern basis and (e) the directors, in case of a

			listed company, had laid down internal financial controls to be followed by the company and that such internal financial controls are adequate and were operating effectively. Explanation: For the purposes of this clause, the term "internal financial controls" means the policies and procedures adopted by the company for ensuring the orderly and efficient conduct of its business, including adherence to company's policies, the safeguarding of its assets, the prevention and detection of frauds and errors, the accuracy and completeness of the accounting records and the timely preparation of reliable financial information. (f) the directors had devised proper systems to ensure compliance with the provisions of all applicable laws and that such systems were adequate and operating effectively.
16.CEO/ CFO certification	*Declaration signed by the chief executive officer* stating that the members of board of directors and senior management personnel have affirmed compliance with the code of conduct of board of directors and senior management.	Clause 49(IX): CEO/CFO certification The CEO, i.e. the Managing Director or Manager appointed in terms of the Companies Act, 1956 and the CFO i.e. the whole-time Finance Director or any other person heading the finance function discharging that function shall certify to the Board that: A. They have reviewed financial statements and the cash flow statement for the year and that to the best of their knowledge and belief: 1. these statements do not contain any materially untrue statement or omit any material fact or contain statements that might be misleading; 2. these statements together present a true and fair view of the company's affairs and are in compliance with existing accounting standards, applicable laws and regulations.	

		B. There are, to the best of their knowledge and belief, no transactions entered into by the company during the year which are fraudulent, illegal or violative of the company's code of conduct. C. They accept responsibility for establishing and maintaining internal controls for financial reporting and that they have evaluated the effectiveness of internal control systems of the company pertaining to financial reporting and they have disclosed to the auditors and the Audit Committee, deficiencies in the design or operation of such internal controls, if any, of which they are aware and the steps they have taken or propose to take to rectify these deficiencies. D. They have indicated to the auditors and the Audit committee: 1. significant changes in internal control over financial reporting during the year; 2. significant changes in accounting policies during the year and that the same have been disclosed in the notes to the financial statements; and 3. instances of significant fraud of which they have become aware and the involvement therein, if any, of the management or an employee having a significant role in the company's internal control system over financial reporting.	
17. Compliance certificate by auditors and practicing company secretary	E. Compliance certificate from either the auditors or practicing company secretaries regarding compliance of conditions of corporate governance shall be annexed with the directors' report.	Clause 49(XI) Compliance A. The company shall obtain a certificate from either the auditors or practicing company secretaries regarding compliance of conditions of corporate governance as stipulated in this clause and annex the certificate with the directors' report, which is sent	

	annually to all the shareholders of the company. The same certificate shall also be sent to the Stock Exchanges along with the annual report filed by the company.		

18.Related Party transactions	**Regulation 23**
	(1).The listed entity shall formulate a policy on materiality of related party transactions and on dealing with related party transactions:
	Explanation - A transaction with a related party shall be considered material if the transaction(s) to be entered into individually or taken together with previous transactions during a financial year, exceeds ten percent of the annual consolidated turnover of the listed entity as per the last audited financial statements of the listed entity.
	(2) All related party transactions shall require prior approval of the audit committee.
	(3) Audit committee may grant omnibus approval for related party transactions proposed to be entered into by the listed entity subject to the following conditions, namely-
	(a) the audit committee shall lay down the criteria for granting the omnibus approval in line with the policy on related party transactions of the listed entity and such approval shall be applicable in respect of transactions which are repetitive in nature;
	(b) the audit committee shall satisfy itself regarding the need for such omnibus approval and that such approval is in the interest of the listed entity;
		Clause 49(VII)Related Party Transactions
		A. A related party transaction is a transfer of resources, services or obligations between a company and a related party, regardless of whether a price is charged.
		
		B. A 'related party' is a person or entity that is related to the company. Parties are considered to be related if one party has the ability to control the other party or exercise significant influence over the other party, directly or indirectly, in making financial and/or operating decisions and includes the following:
		
		1. A person or a close member of that person's family is related to a company if that person:
		a. is a related party under Section 2(76) of the Companies Act, 2013;or
		b. has control or joint control or significant influence over the company; or
		c. is a key management personnel of the company or of a parent of the company; or
		
		2. An entity is related to a company if any of the following conditions applies:
		
		a. The entity is a related party under Section 2(76) of the Companies Act, 2013; or
		b. The entity and the company are members of the same group (which means that each parent, subsidiary and fellow subsidiary is related to the others); or
		c. One entity is an associate or joint venture of the other entity (or an associate or joint venture of a member of a group of which
			Section 188(1), except with the consent of the Board of Directors given by a resolution at a Board meeting and subject to such conditions as may be prescribed, no company shall enter into any contract or arrangement with a related party with respect to:
			  (a) sales, purchase or supply of any goods or materials
			  (b) selling or otherwise disposing of, or buying, property of any kind,
			  (c) leasing of property of any kind
			  (d) availing or rendering of any services
			  (e) appointment of any agent for purchase or sale of goods, materials, services or property,
			  (f) such related party's appointment to any office or place of profit in the company, its subsidiary company or associate company and
			  (g) underwriting the subscription of any securities or derivatives thereof of the company;
			The 2013 Act prescribes that all related party transactions which are not in the ordinary course of business or not at arm's length basis should be approved by the Board.
			The 2013 Act also prescribes that for the companies with the prescribed share capital, no contract or arrangement or transactions exceeding prescribed amount, shall be entered into with its related party, unless, approved by the

(c) the omnibus approval shall specify: (i) the name(s) of the related party, nature of transaction, period of transaction, maximum amount of transactions that shall be entered into, (ii) the indicative base price / current contracted price and the formula for variation in the price if any; and (iii) such other conditions as the audit committee may deem fit: Provided that where the need for related party transaction cannot be foreseen and aforesaid details are not available, audit committee may grant omnibus approval for such transactions subject to their value not exceeding rupees one crore per transaction. (d) the audit committee shall review, at least on a quarterly basis, the details of related party transactions entered into by the listed entity pursuant to each of the omnibus approvals given. (e) Such omnibus approvals shall be valid for a period not exceeding one year and shall require fresh approvals after the expiry of one year: (4) All material related party transactions shall require approval of the shareholders through resolution and the related parties shall abstain from voting on such resolutions whether the entity is a related party to the particular transaction or not. (5) The provisions of sub-regulations (2), (3) and (4) shall not be applicable in the following cases:	the other entity is a member); or d. Both entities are joint ventures of the same third party; or e. One entity is a joint venture of a third entity and the other entity is an associate of the third entity; or f. The entity is a post-employment benefit plan for the benefit of employees of either the company or an entity related to the company. If the company is itself such a plan, the sponsoring employers are also related to the company; or g. The entity is controlled or jointly controlled by a person identified in (1). h. A person identified in (1)(b) has significant influence over the entity (or of a parent of the entity); or **Explanation:** For the purpose of Clause 49(V) and Clause VII (B), the term "control" shall have the same meaning as defined in SEBI (Substantial Acquisition of Shares and Takeovers) Regulations, 2011. C. The company shall formulate a policy on materiality of related party transactions and also on dealing with Related Party Transactions. Provided that a transaction with a related party shall be considered material if the transaction / transactions to be entered into individually or taken together with previous transactions during a financial year, exceeds five percent of the annual turnover or twenty percent of the net worth of the company as per the last audited financial statements of the company, whichever is higher. D. All Related Party Transactions shall require prior approval of the Audit Committee. E. All material Related Party Transactions shall require	shareholders of the company by way of a special resolution. However, the related party shareholders are not permitted to exercise their voting rights, in such special resolution. The 2013 Act also specifies that a company shall not make investments through more than two layers of investment companies, unless the investments are in an overseas company and the company has overseas subsidiaries and such layers are permitted under the local law of the company being acquired or under the law of the acquiring company. Every contract or arrangement entered into with a related party shall be referred to in the Board's report along with the justification for entering into such contract or arrangement.

	(a) transactions entered into between two government companies;	approval of the shareholders through special resolution and the related parties shall abstain from voting on such resolutions.	
	(b) transactions entered into between a holding company and its wholly owned subsidiary whose accounts are consolidated with such holding company and placed before the shareholders at the general meeting for approval.		
	Explanation - For the purpose of clause (a), "government company (ies)" means Government company as defined in sub-section (45) of section 2 of the Companies Act, 2013.		
	(6) The provisions of this regulation shall be applicable to all prospective transactions. (7) For the purpose of this regulation, all entities falling under the definition of related parties shall abstain from voting irrespective of whether the entity is a party to the particular transaction or not. (8) All existing material related party contracts or arrangements entered into prior to the date of notification of these regulations and which may continue beyond such date shall be placed for approval of the shareholders in the first General Meeting subsequent to notification of these regulations.		
19.Performan-ce evaluation of Independent Directors	*Regulation 17(10)*The performance evaluation of independent directors shall be done by the entire board of directors: Provided that in the above evaluation the directors	*Clause 49(II)(B)(5)* The Nomination Committee shall lay down the evaluation criteria for performance evaluation of independent directors. The company shall disclose the criteria for performance	*Section 178(2) read with Schedule IV* The Nomination and Remuneration Committee shall identify persons who are qualified to become directors and who may be appointed in senior management in

	who are subject to evaluation shall not participate	evaluation, as laid down by the Nomination Committee, in its Annual Report. The performance evaluation of independent directors shall be done by the entire Board of Directors (excluding the director being evaluated). On the basis of the report of performance evaluation, it shall be determined whether to extend or continue the term of appointment of the independent director.	accordance with the criteria laid down, recommend to the Board their appointment and removal and shall carry out evaluation of every director's performance. The performance evaluation of independent directors shall be done by the entire Board of Directors, excluding the director being evaluated. On the basis of the report of performance evaluation, it shall be determined whether to extend or continue the term of appointment of the independent director.
20.Number of directorships		Limit on number of directorships a. A person shall not serve as an independent director in more than seven listed companies. b. Further, any person who is serving as a whole time director in any listed company shall serve as an independent director in not more than three listed companies.	According to Section 165(1) of Companies Act 2013, a person cannot have directorships (including alternate directorships) in more than twenty companies, including ten public companies. For determination of public companies, directorship in private companies that are either holding or subsidiary company of a public company shall be regarded as a public company. It is noted that members at their discretion can prescribe a lower number of companies in which a director of the company may act as a director. The 2013 Act provides for one year period from the enactment to comply with this requirement
21.Prohibition of insider trading	Relevant provisions on insider trading highlighted in SECURITIES AND EXCHANGE BOARD OF INDIA (PROHIBITION OF INSIDER TRADING) REGULATIONS, 2015.		New clause has been introduced with respect to prohibition of insider trading of securities under the 2013 Act. The definition of price sensitive information has also been included. No person including any director or Key Management Personnel of a company shall enter into insider trading except any communication required in the ordinary course of business or profession or employment or under any law. Section 195(1).

Chapter 3: Financial Reporting requirements under Companies Act 2013

3.1. Financial Reporting requirements under Schedule III of Companies Act 2013

Amendments to schedule III of the Companies Act 2013 incorporating financial reporting requirements under Indian Accounting Standards (Ind AS)

Division I
Financial Statements for a company Financial Statements of which are required to comply with the Companies (Accounting Standards) Rules, 2006.

GENERAL INSTRUCTIONS FOR PREPARATION OF BALANCE SHEET AND STATEMENT OF PROFIT AND LOSS OF A COMPANY".

3.2. Balance Sheet: (Schedule III – Part I)
Specimen Balance Sheet format as detailed in Schedule III – Part I is reproduced below.
Name of Company............
Balance Sheet as at..........

Particulars	Note no.	Figures as at the end of current reporting period	Figures as at the end of previous reporting period
1	2	3	4
I. Equity and Liabilities			
(1)Shareholders' funds			
a) Share capital			
b) Reserve and surplus			
c) Money received against share warrants			
(2)Share application money pending allotment			
(3)Non-current liabilities			
a) Long term borrowings			
b) Deferred tax liabilities (net)			
c) Other long term liabilities and			
d) Long term provisions and			
(4)Current liabilities which covers			
a) Short term borrowings			
b) Trade payables			
c) Other current liabilities			
d) Short term provisions			
TOTAL			
II. Assets			
Non-current assets			
(I)(a) Fixed Assets			
(i) Tangible assets,			
(ii) Intangible assets,			
(iii) capital work-in-progress			
(iv)Intangibles under development			
(b) Non-current investments			

(c) Deferred tax assets (net)
(d) Long term loans and advances and
(e) other non-current assets and
(2)Current assets
  (a) Current investments
  (b) Inventories
  (c) Trade receivables
  (d) Cash and cash equivalents
  (e) Short term loans and advances and
  (f) Other current assets			

TOTAL			

The format above is followed by General Instructions for preparation of Balance Sheet in Schedule III, which is summarised as under:

3.2.1. Non-current assets

1.An asset shall be classified as current when it satisfies any of the following criteria:	a) It is expected to be realized in, or is intended for sale of consumption in the company's normal operating cycle; b) It is held primarily for the purpose of being traded; c) It is expected to be realized within twelve months after the reporting date ; or d) It is cash or cash equivalent unless it is restricted from being exchanged or used to settle a liability for at least twelve months after the reporting date.

All other assets shall be classified as non-current.

3.2.2. Operating cycle

2. An operating cycle is the time between the acquisition of assets for processing and their realization in cash or cash equivalents. Where the normal operating cycle cannot be identified. It is assumed to have a duration of 12 months.

3.2.3.Non-current liabilities

3. A liability shall be classified as current when it satisfies any of the following criteria	(a) It is expected to be settled in the company's normal operating cycle (b) It is held primarily for the purpose of being traded (c) it is due to be settled within twelve months after the reporting date or (d) The company does not have an unconditional right to defer settlement of the liability for at least 12 months after the reporting date. The terms of a liability , that could , at the option of counter-party result in its

	settlement by the issue of equity instruments do not affect its classification

All other liabilities shall be classified as non-current.

4. A receivable shall be classified as a "trade receivable" if it is in respect of the amount due on account of goods sold or services rendered in the normal course of business

5. A payable shall be classified as a "trade payable" If it is in respect of the amount due on account of goods purchased or services received in the normal course of business.
6. A company shall disclose the following in the notes to accounts

A. Share Capital
For each class of share capital (different classes of preference shares to be treated separately)
    (a) the number of amount of shares authorized
    (b) the number of shares issued, subscribed and fully paid up and subscribed and not fully paid up
    (c) par value of shares

Illustration 3.1 - Specimen format of Share Capital

	As at 31st March 2016	As at 31st March 2015
Authorised Share Capital:		
Equity shares of Rs. each	xxx	xxx
Preference shares of Rs. each	xxx	xxx
Total	xxx	Xxx
Issued, subscribed and paid-up:		
Equity shares of Rs. each	xxx	xxx
Preference shares of Rs. Each	xxx	xxx
Less: Calls in arrears (Rs. (Previous Year Rs.))	xxx	xxx
Total	xxx	Xxx

    (d) a reconciliation of number of shares outstanding at the beginning and at the end of the reporting period

Illustration 3.2 : Reconciliation of number of shares outstanding:

Particulars	As at 31st March 2016 No.of shares	As at 31st March 2016 Amount Rs)	As at 31st March 2015 No.of shares	As at 31st March 2015 Amount (Rs)
Equity shares at the beginning of the year	X	X	X	X
Add: Shares issued on exercise of employee stock Option	X	X	X	X
Less: Shares cancelled on buy back of equity Shares	x	X	X	X
Equity shares at the end of the year	x	X	X	X

    (e) the rights, preferences and restrictions attaching to each class of shares including restrictions on the distribution of dividend and repayment of capital

(f) shares in respect of each class in the company held by its holding company or its ultimate holding company including shares held by or by subsidiaries or associates of the holding or its ultimate holding company in aggregate

(g) shares in the company held by each shareholder holding more than 5% shares specifying the number of shares held

Illustration 3. 3: Specimen format of details of shareholders holding more than 5% shares

Name of the shareholder	As at 31st March 2016		As at 31st March 2015	
	No. of Shares	% held	No. of Shares	% held
Share holder A	X	x	X	x
Share holder B	X	x	X	x
Share holder C	X	X	X	X

(h) shares reserved for issue under options and contracts / commitments for the sale of shares / disinvestment including terms and amounts

(i) for the period of five years immediately preceding the date as at which the Balance Sheet is prepared :

- aggregate number and class of shares allotted as fully paid up pursuant to contracts without payment being received in cash
- aggregate number and class of shares allotted as fully paid up by way of bonus shares
- aggregate number and class of shares boughtback

(j) Terms of any securities convertible into equity / preference shares issued with the earliest date of conversion in descending order starting from the farthest such that

(k) calls unpaid (showing aggregate value of calls unpaid by directors and officers)

(l) forfeited shares (amount originally paid up)

B. Reserves and surplus

(i) Reserves and Surplus shall be classified as:	a) Capital reserve, b) Capital redemption reserve, c) Securities premium reserve, d) Debenture redemption reserve e) Revaluation Reserve; f) Share Options Outstanding Account ; g) Other Reserves – (specify the nature and purpose of each reserve and the amount in respect thereof) h) Surplus i.e. balance in Statement of Profit & Loss disclosing allocations and appropriations such as dividend, bonus shares and transfer to / from reserves etc. (Additions and deductions since last balance sheet to be shown under each of the specific heads)

(ii) A reserve specifically represented by earmarked investments shall be termed as a "fund"

(iii) Debit balance of Statement of Profit and Loss shall be shown as a negative figure under the head "surplus". Similarly balance of "Reserves and surplus" after adjusting the negative balance of surplus. If any, shall be shown under the head "Reserves and surplus" even if the resulting figure is in the negative.

Illustration 3.4: Specimen format of Reserves and Surplus

		As at 31st March 2016	As at 31st March 2015
Revaluation Reserve			
As per last Balance Sheet		xxx	xxx
Less: Transferred to Profit and Loss Account		(xxx)	(xxx)
Less: Utilised ondemerger adjustments		(xxx)	(xxx)
	Sub-total	Xxx	xxx
Capital Reserve			
As per last Balance Sheet		Xxx	xxx
	Sub-total	Xxx	xxx
Capital Redemption Reserve			
As per last Balance Sheet		xxx	xxx
Add: Transferred from Profit & Loss Account on buy back of equity shares			
		xxx	xxx
	Sub-total	Xxx	xxx
Securities Premium Reserve			
As per last Balance Sheet		xxx	xxx
Add: On issue of shares		xxx	xxx
Less: Redemption of debentures / bonds		xxx	xxx
Less: Buy back of equity shares		(xxx)	(xxx)
Less: Calls in arrears – others		(xxx)	(xxx)
		(xxx)	(xxx)
	Sub-total	Xxx	xxx
Debenture redemption reserve			
As per last Balance Sheet		Xxx	xxx
	Sub-total	Xxx	xxx
General Reserve			
As per last Balance Sheet		xxx	xxx
Add: Transfer from Profit and Loss Account		xxx	xxx
	Sub-total	Xxx	xxx
Profit & Loss Account		xxx	xxx
As per last Balance Sheet		xxx	xxx
Add: Profit for the year		xxx	xxx
Less: Appropriations			
Transfer to General Reserve		(xxx)	(xxx)
Transfer to Capital Redemption reserve on buy		(xxx)	(xxx)
Back of equity shares		(xxx)	(xxx)
Proposed dividend on equity shares		(xxx)	(xxx)
(Dividend per share Rs. (Previous Year Rs.))			
Tax on dividend		(xxx)	(xxx)
	Sub-total	Xxx	Xxx
	Total	Xxx	Xxx

C. Long-term borrowings

(i)Long-term borrowings shall be classified as:	a) Bonds / debentures b) Term loans • From banks • From other parties c) Deferred payment liabilities d) Deposits e) Loans and advances from related parties f) Long term maturities of finance lease obligations g) Other loans and advances (specify nature)

(i) Borrowings shall further be sub-classified as secured and unsecured. Nature of security shall be specified separately in each case.

(ii) Where loans have been guaranteed by directors and others, the aggregate amount of such loans under each head shall be disclosed.

(iii) Bonds / debentures alongwith rate of interest and particulars of redemption or conversion as the case may be) shall be stated in descending order of maturity or conversion starting from farthest date of redemption or conversion as the case may be. Where bonds/debentures are redeemable by instalments, the date of maturity for this purpose,must be reckoned as the date on which the first instalment becomes due.

(iv) Particulars of any redeemed bonds / debentures which the company has the power to reissue shall be disclosed.

(v) Terms of repayment of term loans and other loans shall be stated

(vi) Period and amount of continuing default as on the balance sheet date in repayment of loans shall be specified separately in each case

Illustration 3.5 : Specimen format for Long term borrowings

	As at 31st March 2016		As at 31st March 2015	
	Non-current	Current	Non-current	Current
Secured				
Non-convertible debentures	xxx	xxx	xxx	xxx
Term loans from banks	xxx	xxx	xxx	xxx
Long term maturities of finance lease obligations				
	xxx	xxx	xxx	xxx
Unsecured				
Bonds	xxx	xxx	xxx	xxx
Term loans from banks	xxx	xxx	xxx	xxx
Deferred payment liabililies	xxx	xxx	xxx	xxx
Total	xxx	xxx	xxx	Xxx

Illustration 3.6: Specimen format of Maturity profile and rate of interest of Debentures and bonds

Rate of interest	2016-17	2017-18	2018-19	2019-20	2020-21
Xxx	xxx	xxx	Xxx	Xxx	Xxx
Xxx	xxx	xxx	Xxx	Xxx	Xxx
Xxx	xxx	xxx	Xxx	Xxx	Xxx
Xxx	xxx	xxx	Xxx	Xxx	Xxx

Applicable for unsecured term loans as well

D. Other long-term liabilities

Other long term liabilities to be classified as :
(a) Trade payables
(b) Others

Illustration 3.7 : Deferred tax Liability (net)

	As at 31st March 2016	As at 31st March 2015
Deferred tax liability Related to Fixed Assets	xxx	xxx
Deferred tax assets Disallowances under Income tax Act 1961	xxx	xxx
Total	Xxx	Xxx

E. Long term provisions

The amount shall be classified as :	(a) Provision for long term benefits (b) Others (specify nature)

F. Short-term borrowings

(i) Short term borrowings shall be classified as:	(a) loans repayable on demand • From banks • From other parties (b)Loans and advances from related parties (c)Deposits (d)Other loans and advances (specify nature)

(ii)Borrowings shall further be sub-classified as secured and unsecured. Nature of security shall be specified separately in each case.

(iii)Where loans have been guaranteed by directors or others, the aggregate amount of such loans under each head shall be disclosed.

(iv)Period and amount of default as on the balance sheet date in repayment of loans and Interest, shall be specified separately in each case.

Illustration 3.8 : Specimen format of Short term borrowing

	As at 31st March 2016	As at 31st March 2015
Secured loan		
Working capital loan from banks	xxx	xxx
Foreign currency loans	xxx	xxx
Rupee loans	xxx	xxx
Sub-total	xxx	xxx
Unsecured loan		
Other loans and advances from banks	xxx	xxx
Foreign currency loans – buyers credit	xxx	xxx
Rupee loans	xxx	xxx
Sub-total	Xxx	xxx

Note:

Working capital loans are secured by hypothecation of present and future stock of raw materials, stock-in process, finished goods, stores and spares (not relating to plant and machinery), book debts, outstanding monies, receivables, claims, bills, materials in transit, etc. save and except receivables of Oil and Gas Division.

5.2 Other Loans and Advances from banks include commercial paper of `NIL (Previous Year' NIL). Maximum balance outstanding at any time during the year being Rs. NIL (Previous Year   ).

G. Other current liabilities:

The amounts shall be classified as:	(a) Current maturities of long-term debt ; (b) Current maturities of finance lease obligations; (c) Interest accrued but not due on borrowings (d) Interest accrued and due on borrowings (e) Interest received in advance (f) Unpaid dividends (g) Application money received from allotment of securities and due for refund and interest accrued thereon. Share application money includes advances towards allotment of share capital. The terms and conditions including number of shares proposed to be issued, the amount of premium, if any, and the period before which shares shall be allotted should be disclosed. It shall also be disclosed whether the company has sufficient authorized capital to cover the share capital amount resulting from allotment of shares out of such share applicatio money. Further the period for which share application money has been pending beyond the period of allottment as mentioned in the document inviting application of shares along with the reason for such share application money being pending shall be disclosed. Share application money not exceeding the issued capital and to the extent not refundable shall be shown under the head Equity and share application money to the extent refundable i.e. the amount in excess of subscription or in case the requirements of minimum subscription are not met shall be separately shown under "other current liabilities". (h)Unpaid matured deposits and interest accrued thereon (i) Unpaid matured debentures and interest accrued thereon (j) Other payables (specify nature)

Illustration 3.9: Specimen format of Trade payables

	As at 31st March 2016	As at 31st March 2015
Micro, small and medium enterprises	xxx	Xxx
Others	xxx	Xxx
Total	xxx	Xxx

The details of amounts outstanding to Micro, Small and Medium Enterprises based on available information with the Company are as under:

Particulars	As at 31st March 2016	As at 31st March 2015
Principal amount due and remaining unpaid	xxx	Xxx
Interest due on above and the unpaid interest	xxx	xxx
Interest paid	xxx	xxx
Payment made beyond the appointed day during the year	xxx	xxx
Interest due and payable for the period of delay	xxx	xxx
Interest accrued and remaining unpaid	xxx	xxx
Amount of further interest remaining due and payable in succeeding years		
Total	xxx	Xxx

Illustration 3.10: Specimen format: Other current liabilities

	As at 31st March 2016	As at 31st March 2015
Current maturities of long term debt	xxx	Xxx
Current maturities of finance lease obligations	xxx	xxx
Interest accrued but not due on borrowings	xxx	xxx
Unclaimed Dividends	xxx	xxx
Application money received and due for refund	xxx	xxx
Unpaid matured debentures and interest accrued thereon	xxx	xxx
Creditors for Capital Expenditure	xxx	xxx
Advance for Transfer of Participating Interest	xxx	xxx
Other Payables *		
Total	xxx	Xxx

* Includes statutory dues, security deposit and advance from customers.

H. Short term provisions
The amounts shall be classified as :
a) Provision for employee benefits
b) Others (specify nature)

Illustration 3.11: Specimen format: Short term provisions

	As at 31st March 2016	As at 31st March 2015
Provisions for Superannuation/Gratuity/Leave Encashment	xxx	xxx
Proposed Dividend	xxx	xxx
Tax on Dividend	xxx	xxx
Provision for Taxes	xxx	xxx
Other Provisions	xxx	xxx
Total	xxx	Xxx

Illustration 3.12: Provisions for indirect taxes

Excise Duty / Service Tax and Sales Tax / Value Added Tax
Excise duty / Service tax is accounted on the basis of both, payments made in respect of goods cleared / services provided as also provision made for goods lying in bonded warehouses. Sales tax / Value added tax paid is charged to Profit and Loss account.

I. Tangible Assets

(i)Classification shall be given as:	(a) Land (b) Buildings (c) Plant and Equipment (d) Furniture and fixtures (e) Vehicles (f) Office equipment (g) Others (specify nature)

(ii)Assets under lease shall be separately specified under each class of asset.

(iii)A reconciliation of the gross and net carrying amounts of each class of assets at the beginning and end of the reporting period showing additions, disposals, acquisitions through business combinations and other adjustments and the related depreciation and impairment losses / reversals shall be disclosed separately.

iv)Where sums have been written off on a reduction of capital or revaluation of assets or where sums have been added on revaluation of assets, every balance sheet subsequent to date of such write-off, or addition shall show the reduced or increased figures as applicable and shall by way of a note also show the amount of the reduction or increase as applicable together with the date thereof for the first five years subsequent to the date of such reduction or increase.

J. Intangible Assets

(i)Classification shall be given as:	a) goodwill b) brand / trademarks c)computer software d)mastheads and publishing titles e)Mining rights f)Copyrights, patents and other intellectual property rights, services and operating rights g)recipes, formulae, models, designs and prototypes h)licenses and franchise i)Others (specify nature)

ii)A reconciliation of gross and net carrying amounts of each class of assets at the beginning and the end of the reporting period showing additions, disposals, acquisitions through business combinations and other adjustments and the related amortization and impairment losses / reversals shall be disclosed separately.

iii)Where sums have been written off on a reduction of capital or revaluation of assets, every balance sheet subsequent to date of such write-off, or addition, shall show the amount of reduction

or increase as applicable together with the date thereof for the first five years subsequent to the date of such reduction or increase.

Illustration 3.13 : Specimen format : Non-current assets

Description	Gross Block				Depreciation / amortisation				Net Block	
	Op.bal	Add	Delete	Cl. bal	Op.bal	Add	Delete	Cl.bal	31.3.12	31.3. 11
TANGIBLE ASSETS :										
OWN ASSETS :										
Leasehold Land										
Freehold Land										
Buildings										
Plant & Machinery										
Electrical Installations										
Equipments										
Furniture & Fixtures										
Vehicles										
Ships										
Aircrafts & Helicopters										
Sub-total										
LEASED ASSETS :										
Plant & Machinery										
Ships										
Sub-total										
Total (A)										
INTANGIBLE ASSETS : *										
Technical Knowhow fees										
Software										
Development Rights										
Others										
Total (B)										
Total (A+B)										
Previous Year										
Capital Work-in-progress										
Intangible asset under development										

* Other than internally generated

Illustration 3.14: Specimen format : Fixed Assets acquired on Finance Lease

	Total minimum lease payments Outstanding as at 31st March		Future interest on outstanding lease payments		Present value of minimum lease payment as at 31st March	
	2016	2015	2016	2015	2016	2015
Within one year						
Later than one year and not later than five years						
Later than five years						
Total						

General Description of Lease terms:
(a) Lease rentals are charged on the basis of agreed terms.
(b) Assets are taken on lease over a period of 5 to 10 years.

Illustration 3.15: Specimen format: Capital work-in-progress

	As at 31st March 2016	As at 31st March 2015
Opening Balance	xxx xxx	xxx xxx

Add: Transferred from Profit and Loss Account	xxx	xxx
Interest Capitalised	xxx	xxx
Less: Project Development Expenses Capitalised during the year		
Closing Balance	*xxx*	*Xxx*

Illustration 3.16: Specimen format: Intangible asset under development

	As at 31st March 2016	As at 31st March 2015
Opening Balance	xxx	xxx
Add: Transferred from Profit and Loss Account	xxx	xxx
Interest Capitalised	xxx	xxx
Less: Intangible asset under development capitalised during the year	xxx	xxx
Closing Balance	*Xxx*	*Xxx*

K. Non-current investments

(i) Non-current investments shall be classified as trade investments and other investments and further classified as:	(a) investment property ; (b) investment in equity instruments; (c)Investments in preference shares (d)Investments in government or trust securities (e)Investments in debentures or bonds ; (f)Investments in mutual funds ; (g)Investments in partnership firms (h)Other non-current investments (specify nature) Under each classification, details shall be given of names of the bodies corporate (indicating separately whether such bodies are (i)subsidiaries, (ii)associates, (iii)joint ventures or (iv)controlled special purpose entities) in whom investments have been made and the nature and extent of the investment so made in such body corporate (showing separately investments which are partly paid). In regard to investments in the capital of partnership firms, the names of the firms (with the names of all their partners, the total capital and shares of each partner) shall be given.
(ii)Investments carried at other than at cost	should be separately stated specifying the basis of valuation thereof.
(iii)The following shall also be disclosed:	(a) Aggregate amount of quoted investments and market value thereof, (b) Aggregate amount of unquoted investments , (c) Aggregate provision of dimunition in value of investments

Illustration 3.17: Specimen format : Non-current investments

Particulars	As at 31st March 2016	As at 31st March 2015
Trade Investments In Equity Shares - Unquoted, fully paid up In Equity Shares of Associate Companies - Unquoted, fully paid up In Preference Shares of Associate Company - Unquoted, fully paid up		
Total Trade Investments (A)		
Other Investments In Equity Shares of Associate Company - Quoted, fully paid up In Equity Shares of Associate Company - Unquoted, fully paid up In Equity Shares of Subsidiary Companies - Unquoted, fully paid up In Equity Shares of Subsidiary Companies - Unquoted, partly paid up In Preference Shares of Subsidiary Companies - Unquoted, fully paid up In Preference Shares of Subsidiary Company - Unquoted, partly paid up In Debentures of Subsidiary Companies - Unquoted, Fully paid up In Government Securities-Unquoted In Mutual Fund - Quoted fully paid up (face value Rs.)		
Total Other Investments (B) Total Non-Current Investments (A + B) Aggregate amount of quoted investments Market Value of quoted investments Aggregate amount of unquoted investments		

L. Long-term loans and advances

(i) Long-term loans and advances shall be classified as:	(a)Capital advances ; (b)Security deposits ; (c)Loans and advances to related parties (giving details thereof) (d)Other loans and advances (specify nature)
(ii)The above should be separately sub-classified as:	(a) Secured considered good (b) Unsecured considered good (c) Doubtful
(iii)Allowance for bad and doubtful loans and advances	shall be disclosed under relevant heads separately
(iv)Loans and advances due by directors and other officers of the company or any of them whether severally or jointly with any other persons or amounts due by firms or private companies respectively in which any director is a partner or a director or a	should be separately stated

member	

Illustration 3.18 : Specimen format : Long term loans and advances (unsecured and considered good)

Particulars	As at 31st March 2016	As at 31st March 2015
Capital Advances		
Deposits with Related parties		
Loans and Advances to Related Parties		
Advance Income Tax (Net of Provision)		
Loans and Advances in the nature of Loans given to Subsidiaries and Associates		
Other Loans and Advances*		
Total		

*Includes Loans to Employees

Illustration 3.19 : Specimen format : Assets given on finance lease on or after 1st April 2001:

Particulars	Total		Not later than one year		Later than one year and not later than five years		Later than five years	
	2016	2016	2016	2015	2016	2015	2016	2015
Gross Investment								
Less: Unearned Finance Income								
Present Value of Minimum Lease Rental								
Total								

General Description of Lease terms:
• Lease rentals are charged on the basis of agreed rate of interest.
• Assets are given on lease for a period of five years.

M. Other non-current assets

Other non-current assets shall be classified as:	(i)Long term trade receivables (including trade receivables on deferred credit terms)
	 (ii)others (specify nature)
	 (iii)Long term trade receivables, shall be sub-classified as:
	   (i)(a)Secured , considered good ;
	     (b) Unsecured, considered good ;
	     (c)considered doubtful
	   (ii)Allowance for bad and doubtful debts shall be disclosed under relevant heads separately
	   (iii)Debts due by directors and other officers of the company or any of them whether severally or jointly with any other persons or amounts due by firms or private companies respectively in which any director is a partner or a director or a member should be separately stated

N. Current Investments

(i) Current investments shall be classified as:	(a)Investments in equity instruments ; (b)Investments in Preference Shares ; (c)Investment in government or trust securities ; (d)Investments in debentures or bonds ; (e)Investments in mutual funds ; (f)Investments in partnership firms ; (g)Other investments (specify nature) Under each classification, details shall be given of names of the bodies corporate (indicating separately whether such bodies are (i)subsidiaries, (ii)associates, (iii)joint ventures, or (iv) controlled special purpose entities) in whom investments have been made and the nature and extent of the investment so made in each such body corporate (showing separately investments which are partly-paid). In regard to investments in the capital of partnership firms. The names of the firms (with the names of all their partners, total capital and the shares of each partne) shall be given;
(ii)The following shall also be disclosed:	(a)basis of valuation of individual investments (b)aggregate amount of quoted investments and market value thereof (c)aggregate amount of unquoted investments (d)aggregate provision made for dimunition in the value of investments.

Illustration 3.20: Current Investments

Particulars	As at 31st March 2016	As at 31st March 2015
Investment in Government Securities - Quoted, Fully Paid up	xxx	xxx
Investment in Debentures or Bonds - Quoted, Fully Paid up	xxx	xxx
Investment in Mutual Fund - Quoted, Fully Paid up	xxx	xxx
Investment in Units – Quoted	xxx	xxx
Investment in Commercial Paper – Quoted	xxx	xxx
Investment in Certificate of Deposits with Scheduled Banks - Quoted	xxx	xxx
Total Current Investments	xxx	Xxx

Aggregate amount of quoted investments
Market Value of quoted investments

O. Inventories

(i) Inventories shall be classified as :	(a) Raw materials (b) Work-in-progress (c) Finished goods (d) Stock-in-trade (in respect of goods acquire for trading) (e) Stores and spares (f) Loose tools (g) Others (specify nature)
(ii) Goods-in-transit	shall be disclosed under the relevant sub-head of inventories
(iii) Mode of valuation	shall be stated

Illustration 3.21: Specimen Format : Inventories

Particulars	As at 31st March 2016	As at 31st March 2015
Raw Materials	xxx	Xxx
Raw Materials in Transit	xxx	xxx
Stock-in-Process	xxx	xxx
Finished Goods	xxx	xxx
Stores, Chemicals and Packing Materials	xxx	xxx
Stock-in-Trade	xxx	xxx
Total	xxx	Xxx

P. Trade Receivables

(i) Aggregate amount of trade receivables outstanding for a period exceeding six months from the date they are due for payment	should be separately stated
(ii)Trade receivables shall be sub-classified as	(a)secured, considered good (b)unsecured considered good (c)considered doubtful
(iii)Allowance for bad and doubtful debts	shall be disclosed under the relevant heads separately
(iv)Debts due by directors or other officers of the company or any of them either severally or jointly with any other person or debts due by firms or private companies respectively in which any director or partner or a director or a member	should be separately stated

Illustration 3 22: Specimen format: Trade Receivable

Particulars	As at 31st March 2016	As at 31st March 2015
(Unsecured and Considered Good)		
Over six months	xxx	xxx
Others	xxx	xxx
Total	xxx	Xxx

Q. Cash and Cash equivalents

(1)Cash and cash equivalents shall be classified as:	(a)Balances with banks ; (b) Cheques, drafts on hand ; (c)Cash in hand; (d)Others (speciy nature) Earmarked balances with banks (e.g. for unpaid dividend) shall be separately stated.
(2)Balances with banks to the extent held as margin money or security against borrowings, guarantees, other commitment	shall be disclosed separately.
(3)Repatriation restrictions, if any, in respect of cash and bank balances	shall be separately stated
(4)Bank deposits with more than 12 months maturity	shall be disclosed separately.

Illustration 3.23: Specimen format : Cash and Cash equivalents

Particulars	As at 31st March 2016	As at 31st March 2015
Balance with Banks	xxx	Xxx
Cash on hand	xxx	xxx
Fixed deposits with banks *	xxx	xxx
Total	Xxx	Xxx

Balance with Banks includes Unclaimed Dividend of Rs.   crore (Previous Year Rs.   crore)

* Fixed deposits with banks include deposits of Rs. crore (Previous Year Rs. crore) with maturity of more than 12 months

R. Short-term loans and advances

(i)Short term loans and advances shall be classified as:	(a)Loans and advances to related parties (giving details thereof) (b)Others (specify nature)
(ii)The above shall be sub-classified as:	(a)secured, considered good (b)unsecured considered good (c)considered doubtful

(iii)Allowance for bad and doubtful loans and advances	shall be disclosed under the relevant heads separately
(iv)Loans and advances due by directors or otherofficers of the company or any of them either severally or jointly with any other person or debts due by firms or private companies respectively in which any director or partner or a director or a member	should be separately stated

Illustration 3.24: Specimen format : Short term loans and advances

Particulars	As at 31st March 2016	As at 31st March 2015
(Unsecured and Considered Good)		
Loans and Advances to Related Parties	xxx	xxx
Balance with Customs, Central Excise Authorities	xxx	xxx
Deposits	xxx	xxx
Others*#	xxx	xxx
Total	xxx	Xxx

* Netted for Loans and Advances considered doubtful Rs. crore (Previous Year Rs. crore)

\# Includes primarily Interest Receivable on Fixed Deposits with Banks, Advance to sundry creditors and Forward Premium on derivative contracts.

S. Other current assets (specify nature)

This is an all-inclusive heading which incorporates current assets that do not fit into other asset categories e.g. unbilled revenue, unamortised premium on forward contracts etc.

According to Guidance Note on Revised Schedule VI issued by ICAI, in case any amount classified under this category is doubtful, it is advisable that such doubtful amount as well as any provision made against the same should be separately disclosed. It is interpreted that the Guidance Note will be applicable to Schedule III as well.

Illustration 3.25: Specimen format : Other Current Assets

Particulars	As at 31st March 2016	As at 31st March 2015
Interest accrued on Investment	xxx	Xxx
Total	xxx	Xxx

T. Contingent liabilities and commitments (to the extent not provided for)

(i)Contingent liabilities shall be classified as:	(a)Claims against the company not acknowledged as debt ;
	(b)Guarantees ;
	(c)Other money for which the company is contingently liable
(ii)Commitments shall be	(a)Estimated amount of contracts remaining to be executed on

classified as:	capital account and not provided for ; (b)Uncalled liability on shares and otherinvestments partly paid (c)Other commitments (specify nature)

U. The amount of dividend proposed to be distributed to equity and preference shareholders for the period and the related amount per share shall be disclosed separately. Arrears of fixed cumulative dividends on preference shares shall also be disclosed separately.

V. Where in respect of an issue of securities made for a specific purpose, the whole or part of the amount has not been used for the specific purpose at the balance sheet date, there shall be indicated by way of a note, how such unutilised amounts have been used or invested.

W. If in the opinion of the Board, any of the assets other than fixed assets and non-current investments do not have a value on realisation in the ordinary course of business at least equal to the amount at which they are stated, the fact that the Board is of that opinion, shall be stated.

3.2.4. Statement of profit & loss: (Schedule III – Part II)
Specimen format of Statement of Profit & Loss as detailed in Schedule III – Part II is reproduced below.

Name of Company...........
Profit & Loss statement for the year ended ....

S/No	Particulars	Note no.	Figures as at the end of current reporting period	Figures as at the end of previous reporting period
1	2	3		
I	REVENUE FROM OPERATION			
II	OTHER INCOME			
III	**(TOTAL REVENUE (I + II)**			
IV	EXPENSES:			
	(a) Cost of material consumed			
	(b) Purchase of stock-in-trade			
	(c) Changes in inventories of finished goods, work-in-progress and stock-in-trade			
	(d) Employees benefit expenses			
	(e) Finance cost			
	(f) Depreciation and amortisation expenses			
	(h) Other expenses			
	TOTAL EXPENSES			
V	PROFIT BEFORE EXCEPTIONAL AND EXTRA-ORDINARY ITEMS AND TAX (III - IV)			
VI	EXCEPTIONAL ITEMS			
VII	PROFIT BEFORE EXTRAORDINARY ITEMS AND TAX (V-VI)			
VIII	EXTRAORDINARY ITEMS			
IX	PROFIT BEFORE TAX (VII - VIII)			

X	TAX EXPENSES:			
	(a) Current tax			
	(b) Deferred tax			
XI	PROFIT/(LOSS) FOR THE PERIOD FROM CONTINUING OPERATIONS (IX - X)			
XII	Profit / (loss) from discontinuing operations			
XIII	Tax expenses from discontinuing operations			
XIV	Profit / (loss) from discontinuing operations (after tax) (XII-XIII)			
XV	PROFIT/(LOSS) FOR THE PERIOD (XI + XIV)			
XVI	Earning per equity share:			
	(1) Basic			
	(2) Diluted			

The format above is followed by General Instructions for preparation of Statement of Profit & Loss in Schedule III. These are summarised as under:

1. The provisions of this Part shall apply to the Income and expenditure account referred to in sub-section (2) of Section 210 of the Act, in like manner as they apply to a statement of profit and loss.

3.2.4.1. Revenue from operations

2. (A) In respect of a company other than a finance company revenue from operations shall disclose separately in the notes revenue from	(a) Sale of products ; (b) Sale of services ; (c) Other operating revenues ; (d) Less: excise duty
2.(B) In respect of a finance company, revenue from operations shall include revenue from:	(a)Interest (b)Other financial services

Revenue from each of the above heads shall be disclosed separately by way of Notes to Accounts to the extent applicable.

3.2.4.2. Treatment of excise duty, sales tax, service tax, VAT etc under Schedule III

The treatment of excise duty, sales tax, service tax, VAT etc. under Schedule III (similar to Revised Schedule VI) is explained as under:

a) In accordance with *AS 9: Revenue Recognition*, the disclosure in case of excise duty needs to be shown on the face of the Statement of Profit and Loss. Since Accounting Standards override Revised Schedule VI, the presentation in respect of excise duty will have to be made on the face of the Statement of Profit and Loss.

   Accordingly, a company may choose to present the elements of revenue from sale of products, sale of services and other operating revenues also on the face of the Statement of Profit and Loss

b) According to Guidance Note of ICAI on Revised Schedule VI, indirect taxes such as sales tax, service tax, purchase tax etc. are generally collected from the customer on behalf of the government in majority of the cases. However, this may hold true in all cases and in some cases a company may act as principal rather than as agent in collecting these taxes. If the

company is acting as a principal and hence responsible for paying tax on its own account, the revenue should be grossed up for the tax billed to the customer and the tax payable should be shown as an expense. However, in cases where the company is collecting tax only as an intermediary or agent i.e .simply collecting and paying tax on behalf of government, revenue should be presented net of taxes

c) As per Guidance Note on Value Added Tax (VAT), VAT is collected from customers on behalf of VAT authorities and hence is not an economic benefit for the enterprise and result in any increase in the equity of the enterprise. Accordingly VAT should not be recorded as Revenue of the enterprise. At the same time payment of VAT should not be treated as expense in the Financial Statements of the enterprise

d) Further Guidance Note states that, as per the definition of Revenue in the Guidance Note on Terms Used in Financial Statement, it excludes amounts collected on behalf of third parties such as certain taxes.

e) The Guidance Note on VAT states further that, where an enterprise has not charged VAT separately but has made a composite charge, it should segregate the portion of sales which is attributable to tax and should credit the same to VAT Payable Account at periodic intervals.

It is interpreted that the above Guidance Note will be applicable to Schedule III as well.

3. Items to be disclosed as Other Operating Revenue vis-à-vis Other Income under Schedule III

At the outset it is to be noted that Other Operating Revenue has not been defined by Schedule III. According to Guidance Note on Revised Schedule VI issued by ICAI, Other Operating Revenue would include revenue arising from a company's operating activities, but which is not part of revenue arising from the sale of products or rendering of services.

4. Whether a particular income in question would be comprised of Other Operating Revenue or Other Income would be decided based on facts of each case and detailed understanding of the company's activities. The classification of income would depend on the purpose for which the particular asset is acquired or held.

Illustration 3.26: Other Operating Revenue

An industrial conglomerate engaged in manufacture and sale of industrial and consumer products also has a real estate vertical. If the real estate vertical is continuously engaged in leasing of real estate properties, the rent arising from leasing of real estate is likely to be "Other Operating Revenue".

Illustration 3.27: Other Operating Revenue

Sale of manufacturing scrap arising out of the operations for a manufacturing company should be treated as Other Operating Revenue since the same arises on account of the company's main operating activity.

3.2.4.3. Finance costs:

Finance costs shall be classified as:

a) Interest expense

b) Other borrowing costs

Applicable net gain / loss on foreign currency transactions and translation

3.2.4.4. Other income shall be classified as:

a) Interest income (in case of a company other than a finance company);

b) Dividend income;

c) Net gain / loss on sale of investments

d) Other non-operating income (net of expenses directly attributable to such income)

Illustration 3.28: Other Income

A company owns a building having fifteen stories. The company uses ten stories of the building for its business and corporate use and leases out the balance five floors. The rent received from these five floors would not be a part of Other Operating Revenue but would be included under "Other Income".

Illustration 3.29: Other Income

Sale of fixed assets is not an operating activity of a company, and hence, profit on sales of fixed assets should be classified as Other Income and not Other Operating Revenue.

Illustration 3.30: Other Income

Net gain out of foreign exchange transactions should be classified as Other Income , the reason being the income has not been generated out of the business operations of the income i.e. sale of products or rendering of services but owing to fluctuation in foreign exchange rates. However, same would not be the case if the company deals in foreign exchange business.

3.2.4.5. Additional information

A Company shall disclose by way of notes additional information regarding aggregate Expenditure and income on the following items:

(i)(a) Employee benefits expense showing separately
  (i)Salaries and wages
  (ii)Contribution to Provident and other funds
  (iii)Expense on employee stock option scheme (ESOP) and
    Employee Stock Purchase Plan (ESPP)
  (iv)Staff welfare expenses
(b) Depreciation and amortisation expenses
(c) Any item of income or expenditure which exceeds one per
  cent of the revenue from operations or Rs.1,00,000 ,
  whichever is higher,
(d) Interest income,
(e) Interest expense
(f) Dividend income
(g) Net gain / loss on sale of investments
(h) Adjustments to the carrying amount of investments
(i) Net gain or loss on foreign currency transaction and
  translation(other than considered as finance cost)
(j) Payments to the auditor as
  • As auditor
  • For Taxation matters
  • For Company Law Matters
  • For Management services
  • For other service
  • For reimbursement of expenses
(k) In case of Companies covered under section 135, amount of
  expenditure incurred on corporate social responsibility
  activities,
(l) Details of items of exceptional and extraordinary nature,
(m)Prior period items,

(ii)(a) In case of manufacturing companies :
  (1) Raw materials under broad heads
  (2) Goods purchased under broad heads

(b)In case of trading companies, purchases in respect of goods traded in by the company under broad heads

(c) In the case of companies rendering or supplying services, gross income derived from the services rendered or supplied under broad heads

(d) In the case of a company, this falls under more than one of the categories mentioned in (a),(b) and (c) above, it shall be sufficient compliance with the requirements herein if purchases, sales and consumption of raw material and the gross income from services rendered is shown under broad heads

(e) In the case of other companies, gross income derived under the broad heads

(iii)In the case of all concerns having works in progress under broad heads

(iv)(a) The aggregate, if material, of any amount set aside or proposed to be set aside, to reserve, but not including provisions made to meet any specific liability, contingency or commitment know n to exist at the date as to which the balance sheet is made up,

(b)The aggregate, if material, of any amounts withdrawn from such reserves,

(v)(a)The aggregate, if material, of the amounts set aside to provisions made from meeting specific liabilities, contingencies or commitments

(b)The aggregate, if material, of the amounts withdrawn from such provisions, as no longer required

(vi)Expenditure incurred on each of the following items, separately for each item:

(a)Consumption of stores and spares,

(b)Power and fuel

(c)Rent

(d)Repairs to building

(e)Repairs to machinery

(f)Insurance

(g)Rates & taxes (excluding income tax)

(h)Miscellaneous expenditure

(vii) (a)Dividends from subsidiary companies

(b)Provisions for losses of subsidiary companies

(viii)The profit and loss account shall also contain by way of a note the following Information namely,

(a)Value of imports calculated on C.I.F basis by the company during the Financial year in respect of:

i) Raw materials

ii) Components and spare parts

iii) Capital goods

(b) Expenditure in foreign currency during the financial year on account of royalty, know-how, professional and consultation

fees, and other matters

(c) *Total* value of all imported raw materials, spare parts and components consumed during the financial year and the *total* value of all indigenous raw materials, spare parts and components similarly consumed and the percentage of each to the total consumption

(d) The amount remitted during the year in foreign currencies on account of dividends, with a specific mention of the *total* number of non-resident shareholders, the *total* number of shares held by them on which the dividends were due and the year to which the dividends related

(e) Earnings in foreign exchange classified under the following heads, namely:

    I Export of goods calculated on FOB basis

    II Royalty, know-how, professional and consultation fees

    III Interest and dividends

    IV Other income, indicating the nature thereof

Illustration 3.31: Cost of materials consumed: Specimen format

a)Manufacturing company: Consumption (Amount in Rs.)

Particulars	For the year ended 31st March 2016	For the year ended 31st March 2015
Raw materials		
Raw materials A	XXX	XXX
Raw materials B	XXX	XXX
Others	XXX	XXX
TOTAL	XXX	XXX

b) Manufacturing company: Purchases (Amount in Rs.)

Particulars	For the year ended 31st March 2016	For the year ended 31st March 2015
Goods purchased		
Traded item A	XXX	XXX
Traded item B	XXX	XXX
Others	XXX	XXX
TOTAL	XXX	XXX

c) Manufacturing company (Amount in Rs.)

Particulars	Sales value	Closing inventory	Opening inventory
Manufactured goods			
Finished goods A	XXX (XXX)	XXX (XXX)	XXX (XXX)

Finished goods B	XXX (XXX)	XXX (XXX)	XXX (XXX)
Others	XXX (XXX)	XXX (XXX)	XXX (XXX)
TOTAL	XXX (XXX)	XXX (XXX)	XXX (XXX)

d) Manufacturing company: Work in progress (Amount in Rs.)

Particulars	As at 31st March 2016	As at 31st March 2015
Work in progress Goods A WIP Goods B WIP Others	XXX XXX XXX	XXX XXX XXX
TOTAL	XXX	XXX

e) Trading company: (Amount in Rs.)

Particulars	For the year ended 31st March 2016	For the year ended 31st March 2015
Traded goods Traded goods A Traded goods B Others	XXX XXX XXX	XXX XXX XXX
TOTAL	XXX	XXX

f) Service company: (Amount in Rs.)

Particulars	For the year ended 31st March 2016	For the year ended 31st March 2015
Services rendered Service A Service B Others	XXX XXX XXX	XXX XXX XXX
TOTAL	XXX	XXX

A company falling under more than one category will make the above disclosures to the extent relevant.

3.2.4.6. Narrative disclosures

A. Accounting policies	a) all significant accounting policies adopted in preparation and presentation of financial statements should be disclosed b) disclosure of significant accounting policies should form part of the financial statements and should be disclosed in one place c) Any change in the accounting policies which has a material effect in later periods should be disclosed in the year of such change

		d) In the case of a change in accounting policies that has a material effect in the current period, the amount by which any item in the financial statements is affected by such change should also be disclosed to the extent ascertainable and where this is not possible, wholly or in part, the fact should be indicated
B.	**Notes to Accounts**	Some illustrative points to be covered under Notes to Accounts are: 1. Contingent liabilities and capital commitment 2. Disclosure related to Small Scale Industrial Undertaking 3. Payments to auditors 4. Value of imports etc 5. Earnings and expenditure in foreign currencies 6. Prior period items 7. Extraordinary items 8. Government grants 9. Amalgamation 10. Related party transaction 11. Leases 12. Disclosure of interest in Joint venture 13. Disclosure of earnings per share 14. Disclosure of taxes on income

3.2.4.7. Cash flow statement

According to Section 2(40) of the Companies Act 2013, financial statements include Cash flow statement except that the financial statement, with respect to One Person Company, small Company and dormant company, may not include the cash flow statement.

AS 3: Cash flow statement issued by ICAI, has been declared as a specified accounting standard for the purpose of Section 129: Financial Statement to be complied with by the companies. Also as per the requirement of clause 32 of the Listing Agreement, it is mandatory for the listed companies to prepare and present a cash flow statement in accordance with AS 3 following the indirect method. Also any enterprise having turnover more than 50 crores in a year or an enterprise that intends to issue securities is required to prepare and present cash flow statement as a principal financial statements.

AS 3 prescribes three types of activities that generate cash flows for an enterprise. These are:

a) Cash flows generated by operating activities
b) Cash flows generated by investing activities and
c) Cash flows generated by financing activities

The standard specifies two alternative methods for presentation of cash flows: direct method and indirect method mainly related to the presentation of cash flow from operating activities

3.3. Companies which would need to comply with Indian Accounting Standards (Ind AS):

Division II
Financial Statements for a company whose financial statements are drawn up in compliance of Companies (Indian Accounting Standards) Rules, 2015.

GENERAL INSTRUCTIONS FOR PREPARATION OF FINANCIAL STATEMENTS OF A COMPANY REQUIRED TO COMPLY WITH Ind AS".

3.3.1. PART I –BALANCE SHEET

Name of the Company........................
Balance Sheet as at ....
(Rupees in............)

Particulars	Note no.	Figures as at the end of current reporting period	Figures as at the end of the previous reporting period
1	2	3	4
ASSETS			
(1) Non-current assets			
(a) Property, Plant and Equipment			
(b) Capital work-in-progress			
(c) Investment Property			
(d) Goodwill			
(e) Other Intangible assets			
(f) Intangible assets under development			
(g) Biological Assets other than bearer plants			
(h) Financial Assets			
(i) Investments			
(ii) Trade receivables			
(iii) Loans			
(iv) Others (to be specified)			
(i) Deferred tax assets (net)			
(j) Other non-current assets			
(2) Current assets			
(a) Inventories			
(b) Financial Assets			
(i) Investments			
(ii) Trade receivables			
(iii) Cash and cash equivalents			
(iv) Bank balances other than (iii) above			
(v) Loans			
(vi) Others (to be specified)			
(c) Current Tax Assets (Net)			
(d) Other current assets			
Total assets			
Equity and Liabilities			
Equity			
(a) Equity Share capital			
(b) Other Equity			
LIABILITIES			
(1)			

	Non-current liabilities		
	(a) Financial Liabilities		
	(i) Borrowings		
	(ii) Trade payables		
	(iii) Other financial liabilities (other than those specified in (b) below, to be specified)		
	(b) Provisions		
	(c) Deferred tax liabilities (Net)		
(2)	(d) Other non-current liabilities		
	Current liabilities		
	(a) Financial Liabilities		
	(i) Borrowings		
	(ii) Trade payables		
	(iii) Other financial liabilities (other than those specified in (c) below)		
	(b) Other current liabilities		
	(c) Provisions		
	(d) Current Tax Liabilities (Net)		
	Total equity and liabilities		

3.3.2. STATEMENT OF CHANGES IN EQUITY

Name of the Company.........................
Statement of Changes in Equity for the period ended ....
(Rupees in..................)

a) Equity share capital

Balance at the beginning of the reporting period	Changes in equity share capital during the year	Balance at the end of the reporting period

b. Other Equity

	Share application money pending allotment	Equity component of compound financial instruments	Reserves & surplus - Capital Reserve	Reserves & surplus - Securities premium reserve	Reserves & surplus - Other reserves (specify nature)	Reserves & surplus - Retained earnings	Other comprehensive Income - Debt instruments through Other Comprehensive Income	Other comprehensive Income - Equity instruments through Other Comprehensive Income	Other comprehensive Income - Effective portion of Cash Flow Hedges	Other comprehensive Income - Revaluation Surplus	Other comprehensive Income - Exchange differences on translating the financial statements of a foreign operation	Other comprehensive Income - Other items of other comprehensive income (specify nature)	Money received against share warrants	TOTAL
Balance at the beginning of the reporting period														
Changes in accounting policy/prior period errors														
Restated balance at the beginning of the reporting period														
Total Comprehensive Income for the year														
Dividends														
Transfer to retained earnings														
Any other change (to be specified)														
Balance at the end of the reporting period														

Note: Remeasurment of net defined benefit plans, fair value changes relating to own credit risk and share of Other Comprehensive Income in Associates and Joint Ventures shall be recognised as a part

of retained earnings with separate disclosure of such items along with the relevant amounts in the Notes.

Notes

GENERAL INSTRUCTIONS FOR PREPARATION OF BALANCE SHEET

1. An entity shall classify an asset as current when:
>   (a) it expects to realise the asset, or intends to sell or consume it, in its normal operating cycle;
>   (b) it holds the asset primarily for the purpose of trading;
>   (c) it expects to realise the asset within twelve months after the reporting period; or
>   (d) the asset is cash or a cash equivalent unless the asset is restricted from being exchanged or used to settle a liability for at least twelve months after the reporting period.

An entity shall classify all other assets as non-current.

2. The operating cycle of an entity is the time between the acquisition of assets for processing and their realisation in cash or cash equivalents. When the entity's normal operating cycle is not clearly identifiable, it is assumed to be twelve months.

3. An entity shall classify a liability as current when:
>   (a) it expects to settle the liability in its normal operating cycle;
>   (b) it holds the liability primarily for the purpose of trading;
>   (c) the liability is due to be settled within twelve months after the reporting period; or
>   (d) it does not have an unconditional right to defer settlement of the liability for at least twelve months after the reporting period. Terms of a liability that could, at the option of the counterparty, result in its settlement by the issue of equity instruments do not affect its classification.

An entity shall classify all other liabilities as non-current.

4. A receivable shall be classified as a 'trade receivable' if it is in respect of the amount due on account of goods sold or services rendered in the normal course of business.

5. A payable shall be classified as a 'trade payable' if it is in respect of the amount due on account of goods purchased or services received in the normal course of business.

6. A company shall disclose the following in the Notes:

A. Non-Current Assets

I. Property, Plant and Equipment	(i) Classification shall be given as: (a) Land. (b) Buildings. (c) Plant and Equipment. (d) Furniture and Fixtures. (e) Vehicles. (f) Office equipment. (g) Bearer Plants (h) Others (specify nature). (ii) Assets under lease shall be separately specified under each class of assets. (iii) A reconciliation of the gross and net carrying amounts of each class of assets at the beginning and end of the reporting period showing additions, disposals, acquisitions through business combinations and other adjustments and the related depreciation and impairment losses/reversals shall be disclosed separately.
II. Investment Property	A reconciliation of the gross and net carrying amounts of each class of property at the beginning and end of the reporting period showing additions, disposals, acquisitions through business combinations and

	other adjustments and the related amortization and impairment losses/reversals shall be disclosed separately.
III Goodwill	A reconciliation of the gross and net carrying amount of goodwill at the beginning and end of the reporting period showing additions, impairments, disposals and other adjustments.

IV. Other Intangible assets	(i) Classification shall be given as:
	    (a) Brands /trademarks.
	    (b) Computer software.
	    (c) Mastheads and publishing titles.
	    (d) Mining rights.
	    (e) Copyrights, patents, other intellectual property rights, services and operating rights.
	    (f) Recipes, formulae, models, designs and prototypes.
	    (g) Licenses and franchises.
	    (h) Others (specify nature).
	(ii) A reconciliation of the gross and net carrying amounts of each class of assets at the beginning and end of the reporting period showing additions, disposals, acquisitions through business combinations and other adjustments and the related amortization and impairment losses/reversals shall be disclosed separately.

V. Biological Assets other than bearer plants	A reconciliation of the carrying amounts of each class of assets at the beginning and end of the reporting period showing additions, disposals, acquisitions through business combinations and other adjustments shall be disclosed separately.

VI. Investments	(i) Investments shall be classified as:
	    (a) Investments in Equity Instruments;
	    (b) Investments in Preference Shares;
	    (c) Investments in Government or trust securities;
	    (d) Investments in debentures or bonds;
	    (e) Investments in Mutual Funds;
	    (f) Investments in partnership firms;
	    (g) Other investments (specify nature).
	
	Under each classification, details shall be given of names of the bodies corporate that are
	    (i) subsidiaries,
	    (ii) (ii) associates,
	    (iii) (iii) joint ventures, or
	    (iv) structured entities, in whom investments have been made and the nature and extent of the investment so made in each such body corporate (showing separately investments which are partly-paid). Investments in partnership firms along with names of the firms, their partners, total capital and the shares of each partner shall be disclosed separately.
	(ii) The following shall also be disclosed:
	    (a) Aggregate amount of quoted investments and market

	value thereof; (b) Aggregate amount of unquoted investments; (c) Aggregate amount of impairment in value of investments.

VII.Trade Receivables	(i) Trade receivables shall be sub-classified as:
	      (a) Secured, considered good;
	      (b) Unsecured considered good;
	      (c) Doubtful.
	
	(ii) Allowance for bad and doubtful debts shall be disclosed under the relevant heads separately.
	
	(iii) Debts due by directors or other officers of the company or any of them either severally or jointly with any other person or debts due by firms or private companies respectively in which any director is a partner or a director or a member should be separately stated.

VIII. Loans	(i) Loans shall be classified as:
	      (a) Security Deposits;
	      (b) Loans to related parties (giving details thereof);
	      (c) Other loans (specify nature).
	(ii) The above shall also be separately sub-classified as:
	      (a) Secured, considered good;
	      (b) Unsecured, considered good;
	      (c) Doubtful.
	(iii) Allowance for bad and doubtful loans shall be disclosed under the relevant heads separately.
	(iv) Loans due by directors or other officers of the company or any of them either severally or jointly with any other persons or amounts due by firms or private companies respectively in which any director is a partner or a director or a member should be separately stated.

IX.Other non-current assets	Other non-current assets shall be classified as-
	(i) Capital Advances;
	
	(ii) Advances other than capital advances;
	
	    1. Advances other than capital advances shall be classified as:
	      (a) Security Deposits;
	      (b) Advances to related parties (giving details thereof);
	      (c) Other advances (specify nature).
	
	    2. Advances to directors or other officers of the company or any of them either severally or jointly with any other persons or advances to firms or private companies respectively in which any director is a partner or a director or a member should be separately stated.
	
	(iii) Bank deposits with more than 12 months maturity;
	
	(iv) Others (specify nature).

B. Current Assets	

I. Inventories	(i) Inventories shall be classified as:
	    (a) Raw materials;
	    (b) Work-in-progress;
	    (c) Finished goods;
	    (d) Stock-in-trade (in respect of goods acquired for trading);
	    (e) Stores and spares;
	    (f) Loose tools;
	    (g) Others (specify nature).
	(ii) Goods-in-transit shall be disclosed under the relevant sub-head of inventories.
	(iii) Mode of valuation shall be stated.

II. Investments	(i) Investments shall be classified as:
	    (a) Investments in Equity Instruments;
	    (b) Investment in Preference Shares;
	    (c) Investments in government or trust securities;
	    (d) Investments in debentures or bonds;
	    (e) Investments in Mutual Funds;
	    (f) Investments in partnership firms;
	    (g) Other investments (specify nature).
	
	Under each classification, details shall be given of names of the bodies corporate that are
	    (i) subsidiaries,
	    (ii) associates,
	    (iii) joint ventures, or
	    (iv) structured entities, in whom investments have been made and the nature and extent of the investment so made in each such body corporate (showing separately investments which are partly-paid).
	
	ii) The following shall also be disclosed
	
	    (a) Aggregate amount of quoted investments and market value thereof;
	    (b) Aggregate amount of unquoted investments;
	    (c) Aggregate amount of impairment in value of investments.

III. Trade Receivables	(i) Aggregate amount of Trade Receivables outstanding for a period exceeding six
	    months from the date they are due for payment should be separately stated.
	(ii) Trade receivables shall be sub-classified as:
	    (a) Secured, considered good;
	    (b) Unsecured considered good;
	    (c) Doubtful.
	(iii) Allowance for bad and doubtful debts shall be disclosed under the relevant heads separately.
	(iv) Debts due by directors or other officers of the company or any of them either severally or jointly with any other person or debts due by

	firms or private companies respectively in which any director is a partner or a director or a member should be separately stated.
IV. Cash and cash equivalents	Cash and cash equivalents shall be classified as: a. Balances with Banks (of the nature of cash and cash equivalents); b. Cheques, drafts on hand; c. Cash on hand; d. Others (specify nature).

V. Loans	(i) Loans shall be classified as:
	    (a) Security deposits;
	    (b) Loans to related parties (giving details thereof);
	    (c) Others (specify nature).
	(ii) The above shall also be sub-classified as:
	    (a) Secured, considered good;
	    (b) Unsecured, considered good;
	    (c) Doubtful.
	(iii) Allowance for bad and doubtful loans shall be disclosed under the relevant heads separately.
	(iv) Loans due by directors or other officers of the company or any of them either severally or jointly with any other person or amounts due by firms or private companies respectively in which any director is a partner or a director or a member shall be separately stated.

VI. Other current assets (specify nature).	This is an all-inclusive heading, which incorporates current assets that do not fit into any other asset categories.
	Other current assets shall be classified as-
	(i) Advances other than capital advances
	    1. Advances other than capital advances shall be classified as:
	
	        (a) Security Deposits;
	        (b) Advances to related parties (giving details thereof);
	        (c) Other advances (specify nature).
	
	    2. Advances to directors or other officers of the company or any of them either severally or jointly with any other persons or advances to firms or private companies respectively in which any director is a partner or a director or a member should be separately stated.
	
	(ii) Others (specify nature)

C. The following disclosures with regard to cash and bank balances shall be made:
a. Earmarked balances with banks (for example, for unpaid dividend) shall be separately stated.
b. Balances with banks to the extent held as margin money or security against the borrowings, guarantees, other commitments shall be disclosed separately.
c. Repatriation restrictions, if any, in respect of cash and bank balances shall be separately stated.

D. Equity

| I. Equity Share Capital | for each class of equity share capital:
(a) the number and amount of shares authorized;

(b) the number of shares issued, subscribed and fully paid, and subscribed but not fully paid;

(c) par value per share;

(d) a reconciliation of the number of shares outstanding at the beginning and at the end of the period;

(e) the rights, preferences and restrictions attaching to each class of shares including restrictions on the distribution of dividends and the repayment of capital;

(f) shares in respect of each class in the company held by its holding company or its ultimate holding company including shares held by or by subsidiaries or associates of the holding company or the ultimate holding company in aggregate;

(g) shares in the company held by each shareholder holding more than 5 percent shares specifying the number of shares held;

(h) shares reserved for issue under options and contracts/commitments for the sale of shares/disinvestment, including the terms and amounts;

(i) For the period of five years immediately preceding the date as at which the Balance Sheet is prepared:

• Aggregate number and class of shares allotted as fully paid up pursuant to contract(s) without payment being received in cash.
• Aggregate number and class of shares allotted as fully paid up by way of bonus shares.
• Aggregate number and class of shares bought back.

(j) Terms of any securities convertible into equity shares issued along with the earliest date of conversion in descending order starting from the farthest such date.

(k) Calls unpaid (showing aggregate value of calls unpaid by directors and officers)

(l) Forfeited shares (amount originally paid up) |
| II. Other Equity | (i) 'Other Reserves' shall be classified in the notes as:
    (a) Capital Redemption Reserve;
    (b) Debenture Redemption Reserve;
    (c) Share Options Outstanding Account;
    (d) Others– (specify the nature and purpose of each reserve and the amount in respect thereof);
(Additions and deductions since last balance sheet to be shown under each of the specified heads)

(ii) Retained Earnings represents surplus i.e. balance of the relevant column in the Statement of Changes in Equity. |

	(iii) A reserve specifically represented by earmarked investments shall disclose the fact that it is so represented.
	(iv) Debit balance of Statement of Profit and Loss shall be shown as a negative figure under the head 'retained earnings'. Similarly, the balance of 'Other Equity', after adjusting negative balance of retained earnings, if any, shall be shown under the head 'Other Equity' even if the resulting figure is in the negative.
	(v) Under the sub-head 'Other Equity', disclosure shall be made for the nature and amount of each item.

E. Non-Current Liabilities

I. Borrowings	(i) Borrowings shall be classified as: 　　(a) Bonds/debentures 　　(b) Term loans 　　　　• from banks. 　　　　• from other parties. 　　(c) Deferred payment liabilities. 　　(d) Deposits. 　　(e) Loans from related parties. 　　(f) Long term maturities of finance lease obligations 　　(g) Liability component of compound financial instruments 　　(h) Other loans (specify nature). (ii) Borrowings shall further be sub-classified as secured and unsecured. Nature of security shall be specified separately in each case. (iii) Where loans have been guaranteed by directors or others, the aggregate amount of such loans under each head shall be disclosed. (iv) Bonds/debentures (along with the rate of interest, and particulars of redemption or conversion, as the case may be) shall be stated in descending order of maturity or conversion, starting from farthest redemption or conversion date, as the case may be. Where bonds/debentures are redeemable by instalments, the date of maturity for this purpose must be reckoned as the date on which the first instalment becomes due. (v) Particulars of any redeemed bonds/ debentures which the company has power to reissue shall be disclosed. (vi) Terms of repayment of term loans and other loans shall be stated. (vii) Period and amount of default as on the balance sheet date in repayment of borrowings and interest shall be specified separately in each case.
II. Provisions	The amounts shall be classified as: 　　(a) Provision for employee benefits.

	(b) Others (specify nature).
III. Other non-current liabilities	(a) Advances (b) Others (specify nature)

F. Current Liabilities

I. Borrowings	(i) Borrowings shall be classified as:
	    (a) Loans repayable on demand
	      • from banks.
	      • from other parties.
	    (b) Loans from related parties.
	    (c) Deposits.
	    (d) Other loans (specify nature).
	(ii) Borrowings shall further be sub-classified as secured and unsecured. Nature of security shall be specified separately in each case.
	(iii) Where loans have been guaranteed by directors or others, the aggregate amount of such loans under each head shall be disclosed.
	(iv) Period and amount of default as on the balance sheet date in repayment of borrowings and interest, shall be specified separately in each case.

II. Other Financial Liabilities	Other Financial liabilities shall be classified as:
	    (a) Current maturities of long-term debt;
	    (b) Current maturities of finance lease obligations;
	    (c) Interest accrued;
	    (d) Unpaid dividends;
	    (e) Application money received for allotment of securities to the extent refundable and interest accrued thereon;
	    (f) Unpaid matured deposits and interest accrued thereon;
	    (g) Unpaid matured debentures and interest accrued thereon;
	    (h) Others (specify nature).
	'Long term debt' is a borrowing having a period of more than twelve months at the time of origination

III. Other current liabilities	The amounts shall be classified as:
	    (a) Revenue received in advance;
	    (b) Other advances (specify nature);
	    (c) Others (specify nature);

IV. Provisions	The amounts shall be classified as:
	    (i) Provision for employee benefits.
	    (ii) Others (specify nature).

G. The presentation of liabilities associated with group(s) of assets classified as held for sale and non-current assets classified as held for sale shall be in accordance with the relevant Indian Accounting Standards (Ind ASs).

H. Contingent Liabilities and Commitments

(to the extent not provided for)

(i). Contingent Liabilities shall be classified as:

    (a) Claims against the company not acknowledged as debt;

    (b) Guarantees excluding financial guarantees;

    (c) Other money for which the company is contingently liable.

(ii). Commitments shall be classified as:

    (a) Estimated amount of contracts remaining to be executed on capital account and not provided for;

    (b) Uncalled liability on shares and other investments partly paid;

    (c) Other commitments (specify nature).

I. The amount of dividends proposed to be distributed to equity and preference shareholders for the period and the related amount per share shall be disclosed separately. Arrears of fixed cumulative dividends on irredeemable preference shares shall also be disclosed separately.

J. Where in respect of an issue of securities made for a specific purpose the whole or part of amount has not been used for the specific purpose at the Balance Sheet date, there shall be indicated by way of note how such unutilized amounts have been used or invested.

7. When a company applies an accounting policy retrospectively or makes a restatement of items in the financial statements or when it reclassifies items in its financial statements, the company shall attach to the Balance Sheet, a "Balance Sheet" as at the beginning of the earliest comparative period from which the above adjustments are made.

8. Share application money pending allotment shall be classified into equity or liability in accordance with relevant Indian Accounting Standards. Share application money to the extent not refundable shall be shown under the head Equity and share application money to the extent refundable shall be separately shown under 'Other current liabilities'.

9. Preference shares shall be classified and presented as 'Equity' or 'Liability' in accordance with the requirements of the relevant Indian Accounting Standards. Accordingly, the disclosure and presentation requirements in this regard applicable to the relevant class of equity or liability shall be applicable *mutatis mutandis* to the preference shares. For instance, redeemable preference shares shall be classified and presented under 'non-current liabilities' as 'borrowings' and the disclosure requirements in this regard applicable to such borrowings shall be applicable *mutatis mutandis* to redeemable preference shares.

10. Compound financial instruments such as convertible debentures, where split into equity and liability components, as per the requirements of the relevant Indian Accounting Standards, shall be classified and presented under the relevant heads in 'Equity' and 'Liabilities'

11. Regulatory Deferral Account Balances shall be presented in the Balance Sheet in accordance with the relevant Indian Accounting Standards.

3.3.3. PART II – STATEMENT OF PROFIT AND LOSS
Name of the Company..........................
Statement of Profit and Loss for the period ended ....
(Rupees in............)

S/No	Particulars	Note no.	Figures for the current reporting period	Figures for the previous reporting period
1	2	3		
I	Revenue from Operations			
II	Other Income			
III	Total Income (I + II)			
IV	EXPENSES:			
	Cost of material consumed			
	Purchases of stock-in-trade			
	Changes in inventories of finished goods, stock-in-trade and work-in-progress			
	Employees benefit expenses			
	Finance cost			
	Depreciation and amortisation expenses			
	Other expenses			
	Total expenses (IV)			
V	Profit/(loss) before exceptional items and tax (I- IV)			
VI	Exceptional items			
VII	Profit/(loss) before tax (V-VI)			
VIII	Tax expenses:			
	(a) Current tax			
	(b) Deferred tax			
IX	Profit (Loss) for the period from continuing operations (VII-VIII)			
X	Profit / (loss) from discontinued operations			
XI	Tax expenses from discontinued operations			
XII	Profit / (loss) from discontinued operations (X-XI)			
XIII	Profit/(loss) for the period (IX+XII)			
XIV	Other Comprehensive Income A (i) Items that will not be reclassified to profit or loss (ii) Income tax relating to items that will not be reclassified to profit or loss B (i) Items that will be reclassified to profit or loss (ii) Income tax relating to items that will be reclassified to profit			

	or loss			
XV	Total Comprehensive Income for the period (XIII+XIV)(Comprising Profit (Loss) and Other Comprehensive Income for the period)			
XVI	Earning per equity share (for continuing operations): (1) Basic (2) Diluted			
XVII	Earning per equity share (for discontinued operations): (1) Basic (2) Diluted			
XVIII	Earnings per equity share(for discontinued & continuing operations) (1) Basic (2) Diluted			

See accompanying notes to the financial statements

Notes
GENERAL INSTRUCTIONS FOR PREPARATION OF STATEMENT OF PROFIT AND LOSS
1. The provisions of this Part shall apply to the income and expenditure account, in like manner as they apply to a Statement of Profit and Loss.

2. **The Statement of Profit and Loss** shall include:
(1) Profit or loss for the period;
(2) Other Comprehensive Income for the period.
The sum of (1) and (2) above is 'Total Comprehensive Income'.

3. **Revenue from operations** shall disclose separately in the notes
      (a) sale of products (including Excise Duty);
      (b) sale of services;
      (c) other operating revenues;

4. **Finance Costs**
Finance costs shall be classified as:
      (a) interest;
      (b) dividend on redeemable preference shares;
      (c) exchange differences regarded as an adjustment to borrowing costs;
      (d) other borrowing costs (specify nature).

5 **Other income**
Other income shall be classified as:
      (a) Interest Income;
      (b) Dividend Income;
      (c) Other non-operating income (net of expenses directly attributable to such income).

6. **Other Comprehensive Income** shall be classified into:

(A) Items that will not be reclassified to profit or loss	(i) Changes in revaluation surplus;
	(ii) Remeasurements of the defined benefit plans;
	(iii) Equity Instruments through Other Comprehensive Income;

	(iv) Fair value changes relating to own credit risk; (v) Share of Other Comprehensive Income in Associates and Joint Ventures, to the extent not to be classified into profit or loss; (vi) Others (specify nature).
(B) Items that will be reclassified to profit or loss	(i) Exchange differences in translating the financial statements of a foreign operation; (ii) Debt Instruments through Other Comprehensive Income; (iii) The effective portion of gains and loss on hedging instruments in a cash flow hedge; (iv) Share of Other Comprehensive Income in Associates and Joint Ventures, to the extent to be classified into profit or loss; (v) Others (specify nature).

7. Additional Information

A Company shall disclose by way of notes, additional information regarding aggregate expenditure and income on the following items:	(a) Employee Benefits expense [showing separately (i) salaries and wages, (ii) contribution to provident and other funds, share based payments to employees, (iv) staff welfare expenses]. (b) Depreciation and amortization expense; (c) Any item of income or expenditure which exceeds one per cent of the revenue from operations or Rs.10,00,000, whichever is higher, in addition to the consideration of 'materiality' as specified in clause 7 of the General Instructions for Preparation of Financial Statements of a Company. (d) Interest Income; (e) Interest Expense; (f) Dividend income; (g) Net gain/loss on sale of investments; (h) Net gain/loss on foreign currency transaction and translation (other than considered as finance cost); (i) Payments to the auditor as (a) auditor, (b) for taxation matters, (c) for company law matters, (d) for other services, (e) for reimbursement of expenses; (j) In case of companies covered under section 135, amount of expenditure incurred on corporate social responsibility activities; (k) Details of items of exceptional nature;

8. Regulatory Deferral Account Balances shall be presented in the Statement of Profit or Loss in accordance with the relevant Indian Accounting Standards.

3.3.4. Preparation of consolidated Financial Statements

According to Schedule III, where a company is required to prepare Consolidated Financial Statements i.e. consolidated balance sheet and consolidated statement of profit and loss, the company shall *mutatis mutandis* follow the requirements of this Schedule as applicable to a company in the preparation of balance sheet and statement of profit & loss. In addition, the consolidated financial statements shall disclose the information as per the requirements specified in the applicable Accounting Standards including the following:

(i)   Profit & Loss attributable to "minority interest" and to owners of the parent in the statement of profit & loss shall be presented as allocation for the period.

(ii)   "Minority interests" in the balance sheet within equity shall be presented separately from the equity of the owners of the parent.

In the consolidated financial statements, the following shall be disclosed by way of additional information:

Name of the entity in the	Net Assets, i.e. total assets minus total liabilities		Share in profit or loss	
	As % of consolidated net assets	Amount	As % of consolidated profit or loss	Amount
(1)	(2)	(3)	(4)	(5)
Parent Subsidiaries Indian 1. 2. 3.				
Name of the entity in the	Net Assets, i.e. total assets minus total liabilities		Share in profit or loss	
	As % of consolidated net assets	Amount	As % of consolidated profit or loss	Amount
(1)	(2)	(3)	(4)	(5)
Foreign 1. 2. 3.				
Minority Interests in all subsidiaries				
Associates (Investment as per the equity method) Indian 1. 2. 3. Foreign 1. 2. 3.				
Joint Ventures (as per proportionate consolidation / investment as per the equity method) Indian 1. 2.				

3.				
Foreign				
1.				
2.				
3.				
TOTAL				

3.3.5. Amendments to schedule III of the Companies Act 2013 incorporating financial reporting requirements under Indian Accounting Standards (Ind AS)

PART III- GENERAL INSTRUCTIONS FOR THE PREPARATION OF CONSOLIDATED FINANCIAL STATEMENTS

1. Where a company is required to prepare Consolidated Financial Statements, i.e., consolidated balance sheet, consolidated statement of changes in equity and consolidated statement of profit and loss, the company shall *mutatis mutandis* follow the requirements of this Schedule as applicable to a company in the preparation of balance sheet, statement of changes in equity and statement of profit and loss. In addition, the consolidated financial statements shall disclose the information as per the requirements specified in the applicable Indian Accounting Standards notified under the Companies (Indian Accounting Standards) Rules 2015, including the following:

(i) Profit or loss attributable to 'non-controlling interest' and to 'owners of the parent' in the statement of profit and loss shall be presented as allocation for the period. Further, 'total comprehensive income' for the period attributable to 'non-controlling interest' and to 'owners of the parent' shall be presented in the statement of profit and loss as allocation for the period. The aforesaid disclosures for 'total comprehensive income' shall also be made in the statement of changes in equity. In addition to the disclosure requirements in the Indian Accounting Standards, the aforesaid disclosures shall also be made in respect of 'other comprehensive income'.

(ii) 'Non-controlling interests' in the Balance Sheet and in the Statement of Changes in Equity, within equity, shall be presented separately from the equity of the 'owners of the parent'.

(iii) Investments accounted for using the equity method.

Name of the entity in the group	Net Assets, i.e. total assets minus total liabilities		Share in profit or loss		Share in other comprehensive income		Share in total comprehensive income	
	As % of consolidated net assets	Amount	As % of consolidated profit or loss	Amount	As % of consolidated other comprehensive income	Amount	As % of total comprehensive income	Amount
Parent Subsidiaries Indian 1. 2. 3. Foreign 1. 2. 3.								
Non-controlling Interests in all subsidiaries								

Associates (Investment as per the equity method) Indian 1. 2. 3. Foreign 1. 2. 3.								
Joint Ventures (as per proportionate consolidation / investment as per the equity method) Indian 1. 2. 3. Foreign 1. 2. 3.								
TOTAL								

5.8.5.1. All subsidiaries, associates and joint ventures (whether Indian or foreign) will be covered under consolidated financial statements.

5.8.5.2. An entity shall disclose the list of subsidiaries or associates or joint ventures which have not been consolidated in the consolidated financial statements along with the reasons of not consolidating.

117

Chapter 4: Reporting of Internal financial control over financial reporting

4.1. Reporting on internal financial controls under clause (i) of Subsection 3 of Section 143 of the Companies Act, 2013

According to Clause (i) of Sub-section 3 of Section 143 of the Companies Act, 2013 ("the 2013 Act" or "the Act") the auditors' report needs to state whether the company has adequate internal financial controls system in place and the operating effectiveness of such controls.

The scope for reporting on internal financial controls is significantly larger and wider than the reporting on internal controls under the Companies (Auditor's Report) Order, 2015 ("CARO").

Under CARO, the reporting on internal controls is limited to the adequacy of controls over purchase of inventory and fixed assets and sale of goods and services. As such, CARO does not require reporting on all controls relating to financial reporting and also does not require reporting on the "adequacy and operating effectiveness" of such controls.

4.2. Management's responsibility

Rule 8(5)(viii) of the Companies (Accounts) Rules, 2014 requires the Board of Directors' report of all companies to state the details in respect of *adequacy of internal financial controls* with reference to the financial statements.

According to Clause (e) of Sub-section 5 of Section 134 to the Act, the directors' responsibility statement is required to state that the directors, in the case of a listed company, had laid down internal financial controls to be followed by the company and that such internal financial controls are adequate and were operating effectively.

The inclusion of the matters relating to internal financial controls in the directors' responsibility statement is in addition to the requirement for the directors to state that they have taken proper and sufficient care for the maintenance of adequate accounting records in accordance with the provisions of the 2013 Act, for safeguarding the assets of the company and for preventing and detecting fraud and other irregularities.

4.3. Auditors responsibility

The auditor's objective in an audit of internal financial controls over financial reporting is to express an opinion on the effectiveness of the company's internal financial controls over financial reporting, the procedures related to which are carried out along with an audit of the financial statements.

4.4. Definition of internal financial controls

In accordance with Clause (e) of Sub-section 5 of Section 134 explains the meaning of the term, "internal financial controls" as "the policies and procedures adopted by the company for ensuring the orderly and efficient conduct of its business, including adherence to company's policies, the safeguarding of its assets, the prevention and detection of frauds and errors, the accuracy and completeness of the accounting records, and the timely preparation of reliable financial information."

According to Guidance Note on *Internal Financial Controls over Financial Reporting* issued by ICAI, the "internal financial controls over financial reporting" is defined as *"A process designed to provide reasonable assurance regarding the reliability of financial reporting and the preparation of financial statements for external purposes in accordance with generally accepted accounting principles. A company's internal financial control over financial reporting includes those policies and procedures that*

(i) pertain to the maintenance of records that, in reasonable detail, accurately and fairly reflect the transactions and dispositions of the assets of the company;

(ii) provide reasonable assurance that transactions are recorded as necessary to permit preparation of financial statements in accordance with generally accepted accounting principles, and that

receipts and expenditures of the company are being made only in accordance with authorisations of management and directors of the company; and
(iii) provide reasonable assurance regarding prevention or timely detection of unauthorised acquisition, use, or disposition of the company's assets that could have a material effect on the financial statements."

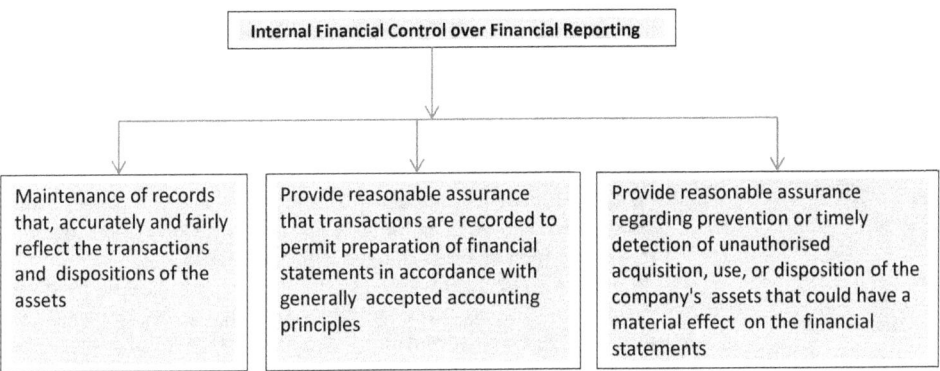

4.5. Components of Internal Control (Auditing Standard: SA 315)

Internal control loop is explained through the following diagram:

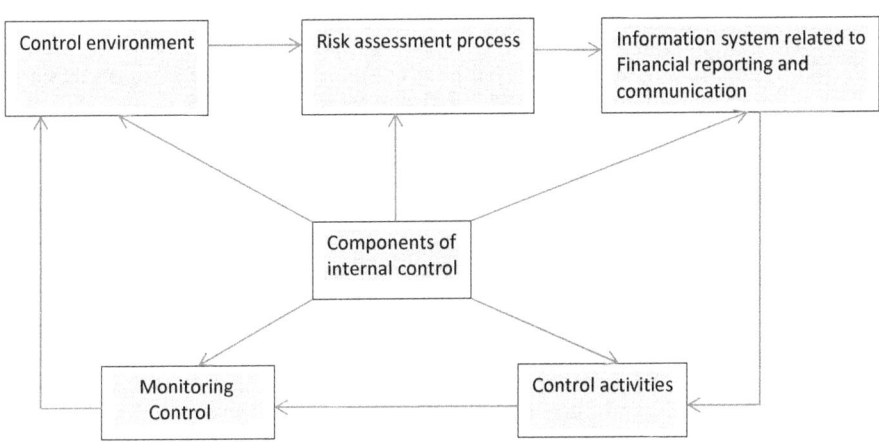

Each component of the loop is explained below in detail.

| a)Control environment | Paragraph 49. The control environment encompasses the following elements:

(a) **Communication and enforcement of integrity and ethical values.** The effectiveness of controls cannot rise above the integrity and ethical values of the people who create, administer, and monitor them. Integrity and ethical behavior is the product of the entity's ethical and behavioral standards, how they are communicated, and how they are reinforced in practice. The enforcement of integrity and ethical values includes, for example, management actions to eliminate or mitigate incentives or temptations that might prompt personnel to engage in dishonest, illegal, or unethical acts. The communication of entity policies on integrity and ethical values may include the communication of behavioral standards to personnel through policy statements and codes of conduct and by example.

(b) **Commitment to competence.** Competence is the knowledge and skills necessary to accomplish tasks that define the individual's job.

(c) **Participation by those charged with governance.** An entity's control consciousness is influenced significantly by those charged with governance. The importance of the responsibilities of those charged with governance is recognised in codes of practice and other laws and regulations or guidance produced for the benefit of those charged with governance. Other responsibilities of those charged with governance include oversight of the design and effective operation of whistle blower procedures and the process for reviewing the effectiveness of the entity's internal control.

(d) **Management's philosophy and operating style.** Management's philosophy and operating style encompass a broad range of characteristics. For example, management's attitudes and actions toward financial reporting may manifest themselves through conservative or aggressive selection from available alternative accounting principles, or conscientiousness and conservatism with which accounting estimates are developed.

(e) **Organisational structure.** Establishing a relevant organisational structure includes considering key areas of authority and responsibility and appropriate lines of reporting. The appropriateness of an entity's organisational structure depends, in part, on its size and the nature of its activities.

(f) **Assignment of authority and responsibility.** The assignment of authority and responsibility may include policies relating to appropriate business practices, knowledge and experience of key personnel, and resources provided for carrying out duties. In addition, it may include policies and communications directed at ensuring that all personnel understand the entity's objectives, know how their individual actions interrelate and contribute to those objectives, and recognize how and for what they will be held accountable.

(g) **Human resource policies and practices.** Human resource policies and practices often demonstrate important matters in relation to the control consciousness of an entity. For example, standards for recruiting the most qualified individuals – with emphasis on educational background, prior work experience, past accomplishments, and evidence of integrity and ethical behavior – |

	demonstrate an entity's commitment to competent and trustworthy people. Training policies that communicate prospective roles and responsibilities and include practices such as training schools and seminars illustrate expected levels of performance and behavior. Promotions driven by periodic performance appraisals demonstrate the entity's commitment to the advancement of qualified personnel to higher levels of responsibility.
b) The entity's risk assessment process	Paragraph 51. Risks relevant to reliable financial reporting include external and internal events, transactions or circumstances that may occur and adversely affect an entity's ability to initiate, record, process, and report financial data consistent with the assertions of management in the financial statements. Management may initiate plans, programs, or actions to address specific risks or it may decide to accept a risk because of cost or other considerations. Risks can arise or change due to circumstances such as the following: a) *Changes in operating environment*. Changes in the regulatory or operating environment can result in changes in competitive pressures and significantly different risks. b) *New personnel*. New personnel may have a different focus on or understanding of internal control. c) *New or revamped information systems*. Significant and rapid changes in information systems can change the risk relating to internal control. d) *Rapid growth*. Significant and rapid expansion of operations can strain controls and increase the risk of a breakdown in controls. e) *New technology*. Incorporating new technologies into production processes or information systems may change the risk associated with internal control. f) *New business models, products, or activities*. Entering into business areas or transactions with which an entity has little experience may introduce new risks associated with internal control. g) *Corporate restructurings*. Restructurings may be accompanied by staff reductions and changes in supervision and segregation of duties that may change the risk associated with internal control. h) *Expanded foreign operations*. The expansion or acquisition of foreign operations carries new and often unique risks that may affect internal control, for example, additional or changed risks from foreign currency transactions. i) *New accounting pronouncements*. Adoption of new accounting principles or changing accounting principles may affect risks in preparing financial statements.
c) Information system relevant to financial reporting and communication	Paragraph 54. An information system consists of infrastructure (physical and hardware components), software, people, procedures, and data. Many information systems make extensive use of information technology (IT). Clause 55. The information system relevant to financial reporting objectives, which includes the financial reporting system, encompasses methods and records that: a) *Identify* and record all valid transactions.

	b) *Describe* on a timely basis the transactions in sufficient detail to permit proper classification of transactions for financial reporting. c) *Measure* the value of transactions in a manner that permits recording their proper monetary value in the financial statements. d) *Determine* the time period in which transactions occurred to permit recording of transactions in the proper accounting period. e) *Present* properly the transactions and related disclosures in the financial statements. Clause 56. The quality of system-generated information affects management's ability to make appropriate decisions in managing and controlling the entity's activities and to prepare reliable financial reports. Clause 57. Communication, which involves providing an understanding of individual roles and responsibilities pertaining to internal control over financial reporting, may take such forms as policy manuals, accounting and financial reporting manuals, and memoranda. Communication also can be made electronically, orally, and through the actions of management.

d) Control activities	Paragraph 52. Generally, control activities that may be relevant to an audit may be categorised as policies and procedures that pertain to the following:
	a) *Performance reviews*. These control activities include reviews and analyses of actual performance versus budgets, forecasts, and prior period performance; relating different sets of data – operating or financial – to one another, together with analyses of the relationships and investigative and corrective actions; comparing internal data with external sources of information; and review of functional or activity performance.
	b) *Information processing*. The two broad groupings of information systems control activities are application controls, which apply to the processing of individual applications, and general IT-controls, which are policies and procedures that relate to many applications and support the effective functioning of application controls by helping to ensure the continued proper operation of information systems.
	c) *Physical controls.* Controls that encompass:
	   • The physical security of assets, including adequate safeguards such as secured facilities over access to assets and records.
	   • The authorisation for access to computer programs and data files.
	   • The periodic counting and comparison with amounts shown on control records (for example, comparing the results of cash, security and inventory counts with accounting records). The extent to which physical controls intended to prevent theft of assets are relevant to the reliability of financial statement preparation, and therefore the audit, depends on circumstances such as when assets are highly susceptible to misappropriation.
	d) *Segregation of duties*. Assigning different people the responsibilities of authorising transactions, recording transactions, and maintaining custody of assets. Segregation of duties is intended to

	reduce the opportunities to allow any person to be in a position to both perpetrate and conceal errors or fraud in the normal course of the person's duties.
	Paragraph 53. Certain control activities may depend on the existence of appropriate higher level policies established by management or those charged with governance. For example, authorisation controls may be delegated under established guidelines, such as, investment criteria set by those charged with governance; alternatively, non-routine transactions such as, major acquisitions or divestments may require specific high level approval, including in some cases that of shareholders.
e) Monitoring of controls	Paragraph 58. An important management responsibility is to establish and maintain internal control on an ongoing basis. Management's monitoring of controls includes considering whether they are operating as intended and that they are modified as appropriate for changes in conditions.
	Monitoring of controls may include activities such as, management's review of whether bank reconciliations are being prepared on a timely basis, internal auditors' evaluation of sales personnel's compliance with the entity's policies on terms of sales contracts, and a legal department's oversight of compliance with the entity's ethical or business practice policies.
	Monitoring is done also to ensure that controls continue to operate effectively over time. For example, if the timeliness and accuracy of bank reconciliations are not monitored, personnel are likely to stop preparing them.
	Paragraph 59. Internal auditors or personnel performing similar functions may contribute to the monitoring of an entity's controls through separate evaluations. Ordinarily, they regularly provide information about the functioning of internal control, focusing considerable attention on evaluating the effectiveness of internal control, and communicate information about strengths and deficiencies in internal control and recommendations for improving internal control.
	Paragraph 60. Monitoring activities may include using information from communications from external parties that may indicate problems or highlight areas in need of improvement. Customers implicitly corroborate billing data by paying their invoices or complaining about their charges. In addition, regulators may communicate with the entity concerning matters that affect the functioning of internal control, for example, communications concerning examinations by bank regulatory agencies. Also, management may consider communications relating to internal control from external auditors in performing monitoring activities.

4.6. Guidance Note on Internal control:

The Guidance provided by the ICAI on the components of Internal control is enumerated as under:

Internal Control Component	Guidance reference
Control environment	*Para 89. Entity-level controls vary in nature and precision:* • Some entity-level controls, such as certain control environment controls, have an important, but indirect, effect on the likelihood that a misstatement will be detected or prevented on a timely basis. These controls might affect the other controls the auditor selects for testing and the nature, timing, and extent of procedures the auditor performs on other controls. • Some entity-level controls monitor the effectiveness of other controls. Such controls might be designed to identify possible breakdowns in lower-level controls, but not at a level of precision that would, by themselves, sufficiently address the assessed risk that misstatements to a relevant assertion will be prevented or detected on a timely basis. These controls when operating effectively, might allow the auditor to reduce the testing of other controls. • Some entity-level controls might be designed to operate at a level of precision that would adequately prevent or detect on a timely basis misstatements to one or more relevant assertions. If an entity-level control sufficiently addresses the assessed risk of misstatement, the auditor need not test additional controls relating to that risk. *Para 90. Entity-level controls include:* • Controls related to the control environment; • Controls over management override; • The company's risk assessment process; • Centralised processing and controls, including shared service environments; • Controls to monitor results of operations; • Controls to monitor other controls, including activities of the internal audit function, the audit committee, and self-assessment programs; • Controls over the period-end financial reporting process; • Controls over recording of unusual transactions; and • Policies that address significant business control and risk management practices. *Para 91. Control environment.* Because of its importance to effective internal financial controls over financial reporting, the auditor must evaluate the control environment at the company. As part of evaluating the control environment, the auditor should assess: • Whether management's philosophy and operating style promote effective internal financial controls over financial reporting; • Whether sound integrity and ethical values, particularly of top management, are developed and understood; and • Whether the board or audit committee understands and exercises

	oversight responsibility over financial reporting and internal control.
	Para 92. Period-end financial reporting process.
	Because of its importance to the auditor's opinions on internal financial controls over financial reporting and the financial statements, the auditor must evaluate the period-end financial reporting process. The period-end financial reporting process includes the following:
	• Procedures used to enter transaction totals into the general ledger;
	• Procedures related to the selection and application of accounting policies;
	• Procedures used to initiate, authorise, record, and process journal entries in the general ledger;
	• Procedures used to record recurring and non-recurring adjustments to the annual and quarterly / interim financial statements / results, if any;
	• Procedures for preparing annual and quarterly financial statements and related disclosures.
	Para 93. As part of evaluating the period-end financial reporting process, the auditor should assess:
	• Inputs, procedures performed, and outputs of the processes the company uses to produce its annual and interim financial statements;
	• The extent of information technology ("IT") involvement in the period-end financial reporting process;
	• Who participates from management;
	• The locations involved in the period-end financial reporting process;
	• The types of adjusting and closing entries; and
	• The nature and extent of the oversight of the process by management, the board of directors, and the audit committee.
	Para 84 – Using the work of others
	The auditor should assess the competence and objectivity of the persons whose work the auditor plans to use to determine the extent to which the auditor may use their work. The higher the degree of competence and objectivity, the greater use the auditor may make of the work.
Risk assessment	***Role of risk assessment***
	Para 76. Risk assessment underlies the entire audit process described by this guidance, including the determination of significant accounts and disclosures and relevant assertions, the selection of controls to test, and the determination of the evidence necessary for a given control.
	Para 77. A direct relationship exists between the degree of risk that a significant deficiency or material weakness could exist in a particular area of the company's internal financial controls over financial reporting and the amount of audit attention that should be devoted to that area. In addition, the risk that a company's internal financial controls over financial reporting will fail to prevent or detect a misstatement caused by fraud usually is higher than the risk of failure to prevent or detect error. The auditor should focus more of his or her attention on the areas of

highest risk. On the other hand, it is not necessary to test controls that, even if deficient, would not present a reasonable possibility of material misstatement to the financial statements.

An illustrative list of risks of material misstatement, related control objectives and control activities is given in **Appendix IV of the Guidance Note.**

Para 78. The complexity of the organisation, business unit, or process, will play an important role in the auditor's risk assessment and the determination of the necessary procedures.

Addressing the risk of fraud

Para 80. When planning and performing the audit of internal financial controls, the auditor should take into account the results of his or her fraud risk assessment. As part of identifying and testing entity-level controls, as discussed beginning at paragraph 88 of this Section, and selecting other controls to test, as discussed beginning at paragraph 105 of this Section, the auditor should evaluate whether the company's controls sufficiently address identified risks of material misstatement due to fraud and controls intended to address the risk of management override of other controls. Controls that might address these risks include:

- Controls over significant, unusual transactions, particularly those that result in late or unusual journal entries;
- Controls over journal entries and adjustments made in the period-end financial reporting process;
- Controls over related party transactions;
- Controls related to significant management estimates; and
- Controls that mitigate incentives for, and pressures on, management to falsify or inappropriately manage financial results.

Para 81. If the auditor identifies deficiencies in controls designed to prevent or detect fraud during the audit of internal financial controls over financial reporting, the auditor should take into account those deficiencies when developing his or her response to risks of material misstatement during the financial statement audit, as provided in SA 240 "The Auditor's Responsibilities Relating to Fraud in An Audit of Financial Statements".

Selecting controls to test

Para 105. The auditor should test those controls that are important to the auditor's conclusion about whether the company's controls sufficiently address the assessed risk of misstatement to each relevant assertion.

Para 106. There might be more than one control that addresses the assessed risk of misstatement to a particular relevant assertion; conversely, one control might address the assessed risk of misstatement to more than one relevant assertion. It is neither necessary to test all controls related to a relevant assertion nor necessary to test redundant controls, unless redundancy is itself a control objective.

Para 107. The decision as to whether a control should be selected for testing depends on which controls, individually or in combination, sufficiently address the assessed risk of misstatement to a given relevant

assertion rather than on how the control is labelled (e.g., entity-level control, transaction-level control, control activity, monitoring control, preventive control, detective control).

Relationship of risk to the evidenced obtained
Para 113. Factors that affect the risk associated with a control include:

- The nature and materiality of misstatements that the control is intended to prevent or detect;
- The inherent risk associated with the related account(s) and assertion(s);
- Whether there have been changes in the volume or nature of transactions that might adversely affect control design or operating effectiveness;
- Whether the account has a history of errors;
- The effectiveness of entity-level controls, especially controls that monitor other controls;
- The nature of the control and the frequency with which it operates;
- The competence of the personnel who perform the control or monitor its performance and whether there have been changes in key personnel who perform the control or monitor its performance; (Refer IG 6)
- The degree to which the control relies on the effectiveness of other controls (e.g., the control environment or information technology general controls); (Refer IG 7 and IG 8)
- Whether the control relies on performance by an individual or is automated (i.e., an automated control would generally be expected to be lower risk if relevant information technology general controls are effective); and
- The complexity of the control and the significance of the judgements that must be made in connection with its operation.

Para 119: Prior to the balance sheet date, management might implement changes to the company's controls to make them more effective or efficient or to address control deficiencies. If the auditor determines that the new controls achieve the related objectives of the control criteria and have been in effect for a sufficient period to permit the auditor to assess their design and operating effectiveness by performing tests of controls, he or she will not need to test the design and operating effectiveness of the superseded controls for purposes of expressing an opinion on internal financial controls over financial reporting. If the operating effectiveness of the superseded controls is important to the auditor's control risk assessment, the auditor should test the design and operating effectiveness of those superseded controls, as appropriate. (Refer IG 17)

Para 122: The additional evidence that is necessary to update the results of testing from an interim date to the company's year-end depends on the following factors:
- The specific control tested prior to the balance sheet date, including the risks associated with the control and the nature of the control, and the results of those tests;

- The sufficiency of the evidence of effectiveness obtained at an interim date;
- The length of the remaining period; and
- The possibility that there have been any significant changes in internal financial controls subsequent to the interim date.

Note: In some circumstances, such as when evaluation of the foregoing factors indicates a low risk that the controls are no longer effective during the roll-forward period, inquiry alone might be sufficient as a roll-forward procedure.

Special considerations for subsequent years' audit

Para 124: Factors that affect the risk associated with a control in subsequent years' audits include those in paragraph 113 and the following:

- The nature, timing, and extent of procedures performed in previous audits,
- The results of the previous years' testing of the control, and
- Whether there have been changes in the control or the process in which it operates since the previous audit.

Para 127: In addition, the auditor should vary the nature, timing, and extent of testing of controls from year to year to introduce unpredictability into the testing and respond to changes in circumstances. For this reason, each year the auditor might test controls at a different interim period, increase or reduce the number and types of tests performed or change the combination of procedures used.

Subsequent events

Para 144: Changes in internal financial controls over financial reporting or other factors that might significantly affect internal financial controls over financial reporting might occur subsequent to the date as of which internal financial controls over financial reporting is being audited but before the date of the auditor's report. The auditor should inquire of management whether there were any such changes or factors and obtain written representations from management relating to such matters, as described in paragraph 150.

Para 145. To obtain additional information about whether changes have occurred that might affect the effectiveness of the company's internal financial controls over financial reporting and, therefore, the auditor's report, the auditor should inquire about and examine, for this subsequent period, the following:

- Relevant internal audit (or similar functions, such as loan review in a financial institution) reports issued during the subsequent period,
- Regulatory agency reports on the company's internal financial controls over financial reporting, and
- Information about the effectiveness of the company's internal financial controls over financial reporting obtained through other engagements.

Control activities	**_Understanding likely sources of misstatement_**
	Para 100. To further understand the likely sources of potential misstatements, and as a part of selecting the controls to test, the auditor should achieve the following objectives: • Understand the flow of transactions related to the relevant assertions, including how these transactions are initiated, authorised, processed, and recorded; (Refer IG 2 and IG 3) • Verify that he/she has identified the points within the company's processes at which a misstatement – including a misstatement due to fraud – could arise that, individually or in combination with other misstatements, would be material; • Identify the controls that management has implemented to address these potential misstatements; and • Identify the controls that management has implemented over the prevention or timely detection of unauthorised acquisition, use, or disposition of the company's assets that could result in a material misstatement of the financial statements. An illustrative list of risks of material misstatement, related control objectives and control activities is given in **Appendix IV of the Guidance Note**. _Para 101._ Because of the degree of judgement required, the auditor should perform the procedures that achieve the objectives in para 100 either by himself or herself or supervise the work of others who provide direct assistance to the auditor. _Para 102._ The auditor should also understand how Information Technology (IT) affects the company's flow of transactions. The auditor should apply the requirements of SA 315, which discuss the effect of information technology on internal financial controls and the risks to assess. **Note:** The identification of risks and controls within IT is not a separate evaluation. Instead, it is an integral part of the top-down approach used to identify significant accounts and disclosures and their relevant assertions, and the controls to test, as well as to assess risk and allocate audit effort as described by this guidance. _Para 103._ Performing walkthroughs. Performing walkthroughs will frequently be the most effective way of achieving the objectives in paragraph 100. In performing a walkthrough, the auditor follows a transaction from origination through the company's processes, including information systems, until it is reflected in the company's financial records, using the same documents and information technology that company personnel use. Walkthrough procedures usually include a combination of inquiry, observation, inspection of relevant documentation, and re-performance of controls. _Para 104._ In performing a walkthrough, at the points at which important processing procedures occur, the auditor questions the company's personnel about their understanding of what is required by the company's prescribed procedures and controls. These probing questions, combined with the other walkthrough procedures, allow the auditor to gain a sufficient understanding of the process and to be able to identify important points at which a necessary control is missing or not designed effectively. Additionally, probing questions that go beyond a narrow focus

on the single transaction used as the basis for the walkthrough allow the auditor to gain an understanding of the different types of significant transactions handled by the process.

Selecting controls to test

Para 105 The auditor should test those controls that are important to the auditor's conclusion about whether the company's controls sufficiently address the assessed risk of misstatement to each relevant assertion.

Para 106. There might be more than one control that addresses the assessed risk of misstatement to a particular relevant assertion; conversely, one control might address the assessed risk of misstatement to more than one relevant assertion. It is neither necessary to test all controls related to a relevant assertion nor necessary to test redundant controls, unless redundancy is itself a control objective.

Para 107. The decision as to whether a control should be selected for testing depends on which controls, individually or in combination, sufficiently address the assessed risk of misstatement to a given relevant assertion rather than on how the control is labelled (e.g., entity-level control, transaction-level control, control activity, monitoring control, preventive control, detective control).

Process flow diagrams

When considering and reviewing the relevant information to developing process flow diagrams, the following questions may be helpful:

- Who is involved in the process (e.g., departments, roles, and people)?
- Are there segregations of duties that are relevant to the process?
- What is the general objective of the processes and what are the related sub-processes?
- When does the process occur?
- Does the process involve, or impact, multiple locations?
- What are the tasks within the process and in what sequence do they occur?
- What are the points in the process at which a misstatement, including a misstatement due to fraud, could arise?
- What control activities address the risks?
- What IPE is involved?
- How is application systems involved within the process?

Understanding IT Environment

IG 4.1 Based on the identification of the relevant flows of transactions or processes, the auditor also identifies the relevant IT environment related to those flows or processes to understand the effect of IT and the risks arising from IT. The term IT environment includes both the application systems and the IT infrastructure supporting those applications systems, including the database, operating system and network.

IG 4.2 The auditor identifies the relevant applications and IT infrastructure to identify the relevant risks arising from IT (IT risks) that need to be addressed for purposes of opining on internal financial controls and for purposes of being able to use a control reliance strategy for those accounts that are impacted by the IT risks (i.e., those accounts where the

risks of material misstatement are addressed by controls that are dependent upon the relevant application systems and IT infrastructure.) He or she then identifies and tests the relevant general IT controls that address those IT risks.

IG 4.3 The auditor's procedures related to IT risks and controls are performed in the context of the relevant flows of transactions related to significant accounts and disclosures. In other words, the auditor is not required to obtain an understanding of all the entity's IT systems; instead, he or she focuses on those aspects of the entity's IT environment that may pose risks to the entity's financial statements. Even when a control-reliance strategy is not planned, the auditor's understanding of IT's role in the entity's processes is important to the identification and assessment of risks of material misstatement and to plan further substantive procedures.

IG 4.4 The auditor should obtain an understanding of the information system, including the related business processes relevant to financial reporting, including the following areas:

- The classes of transactions in the entity's operations that are significant to the financial statements.
- The procedures within both IT and manual systems by which those transactions are initiated, authorised, recorded, processed, corrected as necessary, transferred to the general ledger, and reported in the financial statements.
- The related accounting records supporting information and specific accounts in the financial statements that are used to initiate, authorise, record, process, and report transactions. This includes the correction of incorrect information and how information is transferred to the general ledger. The records may be in either manual or electronic form.
- How the information system captures events and conditions, other than transactions, that are significant to the financial statements.
- The financial reporting process used to prepare the entity's financial statements, including significant accounting estimates and disclosures.
- Controls surrounding journal entries, including non-standard journal entries used to record non-recurring, unusual transactions, or adjustments.

Information system and communication	*IG 8 – Information Produced by the Entity (IPE)* *IPE Diagrams* *IG 2.9* When a control activity is dependent upon IPE that is generated from systems or other sources, it is important that the auditor understands what could go wrong in the generation of the IPE. Illustrative diagrams that depict the auditor's understanding of the report logic, parameters, and source data may be helpful when trying to understand and articulate the risks related to IPE. *IG 2.10* It may be helpful to involve Information Technology (IT) specialists in the creation of IPE diagrams, especially if the IPE is system generated, as much of the information may be generated from the IT systems of the

entity. It is important that IT specialists collaborate with the auditors who use the IPE for audit purposes so everyone gains an appropriate understanding of the purpose and intended use of the IPE.

IG 2.11 IPE may be relevant to the audit due to its relationship with the auditor's tests of controls or substantive procedures. The following are the general reasons that IPE is relevant to the audit:
- IPE is used by entity personnel to perform a relevant control.
- IPE is used by the auditor to test a relevant control.
- IPE is used by the auditor to perform substantive procedures.

IG 2.12 Regardless of the use of the IPE in the context of an audit, the auditor may consider creating IPE diagrams to document his or her understanding of the IPE and assist in determining appropriate procedures to test the accuracy and completeness of the information.

IG 2.13 The following general steps to be performed by auditors to build an IPE diagram assume that the auditor has already identified relevant IPE to the audit:

Step 1 — Identification of and Understanding Report Logic and Parameters

Step 2 — Identification and Understanding Source Data

Step 3 — Building the IPE Diagrams

After the IPE parameters, report logic and source data have been understood, the auditor can develop the IPE diagram.

The following basic elements may be depicted in the diagram to represent the auditor's understanding of the IPE:
- IPE parameters
  - Identification of relevant parameters that impact the results of the IPE.
  - Common parameter combinations used to generate IPE (if there are recurring uses).
- IPE logic
  - Identification of standard or custom IPE logic.
  - Location information on where the source logic is maintained in the system.
  - If a benchmarking strategy is used to test logic, identification of the date that logic was last changed.
  - Information that indicates whether general IT controls are relevant.
- IPE source data
  - Relevant application systems.
  - Sources of information used to generate IPE (e.g., system tables).
  - Information that indicates whether general IT controls are relevant.
  - If general IT controls are not relevant, document alternative methods for validating the accuracy and completeness of the data.
- Reference to IPE on process flow diagram, if applicable.

	Situation in which service organisations are relevant for internal financial controls IG 9.3 If the service organisation's services are part of a company's information system, then they are part of the information and communication component of the company's internal financial controls. When the service organisation's services are part of the company's internal financial controls, the auditor should include the activities of the service organisation when determining the evidence required to support his or her opinion. IG 9.4 The following are the procedures that the auditor should perform with respect to the activities performed by the service organisation – • Obtaining an understanding of the controls at the service organisation that are relevant to the entity's internal control and the controls at the user organisation over the activities of the service organisation, and • Obtaining evidence that the controls that are relevant to the auditor's opinion are operating effectively.
Monitoring activities	**Entity-level controls** **Para 89. Entity-level controls vary in nature and precision:** • Some entity-level controls, such as certain control environment controls, have an important, but indirect, effect on the likelihood that a mis-statement will be detected or prevented on a timely basis. These controls might affect the other controls the auditor selects for testing and the nature, timing, and extent of procedures the auditor performs on other controls. • Some entity-level controls monitor the effectiveness of other controls. Such controls might be designed to identify possible breakdowns in lower-level controls, but not at a level of precision that would, by themselves, sufficiently address the assessed risk that misstatements to a relevant assertion will be prevented or detected on a timely basis. These controls when operating effectively, might allow the auditor to reduce the testing of other controls. • Some entity-level controls might be designed to operate at a level of precision that would adequately prevent or detect on a timely basis misstatements to one or more relevant assertions. If an entity-level control sufficiently addresses the assessed risk of mis-statement, the auditor need not test additional controls relating to that risk. **Para 90: Entity-level controls include:** • Controls related to the control environment; • Controls over management override; • The company's risk assessment process; • Centralised processing and controls, including shared service environments; (Refer IG 9) • Controls to monitor results of operations; • Controls to monitor other controls, including activities of the internal audit function, the audit committee, and self-assessment programs;

- Controls over the period-end financial reporting process;
- Controls over recording of unusual transactions; and
- Policies that address significant business control and risk management practices.

Para 91: Control environment.
Because of its importance to effective internal financial controls over financial reporting, the auditor must evaluate the control environment at the company. As part of evaluating the control environment, the auditor should assess:

- Whether management's philosophy and operating style promote effective internal financial controls over financial reporting;
- Whether sound integrity and ethical values, particularly of top management, are developed and understood; and
- Whether the board or audit committee understands and exercises oversight responsibility over financial reporting and internal control.

Para 93: As part of evaluating the period-end financial reporting process, the auditor should assess:

- Inputs, procedures performed, and outputs of the processes the company uses to produce its annual and interim financial statements;
- The extent of information technology ("IT") involvement in the period-end financial reporting process;
- Who participates from management;
- The locations involved in the period-end financial reporting process;
- The types of adjusting and closing entries; and
- The nature and extent of the oversight of the process by management, the board of directors, and the audit committee.

Indicators of material weakness
Para 135: Indicators of material weaknesses in internal financial controls over financial reporting include:

- Identification of fraud, whether or not material, on the part of senior management;
- Errors observed in previously issued financial statements in the current financial year;
- Identification by the auditor of a material misstatement of financial statements in the current period in circumstances that indicate that the misstatement would not have been detected by the company's internal financial controls over financial reporting; and
- Ineffective oversight of the company's external financial reporting and internal financial controls over financial reporting by the company's audit committee.

(Source: ICAI Guidance Note on Internal Financial Control over Financial Reporting)

Chapter 5: Shareholders funds

5.1. Shareholders' funds: Control environment

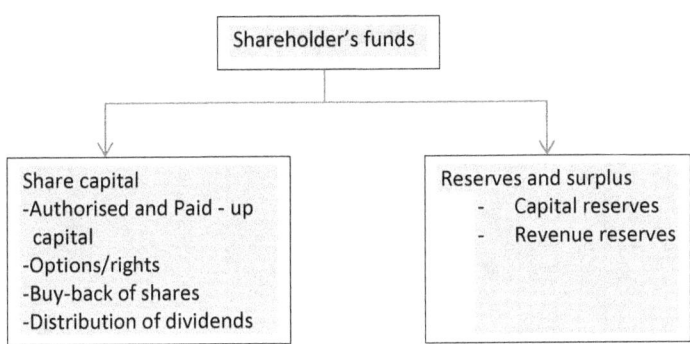

a) Share capital, both authorised and issued and paid-up, has been maintained in the books of accounts as per the stipulations of Companies Act 1956 and Companies Act 2013.

b) Reserves and Surplus – both capital and revenue – has been maintained in the books of accounts in line with the provisions of Companies Act 1956 and Companies Act 2013.

c) Records and returns are maintained in line with the Memorandum and Articles of Association of the entity.

d) All the formalities related to Registrar of Companies have been duly carried out from time to time.

e) There is no qualification / adverse opinion of the Companies Auditors as well as external Company Secretaries related to Share capital as well as Reserves and Surplus.

f) All the relevant transactions related to Shareholders' funds have been adequately backed up by board as well as shareholders' resolution as required from case to case basis.

5.2. Shareholders' funds: Financial Control over financial reporting

Activities	Risk Environment	Preventive control	Detective control	Monitoring control Y/N/NA
Share capital **Issue of share** **capital**	*Core risk and control* Subscribed and fully paid up share capital are: • Recorded for transactions that did not occur • Not recorded for transactions that did occur • Recorded at the incorrect amount.	Finance personnel prepare the journal entry, supporting documentation, and account analysis to record subscribed and paid up share capital. Management reviews and approves the journal entry, supporting documentation, and account analysis before the journal entry is recorded.	Management with knowledge of the entity's share capital transactions and share capital account activity reviews the share capital accounts for unrecorded or inaccurately recorded transactions. Unusual activity or errors are investigated and resolved on a timely basis.	

Issue of Share Capital	**Other risks and control** Options/Rights exercised and purchases of shares of are recorded in the Share capital accounts for transactions that did not occur.	Finance personnel prepare the journal entry, supporting documentation, and account analysis to record subscribed and paid up share capital. Management reviews and approves the journal entry, supporting documentation, and account analysis before the journal entry is recorded.	Bank statements are reconciled to the general ledger regularly and differences are investigated and resolved on a timely basis.	
	Options/Rights to purchase shares are exercised, or shares are purchased through an employee stock option plan, but are: • Not recorded in the equity accounts • Recorded at the incorrect amount	Same as above	Same as above	
Buyback of Shares	Buyback of shares are not recorded.	Finance personnel prepare the journal entry, supporting documentation, and account analysis to record subscribed and paid up share capital. Management reviews and approves the journal entry, supporting documentation, and account analysis before the journal entry is recorded.	Bank statements are reconciled to the general ledger regularly and differences are investigated and resolved on a timely basis Management with knowledge of the entity's share capital transactions and share capital account activity reviews the share capital accounts for unrecorded or inaccurately recorded transactions. Unusual activity or	

			errors are investigated and resolved on a timely basis.	
	Buyback of shares are recorded for transactions that did not occur.	Same as above	Same as above	
Distribution of dividends	Dividends are declared but not recorded.	Bank statements are reconciled to the general ledger regularly and differences are investigated and resolved on a timely basis.		
	Dividends are distributed but not recorded.	Bank statements are reconciled to the general ledger regularly and differences are investigated and resolved on a timely basis.	Management with knowledge of the entity's share capital transactions and share capital account activity reviews the share capital accounts for unrecorded or inaccurately recorded transactions. Unusual activity or errors are investigated and resolved on a timely basis.	
	Dividends are recorded even though no dividends have been declared or distributed	Finance personnel prepare the journal entry, supporting documentation, and account analysis to record dividends. Management reviews and approves the journal entry, supporting documentation, and account analysis before the journal entry is recorded.	Management with knowledge of the entity's equity transactions and share capital account transactions reviews the accounts for unrecorded or inaccurately recorded transactions. Unusual transactions or errors are investigated and resolved on a timely basis.	

	Dividends are inaccurately calculated and recorded.	Finance personnel prepare the journal entry, supporting documentation, and account analysis to record dividends. Management reviews and approves the journal entry, supporting documentation, and account analysis before the journal entry is recorded	Management with knowledge of the entity's share capital and dividend transactions reviews such accounts for unrecorded or inaccurately recorded transactions. Unusual activity or errors are investigated and resolved on a timely basis	
Reserves & surplus	Reserves & surplus: • Recorded for transactions that did not occur • Not recorded for transactions that did occur • Recorded at the incorrect amount.	Finance personnel prepare the journal entry, supporting documentation, and account analysis to record reserves & surplus. Management reviews and approves the journal entry, supporting documentation, and account analysis before the journal entry is recorded.	Management with knowledge of the entity's reserves & surplus transactions and reviews the reserves & surplus accounts for unrecorded or inaccurately recorded transactions. Unusual activity or errors are investigated and resolved on a timely basis.	

5.3. Risk Map – Share capital and reserves and surplus

Risk map for share capital and reserves and surplus is illustrated as under:

5.4. Share capital: Assessment check list

Shareholders' Equity Controls	Yes	No	N/A	Comments
1. Use of registrar				
2. Use of transfer agent				
3. Adequacy of detailed records				
4. Comparison of transfer agent's report with records				
5. Physical control over blank certificates				
6. Physical control over treasury certificates				
7. Authorization for transactions				
8. Tax stamp compliance for canceled certificates				
9. Independent dividend agent				
10. Imprest dividend account				
11. Periodic reconciliation of dividend account				
12. Adequacy of stockholders' ledger				
13. Review of stock restrictions and provisions				
14. Valuation procedures for stock issuances				
15. Other paid-in capital entries				
16. Other retained earnings entries				

Chapter 6: Long term liabilities

6.1. Long term liabilities: Control environment

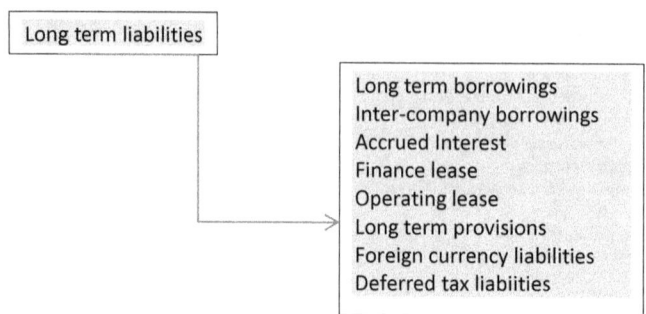

a) Long term liabilities including long term borrowings, have been maintained in the books of accounts as per the stipulations of Companies Act 1956 and Companies Act 2013.

b) Long term borrowings – have been maintained in the books of accounts in line with the provisions of Companies Act 1956 and Companies Act 2013.

c) All the related charges against long term borrowings have been properly entered in Register of Charges as well as filed with Registrar of Companies from time to time.

d) Records and returns are maintained in line with the Memorandum and Articles of Association of the entity.

e) All the formalities related to Registrar of Companies have been duly carried out from time to time.

f) There is no qualification / adverse opinion of the Companies Auditors as well as external Company Secretaries related to Long term borrowings.

g) All the relevant transactions related to long term liabilities have been adequately backed up by board as well as shareholders' resolution as required in case to case basis.

6.2. Long term liabilities: Financial Control over financial reporting

Activities	Risk Environment	Preventive control	Detective control	Monitoring control Y/N/NA
Loans / borrowings *Recording Borrowings*	Loan agreements are entered into and not recorded in the general ledger.	New loan agreements, including finance leases, or modifications to existing loan agreements, are analysed by finance personnel who prepare the journal entry and supporting analysis; management reviews and approves the journal entry and supporting analysis before recording the entry.	Management prepares cash flow analyses to monitor working capital. On a periodic basis, management compares forecasted cash position to actual; significant and/or unusual differences are investigated and resolved.	

	Loan agreements are entered into and are recorded in the general ledger at the incorrect amount.	New loan agreements, including finance leases, or modifications to existing loan agreements, are analysed by finance personnel who prepare the journal entry and supporting analysis; management reviews and approves the journal entry and supporting analysis before recording the entry.		
	Loan is recorded when no borrowing agreement has been entered into or for loan that is not the loan of the entity.	New loan agreements including finance leases, or modifications to existing loan arrangements, are analysed by finance personnel who prepare the journal entry and supporting analysis; management reviews and approves the journal entry and supporting analysis before recording the entry.	Management prepares cash flow analyses to monitor working capital. On a periodic basis, management compares forecasted cash position to actual; significant and/or unusual differences are investigated and resolved.	
	Loan stated in the general ledger does not reconcile to the supporting loan records, and/or the reconciliation contains invalid items.		On a periodic basis, finance personnel perform a reconciliation of the loan register to the general ledger. Management reviews and approves the reconciliation and any reconciling items are reviewed and addressed on a timely basis.	
Recording payments	Loan payments have been:	Management with knowledge of loan	Bank statements are reconciled to	• Existence; Rights and

		agreements, payment schedules, and other debt terms, periodically reviews the transactions within the loan register. Discrepancies are investigated and resolved on a timely basis.	the general ledger regularly and differences are investigated and resolved on a timely basis.	Obligations • Completeness • Valuation and Allocation
	• Made but are not recorded • Recorded, but have not been paid • Recorded at an amount that differs from the actual amount paid.			
Recording Accrued Interest	Accrued interest and Finance cost are initially recorded when no loan exists.	Finance personnel prepare the journal entry, supporting documentation, and account analysis to record accrued finance cost. Management reviews and approves the journal entry, supporting documentation, and account analysis before the journal entry is recorded.	On a periodic basis, finance personnel reconcile accrued interest, to supporting detail.	Completeness
	Accrued interest and finance cost exist but are not recorded.	On a periodic basis, finance personnel meet with members of management (e.g., sales, operational, human resources, legal counsel, Treasury) to discuss developments and/or changes in the business that may affect recorded provision for expenses, or may affect the need to record an provision for expense. Finance personnel prepare a journal entry and supporting documentation, which are reviewed by management before the journal	Management reviews the reconciliation and supporting documentation, and unusual transactions or invalid reconciling items are investigated and resolved on a timely basis.	

		entry is recorded.		
	Accrued interest and finance cost are recorded at incorrect amounts.	Finance personnel prepare the journal entry, supporting documentation, and account analysis to record accrued finance cost. Management reviews and approves the journal entry, supporting documentation, and account analysis before the journal entry is recorded.	Spreadsheets utilised to analyse and calculate significant accrued finance costs are locked from formula editing. On a test basis, finance personnel test the calculations within the spreadsheet for ongoing accuracy.	
Inter-company loan & interest	Intercompany loan transactions occurred but are not recorded in one of the subsidiary general ledgers or are recorded at incorrect amounts.	Finance personnel prepare the journal entry to record intercompany transactions along with supporting documentation. Management reviews and approves the journal entry and supporting documentation before the journal entry is recorded. Finance personnel enter intercompany transactions into the ERP system identifying the affected entities by company code. The ERP system automatically records intercompany transactions to the corresponding entities' general ledger.	Management with knowledge of intercompany transactions reviews the activity within the various intercompany accounts. Discrepancies or unusual activity are investigated and resolved on a timely basis	
Finance lease	Finance leases for fixed assets are incorrectly accounted for as	New lease contracts and lease modifications are reviewed by	New lease contracts and lease modifications recorded in the	

	operating leases	finance personnel to determine whether they meet the criteria for finance or operating lease treatment, including reference to the appropriate accounting framework and principle. The journal entry and supporting documentation are reviewed by management prior to the journal entry being posted.	lease register are periodically reviewed by management to verify that the lease has been properly accounted for as a finance or operating lease.	
Operating lease	Operating leases for fixed assets are incorrectly accounted for as finance leases.	New lease contracts and lease modifications are reviewed by finance personnel to determine whether they meet the criteria for finance or operating lease treatment, including reference to the appropriate accounting framework and principle. The journal entry and supporting documentation are reviewed by management prior to the journal entry being posted.	New lease contracts and lease modifications recorded in the lease register are periodically reviewed by management to verify that the lease has been appropriately accounted for as a finance or operating lease.	
Finance lease	Finance lease obligations are valued and recorded using the incorrect interest rate.	Finance personnel prepare the journal entry and supporting analyses for new finance leases. Management with the requisite expertise and knowledge of the applicable accounting framework and		

		principles reviews the journal entry and supporting analyses prior to the journal entry being recorded.		
Recording payments	Loan re- payments are auto-deducted from the entity's bank account (or otherwise made) and not recorded in the general ledger.	Finance personnel prepare the journal to record loan waiver along with supporting documentation. Management reviews and approves the journal entry and supporting documentation before the journal entry is recorded.	Bank statements are reconciled to the general ledger regularly and differences are investigated and resolved on a timely basis. On a periodic basis, finance personnel perform a reconciliation of the loan register to the general ledger. Management reviews and approves the reconciliation and any reconciling items are reviewed and addressed on a timely basis.	
	Recorded loan obligations are fully or partially waived and the waived amount is not recorded in the general ledger or is recorded at an incorrect amount.		Management with knowledge of loan agreements, payment schedules, and other terms, periodically reviews the activity within the loan register. Discrepancies are investigated and resolved on a timely basis.	
Recording of Other Loan Related Transactions	Loan related account balances or transactions denominated in foreign currencies are valued and recorded using the incorrect exchange rate.	The ERP system automatically calculates the foreign currency translation adjustment for accounts denominated in foreign currencies. The proposed translation adjustment is independently	Management with knowledge of loan agreements, payment schedules, and other terms, periodically reviews the activity within the loan register. Discrepancies are investigated and resolved on a timely basis.	

		reviewed and approved by management prior to recording.		
Foreign currency	Foreign Currency Translation Adjustments	The ERP system automatically calculates the foreign currency translation adjustment for accounts denominated in foreign currencies. The proposed translation adjustment is independently reviewed and approved by management prior to recording.	Management with knowledge of the entity's share capital transactions reviews the share capital for unrecorded or inaccurately recorded transactions. Unusual activity or errors are investigated and resolved on a timely basis.	

6.3. Deferred tax liabilities: Financial Control over Financial Reporting

Activities	Risk environment	Preventive control	Detective control	Monitoring control Y/N/NA
Deferred taxes *Calculate and Record Deferred Income Tax Assets and Liabilities*	*Core risks and controls* Permanent differences are: • Incorrectly classified as timing differences, and vice versa • Recorded at the incorrect amount.	Deferred tax calculation and journal entry to record deferred taxes are (1) prepared by personnel with sufficient training and experience and (2) independently reviewed by management Tax function obtains supporting documentation and analyses for permanent and timing differences in the general ledger accounts and independently evaluates and tests the data for proper inclusion and completeness		
Calculate and Record	Transactions with a deferred income tax	A listing of all types of transactions or	The tax department and finance	

146

Deferred Income Tax Assets and Liabilities	impact are not considered when calculating deferred tax balances.	events affecting the income tax provision and related deferred income tax accounts is utilised to compare captured data and information for completeness.	department meet on a regular basis to discuss changes in the business. Changes that may have an effect on deferred income taxes and income tax expense are analysed and the conclusions are documented.	
Calculate and Record Deferred Income Tax Assets and Liabilities	Provision to return adjustments are not recorded.	Tax department of the entity compares amounts in the tax return to the amounts included in the prior-year income tax provision and records adjustments to the deferred tax accounts, income taxes payable / refund receivable, and income tax expense as applicable.		
Calculate and Record Deferred Income Tax Assets and Liabilities	Tax rate applied in taxable income and deferred tax calculation is incorrect.	Deferred taxes calculation and journal entry to record deferred taxes are (1) prepared by personnel with sufficient training and experience and (2) independently reviewed by management Deferred taxes are processed using a software program. Program's algorithms, calculations, etc., are tested by the entity for accuracy. New releases or updates to the software are separately tested and incorporated on a timely basis.		
Calculate and Record	Recent amendments to the income tax	Income taxes are processed using a		

Deferred Income Tax Assets and Liabilities	code are not reflected in the determination of income tax expense and deferred taxes.	software program that draws financial and tax data from the ERP system. Program's algorithms, calculations, etc., are tested for accuracy. New releases or updates to the software are tested prior to implementation and are implemented on a timely basis. The tax department of the entity agrees the tax rate utilised in determining income tax expense to the enacted rate as per the Income Tax Act, 1961 and considers whether there is substantively enacted tax rates that will affect the balance of deferred taxes.		
Calculate and Record Deferred Income Tax Assets and Liabilities	Tax journal entries are posted at incorrect amounts to the general ledger.	Journal entries to record the adjustments to the income tax accounts have adequate supporting documentation and are independently reviewed and approved prior to recording.		
Calculate and Record Deferred Income Tax Assets and Liabilities	The entity's assessment that there is reasonable/virtual certainty that sufficient future taxable income will be available against which the deferred tax assets can be realised is not appropriate.	Processes exist whereby accounting and tax personnel jointly identify and assess available sources of taxable income, including assessing and weighing all positive and negative evidences. The analysis and conclusion are reviewed and approved by		

		management prior to the journal entry being recorded. Financial forecasts are prepared by accounting personnel with an appropriate level of knowledge of accounting requirements. Management (1) reviews the financial forecast methodology for appropriateness and consistent application to other financial forecasts prepared and (2) reviews, challenges, and approves the significant assumptions applied		
Calculate and Record Deferred Income Tax Assets and Liabilities	Deferred income tax amounts recorded in the general ledger contains invalid items	Deferred taxes calculation and journal entry to record deferred taxes are (1) prepared by personnel with sufficient training and experience and (2) independently reviewed by management Deferred taxes are processed using a software program. Program's algorithms, calculations, etc., are tested by the entity for accuracy. New releases or updates to the software are separately tested and incorporated on a timely basis.		

6.4. Risk Map – Long term liabilities

Risk map for long term liabilities is illustrated as under:

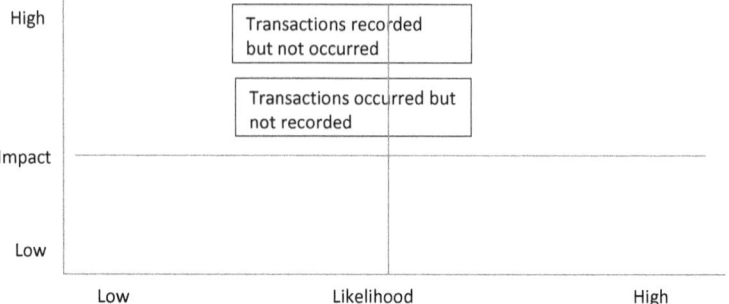

6.5. Long-term liabilities: Assessment check list

Long-Term Liabilities Controls	Yes	No	N/A	Comments
1. Authorization to incur				
2. Executed in company name				
3. Detailed records of long-term debt				
4. Reports of independent transfer agent				
5. Reports of independent registrar				
6. Otherwise adequate records of creditors				
7. Control over unissued instruments				
8. Signers independent of each other				
9. Adequacy of records of collateral				
10. Periodic review of debt agreement compliance				
11. Recordkeeping of detachable warrants				
12. Recordkeeping of conversion features				

Chapter 7: Trade Payables & Other current liabilities

7.1. Trade Payable: Control environment

Control environment related to Trade Payables is explained below through a summary chart:

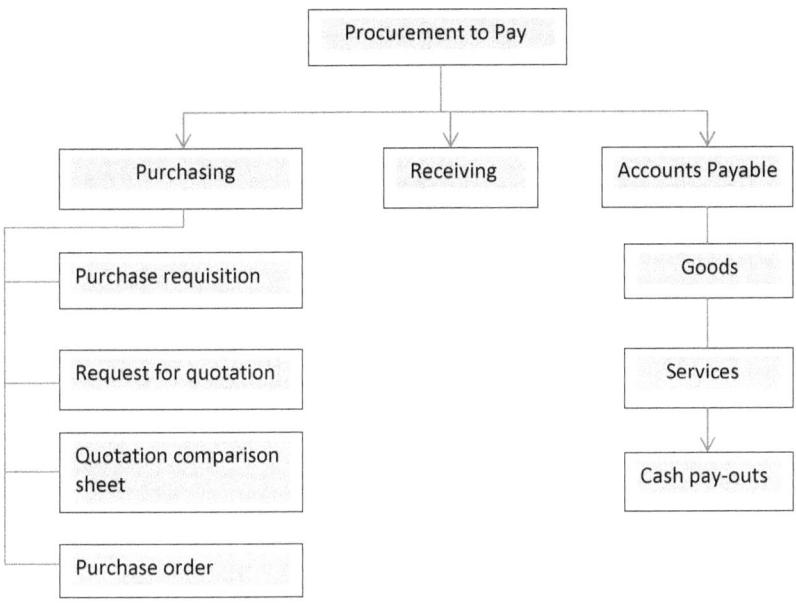

7.1.1. Procurement to pay cycle

A detailed Process flow diagram on Procurement to pay cycle is illustrated below.

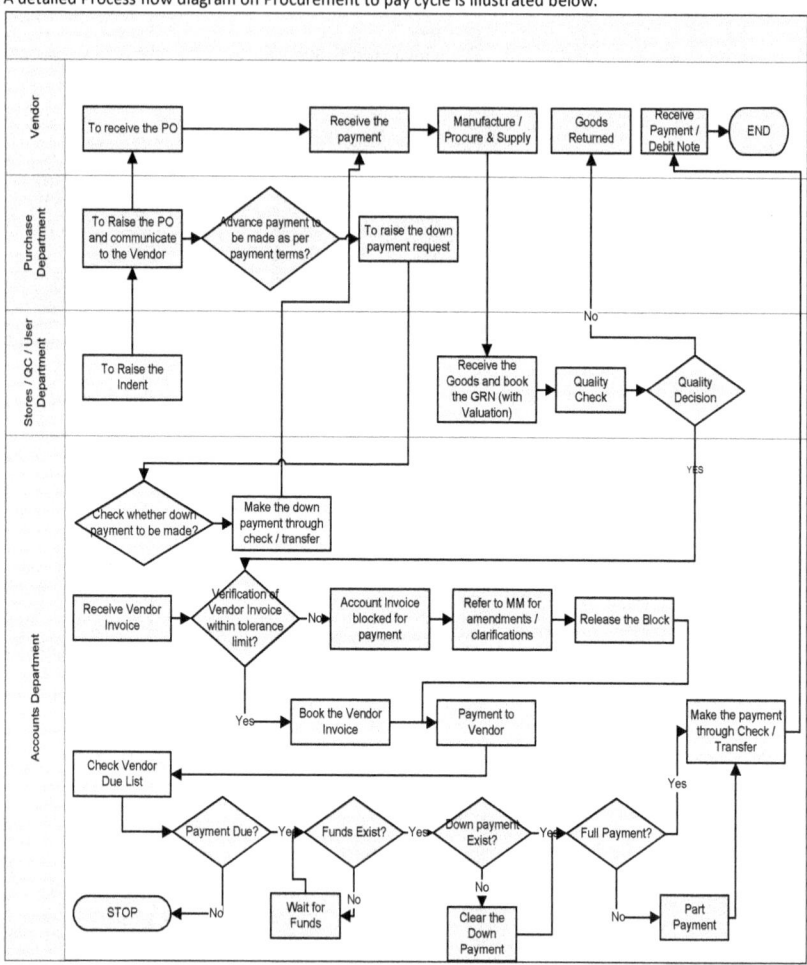

Steps under Procure to pay cycle would cover the following:

Steps	Process Narrative
Step 1	Purchase Requisition (PR)
Step 2	Request for Quotation and Quotation
Step 3	Purchase Order (PO)

Step 4	Goods Receipt Note (GRN)
Step 5	Invoice verification (Three way match)
Step 6	Payment to vendors

Process flow analysis through SIPOC diagrams for each of these processes is detailed below for easy reference.

7.1.2. Purchase Requisition

SIPOC (Supplier Input Process Output Customer) document for Purchase Requisition is shown as under:

Supplier	Input	Process	Output	Customer
Sales Department	Sales Plan from Sales planning team for next three months by 20th of every month	Define Target level inventory for all materials TOTAL REQUIREMENT = PLANNED REQUIREMENT – CURRENT STOCK IN HAND		
Plant	In case of Plants, the requirement of finished goods will be finalised by Plant user department based on Production Plan after approval of HOD	Create MRP run by end of every month		
		Raise PR on target level inventories in system		
		Verify PR, review reasons for rejection of PR if any		
		Approve PR based on Chart of Authority	Approved PR	Sent to Purchase Dept for raising PO

7.1.3. Request for quotations (RFQ) and Quotation

Supplier	Input	Process	Output	Customer
User Dept	Received approved PR	Create Request for Quotation and send to at least five vendors via email		
		Receive quotation		

		from each vendor		
		Create Comparative statement of quotations		
		Approve vendor having lowest rates based on DOA	Approved quotation	Purchase Dept for creation of PO

7.1.4. Purchase Order

SIPOC document for Purchase Order is shown as under:

Supplier	Input	Process	Output	Customer
User Department	List material requirement from user department	Initiate supplier selection and management process for materials to be procured		
	Receive approved PR	Check if Rate Contract is available – if yes then system automatically picks up price and terms and conditions		
		If not then identify vendor through vendor selection process		
		Raise PO		
		Approve PO based on Chart of Authority	Approved PR	E-mail PO to vendor for delivery

7.1.5. Goods Receipt Note (GRN)

Supplier	Input	Process	Output	Customer
PO received by vendor based on quotation sent	Delivered material by vendor based on PO	Make Gate entry on receipt of material and before initiating quality check		
	Receive delivery challan from the vendor indicating quantity and value of material	Receive material at stores		

		Check quality assurance of materials		
		Raise GRN		
		Approve GRN	Approved GRN	Sent approved GRN to Accounts

7.1.6. Invoice verification
7.1.6.1. Vendor invoice without Purchase Order

Vendor Invoices are received in respect of expenses for which Purchase Orders are not created. These Invoices would be accounted for directly in the FI(Finance) Module without any procurement process. Since there are no preceding documents like Purchase Orders, Goods Receipt / Service Entry Sheet, the Invoice would be physically verified and approved by the concerned Department Head responsible for incurring the expense.

For creating a Vendor Invoice, the following minimum information is required in the document header:	• **Vendor Code** • **Posting Date:** This is the date on which the transaction is posted in the General Ledger and vendor sub ledger. It determines the posting. • **Document date:** Issue date of the original document (not necessarily the same as the posting date). For invoices it is called the invoice date. • **Reference:** The Invoice No. (As mentioned by the Vendor in the Invoice) shall be entered as Reference and the system shall check if an earlier Invoice has been entered for the same Vendor with the same Reference detail. An error message will be issued in case of duplication in the Reference field. • **Amount:** The total amount of the Invoice • **Document type** • **Currency** • **Document header text** would be mandatory • **G/L Account number:** To be created from the master Chart of Accounts • **Amount:** All amounts shall be converted to the Company Code currency which is the functional currency. If the

	Document Currency is a foreign currency, then additionally all amounts shall be converted to the Group Currency i.e. INR.

Additional assignments including Cost Center would be required depending on the G/L Account used. The Assignment field (alphanumeric, up to 18 characters) is updated automatically with the data from the field referenced in the Sort Key field of the general ledger account. A value in the Assignment field can also be manually entered.

7.1.6.2. Goods Receipt based vendor invoice verification

The main task of the Invoice Verification component is to complete the procedure of materials procurement by posting the vendor invoice and to pass on information concerning the invoice to Financial Accounting and subsequent applications. Invoices that originate in procurement of services can also be processed.

The entity will use GR based invoice verification for all the other procurement processes.

An Invoice against a Purchase Order will be processed with reference to the Purchase Order Number or the Delivery Note. An invoice for a service will refer to a service entry sheet. Goods-receipt-based Invoice Verification must be defined in all purchase orders. Each invoice item can then be matched up uniquely with the goods receipt item.

All deliveries or services provided by a vendor can be settled in a single invoice. On the item list all purchase order items that match the reference allocation and that are ready to be invoiced will be suggested.

7.1.6.3. Invoice verification (SIPOC diagram)

Supplier	Input	Process	Output	Customer
Accounts receive approved GRN from Stores	Gate Receipt record	Receive approved GRN, PO and vendor Invoice		
Accounts received approved PO from Sourcing Department	Approved Goods Received Note (GRN)	Do a three way match in ERP and approve vendor invoice		
Vendor sending vendor invoice substantiating the material sent	Approved Purchase Order (PO)	Quantity approved from GRN Rate approved		

against the PO		from PO		
	Vendor invoice along-with Delivery Challan	Pass vendor invoice for payment		
			Vendor invoice approved for payment	
			TDS deducted and net amount approved for payment	Funds transferred / cheque payment made to vendor

All invoice items in which the quantity expected to be invoiced is not zero will be selected by default. Only the selected invoice items are copied to the document when you post the invoice. Any invoice items that has been proposed and selected should be manually deselected if they do not appear in the Vendor's invoice.

In the Quantity column, the quantity to be invoiced will be proposed. This quantity will be the difference between the quantity delivered and that invoiced so far for each goods receipt.

In the Amount column, the product of the quantity proposed and the order price will be proposed. This amount will not include taxes.

The following information will be mandatory entry during the Invoice Verification process.

- Document Date i.e. date of invoice
- Posting Date
- Invoice Number
- Invoice Amount
- Purchase Order / Delivery Note or Service Entry Sheet number.

The following information will be then copied from the Purchase Order:

- Vendor, terms of payment (if defined there), currency
- Invoice items

The following information is derived from the Purchase Order history:

- Quantity, amount

Tolerances limits may be specified for different types of variances which are defined in the various Tolerance Keys. When processing an Invoice, each item shall be checked for variances between the invoice and the Purchase Order or Goods Receipt.

If in the master data for the material it has been defined that the Goods Receipt of the material is subject to inspection and that an Invoice for the material should be blocked due to Quality Inspection, then an Invoice for the material would be blocked if no usage decision has been made about the inspection lot for the goods receipt concerned or if the inspection lot is rejected.

It will not be possible to post an invoice before the goods receipt. Also, the invoice quantity will not be greater than the actual delivered quantity.

All Invoices will be initially parked before being posted. For each incoming invoice, Invoice Verification creates an MM (Material Management) invoice document and an FI (Financial Accounting) invoice document. Both these document numbers will be informed via the system message when the document has been successfully processed. When the invoice is posted, the GR/IR clearing account is debited and the vendor account is credited.

After the invoice has been posted, the document appears as an open item on the vendor account. It will also update the purchase order history.

7.1.6.4. Goods Receipt based Invoice Verification for Imports

Purchase Orders in foreign currencies are created for imports of Raw material, or semi-finished goods and capital assets. In case of Invoice Verification in respect of imports, the currency of the document is determined from the Purchase Order currency. The exchange rate differences are calculated from the exchange rate at the time of the goods receipt and the exchange rate at the time of the invoice receipt. The difference between them will be automatically calculated and posted to separate G/L Account so that the amounts posted in Local Currency to GR/IR Clearing Account are identical.

Custom duty paid on the imports purchases is added in the value of the raw material. Also other charges, related to the delivery, like transportation, clearing agent charges are added to the value of material.

7.1.6.5. Invoice for delivery costs

Freight charges are sometimes planned in the purchase order. More often, they are not known in detail when the purchase order is created and are entered only in Invoice Verification on the basis of information in the invoice. Therefore, delivery costs can be divided into:

- Planned delivery costs which are entered at item level in the Purchase Order
- Unplanned delivery costs which are entered at invoice receipt.

For planned delivery costs, postings will be made to the GR/IR clearing account at goods receipt. These postings are cleared when the invoice is posted.

Unplanned delivery cost will be posted to separate expense accounts when the stock is not available.

7.1.6.6. Invoice verification for blanket purchase order

One can use blanket purchase orders to procure consumable materials or services for which it is not worth creating a separate purchase order for each procurement transaction.

Blanket purchase orders are usually valid for a longer period of time. You can directly post the invoices for the materials and services procured for this blanket purchase order. No goods receipt is required in the system. However, Invoice Verification cannot be done for an amount higher than the limits specified in the Blanket Purchase Order.

7.1.6.7. Vendor credit memo processing

In normal business transactions, there are instances whereby vendors will send credit memos in order to reduce invoices. Such cases might arise due to incorrect invoiced amount or rejection of goods. A credit memo is then required to substantiate the adjustment.

Being an adjustment entry, credit memo shall affect Financials module only unless the adjustment is related to MM such as good return etc.

The processes are similar to invoice processing. Only the accounting treatment will be different, where in vendor has over charged or goods is rejected. In ERP for only value related adjustment credit notes, FI can pass direct adjust entry with reference to the particular invoice document. When the goods are rejected, the process of credit note related to quantity and value is routed through Materials Management and this process is similar to vendor bill booking process through logistics invoice verification. Only difference is that accounting entries which will be reverse of invoice booking.

7.1.7. Scheme of entries: Procure to pay cycle: Control environment

Scheme of entries	The following accounting entries will be passed in the Financial Accounts During the Goods Receipt against the Purchase Order • Dr. RM/PM Stock Account • Cr. GR/IR Account

- Cr. Freight Clearing Account

During the Goods Receipt against the Production Order

- Dr. FG inventory A/c
- Cr. Factory output A/c / Cost of production A/c

During the Goods issue against the Production Order

- Dr. Consumption A/c
- Cr. Stock A/c

During the Goods issue against the Cost Center

- Dr. Consumption A/c
- Cr. Stock A/c

During the Return Delivery to Vendor

- Dr. GR/IR Account
- Cr. RM/PM Stock Account

During the invoice verification

- Dr. GR/IR Account
- Cr. Vendor Account

7.1.8. Payment to vendors

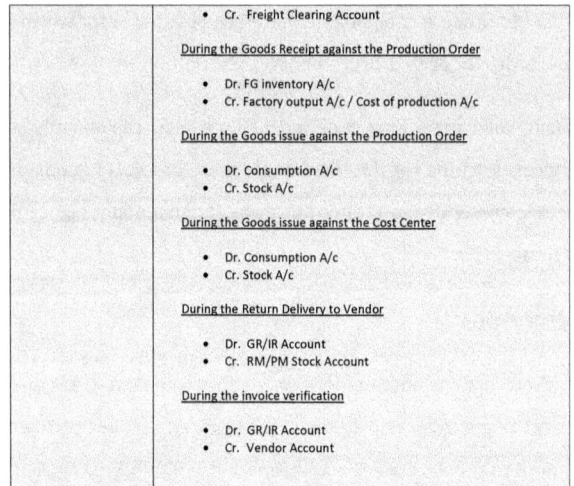
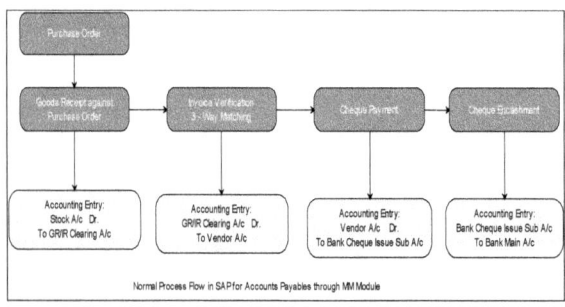

Normal Process Flow in SAP for Accounts Payables through MM Module

The entity will be making both manual payments and automatic payments from time to time to pay the outstanding Vendor Invoices which are due for payment. If the outgoing payment involves a payment in foreign currency, the defaulted local currency would have to be changed to the foreign currency being used for payment. The exchange rate maintained as on the Posting Date which is defaulted can be changed if the buying rate is different.

Separate bank sub-accounts for outgoing payment would be maintained for each Bank master and Account. The bank sub-account from which payment is being made as well as the payment amount and the bank charges, if any for the payment has to be determined in case of manual payment. The bank charges would then be automatically posted to the appropriate G/L Account.

The bank sub-account would be determined automatically from the Bank master.

Both normal open line items and special G/L line items can be selected while making the payment. Additional selections can be made based upon specific fields including Amounts, Document Number, Reference, etc. Additional field of "Net Due Date" will be available in the display and for sorting so that the open items can be sorted based on their due dates.

Any under-payment or over-payments within the tolerance limits shall be accounted for in the specified G/L Accounts. Similarly, in the case of payment in foreign currency any gain / loss between the exchange rate for the payment and the original / revaluated open item will be posted to separate Gain and Loss on realized foreign exchange G/L Accounts.

The entity will be usually making full payments against invoices. Occasionally partial payments will also be made to the vendors. In case of partial payments, the invoice and the partial payment amount shall both appear as open items.

Once the payment document is posted, the items selected for the payment shall be marked as cleared items and no longer appear in the open item list. The number and posting date of the payment document shall be updated in the documents which were cleared against it. Additionally, in case of payment with print, the check shall be printed immediately on posting the payment document and the check information created.

The Remittance Advise and Payment Voucher will be printed subsequently.

The following are the identified scenarios for billing from the System:

01	Payment to Vendors for goods / materials
02	Payment to Suppliers for expenses
03	Payment to Employees
04	Payment to Transport Vendors
05	Payment to Statutory Authorities

7.1.8.1. The scheme of entries to be passed

Scheme of entries	
	a) *At the time of Recording the GRN after entering the Quality Attributes* Dr. Stock a/c Cr. GR / IR Clearing a/c b) *At the time of Invoice Verification* Dr. GR / IR Clearing a/c Cr. Vendor / Procurement A/c c) *At the time of Recovering the Advances / Loans* Dr. Vendor / Procurement A/c Cr. Vendor a/c - Advances Cr. Vendor a/c - User Charges Cr. Customer a/c - E&I Items Cr. Vendor a/c - Loans d) *At the time of Recovering the Advances / Loans* Dr. Vendor / Procurement a/c Cr. Bank Check Issue Sub a/c e) *At the time of generating bank reconciliation statement, the following entry will clear the bank sub account. Entry will be as follows:* Dr. Bank check issue sub a/c Cr. Bank main a/c f) *At the time of levying the penalty on Transporter* Dr. Transporter a/c Cr. Penalties Received a/c g) *At the time of Recovery from Transporter and payment to Vendor* Dr. Transporter a/c Cr. Vendor a/c

7.1.8.2. Payments to Vendors:

Steps	
	1) Process of AP will start from invoice verification / advance payment against down payment request
	2) Payment of advance to the vendor against down payment request.
	3) Invoice verification will be done against the GRN and PO number by finance.
	4) Once the invoice is verified it will be available for payment in finance.
	5) If any advance is outstanding against the vendor, system will prompt while doing the verification and payments.
	6) Adjusting of advances paid against open invoices (Manual /automatic).
	7) Payments can be made by check or by adjusting credit notes issued to supplier. (Manual /automatic)
	8) Payments are proposed to be centralized at the corporate.
	9) Part payments can be made if required.
	10) Once the payment is processed the bank account will get credited and vendor account will get debited.

7.1.8.3. Vendor payment: SIPOC diagram

Supplier	Input	Process	Output	Customer
Accounts department – bill passing section	Approved vendor invoice	Intimate Finance & Accounts team member through email for payment processing		
	TDS deducted and net amount approved for payment	Check terms of payment		
	Posted entry in Accounts Payable ledger and General ledger control Account	Check payment due date as per credit term / credit period		
		Check availability		

		of funds		
		If all positive, release payment on due date through cheque/ NEFT/ RTGS		
		Update Accounts Payable ledger and General Ledger	Vendor invoice open item closed and cheque issued/ NEFT/RTGS made	Vendor – paid
7.1.8.4. Vendor payments:				

Scheme of entries		a) At the time of GR / Service entry sheet update inventory.
		Dr. Inventory (with restricted inventory type) a/c
		Cr. GR/IR Clearing a/c
		
		Inventory will be restricted for further processing before Quality Check but the inventory GL accounts will be updated
		
		b) At the time of QC check if the material is found as per the ordered quality there will be a system entry, which will reverse Restricted Inventory type to Un-Restricted Inventory type.
		
		c) At the time of Invoice verification the system will prompt the user if any advance payment exists. Invoice verification will pass the following entry:
		Dr. GR/IR a/c
		Cr. Vendor (AP) a/c
		
		d) At the time of making payment there are 2 options:
		  i. Automatic payment run –
		    This clears all the open items against the IV & will list down all the cleared items after which automatic check printing will be done by the system. Finally, the FI postings will also be done by the system automatically
		  ii. Manual payment run –
		    Here, the user will have to manually select the parties to whom payment has to be made. Also the check preparation & FI posting will be done manually.
		
		    The entry passed will be:
		    Dr. Vendor a/c
		    Cr. Bank Check Issue Sub a/c
		
		e) At the time of generating bank reconciliation statement, the following entry will clear the bank sub account. Entry		

	will be as follows: Dr. Bank check issue sub a/c Cr. Bank main a/c

7.2. Loans and advances to employees

The entity has various types of transaction excluding salary payments with its employees. For the purpose of recording these transactions separately, the employees shall be created as Vendor Accounts.

Since the majority of transactions with employees are in the form of advances related to their carrying out their official duties, the normal reconciliation account for the Employee Vendor Accounts shall be "Employee Advances". Special G/L Transactions would be used for the purpose of tracking different advances.

7.3. Payment to transporters

The transporter details along with the bank account are maintained in the ERP as vendors with account group as 'Transporters'

Advances (Down Payments) can be given to transporters and it can be entered into SAP FI - payables module as Down payments / Advances.

Also security deposits can be collected from the transporters which will be entered into SAP FI with special G/L Transactions.

This amount will be refunded, once the period is over or the contract terms are over.

Amount to be paid to the transporter as well as transporter penalties (for spillages, damaged cans) are captured in the procurement module and will be shown as a report.

Inward / Outward Transportation charges are recorded through transportation module. Invoice verification have to be done in FI module after receiving the bill from the transporter.

Payment can be made against the invoice after adjusting the pre-payment.

The schemes of entries are as under:

Scheme of entries	a) *At the time of Advances to Transporters* Dr. Vendor - Advance a/c Cr. Bank Check Issue Sub a/c Cr. TDS Payable – Sec 194C a/c (if applicable) b) *At the time of entering Service Entry Sheet in Transportation module*

Dr. Transportation Charges
Cr. GR / IR Transportation Charges

c) *At the time of Invoice Verification*
   Dr. GR / IR Transportation Charges a/c
   Cr. Inward Freight Payable (Vendor) a/c
   Cr. TDS Payable – Sec 194C a/c (If applicable)

d) *At the time of Clearing advance with Vendor Invoice*
   Dr. Vendor a/c
   Cr. Vendor (advance) a/c

e) At the time of outgoing payment
   Dr. Vendor (main) a/c

   Cr. Bank Check Issue Sub a/c

f) At the time of generating bank reconciliation statement, the following entry will clear the bank sub account. Entry will be as follows:
   Dr. Bank check issue sub a/c
   Cr. Bank main a/c

g) Certain contracts entered into with the Transport Vendors, provide for retaining certain amounts from the bills payable to the Transport Vendors as **Security Deposit**. Such amount is withheld and released at a later point of time as per the terms of the Contract.

7.4. Payment to Statutory authorities

Payment to Statutory authorities is classified into the following:

1) Statutory Payments – PF, ESI, Professional Tax
2) Statutory Payment - Excise
3) Statutory Payments – Sales Tax (VAT / CST), Service Tax/work contract tax/cess
4) Statutory Payments – TDS/TCS

7.4.1. Statutory Payments – PF, ESI, Professional Tax

A JV can be entered in Finance module directly for statutory liabilities arising from Wages and the payment can be made for the same.

On creation of Statutory Liabilities:	Salaries / Wages Payables	Dr.
	Company's Contribution to PF	Dr.

	Company's Contribution to ESI Dr. To PF Payable Cr. To ESI Payable Cr. To Prof. Tax Payable Cr.
On Payment	PF Payable Dr. ESI Payable Dr. Prof. Tax Payable Dr. To Bank Check Issue Sub A/c Cr.

Deductions will be based on the local state rules and regulations.

7.4.2. Statutory payment – excise

- Payment by cash/bank is determined after analyzing total liability and total input credit.

Transaction eligible for Input credit
Excise on Packing Materials used in Casein & Lactose CVD on material imported
Transaction eligible for Output liability
Excise duty on sale of Casein & Lactose CENVAT reversal due to return of rejection material

- Payment by cash/bank through PLA and pass Excise JV.
  Debit PLA on Hold

  Credit Bank

- Excise JV: This shall be done for updating PLA register as previous step updated books of Accounts only
  Debit PLA Excise Duty

  Credit PLA on Hold

- Utilization of Input tax credit (Excise Duty), PLA against Output tax liability (Excise Duty); this shall be done on monthly basis.
  Debit Output Excise Duty Payable A/c
  Credit Input CENVAT A/c
  Credit PLA Excise duty

7.4.3. Statutory Payments – Sales Tax (VAT / CST), Service Tax
Tax Accounts will be defined in the system.

Postings to these accounts will be automated while Tax Code is selected while entering the Invoice / Debit Note / Credit Note.

7.4.4. Statutory Payments – TDS
TDS includes the following:

- TDS on Salaries and
- TDS on others
- TCS on sale of scrap

7.4.4.1. TDS on Salaries:

TDS on Salaries should be calculated out of SAP and an accounting entry should be posted. Certificates & all other statutory obligations in this regards should be done manually, out of SAP system.

7.4.4.2. TDS on Others

TDS on Others will be categorized as per the following sections under Income Tax Act.

7.4.4.3. Official Withholding tax key:

The deduction of TDS takes place under various sections of the Income Tax Act. These sections are defined as Withholding Tax keys in the system and mapped to the sections of the Income Tax Act under which TDS is to be deducted. Based on the above the following official Withholding Tax codes shall be created in the system:

Section-193	TDS on Interest on Securities
Section-194	TDS on Dividends
Section-194A	TDS on Interest other than Interest on securities
Section-194C	TDS on payment to Contractors and sub-contractors
Section-194H	TDS on Commission and Brokerage
Section-194I	TDS on Rent
Section-194J	TDS for Professional and Technical services
Section-195	TDS on payments for Foreign services

Any new section which attracts TDS can be configured as Official Withholding Tax Key

7.4.4.4. Recipient type:

The vendors from whom TDS is deducted need to be classified as Company and Others. Recipient type enables categorization of the vendors. This categorization is required for creation of separate challans and printing the TDS certificates

7.4.4.5. Withholding Tax types:

Withholding tax types are defined at client level to represent the various types of withholding taxes for ex: 194C, 194D etc. Withholding tax types are also used to determine whether the deduction of TDS will take place at the time of invoice verification or at the time of payment. These withholding tax types can be used once these are linked to the Company codes. Withholding tax types are configured as per entity requirement. For each withholding tax type minimum and maximum amounts shall be maintained.

7.4.4.6. Withholding Tax Codes:

The various sections of the Income tax Act prescribe the rate at which the Tax is to be deducted. Withholding tax codes are used to define the rate at which tax is to be deducted and the base amount on which the tax is to be calculated. The rate will also include rate of surcharge and Education Cess if any is applicable. Surcharge and Education cess rates shall be maintained separately in tables and printed on the Vendor TDS certificate.

7.4.4.7. Vendor master:

WHT type /codes shall be maintained in the Vendor master as applicable to the vendor. Tax computation will be done by the system based on the WHT type/code maintained in the vendor master at the time of invoice entry and also advance payments. Withholding Tax Type and Withholding Tax code are maintained at the Invoice Entry level and PAN# will be made as a part of Vendor Master

Only tax type is maintained at the Payment level. This will ensure tax will not be deducted both at the time of invoice and payment. In the case of Advance payment, tax type will be maintained and user needs to select the tax code. If multiple TDS sections are applicable to a particular vendor, then all the tax types and tax codes for invoices applicable for those TDS sections must be maintained in the vendor master. However at the time of invoice entry the user has to select the correct tax type and code and exclude those which are not applicable.

System should facilitate manually enter the taxable amount: - At the time of posting user shall amend the base amount.

Once the tax is calculated, it should be posted to the respective account Tax Payable A/c automatically is a standard functionality. TDS Payable Account will be maintained section wise.

Exemptions rates will be maintained at the Vendor Master level for deducting tax to vendors.

a) *Accounting entry at the time of Invoice entry:*

    Dr Expense a/c
        Cr Vendor
        Cr TDS Payable

(Separate GL accounts shall be created section wise like TDS payable – Contractors, TDS payable - Professional fee. etc.)

b) *Accounting entry for advance payment to vendors:*

    Dr. Vendor Advance a/c
        Cr. Bank a/c
        Cr. TDS Payable

7.4.4.8. TDS remittance:

Remittance will be made through the system by standard T-code J1INCHLN. Challans will be updated for each section wise, corporate and Non corporate separately. Due dates will be defined in the configuration for each section wise.

    Dr TDS Payable
        Cr Bank a/c

7.4.4.9. Bank Challan updating:

Bank challan number will be updated in the system. This will link the remittance challans with the external bank scroll number. No accounting entry will be generated.

7.4.4.10. TDS certificate:

Certificates for the vendors can be generated by the system

Certificates cannot be generated more than once. However duplicate certificate can be issued.

7.4.4.11. Quarterly E-Returns:

E-Returns for TDS shall be generated from the system. The return shall be converted into required excel file and can be validated for filing.

Procedures	Remarks
TDS Calculation & posting at the time of down payment	
TDS calculation & posting at the time of invoice verification	
Clearing Down payment with invoice posting	TDS posted at the time of Down payment is adjusted with TDS payable posted during Invoice posting.

Prepare challan for remitting TDS amount	TDS remittance entry is posted in SAP & Bank account is updated.
Updating bank challan number	Update e-payment number or challan
Creating text file for Quarterly return	
Issuing TDS certificate	

7.4.4.12. TDS deducted by Customers:

A separate set of WT tax code & tax type shall have to be created for customers. Following accounting entry shall be generated at the time of receiving the payment:

Dr.   Bank a/c

Dr.   TDS deducted by customer a/c

Cr.   Customer a/c

The system will propose the TDS amount and the user can overwrite the amount, if required.

After receiving the TDS certificate from the customer, J1INCUST transaction shall be run and following accounting entry shall be generated:

Dr.   Advance Tax Paid A/c

Cr.   TDS deducted by customer a/c

7.4.4.13. TCS deducted From Customers:

TCS under section 206 of Income tax act should be deducted, from the customers on   sale of scrap (Manufactured Goods Only). In SAP separate TDS Codes will be maintained for TCS and the same should be maintained in customer master for TCS deduction.
TCS tax rate is generally kept at 1% for deduction of tax at source.

Dr.   Customer A/c

Cr.Sales Revenue A/c

Cr.TCS as per Sec 206 A/c

7.4.4.14. Work contract tax:

Work contract tax is collected from purchase of services such as civil construction work.The entity will be deducting WCT at the rate of 2% on bill value and the amount will be remitted to the Government treasury. The procedure will be like TDS collection from vendors.

In the system separate TDS Codes will be maintained for WCT and the same should be maintained in Vendor master for WCT deduction.

Dr. GR/IR Clearing A/c
    To Vendor A/c
    To TDS on WCT A/c

7.5. Accounts Payable – process steps summary

Main process	Description	Process as per ERP
1. General	Reconciliation GL & Vendor master will be Created	Creation of GL accounts (for all sundry creditors, inventories etc)
		Creation of Vendor master (in sync with MM)
		If Withholding tax is applicable to the vendor Attach withholding tax codes to the vendor master
		Invoice posting (if FI vendors)
		To See the party wise account
		Payment posting and printing the checks
2. Advance Payment	When a particular vendor asked for any down payment before sending the goods it will be collected in a special GL account by using Special GL indicator and after goods are received it will be cleared.	Creating the special GL accounts
		Down payment request
		Advance Payment posting
		Invoice posting
		Clearing advance payment by transferring to normal account
		Clearing the normal item
3. Banks:	Payment to Vendor by Cheque/NEFT/RTGS	Creation of cheque lots
		Payment through bank

Main process	Description	Process as per ERP
		Manual cheque updating or when automatic payment program is configured system takes the next available cheque number and prints it and matches to the invoice.
		Cheque register
		To enter cheque encashment date
		Un-issued cheque cancellations
		Issued cheque cancellations
4. Vendor account analysis	By using ERP we can see the line items / balances of vendors and also change the layout of display by adding any necessary fields like cost center, etc., into display	Vendor line item analysis
		Vendor balance analysis.
5. Account Clearing	After the outgoing payment has been posted all vendor invoices can be cleared either age wise or one by one.	Manual Clearing

7.6. Trade Payables: Financial Control over Financial Reporting

Activities	Risk Environment	Preventive control	Detective control	Monitoring control Y/N/NA
Trade Payables Recording Payables	*Core risks and controls* Goods received by, or services rendered to, the entity are: • Not recorded in	Trade payables and other expenses are recorded automatically by the ERP system upon matching the purchase order,	On a periodic basis, management compares actual results with budgeted and prior-year amounts; significant and/or unusual	

	trade payables or other expenses • Recorded at the incorrect amount.	completed vendor work order, or GRN On a periodic basis, finance personnel review open purchase orders and record other expenses and accrued payables for goods received or services rendered for which a completed service order or vendor invoice has not been received. The journal entry and supporting documentation are reviewed and approved by management before the journal entry is recorded.	differences are investigated and resolved.	
Recording Payables	The reconciliation between the trade payables sub-ledger and the general ledger may contain invalid reconciling items, which may result in a misstatement of trade payables.		On a periodic basis, finance personnel perform a reconciliation of the trade payables sub-ledger to the general ledger. Management reviews and approves the reconciliation and any reconciling items are reviewed and addressed on a timely basis	
Recording Payables	Amounts recorded to trade payables and other expenses do not relate to goods or services received.	Trade payables and other expenses are recorded automatically by the ERP system upon matching the purchase order, completed vendor work order, or GRN. Manual journal entries to trade payables, inventory, or other expenses, including period-end payable accruals and supporting documentation, are reviewed and approved by		

		management before the journal entry is recorded.		
Recording Payables	Inventory and trade payables are recorded prior to receipt and/or title transfer of the inventory.	Inventory and trade payables entries are recorded automatically by the ERP system upon matching the purchase order and GRN. Management reviews and approves the journal entry and supporting documentation for inventory and trade payables recorded for goods not yet received, but title has transferred to the entity. On a periodic basis, finance personnel review open purchase orders and record inventory and accrued payables for goods received or for goods not yet received where title has transferred to the entity. The journal entry and supporting documentation is reviewed and approved by management before the journal entry is recorded.	Physical inventory is counted periodically and discrepancies are investigated and corrected within the inventory records. Inventory records based on the physical inventory are reconciled to the general ledger with any differences being recorded as a book-to-physical inventory adjustment.	
Recording Payables	Inventory and trade payables are recorded at the incorrect amount.	Inventory and trade payables entries are recorded automatically by the ERP system upon matching the purchase order and GRN.		
Recording Payables	Acquisitions of fixed assets are not recorded.	A 3-way match process is performed for fixed assets purchases that utilise the purchase order, GRN, and	Periodic counts of fixed assets are performed. Selections are made from the floor and reconciled to the fixed assets	

		vendor invoice. Once the 3-way match process is performed and the key terms of the purchase are agreed to supporting documentation, a transaction is posted in the fixed assets sub-ledger and general ledger to record the addition.	register, and any differences are investigated and resolved
Recording Payables	Inventory is received and not recorded in the inventory system.	Inventory and trade payables entries are automatically recorded by the ERP system upon matching the purchase order and GRN. On a periodic basis, finance personnel review open purchase orders and record inventory and accrued payables for goods received or for goods not yet received where title has transferred to the entity. The journal entry and supporting documentation are reviewed and approved by management before the journal entry is recorded.	Physical inventory is counted periodically and discrepancies are investigated and corrected within the inventory records. Inventory records based on the physical inventory are reconciled to the general ledger with any differences being recorded as a book-to-physical inventory adjustment.
Recording Disbursements	Cash disbursements are: • Not recorded • Recorded in the general ledger when no cash disbursement has been made • Recorded at the incorrect amount.	Cash disbursements are generated through the ERP system. The ERP system automatically records the journal entry for cash disbursements to the trade payables and cash sub-ledgers. All manually generated cheques, including supporting documentation and the related journal entry, are reviewed	Bank statements are reconciled to the general ledger regularly, and differences are investigated and resolved on a timely basis.

		and approved by management before the journal entry is recorded.		
Recording Debit Memos	Inventory returned to suppliers is: • Not removed from the inventory and trade payables records • Recorded at the incorrect amount.	The ERP system automatically records entries to reduce inventory and trade payables per the sub-ledgers upon matching the goods return order, shipping document, and debit memo, completing a 3-way match	Inventory returned to suppliers is separately logged. On a periodic basis, the return log is utilised to verify inventory is removed and trade payables is reduced for inventory returned to suppliers.	
Recording Debit Memos	Inventory recorded as returned to vendors (removed from the inventory and trade payables records) is not actually returned.		Inventory returned to suppliers is separately logged. On a periodic basis, the return log is utilised to verify inventory is removed and trade payables is reduced for inventory returned to suppliers.	
Recording Payables	Inventory and trade payables are not recorded upon transfer of ownership prior to actual receipt.	Management reviews and approves the journal entry and supporting documentation for inventory and trade payables recorded for goods not yet received, but title has transferred to the entity.		
Recording Payables	*Other Possible Risks and Controls* The trade payables balance includes amounts due to unauthorised vendors.	New vendors to be added to the vendor master file are submitted to the accounting function by purchasing personnel. New vendors are independently verified by the accounting function for appropriateness and approved by management before the vendor is added to the vendor master file. Trade payables and other expenses are		

		recorded automatically by the ERP system upon matching the purchase order, completed service order, and the invoice received, completing a 3-way match. Completed matches are only posted for those vendors included in the vendor master file.		
Recording Payables	Foreign trade payables are translated using an incorrect foreign exchange rate.	On a periodic basis, a schedule of all foreign trade payables is prepared by accounting personnel reflecting the foreign trade payables, the applicable foreign exchange rate at period-end, and the foreign currency adjustment to be recorded. The schedule, supporting documentation, and journal entry are reviewed and approved by management before the foreign exchange adjustment is recorded. The ERP system automatically calculates the translation amounts for foreign trade payables and other expenses, which is independently verified by management.		
Recording Debit Memos	Volume or purchase discounts from suppliers are recorded in improper accounts (e.g., cost of sales, inventory) or at incorrect	On a periodic basis, purchasing provides the accounting function with analysis of inventory purchases related to all supplier volume/discount	Management subsequently compares volume discount cash received to the recorded volume rebate estimate for accuracy. Discrepancies are	

Activities	Risk Environment	Preventive control	Detective control	Monitoring control Y/N/NA
		agreements. Accounting personnel calculate the estimated volume discounts. Prior to recording the journal entry, management reviews the calculation, methodology, significant assumptions used, supporting documentation, and the journal entry for accuracy and proper classification.	investigated and corrected, as necessary.	
Recording Debit Memos	Debit memos are incorrectly recorded resulting in amounts removed from trade payables when a liability still exists.	The ERP system automatically records entries to reduce inventory and trade payables per the sub-ledgers upon matching the goods return order, shipping document, and debit memo, completing a 3-way match.		
7.7.Provision for expenses	**Financial Control over Financial Reporting**			
Activities	**Risk Environment**	**Preventive control**	**Detective control**	**Monitoring control Y/N/NA**
Recording Provision for expenses	*Core Risks and Controls* Provision for expenses exist but are not recorded.	On a periodic basis, finance personnel meet with members of management (e.g., sales, operational, human resources, legal counsel) to discuss developments and/or changes in the business that may affect recorded provision for expenses, or may affect the need to record an provision for expense. Finance personnel prepare a journal entry and supporting		

		documentation, which are reviewed by management before the journal entry is recorded.		
Recording Provision for expenses	The entity uses an inappropriate methodology or incorrect significant assumptions [*specify assumptions*] or underlying data [*specify underlying data*] to calculate and record provision for expenses.	On a periodic basis, provision for expenses is recorded based on an analysis performed by qualified personnel at the entity or by a qualified third-party specialist. The methodology, significant assumptions, and underlying data used, as well as the journal entry, are reviewed, evaluated, and approved by management with appropriate knowledge before the journal entry is recorded.	On a periodic basis, management retrospectively reviews prior-year provision for expenses; including the methodology used, significant assumptions utilised, and the underlying data relied upon in developing such estimates. Revisions are made to the methodology or significant assumptions and underlying data used in the current-period estimation process as necessary	
Recording Provision for expenses	Accruals and other expenses are initially recorded when no liability exists.	Finance personnel prepare the journal entry, supporting documentation, and account analysis to record provision for expenses. Management reviews and approves the journal entry, supporting documentation, and account analysis before the journal entry is recorded.	On a periodic basis, finance personnel reconcile provision for expenses to supporting detail. Management reviews the reconciliation and supporting documentation, and unusual activity or invalid reconciling items are investigated and resolved on a timely basis.	
Adjusting Provision for expenses	Provision for expenses is not reversed when a liability no longer exists (e.g., settled).	On a periodic basis, finance personnel meet with members of management (e.g., sales, operational, human resources, legal counsel) to discuss developments and/or changes in the business that may affect recorded provision for	On a periodic basis, management analyses recorded provision for expenses for ongoing relevance. Inconsistencies or discrepancies are investigated and resolved on a timely basis.	

		expenses, or may affect the need to record an provision for expense. Finance personnel prepare a journal entry and supporting documentation, which are reviewed by management before the journal entry is recorded.		
Adjusting Provision for expenses	Previously recorded provision for expenses is incorrectly reversed when a liability still exists.		On a periodic basis, finance personnel meet with members of management (e.g., sales, operational, human resources, legal counsel) to discuss developments and/or changes in the business that may affect recorded provision for expenses, or may affect the need to record an provision for expense. Finance personnel review the list of recorded provision for expenses, and prepare a journal entry and supporting documentation, which are reviewed by management before the journal entry is recorded	
Adjusting Provision for expenses	Adjustments to provision for expenses are recorded in the general ledger at incorrect amounts.	On a periodic basis, finance personnel meet with members of management (e.g., sales, operational, human resources, legal counsel) to discuss developments and/or changes in the business that may affect recorded provision for expenses, or may affect the need to record an provision for expense. Finance personnel prepare a	On a periodic basis, management analyses recorded provision for expenses for ongoing relevance. Inconsistencies or discrepancies are investigated and resolved on a timely basis	

		journal entry and supporting documentation, which are reviewed by management before the journal entry is recorded.		
Recording Disbursements	Cash disbursements are: • Not recorded • Recorded in the general ledger when no cash disbursement has been made • Recorded at the incorrect amount.	Cash disbursements are generated through the ERP system. The ERP system automatically records the journal entry for cash disbursements to the trade payables and cash sub-ledgers. All manually generated cheques, including supporting documentation and the related journal entry, are reviewed and approved by management before the journal entry is recorded.	Bank statements are reconciled to the general ledger regularly, and differences are investigated and resolved on a timely basis.	
Recording Provision for expenses	*Other Possible Risks and Controls* Accrued bonuses are incorrectly calculated and recorded due to misapplication of the bonus criteria.	Finance personnel calculate accrued bonuses based on the provisions of the bonus program. Management reviews and approves the bonus calculation and journal entry before the journal entry is recorded. Management bonuses are reviewed and approved by the CEO and/or a board of governance (e.g., Board of Directors, Remuneration Committee of the Board of Directors) before the management bonuses are recorded.	On a periodic basis, management compares actual results with budgeted and prior-year amounts; significant and/or unusual differences are investigated and resolved.	

Recording Provision for expenses	Accrued payroll, taxes, and other employee benefit costs are recorded at incorrect amounts.	Finance personnel prepare the journal entry, supporting documentation, and account analysis to record provision for expenses. Management reviews and approves the journal entry, supporting documentation, and account analysis before the journal entry is recorded.	Management periodically reviews actual inventory, cost of sales, gross profit, and other expense amounts in comparison to budget, historical amounts, or current-year trends, and investigates and resolves any significant variances. This review is performed at a sufficient level of detail and disaggregation (e.g., by type of product line, type of services).	
Recording Provision for expenses	Accrued compensated absences are incorrectly calculated and recorded (i.e., not consistent with the stated human resource policy).	On a periodic basis, finance personnel calculate accrued compensated absences and prepare the supporting documentation and related journal entry. Management, including human resource management, reviews the calculation and journal entry for consistency with the stated policy and approves the journal entry before it is recorded.	On a periodic basis, management compares actual results with budgeted and prior-year amounts; significant and/or unusual differences are investigated and resolved.	
7.8. Provision for Income tax	**Financial Control over Financial Reporting**			
Activities	**Risk environment**	**Preventive control**	**Detective control**	**Monitoring control Y/N/NA**
Provision for Income tax / advance income tax *Calculate and Record Provision for income taxes*	*Core risks and controls* Estimated Advance income tax payments made are: • Not recorded • Recorded at incorrect amounts.		Tax department of the entity prepares estimated tax payment calculations on a quarterly basis and maintains an income tax payment schedule. Payments as	

or Advance Taxes.			per the payment schedule are compared to the actual payment recorded in the general ledger and investigated for proper recording. Bank statements are reconciled periodically, and reconciling items are investigated for proper recording in the general ledger.	
Calculate and Record Provision for income taxes or Advance Taxes	Income tax /deduction/exemption is incorrectly calculated due to: • Exclusion of valid tax deductions or exemptions or under-recorded tax deductions or exemptions • Inclusion of invalid tax deductions or exemptions or over-recorded deductions or exemptions.	The calculation is prepared by staff with sufficient training and experience. Calculations and supporting analyses are independently reviewed by management	Deductions taken on the prior-year tax return are reconciled to the current-year income tax calculation and significant differences are investigated	
Calculate and Record Provision for income taxes or Advance Taxes	Calculation of income tax expense / deductions / exemptions does not include all jurisdictions.	Tax department of the Company reviews the list of countries where the company has business operations with the marketing department and also with other relevant department in order to identify foreign jurisdictions where obligation to pay income tax may arise.	Listing of all taxable subsidiaries and other legal entities affecting income tax is compared to the income tax calculation for completeness. The tax department and finance department meet on a regular basis to discuss changes in the business. Changes that may have an effect on deferred income taxes and income tax expense are analysed and the conclusions are documented.	
Calculate and Record	Tax adjustments, penalties, or interest	Journal entries to record tax and	On a periodic basis, tax department of the	

Provision for income taxes or Advance Taxes	resulting from income tax assessment orders/appellate orders are: • Not recorded • Inaccurately recorded.	related penalties and interest as a result of income tax assessment orders/appellate orders are prepared by tax personnel on a timely basis. Entries are reviewed and approved by management prior to the journal entry being recorded.	entity provides status updates to finance management on income tax assessments/appellate orders and inquiries with respect to Income tax assessment years open, for proper accounting treatment.	
Calculate and Record Provision for income taxes or Advance Taxes	Provision for income tax to Income tax return adjustments is not recorded	Tax department of the entity compares amounts in the tax return to the amounts included in the previous financial year income tax provision and records adjustments to the deferred tax accounts, income taxes.		
Calculate and Record Provision for income taxes or Advance Taxes	Recent amendments to the income tax (domestic or international) are not reflected in the determination of income tax and deferred taxes.	Income taxes are processed using a software program which draws financial and tax data from the ERP system. Program's algorithms, calculations, etc., are tested for accuracy. New releases or updates to the software are tested prior to implementation and are implemented on a timely basis. The tax department of the entity agrees the tax rate utilised in determining income tax to the enacted rate as per the Income Tax Act, 1961 and considers whether there are substantively enacted tax rates that will affect the balance of deferred		

		taxes		
Calculate and Record Provision for income taxes or Advance Taxes	*Other Possible Risks and Controls* Sales, purchases, and other transactions with Associated enterprises are not at arm's length, resulting in concern regarding transfer pricing matters.	Management establishes policies for transactions to associated enterprises. This policy covers all terms and conditions, including the price to be charged. The policy is reviewed and monitored by the tax department of the entity in order to identify potential transfer pricing considerations. Transactions between associated enterprises entities strictly adhere to this policy.		

7.9. Procurement to Trade Payable: Detailed Risks and system controls

Risks	System controls
1. New vendors are not investigated and approved before being added to the vendor master list.	• Accounts Payable. The system can be set up to place a vendor on "approval hold" when created or modified. This will prevent payment of the vendor until approved. • Accounts Payable. Access to the vendor approval function and to other vendor maintenance functions should be restricted. Only authorized personnel should be permitted to add or change vendors. • Expense Cycle Management (add-on to AP) can automatically route invoices for a new vendor to an authorized user who then does the necessary verification, adds the vendor to the master list, and routes the invoice back to the appropriate person for entry. • Other. Some entities check business directories to verify that the vendor is an existing business. Some compare vendor remit addresses to an employee address file.
2. Vendors no longer used are not inactivated or purged from the vendor master list.	• Accounts Payable. Use the Vendor Purge function to select vendors without activity after a specified date and either purge or inactivate the vendors so that they cannot be paid. • Accounts Payable. Use the Consolidate Vendor function to consolidate vendor activity and eliminate old vendors when appropriate.

3. Vendors are not properly evaluated when purchases are made. Competitive prices are not obtained.	• Purchasing. Integrate AP with the ERP system. PO facilitates establishment and maintenance of up-to-date catalogs reflecting company policy (preferred vendors and pricing agreements). Define what items can be purchased from which vendors. Use the Vendor Performance report to evaluate vendors on pricing, quality, and timeliness of delivery. • Purchasing Cycle Management. Use Purchasing Cycle Management (add-on to PO) to automatically route requisitions for approval or sourcing based on business rules. An easy-to-use web interface (Procurement Portal) allows users outside the purchasing department to submit requisitions for approval. Administrator determines who can order what items and from which vendors.
4.Duplicate vendor numbers and names appear in the vendor master file	• Accounts Payable. The AP system does not permit duplicate vendor numbers (ID's). • Accounts Payable. Prior to setting up a new vendor, the user can search on vendor Sort Name to determine if a vendor already exists. • Accounts Payable. The vendor Full Name and vendor Tax ID can be made soft keys and used for searching. The key can be set up so that duplicates are not allowed. • Accounts Payable. Use the Consolidate Vendor function to consolidate vendor activity when a duplicate vendor is discovered. • Refer discussion under Risk 1 for additional controls pertaining to maintenance of the vendor master file.
5. Purchases are made that exceed department's budget.	• Corporate Budgeting. Use Corporate Budgeting (add-on module) to have the system automatically warn the user when a purchase will cause the budget to be exceeded for a specific account/department
6. Purchases are made without proper approval. Purchase orders are not prepared or authorized.	• Purchasing. Where applicable, set up vendors to require entry of a valid purchase order number before vouchers are entered. If the company has an external Purchasing system, purchase order and receipt information can be loaded into the ERP system to enable two- and three-way matching. • Purchasing Cycle Management. Use Purchasing Cycle Management to automatically route requisitions for approval based on business rules. A purchase order is created automatically when a requisition is approved and can be automatically printed or sent to the vendor via email, fax, or XML. An easy-to-use web interface (Procurement Portal) allows users outside the purchasing department to submit requisitions for approval.
7. Receipt of goods is not documented.	• Purchasing. PO includes a function for recording receipts. Set up the AP system to require matching of invoices and purchase orders with receipts prior to payment. If the company has an external Purchasing system, receipt information can be loaded into ERP to enable matching. • Purchasing Cycle Management. Use PCM to automatically alert users when goods have been received. Matching errors can be automatically routed to the appropriate users for quicker resolution.
8. A/P duties are not effectively segregated to	• Accounts Payable. Each AP user is assigned a security level that determines which functions are available from system menus. • Review your user file and menu security setup to ensure that

minimize the risk of fraud.	segregation of duties is being enforced. For example, this setup can prevent users who add vendors or maintain vendor information from entering vouchers.
	• • Expense Cycle Management and Procurement Cycle Management. Users are restricted to specific functions based on the workgroups to which they are assigned. Menus are automatically generated.
9. Disbursements are made without proper approval.	• Accounts Payable. The system can be set up so that all vouchers are created with a "hold payment" status. The vouchers can then be reviewed by a manager and released for payment using the Voucher Hold/Release function. Approval level codes may also be used to prevent changes to a voucher or payment until reviewed by one or more managers. Access to the Voucher Hold/Release function should be restricted
	• Expense Cycle Management. Use Expense Cycle Management to automatically route vouchers for review/approval based on business rules (for example, based on monetary amounts or vendor).
	• The system can be set up to require multiple approvals for high value invoices. Based on the rules, a voucher's payment status and GL posting status can be set to "hold" initially, and then changed to "release" when the necessary approvals have been given. If there is a dispute with a vendor, all invoices for that vendor can be set up for electronic routing for review/approval prior to payment.
	• Expense Cycle Management. ECM enforces segregation of duties between those who enter invoices and those who have the authority to approve an invoice for payment. All approval routing steps are logged by ECM (who, what, when) for full transaction transparency.
	• ECM Executive. ECM Executive incorporates ECM functionality and also allows managers to review and approve invoices via email or a website.
10. Prices charged on invoice do not match the purchase order or pricing program.	• Purchasing. If the company does not currently have a Purchasing system, Set up the AP system to require matching of invoices and receipts with purchase orders prior to payment.
	• If the company has an external Purchasing system, purchase order information can be loaded into the system.
	• Purchasing Cycle Management. Matching errors can be automatically routed to the appropriate users for quicker resolution
11. Amounts recorded/paid do not match the approved invoices.	• Accounts Payable. The AP system does permit payment for an individual voucher to exceed the voucher due amount.
	• Accounts Payable. During voucher entry, the system requires the voucher due amount to tie out with the accounting distribution. If the totals do not match, the voucher cannot be completed and cannot be paid.
	• Accounts Payable. Use batch control totals to further ensure accuracy in entry of voucher amounts.
	• Expense Cycle Management. Invoices may be scanned and indexed in the mailroom, then routed to users for voucher entry. When indexed, the voucher data may be pre-populated from the invoice. Users can view invoice images when entering vouchers, rather than working with paper invoices which are easily lost or damaged.

	• Expense Cycle Management. ECM allows managers to audit the voucher entry and approval process through sampling to determine accuracy of data entry and conformity to company procedures. The system can send every nth invoice to an audit queue or all invoices over a specific monetary amount.
12. Discounts allowed are not taken.	• Accounts Payable. Payment terms may be established for each vendor so that discount and payment dates are automatically calculated. • Accounts Payable. The AP system provides many options for taking discounts. For example, payment can be scheduled based on the discount date. The system can also be set up to always take discounts even when payment is made after the discount date. • Expense Cycle Management. ECM can alert users when an invoice has not been reviewed / approved in a timely fashion. This process may be tailored to alert managers of high value invoices where discounts are about to be lost.
13. Duplicate invoices are recorded.	• Accounts Payable. The AP system can be set up to disallow a duplicate invoice number from being processed. • Accounts Payable. The system displays information about the original voucher when a duplicate invoice number is entered. The system may be set up to allow override of a duplicate condition within certain restrictions. • Expense Cycle Management. ECM provides for scanning of incoming invoices. The user can display the image associated with the original voucher to determine if the new invoice is actually a duplicate. • Accounts Payable. The system can search several years of A/P history for duplicates. Duplicate invoices are checked across paying companies within a vendor number and across multiple remittance addresses. • Accounts Payable. The system can be set up to detect potential duplicates – invoices that have the same dates and/or amounts.
14. The system allows an invoice to be paid more than once.	• Accounts Payable. The AP system does not permit this. Once a voucher has been paid in full by the system, the voucher status changes to closed so that it cannot be selected for payment in a subsequent check run.
15. Outstanding credit memos are not applied to current or future invoices.	• Accounts Payable. Credits entered into the AP system are automatically deducted from future payments.
16. Invoices are not coded to the appropriate account.	• Accounts Payable. Default AP control account codes are established for each vendor and a default standard distribution can also be set up for the expense lines. Posting accounts are validated when entered online. • Accounts Payable. The Open Voucher reports may be used to produce a list of transactions charged to a specific AP control account to help identify incorrectly coded transactions.
17. Payment is recorded but not made.	• Accounts Payable. The same process (Pay Vouchers/Write Checks) is used to update the payment history and generate a check image file for printing or a file for electronic funds transfer.

	• Accounts Payable. Restrict access to the check processing functions to authorized persons using menu security. • Accounts Payable. Use Statement Reconciliation to automate reconciliations using electronic feed from the bank.
18. Payment is not recorded in the proper period.	• Accounts Payable. The AP system automatically records all payments in the appropriate period when the cash disbursements journal is posted. The period is determined based on the default posting date, which may or may not be overridden by the user, at the time payment is made.
19. Purchases made are not recorded / paid or not recorded / paid timely.	• Expense Cycle Management. Use ECM to scan invoices in mailroom and route for voucher entry and approval. Invoices can also be loaded from an external system using (XML format is supported). Avoid misplacing paper invoices. • Accounts Payable. Establish payment terms in the system so that vendors are paid on a timely basis, reflecting company policy. The voucher entry function automatically defaults the scheduled payment date based on the payment terms. Set up recurring vouchers to ensure that regular bills are paid on time. • Expense Cycle Management. ECM can alert users when an invoice has not been reviewed / approved in a timely fashion. Managers can also track workloads in the AP department and reassign work to ensure timely processing. • Accounts Payable. When a voucher is created, GL accounting distributions are also created, and this information is subsequently posted to the GL. The accounting period is determined based on the default posting date, which may or may not be overridden by the user, at the time the transaction is entered (system parameter). This ensures that the expense is recorded to the appropriate period regardless of the date of payment.
20. Payment is made but not recorded.	• Accounts Payable. The AP system does not allow payments to be issued without updating the AP database. The same process (Pay Vouchers/Write Checks) is used to update the payment history and generate a check image file for printing or a file for electronic funds transfer. • Accounts Payable. Create a "positive pay" file to send to the bank. This contains the list of check numbers, payees, and amounts. The bank pays only checks listed in this file. Some clients have the bank print the checks for them. • Accounts Payable. Use Statement Reconciliation to automate reconciliations using electronic feed from the bank.
21. The Accounts Payable detail is not properly summarized / posted to the General Ledger.	• Accounts Payable. Accounting distributions resulting from voucher entry, voucher changes, reversals, and so on, are generated automatically. These are posted to the proper period when journals are posted to the General Ledger. Several options are available for automatic summarization of postings to GL. • Accounts Payable. Several reports are available to assist with reconciling AP with the General Ledger, including the Aged As Of Requirements Report. To check for AP journals that have not been posted, run the AP Register Query Report and select "Unposted" items.

22. Disbursements are not properly summarized/posted to the General Ledger.	• Accounts Payable. Accounting transactions resulting from payments are generated automatically. These are posted to the proper period when the cash journal is posted. Several options are available for automatic summarization of postings to GL. • Accounts Payable. Several reports are available to assist with reconciling AP with the General Ledger, including the Aged As Of Requirements Report. To check for AP journals that have not been posted, run the AP Register Query Report and select "Unposted" items.
23. There is no audit trail of payables or purchasing related activities.	• Accounts Payable and Purchasing. The systems can be set up to automatically maintain audit trails for changes to transaction and master files. Information tracked includes the User ID, date and time that a specific transaction was entered or modified. The audit trail may also track additions or changes to vendor information. • Accounts Payable and Purchasing. Purge functions allow historic transaction data to be archived for possible future retrieval. • Expense Cycle Management and Procurement Cycle Management. The Workflow Activity Log tracks all the steps (who, what, when) in the process, from requisition to PO to voucher to check, including approvals. For additional protection, store scanned images of original documents, such as invoices and purchase orders, and associate with transactions. Notes may be used to track conversations with vendors. The Activity Log, images, and notes are available from many system inquiries.

7.10. Illustrative Risk map: Purchases

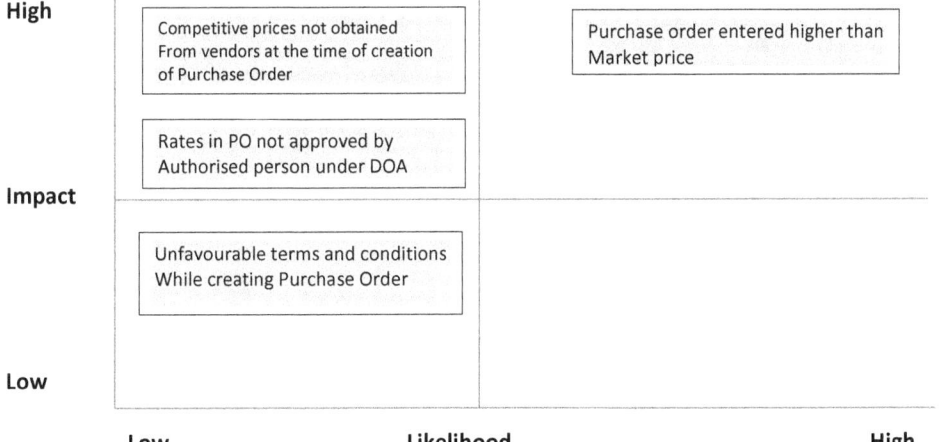

7.11. Illustrative Risk map: Accounts Payable

High

Vendor invoices approved at prices higher than PO		Fictitious or duplicate payment for goods and services
Vendor invoice shows quantities not as per GRN		Vendor invoices not approved as per Delegation of Authority

Impact

Unauthorised cash purchases

Low

    Low   **Likelihood**   **High**

7.12. Self-Assessment Check list

Accounts Payable Controls	Yes	No	N/A	Comments
1. Designation of responsibility				
2. Independence of A/P personnel from purchasing, cashier, receiving functions				
3. Periodic comparison of detail and control				
4. Control over purchase returns				
5. Clerical accuracy of vendors' invoices				
6. Matching of purchase order, receiving report and vendor invoice				
7. Reconciliation of vendor statements with A/P detail				
8. Control over debit memos				
9. Control over advance payments				
10. Review of unmatched receiving reports				
11. Mutilation of supporting documents at payment				
12. Review of debit balances				
13. Investigation of discounts not taken				

Accrued Liabilities and Other Expenses Controls	Yes	No	N/A	Comments
1. Proper authorization for expenditure and incurrence				
2. Control over partial deliveries				
3. Postage meter				
4. Purchasing department				
5. Bids from vendors				
6. Verification of invoices				
7. Imprest cash account				
8. Detailed records				
9. Responsibility charged				
10. Independence from G/L and cashier functions				
11. Periodic comparison with budget				

7.13. Risk Control Matrix summary: Accounts Payable (specimen format)

Item	1	2	3	4	5
Mega process	Purchase & expenses	Purchase & expenses	Purchase & expenses	Purchase & expenses	Purchase & expenses
Process	Accounts payable	Accounts payable	Accounts payable	Accounts payable	Accounts payable
Activity	Tracking of vendor payments	Vendor payments	Payment bookings	Vendor advances	Vendor balance reconciliation
Risk description	Inaccurate/ delayed payment to vendors	Inaccurate/ unapproved vendor payments	Inappropriate booking of payments to vendors	Unauthorized/ inappropriate vendor advances given	Incorrect reporting of vendor balances
Control objective	To ensure that vendors are paid timely and accurately	To ensure that vendor payments are duly authorized	To ensure that vendor payments are correctly recorded	To ensure that vendor advances are given after due approval and adjusted appropriately	Incorrect reporting of vendor balances
Control environment – to be certified by the process owner	The list of vendor invoices due during the month is extracted from GP by Executive Accounts, reviewed by Senior Executive Accounts and approved by Manager Finance.	1. The cheque /NEFT/RTGS advice is prepared by Account Executive and signed by authorized signatories as per bank records. 2. The cheques are handed over by Accounts Team to Admin /IT Team who dispatches the same to the vendor or hand it over directly to vendor's representative. 3. NEFT and RTGS advice is submitted to bank for processing which is based on approved advice from country head/authorized signatory. 4. In case of payment by online mode,	The payment entry is recorded by Executive Accounts and reviewed by Senior Executive Accounts to ensure adjustment in correct vendor ledger.	1. The Procurement executive sends email to Accounts duly approved by Procurement head for processing of vendor advances as per purchase order. 2. The Accounts Executive processes vendor advance request based on specific approval from Country head and considering PO terms. 3. The request for release of balance payment is submitted by Procurement Manager to Manager Finance on mail. 4. The balance payment is released on confirmation of receipt of material/services	The Company receives vendor balance confirmation letter yearly from the major vendors. The Executive accounts confirms the balance through the email along with the reconciliation, if there is any.

				by Concerned
		approval of country head is obtained and the payment is also made by Country head.		by Concerned dep't. to Manager Finance.	
Risk category					
Fraud risk – yes / no	No	Yes	No	No	No
Risk category – high / medium / low	Low	Low	Low	Low	Low
Internal financial control over financial reporting – yes / no	No	Yes	Yes	Yes	Yes
IFC/IFCR Component	Prevention and detection of frauds and errors	Prevention and detection of frauds and errors	Accuracy and completeness of the accounting records	Accuracy and completeness of the accounting records	Accuracy and completeness of the accounting records
Prevention / detection of frauds – yes / no	Yes	Yes	No	No	No
Key Control – yes / no	No	Yes	Yes	No	Yes
Control category					
Completeness					xx
Existence	xx	xx	xx	xx	xx
Accuracy	xx	xx	xx	xx	xx
Valuation					
Rights / obligation					
Presentation					
Manual / Automatic	Manual	Manual	Manual	Manual	Manual
Preventive / detective	Preventive	Preventive	Preventive	Preventive	Detective
Frequency of measurement	Fortnightly	Event based	Event based	Event based	Yearly
Document if any	Vendor invoice list	Payment voucher	Payment voucher	Email	Vendor Invoice & Reconciliation
Prepared by (maker)	Senior Executive - Accounts	Account Executive	Account Executive	Procurement Executive	Accounts Executive
Checked by (checker)	Manager - Finance	Director/ Country head	Senior Executive - Accounts	Manager - Finance	Senior Executive Accounts
System solution – ERP – Yes/no	No	No	Yes	No	**Yes**
Whether covered under SOP – Yes / no	Yes	Yes	Yes	Yes	**Yes**
Process design gap – Yes / no	No	No	No	No	**Yes**

Chapter 8: Non-current Assets

8.1. Non-current Assets: Control environment

8.1.1. Asset accounting: An overview

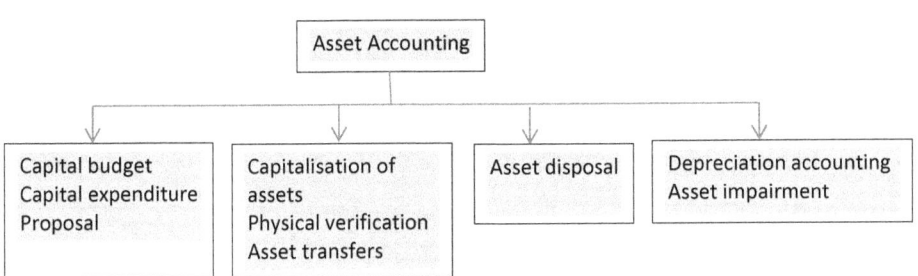

The Asset Accounting module provides most of the processes required for the management of fixed assets. The module is integrated with all other modules and data for all asset-related transactions is updated into GL online. Accounting for assets is done on the concept of sub ledger - all postings made to any asset are updated in the GL account and there is never any difference between the values as shown by the asset reports and the GL balances.

The depreciation calculation process is also automatic, and depreciation is posted to the books of accounts at pre-defined periodical intervals (generally monthly). Depreciation can be calculated according to different principles for the same asset, based on business requirements. For example, the depreciation rates for accounting purposes and for tax purposes can be different.

The asset master contains all the important information required, and the depreciation calculation, postings to cost centers etc. depends upon the assignments made in the master data.

Asset Accounting (FI-AA) transfers data directly to and from other SAP components. It is possible to post from the Materials Management (MM) component directly to FI-AA. When an asset is purchased or produced in-house, you can directly post the invoice receipt or goods receipt, or the withdrawal from the warehouse, to assets in the Asset Accounting component. At the same time, you can pass on depreciation directly to the Financial Accounting (FI) and Controlling (CO) components.

The entity requires the asset to be classified with four levels G/L Accounts/Asset class/Asset and Evaluation groups.

8.1.2. Creation of asset master

Asset master will have the following information:	<ul><li>Assets Class</li><li>Company Code</li><li>Description of assets</li><li>Serial number</li><li>Quantity & Unit of Measure</li><li>Location</li><li>Cost Center</li><li>Control Account link in General Ledger</li><li>Vendor Name</li></ul>

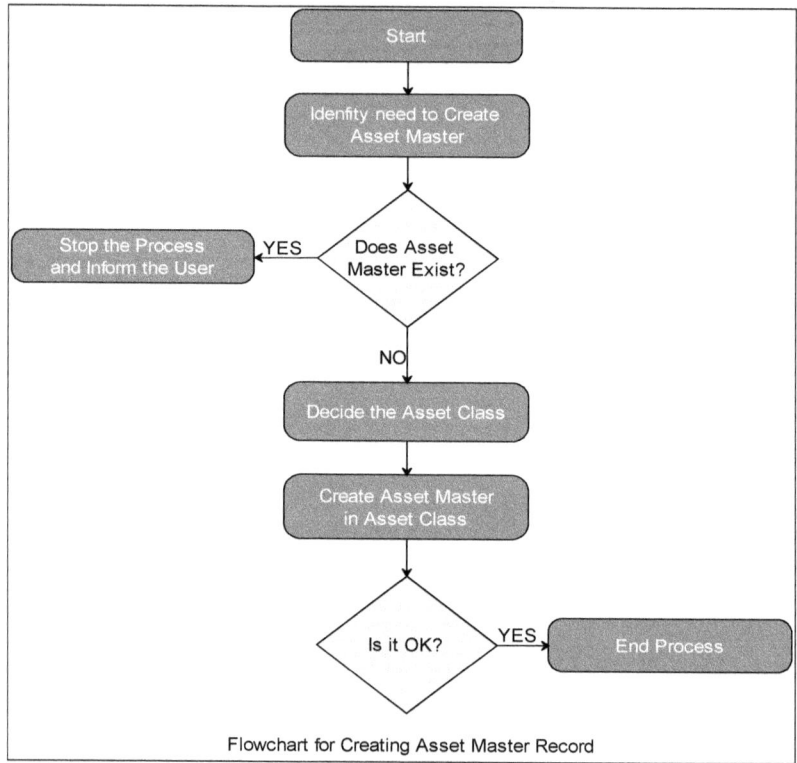

Flowchart for Creating Asset Master Record

8.1.3. Asset Acquisition

The primary business process in asset accounting is the purchase of assets and/or the capitalization of in-house produced goods or services. The Asset Accounting component supports various methods of handling this business process.

8.1.4. Direct Capitalization

Direct capitalization refers to asset acquisitions that do not have an asset under construction phase. Instead, they are capitalized and begin depreciation immediately.

An external asset acquisition is a business transaction resulting from the acquisition of an asset from a business partner (in contrast to an acquisition from in-house production). You can post the acquisition of a purchased asset in several different ways, using different application components:

- In Materials Management (MM) at goods receipt or invoice receipt
- In Asset Accounting (FI-AA) in integration with Accounts Payable (FI-AP), but without reference to a purchase order
- In Asset Accounting, without reference to a purchase order, without integration with Accounts Payable (posting to a clearing account – with or without clearing).

8.1.5. Acquisition through Material Management (MM)

Asset Accounting is integrated with all other relevant ERP modules. There are no interface requirements as such for asset accounting. Asset procurement is linked with Materials Management module, Asset which can be used immediately on receipt like Furniture, computers, office equipments, vehicles etc. In all these cases capitalization will be done based on GRN date. Acquisition of asset by purchase department, like other standard purchases in SAP is integrated with MM. The following activities are involved:

8.1.5.1. SIPOC diagram: Asset capitalisation

Supplier	Input	Process	Output	Customer
User department	Requirement via email based on approved capital budget and capital expenditure proposal	a)Creation of a purchase requisition	Approved PR	Purchase Department
Accounts department	Details of material required to be capitalised	b)Creation of an asset master record	Asset master record	User Department

Purchase Department	Details of material based on PR	c)Creation of the purchase order	Approved PO	Authorised Vendor
Authorised vendor	Material receipt at gate and stores	d)Goods receipt on quality assurance and acceptance of materials	Approved GRN	Accounts Department
Vendor	PR, PO, GRN and Vendor invoice	e)Invoice receipt and process for payment based on three way match	Approved vendor invoice for payment	Vendor
Accounts Department	Asset master, PR,PO, GRN and vendor invoice and installation certificate	f)Capitalisation of materials based on asset master created	Approved capitalisation voucher	User department

8.1.5.2. Scheme of entries

Scheme of entries	
	a) **At the time of Advance Payment against Capital Purchase Order** Dr. Capital Vendors - Advance A/c Cr. Bank – Check Issue Sub A/c b) **At the time of GR.** Excise Entries if applicable will be updated c) **At the time of Invoice verification the system will prompt the user to notify if any advance payment exists.** Dr. Fixed Assets a/c Cr. Capital Vendor (AP) a/c d) **At the time of clearing the advance against the Invoice** Dr. Capital Vendor (AP) a/c Cr. Capital Vendors - Advance A/c e) **At the time of making payment** Dr. Capital Vendor (AP) a/c Cr. Bank – Check Issue Sub A/c f) **At the time of generation of the bank reconciliation statement, the following entry will clear the bank sub account. Entry will be as follows:** Dr. Bank – Check Issue Sub A/c

	Cr. Bank – Main A/c

8.1.6. Acquisition in Asset Accounting with Vendor

Asset can be acquired in Finance – Asset accounting module in integration with FI – AP module.

Process flow for acquisition of assets with vendor comprise:	a) *Creation of an asset master record* b) *FI will post the capital items invoice.* c) *At this stage the system will prompt in case an advance is already paid to the vendor.* d) *In the next step payment is processed for the fixed assets purchased while adjusting the advance already received.* e) *Respective bank a/c is updated & vendor liability cleared.*

Scheme of entries	a) *At the time of Advance Payment against Capital Purchase Order*
	
	      Dr. Capital Vendors - Advance A/c
	      Cr. Bank – Check Issue Sub A/c
	
	 b) *At the time of Posting Invoice*
	
	      Dr. Fixed Assets a/c
	      Cr. Capital Vendor (AP) a/c
	
	 c) *At the time of clearing the advance against the Invoice*
	
	      Dr. Capital Vendor (AP) a/c
	      Cr. Capital Vendors - Advance A/c
	
	 d) *At the time of making payment*
	
	      Dr. Capital Vendor (AP) a/c
	      Cr. Bank – Check Issue Sub A/c
	
	 e) *At the time of generation of the bank reconciliation statement, the following entry will clear the bank sub account. Entry will be as follows:*
	
	      Dr. Bank – Check Issue Sub A/c
	      Cr. Bank – Main A/c

8.1.7. Acquisition in Asset Accounting without Vendor

Asset can be acquired in Finance – Asset accounting module without integration with Finance – Accounts Payable module.

The Process flow for acquisition of assets without vendor is given below:	a) Creation of an asset master record
	b) FI will post the capital items invoice while debiting the asset account and crediting the asset acquisition clearing account.
	c) In the next step payment is processed for the fixed assets purchased
	d) Respective bank a/c is updated & Asset Acquisition clearing account will be cleared.

Scheme of entries	a) At the time of Posting Invoice
	Dr. Fixed Assets a/c
	Cr. Asset Clearing a/c
	b) At the time of making payment
	Dr. Asset Clearing a/c
	Cr. Cash / Bank A/c

8.1.8. Asset under Construction / Capital WIP

Assets under construction (AUC) are a special form of tangible asset. They are usually displayed as a separate balance sheet item and, therefore, require separate account determination and asset classes. During the phase in which an asset is under construction, all actual postings are assigned to the AUC. Once the asset is completed, a transfer is made to a master record that has to be created in the completed fixed assets.

8.1.9. Assets under Construction without Internal Order

Assets under construction are acquisitions to fixed assets that are not permitted to be capitalized and depreciated immediately.

During the construction phase, all the assets are initially booked to the assets under construction account (capital works in progress Account).After the completion of the construction and when the assets are put to use the assets under construction need to be transferred to the assets account. This transfer of assets from assets under construction to the assets is known as settlement in SAP. Before making the settlement, it is to be clearly known, as to in which proportion the line items

under assets under construction are to be settled to the assets. Basing on this, the distribution rules are defined and then assets can be settled.

8.1.10. Assets under Construction with Internal Order

Statistical Internal Orders will be used to control the budgets and when certain business transactions are entered that create costs on the corresponding Internal Order, the system checks whether the available budget or available released budget is sufficient. It uses the tolerance limits specified in Customizing for this check. Tolerance limits can be defined as the usage level from the current budget or the release.

Step 1:	Create an Internal Order
Step 2:	Maintain Budget for the Internal Order
Step 3	Create the AUC – Asset Master
Step 4:	Assign the Internal Order in the Origin Tab of the AUC – Asset Master
Step 5:	Release the Internal Order
Step 6	Execute Any Business Transaction against this AUC
Step 7	Availability Check for Budget will perform whenever any business transaction is executed against the asset
Step 8	When the Asset is commissioned or put to use settle the AUC to the main asset

Scheme of entries	
	a) **At the time of Advance Payment against Capital Purchase Order** Dr. Capital Vendors - Advance A/c Cr. Bank – Check Issue Sub A/c b) **Accounting entry at the time of Goods Receipt** Dr. Capital WIP asset A/c Cr. GR/IR Capital Account c) **Accounting entry at the time of Invoice Receipt** Dr. GR/IR Capital Account Cr. Capital Vendor Account d) **At the time of clearing the advance against the Invoice** Dr. Capital Vendor (AP) a/c

	Cr. Capital Vendors - Advance A/c **e) At the time of making payment** Dr. Capital Vendor (AP) a/c Cr. Bank – Check Issue Sub A/c **f) At the time of generation of the bank reconciliation statement, the following entry will clear the bank sub account. Entry will be as follows:** Dr. Bank – Check Issue Sub A/c Cr. Bank – Main A/c **g) Accounting entry at the time of Settlement of Capital WIP A/c to Final Asset:** Dr. Asset Account Cr. Capital WIP asset A/c

8.1.11. Asset Retirement

The asset disposal process includes activities for identifying, approving and accounting for the disposal of fixed assets. Generally, when an asset is destroyed, obsolete, or is no longer needed, it will either be re-deployed to another business unit that may have a need for the asset or the company may dispose of the asset in partial or full. For assets that are re-usable, the company may try to re-deploy the asset. After a re-deployment effort is pursued and a new owner cannot be identified, the asset will then become available for sale or scrap/abandonment.

8.1.12. Asset Retirement with Revenue - Asset Sale

By using Asset Retirement with Revenue from Customer option the sales process can be initiated in the system. While booking the Retirement, system will calculate the Loss or Gain on the Asset disposal and post necessary accounting entries. User will have option to retire completely or he can choose partially. Accordingly system will reduce the Gross block as well as Accumulated depreciation.

Scheme of entries	Dr. Customer A/c
	
	    Cr. Sale of Asset Clearing A/c
	
	Dr. Sale of Asset Clearing A/c
	
	Dr. Accumulated Depreciation A/c
	
	    Cr. Fixed Assets – Gross Block A/c
	
	Dr. Loss on Sale of Asset A/c
	
	    Cr. Profit on Sale of Asset A/c

8.1.13. Asset Retirement without Revenue - Asset Donation

When an asset is no longer needed and cannot be re-deployed nor sold to a third party, the asset should then be examined for possible donation opportunities. By using the Asset Retirement without Revenue from the Customer option can be used to book the necessary entries in the system.

Scheme of entries	Dr. Customer A/c
	Cr. Sale of Asset Clearing A/c
	Dr. Sale of Asset Clearing A/c
	Dr. Accumulated Depreciation A/c
	Cr. Fixed Assets – Gross Block A/c
	Dr. Loss on Sale of Asset A/c
	Cr. Profit on Sale of Asset A/c

8.1.14. Asset Retirement – Scrapping - Asset Abandonment

In the instance that an asset cannot be re-deployed, sold, or donated (due to damage, obsolescence, etc.) within a reasonable period of time, the asset will then be scrapped. The fixed asset accountant will then remove the asset from the books by performing disposition posting for loss on abandonment.

Scheme of entries	Dr. Accumulated Depreciation A/c
	Cr. Fixed Assets – Gross Block A/c
	Dr. Loss on Sale of Asset A/c
	Cr. Profit on Sale of Asset A/c

8.1.15. Asset Transfers

8.1.15.1. Asset Transfer – Location transfer

In case of transfers within the same company i.e. Intra Company transactions, the new location need to be updated in the location field in the asset master record. The different locations wherein the asset was located at different time intervals can be viewed in the asset master record.

8.1.15.2. Asset Transfer – Cost center transfer

In case of transfers from one cost center to another, the same needs to be updated in the cost center field in the asset master record using AS02. The different cost centers wherein the asset was located at different time intervals can be viewed in the asset master record.

8.1.15.3. Asset Transfer – Wrong to correct asset class

In case of postings to a wrong asset class, transfers can be made through the system in order to transfer the assets to its correct asset class.

All the above transfers' i.e. from one location to another, from one cost center to another can be tracked through the standard reports available in the system. In case of any change in cost centers in the asset master record, depreciation will get charged to the respective cost centers based on specific time intervals for which they were held by each cost center. In case the location change happens for the earlier period, the revised cost centre wise depreciation will not be updated for the previous period.

8.1.16. Revaluation of Assets

Revaluation of Assets can be posted using the Transaction 'Manual Value Correction'. The respective Asset Class will be debited and Revaluation Reserve A/c will be credited with the revaluated amount. The depreciation on the revaluated portion will be adjusted against Revaluation Reserve A/c. The System provides for accommodating revaluation requests and updating of asset records.

8.1.17. Physical Inventory of Assets

The Finance – Asset Accounting component provides the following functions to support the physical inventory – Inventory list.

The system provides an inventory list to assist with physical inventory. You find this list in the standard Information System for Asset Accounting. You adapt the structure and sorting of the list to meet your specific needs. You make these modifications using standard report. The list displays only those assets in which the inventory indicator is set in the asset master record.

8.1.18. Asset Depreciation

- Evaluation of useful life of assets
- Apply depreciation methods
- Ensure consistency in applying depreciation policy
- Follow guidelines as per Schedule II of Companies Act 2013 and Accounting Standard AS 10 and Indian Accounting Standard Ind AS 16

8.1.18.1. Calculation of Depreciation

The depreciation areas specify the different methods for calculating depreciation for the asset to which they are assigned. Each asset of the entity will have at least one depreciation areas which are

defined in the Chart of Depreciation and depreciation is calculated on WDV method for all the assets.

For every asset, depreciation key is assigned in the asset class in accordance with the information provided in the depreciation areas to calculate the depreciation/expense and post it to the general ledger. The useful life in years shall be maintained for each Asset Class. When an Asset Master is created, this useful life maintained in the Asset Class shall be defaulted.

While calculating the book depreciation for the asset, depreciation will be calculated both diminishing balance method and straight line methods. In case of leased assets, system has to calculate depreciation on the life of the asset. Separate general ledger accounts will be established to collect the values for depreciation for different Asset Classes.

The system determines the start or end of depreciation based on the asset value date of a transaction (of the acquisition or retirement) using period controls. For VRSFL depreciation will be calculated at WDV method and depreciation starts from the day of acquisition.

8.1.18.2. Posting of Depreciation
Depreciation shall be calculated and posted every month end as part of the monthly closing process. The depreciation values will be posted to the corresponding expense and asset balance sheet accounts in the General Ledger. The periodic posting will take place using a batch input session. Only summarized postings will be made per G/L Account instead of individual documents.

8.2. Asset Accounting – Process steps

Main process	Description	Process of ERP
Asset Maintenance	In this step asset master record will be created, any changes can be done and also asset retirement can be done. Group asset can be identified based on asset classes defined.	Creation of master record
		Creation of group asset
		Asset shutdown
Receipts	Once asset master record is made, asset acquisition shall be posted depending on	Direct acquisition with vendor

	with PO / without PO and with vendor / without vendor. All down payments to be taken care of and also any subsequent acquisition posted as asset sub number.	Acquisition and clearing with offsetting entry
		Down payments
Retirements	All the asset retirements will be taken care of in this step and any profits / losses posted.	Retirement with Revenue with Customer
		Asset sale without customer
		Asset Retirement by Scrapping
Depreciation	While calculating the depreciation first depreciation planning can be done which will be processed along with cost centers and overhead orders if any and then depreciation posting run will be made periodically. This is a batch input transaction that will be run at the time of period closing.	Depreciation Planning
		Depreciation Processing
		Depreciation posting
Business transactions	All the transactions relating to asset under construction will be collected separately and after finishing they will be capitalized.	Settlement of AUC
Closing operations	The existing asset inventory can be taken out by using the ERP standard report. Changes to the fiscal year will be carried out and the previous year is closed. Before opening the new period, depreciation postings will be made.	Physical asset inventory
		Fiscal year change
		Preparations for yearend closing for assets.
		Mass change of assets

		Depreciation postings
Specific valuations	Separate depreciation area will be defined to make revaluation postings.	Revaluation of Assets

8.3. Non-current Assets: Financial Control over Financial Reporting

Activities	Risk environment	Preventive control	Detective control	Monitoring control Y/N/NA
Non-current Assets *Disposal of Fixed Assets*	*Core risk and control* The sale, disposal, or theft of fixed assets, including assets held for sale, has not been recorded.		Periodic counts of fixed assets are performed. Selections made from the property, plant, and equipment register are verified for existence, and agreed to supporting documentation that legal title and rights to the asset are held. On a periodic basis, operations management reviews the fixed assets register to verify existence and rights to the assets, and communicates errors identified to accounting management for investigation and correction.	
Acquisition of Fixed Assets	Additions are recorded: • For fixed assets that do not exist • When the entity does not have legal title to the fixed assets • At the incorrect amount.	A 3-way match process is performed for fixed assets purchases that utilise the purchase order, receiving document, and vendor invoice. Once the 3-way match process is performed and the key terms of the purchase are verified, a transaction is posted	Periodic counts of fixed assets are performed. Selections are reconciled to the fixed assets register, verified for existence and ownership, and agreed to supporting documentation that legal title is held. On a periodic basis, operational management reviews the fixed assets register to verify	

		in the fixed assets sub-ledger and general ledger to record the addition.	existence and ownership, and communicates errors identified to accounting management for investigation and correction.	
Acquisition of Fixed Assets	Expenditures of a non-capital nature (e.g., repairs and maintenance) have been incorrectly capitalised.	Expenditures of a non-capital nature are reviewed and approved by finance personnel with knowledge of the entity's capitalisation policy. Journal entry and supporting documentation for expenditures of a non-capital nature are reviewed by management prior to the journal entry being posted.	Recorded capital expenditures and other expenses are compared to budget regularly; management investigates and resolves significant variances	
Acquisition of Fixed Assets	Acquisitions of fixed assets are not recorded	A 3-way match process is performed for fixed assets purchases that utilise the purchase order, receiving document, and vendor invoice. Once the 3-way match process is performed and the key terms of the purchase are agreed to supporting documentation, a transaction is posted in the fixed assets sub-ledger and general ledger to record the addition.	Periodic counts of fixed assets are performed. Selections are made from the floor and reconciled to the fixed assets register, and any differences are investigated and resolved	
Acquisition of Fixed assets	Subsequent improvements made to fixed assets (e.g., remodels, additions) are incorrectly expensed.	Subsequent improvement project plans are reviewed by finance personnel with knowledge of the entity's capitalisation policy. The journal entry and supporting documentation for	Recorded other expenses are compared to budget regularly; management investigates and resolves significant variances.	

		subsequent improvement expenditures are reviewed by management prior to the journal entry being posted.		
Depreciating Fixed assets	Depreciation expense is: • Calculated using an inappropriate rate or using an inappropriate methodology • Recorded at the incorrect amount • Not calculated for all fixed assets.		Management reviews fixed assets additions for appropriate assignment of depreciable lives and methodology, and performs a periodic review of depreciable lives and depreciation methodology for all fixed assets for ongoing appropriateness . On a periodic basis, management performs a retrospective analysis of fixed assets disposals to challenge the depreciable lives and methodology being applied to fixed assets	
Depreciating Fixed assets	Depreciation expense is recorded for assets of a non-capital nature or for assets that have been disposed.	Expenditures of a non-capital nature are reviewed and approved by finance personnel with knowledge of the entity's capitalisation policy. Journal entry and supporting documentation for expenditures of a non-capital nature are reviewed by management prior to the journal entry being posted.	Management reviews fixed assets additions for appropriate assignment of depreciable lives and methodology, and performs a periodic review of depreciable lives and depreciation methodology for all fixed assets for ongoing appropriateness	
Fixed assets Valuation	Fixed assets stated in the general ledger does not reconcile to the subsidiary ledger and/or the reconciliation contains invalid items.		On a periodic basis, a roll-forward of fixed assets is performed by the ERP system or manually using computer-generated information and reconciled to the general ledger;	

			differences are investigated and corrected	
Fixed assets Valuation	Impairment indicators may exist for fixed assets, but are not known to management	On a periodic basis, accounting and operations management meet to assess internal or external factors that may be indicators of impairment	Management periodically reviews budgeted versus actual results for the entity, including its product lines and segments. The results of this review are utilised by management in assessing whether impairment indicators may be present.	
Non-current Assets *Acquisition of Fixed assets*	*Other Possible Risks and Controls* Operating leases for fixed assets are incorrectly accounted for as finance leases.	New lease contracts and lease modifications are reviewed by finance personnel to determine whether they meet the criteria for finance or operating lease treatment, including reference to the appropriate accounting framework and principle. The journal entry and supporting documentation are reviewed by management prior to the journal entry being posted.	New lease contracts and lease modifications recorded in the lease register[i] are periodically reviewed by management to verify that the lease has been properly accounted for as a finance or operating lease.	
Acquisition of Fixed assets	Finance leases for fixed assets are incorrectly accounted for as operating leases	New lease contracts and lease modification are reviewed by finance personnel to determine whether they meet the criteria for finance or operating lease treatment, including reference to the appropriate accounting framework and principle. The journal entry and supporting documentation are	New lease contracts and lease modifications recorded in the lease register are periodically reviewed by management to verify that the lease has been properly accounted for as a finance or operating lease.	

		reviewed by management prior to the journal entry being posted.		
Acquisition of Fixed assets	Capital Work in progress (CWIP) is not transferred to fixed assets when the asset is placed into service.		Operations management periodically reviews the listing of CWIP and communicates to accounting management any CWIP assets that have been put into service	
Acquisition of Fixed assets	Capitalised interest is: • Inappropriately recorded for assets directly purchased and put into service • Not recorded for assets constructed • Recorded at the incorrect amount.	CWIP is reviewed by finance personnel with knowledge of the entity's capitalisation policy. Finance personnel consider whether the assets constructed qualify for capitalised interest based on nature of the asset, and amount of interest incurred in the period, and calculate the amount of interest to be capitalised [As per Accounting Standard 16 – Borrowing Costs"]. The journal entry and supporting documentation for capitalised interest are reviewed by management prior to the journal entry being posted		
Fixed assets Valuation	Cash flow projections or significant assumptions used in the impairment test are inconsistent with cash flow projections or significant assumptions used for other purposes (e.g., going concern, deferred tax asset, fixed asset impairment).	Financial forecasts are prepared by finance personnel with an appropriate level of knowledge of accounting requirements. Management (1) reviews the financial forecast methodology for appropriateness and consistent application to other		

		financial forecasts prepared and (2) reviews, challenges, and approves the significant assumptions applied.		
Fixed assets Valuation	The valuation methodology used for impairment purposes is: • Inappropriate under the circumstances • Based on underlying significant assumptions [*specify assumptions*] that are inappropriate, lack sufficient basis, or lack sufficient support.	A valuation analysis is performed by qualified personnel at the entity or by a qualified third-party appraiser. The valuation methodology, significant assumptions, and underlying data used are reviewed, evaluated, and approved by management with appropriate knowledge of valuation techniques.		
Disposal of Fixed assets	The entity incorrectly records the disposal of fixed assets for assets still owned by the entity.	All fixed assets disposals and supporting documentation are reviewed and approved by management prior to the journal entry being recorded.	Periodic counts of fixed assets are performed. Selections made from the floor are reconciled to the fixed assets register, and differences are investigated and resolved.	
Disposal of Fixed assets	Disposals of fixed assets are recorded in the general ledger at incorrect amounts.	Finance personnel obtain supporting documentation for all fixed assets disposals and prepare the related journal entry. Supporting documentation and the journal entry are reviewed and approved by management prior to the journal entry being recorded.	Management periodically compares actual fixed assets disposals to budget. Significant differences or discrepancies are investigated and resolved	

Depreciating Fixed assets	CWIP is not transferred to fixed assets when the asset is placed into service and therefore is not depreciated.		Operations management periodically reviews the listing of CWIP assets and communicates to accounting management any CWIP assets that have been put into service	
8.4.Intangible Assets	**Financial Control over Financial Reporting**			
Activities	**Risk environment**	**Preventive control**	**Detective control**	**Monitoring control Y/N/NA**
Intangible assets and goodwill *Recording Intangible Assets*	*Core Risks and Controls* Intangibles for which no future economic benefit is expected: • Are recorded • Are recorded in excess of the asset amount rather than as another expense.		Finance personnel periodically reconcile intangible asset balances to supporting documentation; management reviews and approves the reconciliations, including supporting documentation for account transactions. Unusual transactions or invalid reconciling items are investigated and resolved on a timely basis and adjusted to other expense. Finance personnel maintain a listing of recorded goodwill and intangible assets. The listing is reviewed by operational management, including in-house legal counsel, as appropriate, for existence and completeness. Discrepancies are investigated and resolved on a timely basis and adjusted to other expense	
Goodwill and Intangible Asset	Goodwill and intangible assets included in the		Finance personnel periodically reconcile intangible asset	

Valuation	valuation analysis: • Do not reconcile to the subsidiary ledger and/or the reconciliation contains invalid items. • Do not exist or the entity no longer has rights to such assets • Do not include all goodwill and intangible assets.		balances to supporting documentation; management reviews and approves the reconciliations, including supporting documentation for account transactions. Unusual transactions or invalid reconciling items are investigated and resolved on a timely basis and adjusted to other expense. Finance personnel maintain a listing of recorded goodwill and intangible assets. The listing is reviewed by operational management, including in-house legal counsel, as appropriate, for existence and completeness. Discrepancies are investigated and resolved on a timely basis and adjusted to other expense.	
Goodwill Valuation	Reporting units are incorrectly identified or inappropriately aggregated for purposes of the goodwill impairment test.	Finance personnel prepare documentation with reference to the applicable accounting framework and principle addressing the identification of the entity's reporting units and the assets and liabilities underlying each reporting unit. The documentation is reviewed and approved by management before the entity performs the goodwill impairment test.		
Amortisation of Intangible Assets	Intangible assets are amortised using an inappropriate useful	On a periodic basis, finance personnel analyse intangible	On a periodic basis, management performs a	

	life or method that is inappropriate under the circumstances	assets for the best estimate of useful lives, and an amortisation method that reflects the pattern in which economic benefits of the intangible asset are consumed or otherwise used up. Management reviews and approves the analysis and supporting documentation.	retrospective analysis of intangible assets that have been fully amortised in prior periods to challenge the useful lives and methodology being applied to intangible assets.	
Amortisation of Intangible Assets	Amortisation is not calculated for all recorded intangible assets.		Management reviews intangible asset additions for appropriate assignment of useful lives and methodology, and performs a periodic review of useful lives and amortisation methodology for all intangible assets for ongoing appropriateness.	
Amortisation of Intangible Assets	Amortisation is recorded for intangible assets that have been disposed, fully amortised, or for which the entity does not have legal ownership.		Finance personnel periodically reconcile intangible asset balances, and related amortisation, to supporting documentation; management reviews and approves the reconciliations, including supporting documentation for account transactions. Unusual transactions or invalid reconciling items are investigated and resolved on a timely basis and adjusted to other expense.	
Goodwill and Intangible Asset Valuation	Management uses a valuation technique that is inappropriate under the circumstances or only utilises a single valuation technique	Management reviews the calculations performed and assumptions used within the goodwill impairment	.	

	for circumstances that indicate multiple valuation techniques are appropriate.	assessment for consistency with commonly accepted valuation practices, prior-year assumptions, and publicly available peer company and industry information		
Goodwill and Intangible Asset Valuation	Management's impairment assessment uses business and valuation assumptions that are not based on its best and most supportable estimates.	Finance management reviews the business assumptions (including the reporting unit carrying amounts and assessment date) for appropriateness prior to being provided to management's valuation expert. Management from different areas of the entity meet to review the forecast for appropriateness using historical performance, their knowledge of the entity's strategic plans, industry projections, and peer company data. Management reviews the calculations performed and assumptions used within the goodwill impairment assessment for consistency with commonly accepted valuation practices, prior-year assumptions, and publicly available peer company and industry information.		

Recording Goodwill	*Other Possible Risks and Controls* Goodwill acquired in business acquisitions is: • Not appropriately recorded in the year of the acquisition • Recorded at the incorrect amount.	Controls will vary by entity	Controls will vary by entity	
Recording Intangible Assets	The entity inappropriately capitalises costs related to internally developed intangible assets rather than expense such costs.	Finance personnel with the requisite expertise and knowledge of the applicable accounting framework, review costs incurred related to intangible assets. Supporting documentation and the journal entry are prepared by finance personnel, and reviewed and approved by management before the journal entry is recorded.	Finance personnel reconcile intangible asset balances to supporting documentation. Management reviews and approves the reconciliations, including supporting documentation for account activity. Unusual activity or invalid reconciling items are investigated and resolved on a timely basis.	
Recording Intangible Assets	Internally developed intangible assets (e.g., copyrights, trademarks, patents) are inappropriately recorded as expenses.	Finance personnel with the requisite expertise and knowledge of the applicable accounting framework, review costs incurred related to intangible assets. Supporting documentation and the journal entry are prepared by finance personnel, and reviewed and approved by management before the journal entry is recorded.		
Recording Intangible Assets	Intangible assets acquired are: • Recorded for intangible assets not acquired • Not recorded • Not recorded at	Controls will vary by entity.	Controls will vary by entity.	

	the correct amount • Not assigned an appropriate useful life			
Recording Intangible Assets	Rights to intangible assets offered as security for debt no longer exist.	On a periodic basis, finance personnel assess compliance with debt covenants and changes in rights to assets offered as security. This assessment, along with supporting documentation and the journal entry, if necessary, is reviewed by management before the journal entry is recorded.		
Goodwill and Intangible Asset Valuation	Management does not obtain an appropriate understanding or perform a review of the work of management's expert, thereby evidencing a lack of appropriate responsibility over the projections made and assumptions used.	Management reviews the data used and calculations performed by management's valuation expert for accuracy and consistency with cash flow information provided. Management reviews the calculations performed and assumptions used within the goodwill impairment assessment for consistency with commonly accepted valuation practices, prior-year assumptions, and publicly available peer company and industry information.		
Disposing Goodwill and Intangible Assets	Goodwill and intangible assets disposed in a sale transaction are not removed from the	On a periodic basis, finance personnel obtain contracts and other documentation	On a periodic basis, finance personnel reconcile goodwill and intangible asset balances to	

	general ledger.	related to business unit disposals and other sale/disposal transactions. Finance personnel prepare a journal entry, along with supporting documentation, to record the sale or disposal. The journal entry and supporting documentation are reviewed by management before the journal entry is recorded.	supporting documentation. Management reviews and approves the reconciliations, including supporting documentation for account transactions. Unusual transactions or invalid reconciling items are investigated and resolved on a timely basis	
Disposing Goodwill and Intangible Assets	The entity incorrectly records the disposal of goodwill or intangible assets when rights to those assets still exist.	All transactions involving goodwill and intangible asset disposals and supporting documentation are reviewed and approved by management prior to the journal entry being recorded.	On a periodic basis, finance personnel roll forward and reconcile goodwill and intangible asset balances to supporting documentation. Management reviews and approves the roll forward and reconciliation, including supporting documentation for account transactions. Unusual activity or invalid reconciling items are investigated and resolved on a timely basis.	

8.5. Illustrative Risk map: Non-current assets

High	

Delay in capitalisation of assets	Non-traceability of assets
No identification of impaired assets	

Impact

Asset capitalised exceed budget / capital expenditure proposal	Transfer of assets not properly controlled leading to incorrect depreciation calculation
	Incorrect depreciation calculation based on incorrect rates and wrong useful lives

Low

Low	Likelihood	High

8.6. Audit check-list

Non-Current Assets Controls	Yes	No	N/A	Comments
1. Detailed property records				
2. Periodic comparison with control accounts				
3. Proper authorization for acquisitions				
4. Written policies for acquisition				
5. Control over expenditures for self-construction				
6. Use of work orders				
7. Individual asset identification plates				
8. Written authorization for sale				
9. Written authorization for retirement				
10. Physical safeguard from theft				
11. Control over fully depreciated assets				
12. Written capitalization–expense policies				
13. Responsibilities charged for asset and depreciation records				
14. Written, detailed depreciation records				
15. Depreciation adjustments for sales and retirements				
16. Control over intracompany transfers				
17. Adequacy of insurance				
18. Control over returnable containers				

Intangibles Controls	Yes	No	N/A	Comments
1. Authorization to incur				
2. Detailed records				
3. Authorization to amortize				
4. Periodic review of amortization				

8.7. Risk Control Matrix summary: Fixed Assets (specimen format)

Item	1	2	3	4	5
Mega process	Fixed Assets	Fixed Assets	Fixed Assets	Fixed Assets	Fixed Assets
Process	Indent	Purchase Order	Receipts of material and	Safeguarding of Fixed assets	Disposal of Fixed Assets

Activity	Request for Capex	Vendor selection and creation of PO	Creation of GRN and payable management	Safeguarding and physical verification of Fixed assets	Disposal of Fixed Assets
			payable		
Risk description	Unauthorized Request for purchase of FA	Selection of Improper Vendor and PO without approval	Unauthorized Material entry and wrong entries	Damage to assets and maintenance of idle assets	Improper valuation
Control objective	To ensure that the Capex requested is approved and made by authorised person	To ensure vendors are identified by obtaining quotation for the requisite product & selected based on quality and price parameter and PO are approved.	To ensure that material is received after authorization and FA related entries are made correctly	To ensure that proper insurance has been done or not. To ensure that the fixed assets as per books of accounts are available physically	To ensure that defective assets are sold / disposed off after appropriate approvals. To ensure that asset sale/disposal is accounted completely and accurately. To ensure there is no false entry recorded for any disposal of assets which is still owned by the entity
Control environment – to be certified by the process owner	1. User sends email to reporting Manager for FA requirement, 2. Reporting manager sends email to BU Head for approval 3. After approval Reporting manager sends email to IT/admin/HR member depending upon the type of asset 4. Concerned department	1. Procurement department is responsible for negotiation with Vendors and selects the vendor basis lowest price. 2. After finalization of vendor, Procurement head sends email to Country head for approval in cases of goods and services costing more than $ 10,000 and Business head in case less than $ 10,000. PO is made after	Once material received admin person sign the GRN or makes the entry in register (wherever applicable). Goods received by admin/IT transferred to user who has raised the requirement and invoice is being sent to Finance IOC Team after approval from respective department. Once the FA	Insurance of all assets is being done and Insurance is being renewed on timely basis. Management representation letter submitted to auditor at the year end after physically verification.	Assets are being sold by IT/admin after taking approval from concerned department. The Information and amount is then shared with Finance department for recording in books of account and deposit of amount in bank.

	sends email to Procurement with specifications.	approval from country head for material amounting to $.10,000 or more and BU head for less than $ 10,000. PO is prepared by Finance team and send the same to procurement for review. All the PO's has unique PO number and particulars are entered in PO tracker by the finance Team.	invoice is received with approved PO and GRN then accountant makes entry into accounts for FA. He ensures that FA Invoice is approved by appropriate person before making entry in the books of accounts and Invoice amount and PO amount is matching.		
Risk category					
Fraud risk – yes / no	No	Yes	No	Yes	No
Risk category – high / medium / low	Low	High	Medium	Medium	Medium
Internal financial control over financial reporting – yes / no	No	Yes	Yes	Yes	Yes
IFC/IFCR Component	Prevention and detection of frauds and errors	Prevention and detection of frauds and errors	Policies and procedures Accuracy and completeness of the accounting records	Prevention and detection of frauds and errors	Prevention and detection of frauds and errors
Prevention / detection of frauds – yes / no	Yes	Yes	No	Yes	Yes
Key Control – yes / no	Yes	Yes	Yes	No	Yes
Control category					
Completeness	xx	xx	xx		xx
Existence	xx	xx	xx	xx	xx
Accuracy	xx	xx	xx	xx	xx
Valuation			xx		xx
Rights / obligation				xx	
Presentation					
Manual / Automatic	Manual	Manual	Manual	Manual	Manual
Preventive / detective	Preventive	Preventive	Preventive	Preventive	Preventive
Frequency of	Event based	Event based	Event based	Event based	Yearly

measurement					
Document if any	Approval email	Purchase Order	GRN or FA entry register FA Invoice and FA ledger	Insurance Policies Management Representation letter	Email , quotations from buyers and internal approval
Prepared by (maker)	User of Asset	IT/Admin/HR member	Account Executive	Finance Manager	Admin/ IT/ HR team member
Checked by (checker)	Reporting manager	Procurement team member	Senior Executive - Accounts	Board	Senior Executive Accounts
System solution – ERP – Yes/no	yes	Yes	Yes	Yes	Yes
Whether covered under SOP – Yes / no	Yes	Yes	Yes	Yes	Yes
Process design gap – Yes / no	No	No	No	No	No

Guide to Risk Management and Internal Financial Control

Chapter 9: Inventories

9.1. Inventories: Control Environment

Inventory control environment would encompass the following:

Inventory Management

Inventory planning	Inventory movement	Inventory monitoring
Material classification	Gate entry	Physical verification
Stock level management	Goods receipt	Warehouse management
Min/max/reorder level	Goods issue to shop-floor	Storing, Stacking and
Master maintenance	Stock transfer	Preservation at right temperature
	Returnable Gate Pass	Identification of slow/non-moving
	Non-returnable gate pass	and obsolete stocks

Control Environment	Yes	No	N/A	Comments
All inventory movements are authorised				
Inventory included in the statement of financial position physically exists				
All purchases and sales of inventory have been recorded in the accounting system				
Inventory records only include items that belong to the entity				
Inventory quantities have been accurately determined				
Inventory is properly stated at the lower of cost and net realisable value				
All purchases and sales of inventory are recorded in the correct accounting period				
Inventory transactions and balance are properly identified and classified in the financial statements				
Disclosures relating to classification and valuation are sufficient				

9.2. Inventories: Procurement : Revisited

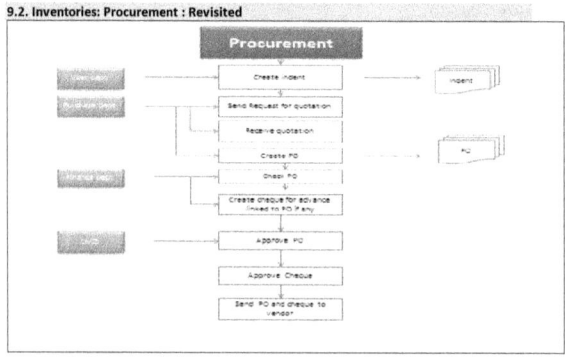

224

9.3. Inventories: Receiving: Revisited

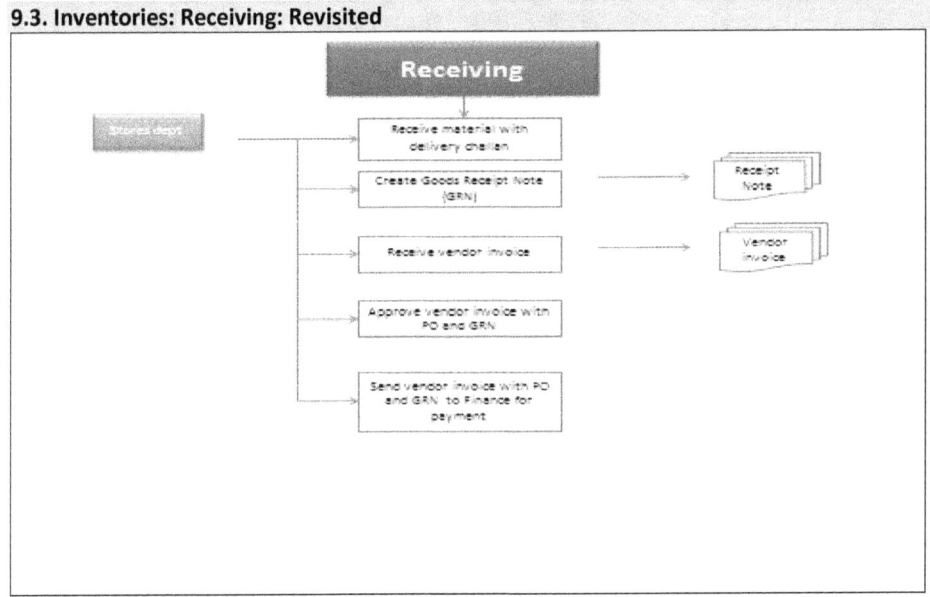

9.4. Inventories: Financial Control over Financial Reporting

Activities	Risk environment	Preventive control	Detective control	Monitoring control Y/N/NA
Inventories Recording Inventory	*Core Risks and Controls* Inventory and trade payables are recorded prior to receipt and/or title transfer of the inventory	Inventory and trade payables entries are recorded automatically by the ERP system upon matching the purchase order and goods received note (GRN). Management reviews and approves the journal entry and supporting documentation for inventory and trade payables recorded for goods not yet received, but title has transferred to the entity. On a periodic basis, finance personnel review open purchase orders and record inventory and accrued payables for	Physical inventory is counted periodically and discrepancies are investigated and corrected within the inventory records. Inventory records based on the physical inventory are reconciled to the general ledger with any differences being recorded as a book-to-physical inventory adjustment	

		goods received or for goods not yet received where title has transferred to the entity. The journal entry and supporting documentation is reviewed and approved by management before the journal entry is recorded.	
Recording Inventory	Inventory and trade payables are recorded at the incorrect amount.	Inventory and trade payables entries are recorded automatically by the ERP system upon matching the purchase order and GRN	
Recording Inventory	Inventory and trade payables are not recorded upon transfer of ownership prior to actual receipt.	Management reviews and approves the journal entry and supporting documentation for inventory and trade payables recorded for goods not yet received, but title has transferred to the entity	
Recording Inventory	Inventory is received and not recorded in the inventory system.	Inventory and trade payables entries are automatically recorded by the ERP system upon matching the purchase order and GRN On a periodic basis, finance personnel review open purchase orders and record inventory and accrued payables for goods received or for goods not yet received where title has transferred to the entity. The journal entry and supporting documentation are reviewed and	Physical inventory is counted periodically and discrepancies are investigated and corrected within the inventory records. Inventory records based on the physical inventory are reconciled to the general ledger with any differences being recorded as a book-to-physical inventory adjustment.	

		approved by management before the journal entry is recorded.		
Recording Inventory	Inventory stated in the general ledger does not reconcile to the inventory records and/or the reconciliation contains invalid items.		Management reviews and approves the reconciliation of the inventory records to the general ledger and any reconciling items are reviewed and addressed on a timely basis	
Recording removal of Inventory	Inventory may be removed from inventory records and recorded as a cost of sales when it has not actually been sold.	Cost of sales is recorded and inventory is relieved automatically by the ERP system upon matching the customer sales order, shipping documents, and the invoice generated, completing a 3-way match	Physical inventory is counted periodically and discrepancies are investigated and corrected within the inventory records. Inventory records based on the physical inventory are reconciled to the general ledger with any differences being recorded as a book-to-physical inventory adjustment	
Recording removal of Inventory	Inventory records include inventory that was sold to customers and not recorded as cost of sales.	Cost of sales is recorded and inventory is relieved automatically by the ERP system upon matching the customer sales order, shipping documents, and the invoice generated, completing a 3-way match	Physical inventory is counted periodically and discrepancies are investigated and corrected within the inventory records. Inventory records based on the physical inventory are reconciled to the general ledger with any differences being recorded as a book-to-physical inventory adjustment.	
Recording removal of Inventory	Inventory may be removed from inventory records and recorded as a cost of sales upon shipment prior to transfer of ownership.	Management reviews and approves the journal entry and supporting documentation for inventory and cost of goods sold for goods that have been dispatched prior to transfer of ownership		
Recording	Inventory that was	Cost of sales is	Physical inventory is	

removal of Inventory	sold to customers and recorded as cost of sales are recorded in the incorrect period.	recorded and inventory is relieved automatically by the ERP system upon matching the customer sales order, shipping documents, and the invoice generated, completing a 3-way match.	counted periodically and discrepancies are investigated and corrected within the inventory records. Inventory records based on the physical inventory are reconciled to the general ledger with any differences being recorded as a book-to-physical inventory adjustment	
Recording removal of Inventory	Inventory has been sold that is removed from the accounts at incorrect amounts.	On a periodic basis, accounting personnel calculate the inventory cost under the costing method utilised by the entity. Prior to recording the journal entry, management reviews the calculation, methodology, significant assumptions used, supporting documentation, and the journal entry for accuracy and proper account classification. Cost of sales is recorded and inventory is relieved automatically by the ERP system upon matching the customer sales order, shipping documents, and the invoice generated, completing a 3-way match		
Physical Inventory	Physical inventory counts are not performed on a periodic basis, potentially resulting in inaccurate inventory records.		Physical inventory is counted periodically and discrepancies are investigated and corrected within the inventory records. Inventory records based on the physical inventory are reconciled to the general ledger with	

			any differences being recorded as a book to physical inventory adjustment	
Physical Inventory	Physical inventory counts: • Count inventory that does not exist • Do not include counts of all inventory • Do not include consideration of movement of inventory during the physical inventory • Are not valued at the appropriate cost • Book to physical adjustments are not recorded or recorded at the incorrect amount.		Physical inventory is counted periodically, and discrepancies are investigated and corrected within the inventory records. Inventory records based on the physical inventory are reconciled to the general ledger, with any differences being recorded as a book-to-physical inventory adjustment.	
Inventory Held by Third Parties	Inventory held by a third party that has been sold to a final customer has not been removed from inventory or recorded as a cost of sales.		On a periodic basis, the reports provided by the third party to the entity, either directly or by confirmation, are reviewed and reconciled to internal records and used by the entity to relieve inventory and record cost of sales.	
Inventory Held by Third Parties	Inventory held by a third party and not yet sold is improperly removed from inventory and recorded as cost of sales.		On a periodic basis, the reports provided by the third party to the entity, either directly or by confirmation, are reviewed and reconciled to internal records and used by the entity to relieve inventory and record cost of sales.	
Inventory Valuation	Inventory records include inventory that is not in a saleable condition.		Physical inventory is counted periodically, and discrepancies are investigated and corrected within the inventory records.	

			Inventory records based on the physical inventory are reconciled to the general ledger, with any differences being recorded as a book-to-physical inventory adjustment	
Inventory Valuation	Inventory may be recorded at the incorrect cost under the entity's costing method.	On a periodic basis, accounting personnel calculate the inventory cost under the costing method utilised by the entity. Prior to recording the journal entry, management reviews the calculation, methodology, significant assumptions used, supporting documentation, and the journal entry for accuracy and proper account classification. Changes made to inventory costing methods are approved by management before becoming effective.	On a quarterly basis, accounting personnel compare the costs automatically calculated by the ERP system to manually calculated inventory costs using the selected costing method for a sample of inventory items. Management meets monthly in product cost review meeting to discuss results of operations, specifically focused on production cost evaluation including a comparison of current-period productions cost to the current-year budget and prior-period benchmarks	
Inventory Valuation	The entity uses inappropriate standard costs in valuing its inventory, including incorrectly calculating the allocation of labour and overhead.	Management reviews the new standard cost analysis and supporting documentation and approves changes to standard costs, including labour and overhead allocation assumptions, before the changes are made to the inventory ERP system. Management compares the revised standard cost master file to		

		the approved standard cost per the New Standard Cost Report.		
Inventory Valuation	Inventory costs are inaccurate due to the inaccurate calculation of product cost variances.	Periodically, management reviews and evaluates the process to account for and calculate product cost variances The report logic used to generate the Cost Variance Report is non-configurable by system users. Any changes to the Cost Variance Report parameters or configuration can only be made by the System Administrator — Inventory and require approval by the Corporate Controller, evidenced by signoff on the Change Request Form before becoming effective.		
Inventory Valuation	Product cost variances have been inaccurately allocated between period costs and period-end inventory.		Prior to recording the monthly journal entry to allocate product cost variances to period-end inventory, management reviews the product cost variance calculation, which includes an assessment of the methodology, significant assumptions used, supporting documentation, and mathematical accuracy.	
Inventory Valuation	Inventory may be recorded at an amount that exceeds the lower of cost or net realisable value (NRV) as the		Management reviews and approves the cost v/s NSR evaluation prepared by finance personnel and the resulting journal entry	

	significant assumptions [*specify assumptions*] utilised in the lower of cost or NRV analysis are inappropriate, do not have a sufficient basis, or do not have sufficient support.		
Inventory Valuation	The adjustment for lower of cost or NRV is recorded in the incorrect accounting period.	Management reviews and approves the cost v/s NSR evaluation prepared by finance personnel and the resulting journal entry	
Inventory Valuation	The adjustment for lower of cost or NRV stated in the general ledger does not reconcile to the calculation and/or contains mathematical errors.	Management reviews and approves the cost v/s NSR evaluation prepared by finance personnel and the resulting journal entry	
Inventory Valuation	In evaluating the adjustments for obsolete, slow moving, or excess inventory : Management's method for determining the E&O (excess and obsolete) adjustments is inappropriate or has not been applied consistently. The estimates are based on assumptions that are unreasonable, lack sufficient basis, or lack sufficient support. Assumptions used in estimating E&O adjustments include: [*specify assumptions*].	Management reviews and approves the excess and obsolete adjustment calculation prepared by finance personnel and resulting journal entry.	
Inventory Valuation	Obsolete, slow moving, or excess inventory exists but no adjustment is recorded against inventory and as a component of cost of	Management reviews and approves the excess and obsolete adjustment calculation prepared by finance personnel	Physical inventory is counted periodically and discrepancies are investigated and corrected within the inventory records. Inventory records

	sales.	and resulting journal entry.	based on the physical inventory are reconciled to the general ledger with any differences being recorded as a book to physical inventory adjustment	
Inventory Valuation	Obsolete, slow moving, or excess inventory does not exist but an adjustment is recorded against inventory and as a component of cost of sales.	Management reviews and approves the excess and obsolete adjustment calculation prepared by finance personnel and resulting journal entry.	Management periodically reviews actual inventory, cost of sales, gross profit, and other expense amounts in comparison to budget, historical amounts, or current-year trends, and investigates and resolves any significant variances. This review is performed at a sufficient level of detail and disaggregation (e.g., by type of product line, type of services).	
Inventory Valuation	The calculations for obsolete, slow-moving, or excess inventory and related adjustments are based on inaccurate inventory usage / movement data.		The inventory management system generates the Inventory Usage/Movement Report based on parameters in the inventory management system.	
Inventory Valuation	The adjustment for obsolete, slow moving, or excess inventory is recorded at the incorrect amount, in the incorrect general ledger account, or in the incorrect accounting period	Management reviews and approves the excess and obsolete adjustment calculation prepared by finance personnel and resulting journal entry.		
Inventory Valuation	The adjustment for obsolete, slow-moving, or excess inventory stated in the general ledger does not reconcile to the calculation and/or contains mathematical errors.	Management reviews and approves the excess and obsolete adjustment calculation prepared by finance personnel and resulting journal entry.		
Inventory	Inventory returned to	The ERP system	Inventory returned to	

Returns	suppliers is: • Not removed from the inventory and trade payables records • Recorded at the incorrect amount	automatically records entries to reduce inventory and trade payables as per the sub-ledgers upon matching the goods return order, shipping document, and debit note, completing a 3-way match	suppliers is separately logged. On a periodic basis, the return log is utilised to verify inventory is relieved and trade payables is reduced for inventory returned to suppliers.	
Inventory Returns	Inventory recorded as returned to vendors (removed from the inventory and trade payables records) is not actually returned.		Inventory returned to suppliers is separately logged. On a periodic basis, the return log is utilised to verify inventory is relieved and trade payables is reduced for inventory returned to suppliers.	
Sales Returns	Inventory returns from customers are recorded: • Prior to receipt • At the incorrect amount • In the incorrect period.	Manual journal entries to record inventory purchases or returns and related accrued payable adjustments are prepared by finance personnel and supported by documentation that the inventory has been received or title has transferred to the entity prior to recording the entry. Management reviews and approves the journal entry and underlying supporting documentation	Physical inventory is counted periodically and discrepancies are investigated and corrected within the inventory records. Inventory records based on the physical inventory are reconciled to the general ledger with any differences being recorded as a book-to-physical inventory adjustment.	
Sales Returns	Goods returned by customers are: • Not recorded • Recorded at the incorrect amount • Recorded in the incorrect period.	Warehouse personnel enter all goods received into the ERP system on the date of receipt, and the ERP system automatically records an adjustment to the inventory subsidiary ledger and to cost of sales in the general ledger.	All returned goods are logged when received. On a periodic basis, return details as per the log are compared to the inventory records to verify the returned inventory is properly recorded in the inventory sub-ledger, and to verify cost of sales has been reduced in the general	

			ledger.	
	Other possible risks and controls			
Recording Inventory	Inventory issued on consignment and not yet sold is improperly removed from inventory and recorded as cost of sales.		Consigned inventory is confirmed and confirmations are reconciled to inventory records and the general ledger. On a periodic basis, consigned inventory is physically verified by company personnel and reconciled to the inventory records Inventory consignee provides periodic reporting of consigned inventory sold to third parties, and consigned inventory held. These reports are reviewed and reconciled to internal records, and used by the entity to record cost of sales and relieve inventory.	
Recording Inventory	Inventory held on consignment and subsequently sold has not been invoiced and recorded as a sale and receivable.		Consigned inventory is confirmed and confirmations are reconciled to inventory records and the general ledger. Randomly, consigned inventory is physically verified by company personnel. Inventory consignee (third party) provides periodic reporting of consigned inventory held. These reports are reviewed and reconciled to internal records and differences are investigated.	

Recording Inventory	Inventory held at offsite locations is improperly removed from inventory and recorded as cost of sales.		Physical inventory, including inventory held at offsite locations, is counted periodically and discrepancies are investigated and corrected within the inventory records. Inventory records are reconciled to the general ledger.	
Recording Inventory	Inventory records include inventory that does not exist due to shrinkage, which has not been recorded as a component of cost of sales.		Physical inventory is counted periodically and discrepancies are investigated and corrected within the inventory records. Inventory records are reconciled to the general ledger On a periodic basis, consigned inventory is physically verified by company personnel and reconciled to the inventory records.	
Recording Inventory	Inventory previously issued on consignment that has been sold to a third party has not been removed from inventory or recorded as a cost of sale.		On a periodic basis, consigned inventory is physically verified by company personnel and reconciled to the inventory records On a periodic basis, the inventory consignee provides the entity reporting of consigned inventory sold to third parties and consigned inventory still held, or the entity confirms consigned inventory with the consignee. These reports or confirmations are reviewed and reconciled to internal records, and used by the entity to record cost of sales and relieve inventory	

Inventory Valuation	Intercompany profits are: • Not eliminated from inventory • Eliminated at the incorrect amount.	Intercompany sales are analysed at period-end to calculate the amount of intercompany profit in inventory to be eliminated. Finance personnel prepare the journal entry, supporting documentation, and account analysis for intercompany profit in inventory to be eliminated. Management reviews and approves the journal entry, supporting documentation, and account analysis before the journal entry is recorded.		
Inventory Valuation	Volume or purchase discounts from suppliers are recorded in improper accounts (e.g., cost of sales, inventory) or at incorrect amounts.	On a periodic basis, purchasing provides the accounting function with analysis of inventory purchases related to all supplier volume/rebate agreements. Accounting personnel calculate the estimated volume discount. Prior to recording the journal entry, management reviews the calculation, methodology, significant assumptions used, supporting documentation, and the journal entry for accuracy and proper classification.	Management subsequently compares volume discount cash received to the recorded volume discount estimate for accuracy. Discrepancies are investigated and corrected, as necessary. Physical inventory is counted periodically and discrepancies are investigated and corrected within the inventory records. Inventory records are reconciled to the general ledger.	

9.5. Illustrative Risk map: Inventories Management

High

| Material going out of gate without any book entry / payment of excise | Incorrect classification of materials leading to incorrect MRP run |

No identification of materials leading to shortage in inventories

Incorrect material coding – one item having multiple codes impacting incorrect reporting of inventory

Unauthorised updation of stocks leading to mis-statement of stock ledger

Inventory in books and physically they do not exist

Incorrect stock monitoring data leading to stock out situation

Incorrect inventory valuation leading to incorrect reporting of financial results

Impact

Material received without PO

No Gate entry made for incoming material

Obsolescence of materials owing to technology change

Low   **Likelihood**   **High**

9.6. Inventories: Audit of controls

Inventory : Test of Controls	Yes	No	N/A	Comments
1. Periodic inventory counts				
2. Written inventory instructions				
3. Counts by noncustodians				
4. Control over count tags				
5. Control over inventory adjustments				
6. Use of perpetual records				
7. Periodic comparison of G/L and perpetual records				
8. Investigation of discrepancies				
9. Control over consignment inventory				
10. Control over inventory stored at warehouses				
11. Control over returnable containers left with customers				
12. Preparation of receiving reports				
13. Prenumbered receiving reports				
14. Receiving reports in numerical order				
15. Independence of custodian from recordkeeping				
16. Adequacy of insurance				
17. Physical safeguards against theft				
18. Physical safeguards against fire				
19. Adequacy of cost system				
20. Cost system tied into general ledger				
21. Periodic review of overhead rates				
22. Use of standard costs				
23. Use of inventory requisitions				
24. Periodic summaries of inventory usage				
25. Control over intracompany inventory transfers				
26. Purchase orders prenumbered				
27. Proper authorization for purchases				
28. Review of open purchase orders				

Chapter 10: Trade Receivables

10.1. Trade Receivable: Control environment

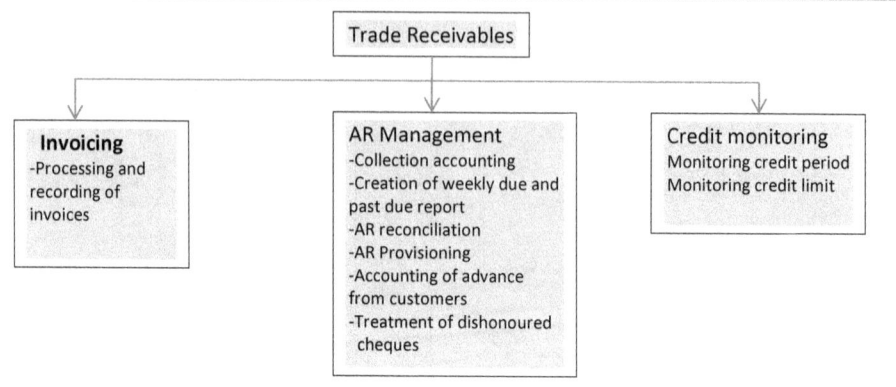

10.1.1. Trade Receivable: Process summary

- ❑ Create a sub-ledger for Trade receivable

- ❑ Create customer master

- ❑ Integrate customer invoicing with Trade Receivable

- ❑ Update customer payments

- ❑ Enable creation of credit notes

- ❑ Total and partial clearing of open items in Trade Receivables

- ❑ Create customer ageing analysis

- ❑ Prepare to send dunning letters to customers > three months

- ❑ Creation of budget and comparison with actuals month and YTD

- ❑ Multi currency posting

- ❑ Drill down from financial statements to voucher level

- ❑ Import and export of data to and from the system

10.1.2. Trade Receivable: Process

Accounts Receivable is the sub-module in which the financial accounting transactions involving customers are recorded and administered. All postings in Accounts Receivable are also recorded simultaneously in General Ledger. The components of Accounts Receivable are closely integrated with components of Sales and Distribution and Materials Management which will support an automated sales cycle.

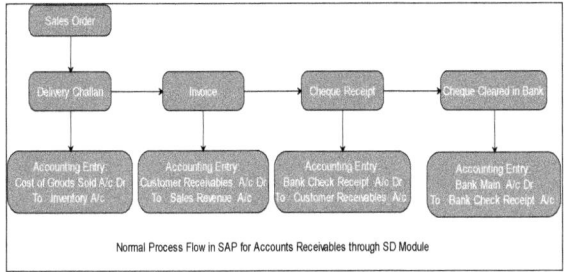

Normal Process Flow in SAP for Accounts Receivables through SD Module

10.1.3. Process Flow for Accounts Receivables through Sales:

Normal process flow (SIPOC) of Accounts Receivables is mapped as under:

Supplier	Input	Process	Output	Customer
Sales department	-Customer Purchase Ord -Approved Sales Order -Customer confirmation for delivery -Availability of finished goods	-Delivery note will be generated in ERP based on which a picking list is generated by the system -Prepare Despatch Clearance after checking all parameters by Sales department - A financial entry is also automatically generated which debits the Cost of Goods Sold account and credits the inventory account.	Approved Delivery note	Send to customer
		Check whether customer is a channel partner, modern trade or non-government retail customer		
		Check whether Despatch clearance and		

		receivables exceed credit limit		
		-Prepare invoice based on all inputs received and attach documents with invoice - This process also results in financial document creation, which debits the customer and credits revenue account.	Invoice	Send to customer
Customer	Cheque receipt / bank transfer	When the cheque is received from the customer, the same is entered into the system along with clearing of outstanding.	Cheque receipt voucher -Updated Customer statement of account	-Accounts department -Receipted acknowledgement of payment to customer
		A deposit slip format will be generated for the same. The same transaction in ERP will also post into the bank cheque receipt sub account and clear the customer outstanding. Any interest on overdue received from the customer is also accounted for here	Deposit slip	Accounts Department
	Bank Statement	Generate bank reconciliation statement. This clears all the open items in the bank cheque receipt sub account and debits the main bank account	Bank Reconciliation statement	Accounts Department

10.1.4. Scheme of entries are as under:

Scheme of entries	

	a) At the time of Delivery challan
	    Dr. Cost of Goods Sold a/c
	    Cr. Inventory a/c
	
	b) At the time of Invoice generation
	    Dr. Customer a/c (AR)
	    Cr. Revenue/Sales a/c
	    Cr. Sales Tax Payable a/c
	
	c) At the time of Receipt of Payment from Customer
	    Dr. Bank Check Receipt Sub a/c
	    Cr. Customer a/c
	
	d) At the time of Check Clearing & Generating BRS
	    Dr. Bank Main a/c
	    Cr. Bank Check Receipt Sub a/c

10.2. Sales invoicing posting to Accounts

The billing document is a document which supports the creation of customer invoices, credit or debit memos, and the recording of the financial impact of these transactions in the general ledger. The Billing Document or Sales Invoices created in Sales & Distribution Module will automatically create an Accounting Document. The Accounts Department shall as part of the closing process verify that the policies in respect of Revenue recognitions have been followed for the Sales Invoices. The Billing Document and the Delivery Documents in respect of the Sales Invoices which do not meet the Revenue recognition criteria will be cancelled / reversed.

As a result of the creation of a billing document, integration to the Financial Accounting module occurs with the automatic creation of an accounting document containing the following accounting entries:

- Debit to the customer account (sub-ledger) and the appropriate general ledger reconciliation account assigned to it
- Credit to the appropriate general ledger revenue account
- Debit to Commission account (if applicable)
- Credit to Accrual commission account (if applicable)
- Debit to Discount account (if applicable)

The Payment Term maintained in the Sales Area segment of the Customer should be the same as in the Accounting Document. Consequently no changes in the Payment Term will be allowed while

creating the Sales Order or Billing Document. A change in the Payment Terms in the Sales Order would be considered as a credit-sensitive field for the purpose of Credit Management.

The following are the identified scenarios for billing from ERP System:

01	Route Sales Processing
02	Product Sales Processing
03	Consignment Sales Processing
04	Sample Sales Processing
05	Free of Charge / Replacement Order Processing
06	Sales Returns Processing
07	Export Sales Process
08	Scrap Sales

10.3. Route sales processing (For FMCG business)

Route Sales involves selling of product under the entity brand to various types of end customers viz. Retailers, Distributors, Parlours, institutions.

This has been identified as a separate process and covered in Selling and distribution module.

The financial implication / accounting entries passed during the process are given below:

Scheme of entries	a) At the time of Goods Issue at Delivering Plant
	    Dr. – Cost of Goods Sold A/c
	    Cr. – Finished Goods Inventory A/c
	
	b) At the time of Invoice generation
	    Dr. – Customer A/c (AR)
	    Cr. – Sales Revenue A/c
	    Cr. – VAT Payable A/c
	
	c) Transportation Cost (Secondary)
	    Dr. – Outward Freight A/c (Secondary - product)
	    Cr. – Outward Freight Payable A/c (secondary – product)
	
	d) Cash Receipt
	    Dr. – Cash / Bank Receipt Sub Account A/c

	Cr. – Customer A/c (AR)

10.4. Product sales processing

Product sales of the entity comprise a direct type of sales to consignee agents and direct customers handled through sales / marketing persons.

This has been identified as a separate process and covered in Selling and distribution module.

The financial implication / accounting entries passed during the process are given below:

Scheme of entries	a) *At the time of Goods Issue at Delivering Plant* Dr. – Cost of Goods Sold A/c Cr. – Finished Goods Inventory A/c b) *At the time of Invoice generation* Dr. – Customer A/c (AR) Cr. – Sales Revenue A/c Cr. – VAT Payable A/c Cr. – Freight Payable A/c c) *Cash / Cheque Receipt* Dr. – Cash / Bank Receipt Sub Account A/c Cr. – Customer A/c (AR)

10.5. Consignment sales processing

Consignment sales process starts with the movement of goods to the customer place as an inventory movement. This initial movement has no sales impact with respect to accounting. This is termed an inventory movement. The customer primarily acts as a stockiest for the company. As and when the stock is being sold out, the company is notified by the consignment agent about the transaction through a document – "Sale Patti".

This forms the basis for sale process to be initiated from the company's perspective. Based on the information provided in the Sale Patti, the company books sale order and invoices the same to the Consignment agent. Payment is received and the invoice is settled off. Forms (Form – H) collected from the consignment customers' needs to be maintained. At any point of time, the

stock held by the consignment agent may be returned to the company. This is again to be tracked as an inventory transfer and not as return sales.

This has been identified as a separate process and covered in Selling and distribution module. The financial implication / accounting entries passed during the process are given below:

Scheme of entries

Based on the 'Sale Patti' received, a Consignment Issue sales order to be created in SAP system, when the customer removes consignment stock to use or sell.

Delivery document has to be created with reference to the sales order. System will identify the stock at the consignment location and delivery items to be maintained with the details of the batch and quantities. On post goods issue the relevant quantity to be deducted from both the customer's special stock and to the entity's own total valuated stock.

Dr. – Cost of Goods Sold A/c

Cr. – Finished Goods Inventory A/c

The transaction to be relevant for pricing since the goods now becomes the property of the customer. After creation of delivery, the invoice will be created with reference to the delivery only. The data of delivery / goods issue will be copied into Invoice (Bill) document from delivery document. New Pricing and taxes to be carried out based on the requirements. While saving the Invoice accounting postings to be done automatically.

Dr. – Customer A/c (AR)

Cr. – Sales Revenue A/c

Cr. – VAT Payable A/c

Cr. – Freight Payable A/c

When Cash / Cheque Receipt against the Sales Revenue the following accounting entry will be generated:

Dr. – Cash / Bank Receipt Sub Account A/c

Cr. – Customer A/c (AR)

10.6. Sample sales processing

Sometimes samples may be sent across to Institutions. Institutions may check for various factors based on the sample item sent including quality etc. The quantity sent is accounted as samples and are not reflected in account books. If not accounted in account books the same will reflect in stock

registers as samples. The consignment is passed through regular quality checks before being delivered. Stock is delivered against Performa Invoice/Delivery Challan, which is acknowledged by the customer.

- Sample sales orders should be processed with one-time customer codes specific to sales offices.
- While sending trade samples to the customer, we need to have two options to post those values into accounting i.e. 1. Cost of goods sold or 2.Sales promotion (Visibility, Distribution expansion, Trade budget)

This has been identified as a separate process and covered in Selling and distribution module. The financial implication / accounting entries passed during the process are given below:

Flow of Journal entries in ERP:

Dr. – Cost of Goods Sold A/c

Cr. – Finished Goods Inventory A/c

10.7. Free of charge / replacement sale processing

Whenever the product cannot be salvaged or it is not desirable to take back the product, the plant is advised to destroy the product.

This has been identified as a separate process and covered in Selling and distribution module. The financial implication / accounting entries passed during the process are given below:

Scheme of entries	*At the time of GR* Dr. FG Inventory A/c Cr. Finished goods change a/c *At the time of GI* Dr. Cost of Goods Sold A/c Cr. FG Inventory A/c *For scrap of material* Dr. Loss on scrapped material a/c Cr. FG Inventory a/c

10.8. Sales returns processing

When the goods are returned by the customer the same are checked for its condition as to whether they are re-saleable or not. If yes, then a GR entry is done for this material quantity updating the FI records in Inventory a/c.

A credit note is raised in the name of customer for the value of sales quantity returned & simultaneously reversing the Sales revenue a/c.

In case the material is not found to be in good condition, it is assessed whether that material has expired or damaged. In case, the material is not re-workable then it is scrapped with proper sanctions & losses booked in the respective P & L a/c.

SIPOC diagram on Sales return process is as under:

Supplier	Input	Process	Output	Customer
Customer	-Intimation received from customer on email for sales return	Understand the reasons for decision of customer to return and the goods purchased		
		Discuss with customer and resolve issues if any		
		If not initiate return process on approval from HOD		
		Inform customers and communicate refundable amount		
		Generate Return sales order and get it approved by HOD	Return sales order	
		Finalise the amount to be refunded to customers after making necessary tax adjustments in consultation with the user department		
		Create pick-up request as per logistics management process		
		Raise Gate entry and GRN on quality check related to material received on return	Goods Receipt Note	
		Intimate GRN no.	Credit Note	

		and amount and raise Credit Note to customers for sales return		
		Finance and Accounts to refund amount to customer through NEFT / RTGS / cheque	Payment voucher and transaction reference for NEFT/ RTGS	Customer

Where the material is partly damaged & can be processed again, it is taken back into FG stocks as a separate return type. This material can further be issued to process order, packing order or any other re-work job necessary to make the goods re-saleable.

This has been identified as a separate process and covered in Selling and distribution module. The financial implication / accounting entries passed during the process are given below:

Scheme of entries	At the time of GR for re-saleable material
	Dr. FG inventory a/c
	Cr. Finished goods change a/c
	At the time of raising the Credit note.
	Dr. Revenue / Expense a/c
	Dr. Sales Tax Payable (if less than 6 months)
	Cr. Customer a/c
	For scrap of material
	Dr. Loss on scrapped material a/c
	Cr. FG Inventory a/c
	Upon issue of returned material to process / packing order (through return type material issue)
	Dr. Material consumption a/c
	Cr. Material Inventory a/c

10.9. Export sales processing

Based on the purchase order received from the export customer towards product requirements, an Export Sales Order has to be created in the system with the customer & product details.

While creating the sale order, system will propose the prices, discounts, freight & taxes based on material, price group / customer group etc. In some cases, details of price, Letter of credit, exchange rates have to be entered manually

Scheme of entries	a) At the time of Delivery challan

	Dr. Finished goods change a/c Cr. FG Inventory a/c b) *At the time of Invoice generation* Dr. Customer a/c (AR) Cr. Revenue/Sales a/c

10.10. Scrap sales processing

At predetermined intervals, as the scrap material accumulates, the party is intimated.

Based on the net weight of the scrap, Delivery Challan cum Invoice is raised to the party.

This has been identified as a separate process and covered in Selling and distribution module. The financial implication / accounting entries passed during the process are given below:

Scheme of entries	a) *At the time of Goods Issue at Delivering Plant* Dr. – COGS (SCRAP) A/c Cr. – Scrap Inventory A/c b) *At the time of Invoice Generation* Dr. – Customer A/c Cr. – Other Revenue A/c

10.11. Credit memo processing

Credit memo will be created when a customer is over-billed. It adjusts previous entries that were overstated. Therefore, posting a credit memo always leads to a credit posting on the customer account. A credit memo will only be prepared if the corresponding invoice was created and sent out to the customer. A credit memo will not be created if the invoice has not been sent to the customer, as user is able to cancel the original invoice, reversing the relevant G/ L entries and create a new invoice.

For credit memo with reference to AR invoice, the credit memo must be created with reference to the original invoice in order to correctly reflect customer outstanding balance. This is done by updating "Invoice Reference" field during the creation of the credit memo.

10.12. Credit Management

The entity will define Credit Limits for each Customer to minimize its Credit risks. Automatic Credit check will be applied for each Customer at the point of creation of Sales Order.

In case a new Sales Order leads to the credit limit being exceeded for the Customer, a warning message will be issued and the Sales Order will be blocked for further process until it is released by concern authority. However, the Sales Order will be blocked for delivery till it is released by the Treasury function.

Also if the Payment Term in the Sales Order is different from the Payment Term maintained in the Sales Area Customer Master Data, the Sales Order would be automatically blocked for delivery.

10.13. Customer incoming payment

This function allows user to record receipts from customers in the system and adjust them against invoices and debit memos. In the case of payments received against invoices, the invoices can be adjusted against the payments. In case the payment is not with reference to specific Invoices, the receipt is recorded as an "On Account" receipts, and linked to one or more invoices later or the oldest invoice is adjusted. Invoices, advances and debit memos can be settled to the extent of the outstanding amount. Incoming payment can be booked partially. Invoices, advances and debit memos can be partially settled.

In case the receipt currency is not the local currency, the same is converted into local currency for accounting purposes. However, the receipt details are stored in the entered currency but can be viewed in local and foreign currency as and when required.

10.14. AR Process steps are as under:

Main process	Description	Process in ERP
1. General	Reconciliation GL & customer master will be created	Creation of GL accounts (sundry debtors, etc.,)
		Creation of customer master (in sync with SD)
		Customer invoice posting (in case of FI customers)

Main process	Description	Process in ERP
		View the customer accounts
		Incoming payment and clearing the customer invoice
2. Advance Payment:	When a customer paid any down payment before sending the goods it will be collected in a special GL account by using Special GL indicator and after goods are received it will be cleared.	Creation of Special GL accounts for advance payments
		Advance receipt
		Invoice posting (in case of FI customers)
		Transfer of advance from special GL to normal account by clearing
		Clearing of normal item
3. Bills of Exchange	In the cases of payments by LC (bills of exchange) it will be recorded into SAP system and can be checked periodically.	Creation of Special GL accounts for bills of exchanges
		Invoice posting
		Receipt of BOE
		Discounting with the bank
		Party wise due list
		Reverse Contingent liability
4. Customer Payments	Any payments from customer can be checked with the down payments, bills of exchange and pending invoices and cleared.	Manual Incoming Payments

Main process	Description	Process in ERP
5. Customer account analysis	By using SAP we can see the line items / balances of Customers and also change the layout of display by adding any necessary things like cost center etc., into display	Customer line item analysis
		Customer balance analysis.
6. Account Clearing	After the outgoing payment has been posted all Customer invoices can be cleared either age wise or one by one.	Manual Clearing

10.15. Trade Receivable: Financial Control over Financial Reporting

Activities	Risk environment	Preventive control	Detective control	Monitoring control Y/N/NA
Accounts receivable Recording of sales	*Core Risks and Controls* Sales and trade receivables are recorded: <ul><li>That do not relate to valid sales/shipments</li><li>At the incorrect amount</li><li>In the incorrect period.</li></ul>	Invoices are generated only upon matching the purchase order and shipping documents, completing a 3-way match. The 3-way match process is performed within an ERP system that identifies the purchase order and shipping document and generates an invoice within established limits. Proof of delivery is provided by third-party shippers for all		

		shipments made. The proof of delivery is required in order for the invoice to be generated.	
Recording of sales	Side agreements or credit memos exist that are not known to accounting.		Representations are received on a quarterly basis from sales personnel and management regarding the existence of customer side agreements or credit memos not yet communicated to accounting. Credit notes issued after period-end are verified by finance manager for association with side agreements and proper accounting	
Recording of sales	Sales are recorded prior to all necessary revenue recognition criteria being met.	Sales agreements are reviewed by personnel with requisite experience to determine if the revenue recognition criteria are met		
Recording of sales	Goods are shipped to customers and no invoice is generated and recorded.		Shipments of goods to customers are logged. The log is used to determine that all shipments are invoiced and that all invoices are recorded. Management reviews relevant sales, trade receivables, costs of sales, and inventory reports related to sales order entry, shipping/dispatch, and invoicing; significant, unusual relationships are monitored and acted upon.	
Recording of Sales	Trade receivables stated in the general ledger does not		Reconciliation is performed between trade receivables in	

	reconcile to the trade receivables records and/or the reconciliation contains invalid items.		the general ledger and trade receivables subsidiary ledger amounts, and is then reviewed by finance manager. Any reconciling items are reviewed and addressed on a timely basis.	
Provision for doubtful trade receivables	Inappropriate methodology for calculating the provision for doubtful trade receivables could result in misstated net receivables and bad debt expense.		Management reviews the provision for doubtful trade receivables methodology, assumptions, and underlying calculation for appropriateness on a periodic basis.	
Provision for doubtful trade receivables	Provision for doubtful trade receivables calculation is based on inaccurate receivables aging data.	The ERP system ages the trade receivables based on the parameters established within the ERP system and this computer-generated information is used in the calculation of the provision for doubtful trade receivables		
Provision for doubtful trade receivables	Receivables included in the provision for doubtful trade receivables calculation: • Do not exist or the entity no longer has rights to such receivables • Do not include all receivables.	The ERP system ages the trade receivables based on the parameters established within the ERP system and this computer-generated information is used in the calculation of the provision for doubtful trade receivables	Finance Manager reviews the provision for doubtful trade receivables methodology, assumptions, and underlying calculation for appropriateness on a periodic basis	
Sales Returns and Credit Memos	Credit notes are issued or committed to the customer but not recorded.		All sales returns are logged when goods received. Return details per the log are compared to credit notes issued and recorded to determine that credit notes are issued in accordance with company policy	

			Representations from operations and sales personnel are obtained indicating that no verbal or unrecorded credit memos exist that have not been reported to finance manager	
Sales Returns and Credit Memos	Credit notes are not issued and recorded for goods returned by customers.		All sales returns are logged when received. Sales return details per the log are compared to credit notes issued to determine that credit notes are issued in accordance with company policy	
Sales Returns and Credit Memos	Credit notes are issued to customers without the receipt of returned goods.	All sales returns are logged when received and the returned goods log automatically generates the credit notes.	All sales returns are logged when received. Credit notes issued are compared to the return log to determine that credits issued are for valid returns	
Sales Returns and Credit Memos	Credit notes are issued for the incorrect amount.	Credit notes are generated by the ERP system. Credit pricing information is obtained from the original sales invoice ERP system validates the amount of the issued credit note against the original invoice. Credit notes issued in excess of the original invoice are flagged and must be reviewed and approved by finance manager. Policy requires that credit notes are not issued in amounts in excess of the original invoice amount; compliance with this policy is monitored by finance manager.		

Sales Returns and Credit Memos	Sales returns reserves are not accurately estimated as a result of: • An inappropriate methodology • Significant assumptions [*specify assumptions*] being inappropriate, lacking sufficient basis, or lacking sufficient support.	Sales return methodology, significant assumptions, and supporting documentation are reviewed by top management prior to recording the journal entry	Management performs a retrospective review supporting the appropriateness of the methodology and significant assumptions. Sales returns are analysed on a monthly basis and compared to budget. Explanations are obtained for any significant variances and differences. The analysis is reviewed by senior management and taken into consideration when estimating the sales return reserve	
Sales Returns and Credit Memos	Sales return transactions occurring around period-end are not recorded in the correct period.		Returned goods received and credit memos issued at, before, or after the end of an accounting period are scrutinised by accounting personnel and/or reconciled to make certain the sales return is recorded in the appropriate accounting period. Manual sales return entries made to the general ledger are reviewed and approved by management for proper inclusion in the correct accounting period	
Cash/bank Receipts	Cash/bank receipts: • Have been recorded (when there are non-existent cash receipts), or have improperly been recorded • Have not been recorded/applied • Are not accurately	On a daily basis, cash/bank receipts recorded to the general ledger are agreed to bank deposit slips by accounting personnel. Discrepancies are investigated and resolved.	Bank statements are reconciled to the general ledger regularly and differences are investigated and resolved on a timely basis.	

	recorded.			
	Other Possible Risks and Controls			
Recording of Sales	Invoices are issued and recorded for shipments to non-customer offsite locations.	The ERP system only permits invoices to be issued for shipments to valid customer locations based on information contained in the customer master file	The customer master file is reviewed for ongoing relevance	
Recording of Sales	Invoices are generated and sales recorded for shipments to fictitious customers.	Invoices can only be generated for customers that exist in the customer master file. Access to add, change, or delete information in the customer master file is limited to approved personnel	The customer master file generates an exception report listing new and deleted customers, shipping address changes, etc., and the report is reviewed by the credit manager and controller Customer master file data is periodically reviewed by management for accuracy and ongoing pertinence	
Recording of Sales	Invoices are generated and recorded for sales of consigned inventory based on incorrect data provided to the entity by the consignee.		Consigned inventory is confirmed and confirmations are reconciled to inventory records and the general ledger. Randomly, consigned inventory is physically verified by company personnel Customers who receive consigned goods are specifically identified as consignment customers in the ERP customer master file. The ERP system generates a report of invoices to consignment customers that is scrutinised by management for proper revenue recognition	
Recording of	Sales and trade	Management	Sales transactions,	

Sales	receivables are inappropriately presented (either over- or understated) from the misapplication of GAAP when acting as a principal or agent in a revenue transaction.	prepares an analysis of the terms and conditions of significant sale transactions, including reference to the appropriate accounting framework and principles. This analysis is reviewed and approved by senior management	volumes, and values are analysed on a monthly basis and compared to budget. Explanations are obtained for any significant variances and differences. The analysis is reviewed by senior management	
Recording of Sales	Foreign sales and trade receivables are restated at the incorrect foreign exchange rate.	Foreign sales and trade receivables restatement is prepared by staff personnel and reviewed/approved by finance manager. Analysis reviewed/approved by finance manager includes supporting documentation for the translation rate calculation ERP system calculates the foreign sales and trade receivables restatement rate, which is independently verified by finance manager		
Recording of Sales	Inventory held on consignment and subsequently sold has not been invoiced and recorded as a sale and receivable		Consigned inventory is confirmed and confirmations are reconciled to inventory records and the general ledger. Randomly, consigned inventory is physically verified by company personnel Inventory consignee (third party) provides periodic reporting of consigned inventory held. These reports are reviewed and reconciled to internal records and differences are	

			investigated.	
Provision for Doubtful Trade receivables	Sales are made to customers with poor credit, which may affect revenue recognition criteria being met and the ultimate write-off of uncollectible trade receivables.	Credit limits are established by the credit manager based on the customer's ability to pay and past collection results, and are reviewed on a regular basis		
Provision for Doubtful Trade receivables	Invoices are generated in excess, individually or in the aggregate, of customer credit limits, which may affect revenue recognition criteria being met and the ultimate write-off of uncollectible trade receivables.	ERP system suspends purchase orders that individually or aggregately exceed customer credit limits. Approval by the credit manager is required prior to the ERP system recording the purchase order.		
Provision for Doubtful Trade receivables	Provision for doubtful trade receivables is insufficient in reserving for both unknown but historically predictable bad debt and specific known bad debt.		Management reviews the provision for doubtful trade receivables methodology, assumptions, and underlying calculation for appropriateness on a periodic basis.	
Provision for Doubtful Trade receivables	Management does not appropriately consider economic, industry, or customer financial considerations in the calculation of provision for doubtful trade receivables.	Management reviews the assumptions utilised in calculating the provision to assess and conclude whether the assumptions take into consideration the current economic environment, specific customer financial conditions, regulatory changes, industry issues, etc. Based on their review, management approves the provision for		

		doubtful trade receivables		
Provision for Doubtful Trade receivables	Provision for doubtful trade receivables is overstated due to possible management bias concerning specific customer reserves.	Credit manager reviews aged trade receivables and documentation of collection activities performed by the credit personnel supporting the specific reserve and approves the recorded specific reserves		
Write-off of Uncollectible trade receivables and adjustments to the Provision for Doubtful debts Account	Trade receivables are incorrectly written off.	Management reviews and approves write-offs of trade receivables.		
Write-off of Uncollectible trade receivables and adjustments to the Provision for Doubtful debts Account	Receivables write-offs using the direct write-off method are not authorised in accordance with the established policy and, as a result, may be invalid.		Trade receivables write-offs are performed by accounting personnel in accordance with the write-off policy. Management reviews trade receivables write-offs for compliance with the established policy.	
Recoveries of Trade receivable	Recoveries of trade receivables previously written off are improperly recorded in the Statement of Profit and Loss	Management reviews recoveries of trade receivables previously written off. Journal entries made to record trade receivables recoveries are reviewed and approved by management prior to recording.		
Sales Returns and Credit Notes	Credit notes are issued at an amount in excess of the original invoice.	Policy requires that credit notes are not issued in amounts in excess of the original invoice amount;	ERP system validates the amount of the issued credit note against the original invoice and creates an	

		compliance with this policy is monitored by management via review of credit notes prior to issuance.	exception report for credit notes in excess of the original invoices. Management reviews, then approves or corrects, items on the exception report based on documentation and support provided	
Sales Returns and Credit Notes	For sales transactions that trigger promotional allowances or volume rebates, the promotional allowance or volume rebate is not appropriately recorded.	For sales transactions that trigger promotional allowances or volume discounts, the calculation for promotional allowances and volume rebates and supporting documentation are reviewed by management prior to recording the journal entry	For customers receiving promotional allowances or volume discounts, management periodically analyses goods returned that may indicate inappropriate recording of promotional allowances or volume discounts. Promotional allowances and volume discounts are analysed on a monthly basis and compared to budget. Explanations are obtained for any significant variances and differences. The analysis is reviewed by senior management	
Sales Returns and Credit Memos	Provision for promotional allowances or volume discounts are not accurately estimated as a result of: • An inappropriate methodology • Significant assumptions [specify assumptions] being inappropriate, lacking sufficient basis, or lacking sufficient support	The methodology for accruing for promotional allowances/volume discounts, significant assumptions used, and supporting documentation are reviewed by management prior to recording the journal entry.	Management performs a retrospective review supporting the appropriateness of the methodology and significant assumptions. Promotional allowances and volume discounts are analysed on a monthly basis and compared to budget. Explanations are obtained for any significant variances and differences. The analysis is reviewed by senior management and taken into	

		consideration when estimating the reserve for promotional allowances and rebates	
Other Receivables	Receivables recorded for insurance recoveries are recorded: • When the entity does not have the right to the insurance proceeds or • At an inappropriate amount as the insurance company's creditworthiness was not appropriately considered.	Management periodically evaluates insurance receivable by obtaining the insurance contracts and determining whether the insurance receivable recorded is appropriate based on the terms of the insurance contract. Management evaluates the creditworthiness of the insurance company in determining the value of the insurance receivable recorded.	

10.16. Trade Receivable: Risk and System controls

Risks	System controls
1. Customers are not properly evaluated when sales are made. Appropriate credit limits are not established.	• **Accounts Receivable**. The system can be configured to require entry of customer credit limits when the customer is added to the system. The Credit Status Report flags customer variances (balance versus credit limit). Use Job Scheduler (Batch Stream Processing) to generate this report on a regular basis. • **Credit Management Portal** runs in tandem with the Credit Managers' Workbench to scrutinize customer data and automatically route possible problem accounts for credit reviews by appropriate personnel. • **Credit Management Portal** lets sales and other customer service personnel access customer balances and payment history real-time via a secure website. This information can also be made available via web services.
2. Billings or invoices are not properly authorized before being sent to customers.	• **Invoicing**. Invoices can be placed on hold and routed for approval before being released for printing.
3. Billings or invoices sent to customers are not	• **Invoicing.** Problems may arise because invoices do not reflect pricing agreed on with customers. DI addresses this issue by providing a sophisticated deal module that lets the user define

complete and accurate.	pricing for a given customer as of a certain date. Also, invoices can be routed for approval prior to printing.
4. Billings or invoices are not sent to customers or not sent on a timely basis.	• Production of bills can be automated through either recurring or cycle billing modules.
5. Billings or invoices are not recorded in the accounts receivable system or are not recorded on a timely basis.	• **Invoicing** is fully integrated into the AR system. An invoice created in DI is automatically recorded in AR upon printing. The AR Zoom inquiry provides for drill-down to DI for auditing and reconciliation purposes. • **Accounts Receivable** allows for both batch and real-time interfaces. The real-time interface can be called as a web service and can be seamlessly integrated with an external billing system.
6. Amounts recorded in accounts receivable do not match invoice amounts.	• **Invoicing** is fully integrated into the AR system. An invoice created in DI is automatically recorded in AR upon printing. The AR Zoom inquiry provides for drill-down to DI for auditing and reconciliation purposes. • **Accounts Receivable** allows for both batch and real-time interfaces. The real-time interface can be called as a web service and can be seamlessly integrated with an external billing system.
7. Invoices are not linked to the appropriate AR account.	• **Accounts Receivable**. During item entry, control accounts default from a "transaction control" table and can be overridden by a default AR account on the customer master. Control accounts can also be dynamically created per customer. During cash application, cash discrepancies such as overpayments can be attributed to an individual invoice and pick up the control account of the invoice. • **Invoicing**. Invoices are automatically recorded in the AR using the appropriate default AR accounts, as described above.
8. Cash receipts or electronic fund transfer receipts on accounts receivable are not recorded completely and accurately.	• **Accounts Receivable** has a flexible lockbox interface compatible with the latest electronic standards. The interface maintains a register to check for duplicate feeds. The interface is integrated with the restart/recovery module to prevent record loss in the event of system failure. The system achieves a high cash to invoice "hit" rate as a result of its support for industry standard file formats, including EDI, and the application of user-defined "cash rules" (see below).
9. Amounts received from customers do not match the invoiced amounts.	• **Accounts Receivable** includes a sophisticated cash management module (This reconciles payments with outstanding items through various cash algorithms or through the adjusting of remittance feeds by user defined "cash rules". Further, adjustments credited against an invoice can be summarized on the fly, allowing matching when customers have subtracted disputed amounts from the invoice.
10. Credit memos are issued to customers without being properly authorized.	• **Accounts Receivable**. Credit memos can be placed on hold (stopped from use) in any of the cash processing modules. • **Credit Management Portal may be used** to route memos to appropriate personnel for review and possible release. Once released, credit memos can be applied against existing items or rebated through the disbursement module. • **Invoicing.** Credit memos can be routed for approval just as invoices are prior to printing.

11. Payments are issued to customers without proper authorization or are not recorded completely and accurately.	• **Accounts Receivable**. Payment batches can be created as work-in-progress files that are not processed until approved. Processed payments, including checks and electronic funds transfers, are automatically recorded in the AR system.
12. There is insufficient supporting documentation for sales and accounts receivable transactions.	• **Electronic Document Management system** may be used to archive invoice files as well as many documents produced by the AR system, including dunning notices and statements. These can be viewed on the web using **Credit Management Portal**.
13. Customers are late in remitting payments.	• **Accounts Receivable**. Customers may be notified through the dunning module or through the Credit Managers' Workbench integrated with **Credit Management Portal**.
14. Credit and collection processes are not established or are not enforced.	• **Accounts Receivable and Credit Management Portal**. Collection processes need to be automated through credit management workbench. Items or accounts past due can be routed via workflow to the appropriate personnel for resolution. Supervisors can monitor personnel performance via Credit Management Portal. Unresolved issues can be automatically escalated and alerts sent to supervisors to guarantee compliance with policies and insure efficiency.
15. Policies for resolving disputes with customers are not established or are not enforced.	• **Credit Management Portal** uses workflow to manage the dispute process through evaluation and approval. Disputes created through Credit Management Portal or the cash application process can be routed to the appropriate persons for resolution. Supervisors can monitor personnel performance via Credit Management Portal. Unresolved issues can be automatically escalated and alerts sent to supervisors to guarantee compliance with policies and insure efficiency.
16. Accounts receivable items are not recorded to the proper period.	• **Accounts Receivable**. The system automatically records all items in the appropriate period when the sales journals are posted. The period is determined based on the default posting date, which may or may not be overridden by the user, at the time the item is entered.
17. Receipts or disbursements are not recorded to the proper period.	• **Accounts Receivable**. The system automatically records all receipts and payments in the appropriate period when the cash journals are posted. The period is determined based on the default posting date, which may or may not be overridden by the user, at the time the receipt or payment is entered.
18. Accounts receivable detail is not properly Summarized / posted to the General Ledger.	• **Accounts Receivable**. Accounting distributions resulting from item entry, item changes, reversals, and so on, are generated automatically. These are posted to the proper period when sales journals are posted to the General Ledger. Several options are available for automatic summarization of postings to the GL. • **Accounts Receivable**. The AR Reconciliation Report is available to assist with reconciling AR with the General Ledger. Also, the General Ledger provides inquiries that allow the user to drill-down from GL balances to the originating AR transactions.

19. Receipts or disbursements are not properly summarized / posted to the General Ledger.	• **Accounts Receivable.** Accounting distributions resulting from cash processes are generated automatically. These are posted to the proper period when cash journals are posted to the General Ledger. Several options are available for automatic summarization of postings to the GL. • **Accounts Receivable.** The AR Reconciliation Report is available to assist with reconciling AR with the General Ledger. Also, the General Ledger provides inquiries that allow the user to drill-down from GL balances to the originating AR transactions.
20. Accounts Receivables duties are not effectively segregated to minimize the risk of fraud.	• **Accounts Receivable.** Each user is assigned a security level that determines which functions are available from the system menus. Review your user file and menu security setup to ensure that segregation of duties is being enforced. For example, this setup can prevent users who add customers or maintain customer information from entering items. • **Credit Management Portal.** Credit Management Portal users are restricted to specific functions based on the workgroups to which they are assigned. Within functions, actions are restricted by workgroup and company.
21. There is no audit trail of receivables or billing related activities.	• **Accounts Receivable.** The systems can be set up to automatically maintain audit trails for changes to transaction and master files. Information tracked includes the User ID, date and time that a specific transaction was entered or modified. The audit trail may also track additions or changes to customer information. • **Accounts Receivable.** Purge functions allow historic transaction data to be archived for possible future retrieval. • **Credit Management Portal.** The Workflow Activity Log tracks all the steps (who, what, when) in the process underpinning Credit Management Portal. Key documents (invoices, emails) may be attached to cases or workflow notes concerning collection issues. Conversations with customers may be summarized in workflow notes.
22. AR balances overstate the amounts that can be realistically collected from customers.	• **Accounts Receivable.** Use the Bad Debt Transfer and Write-off function to evaluate AR assets. Problem receivables can be transferred to bad debt reserves or written off.
23. AR balances of foreign subsidiaries are not adjusted to reflect currency fluctuations.	• **Accounts Receivable.** The system supports several methods for revaluation of assets to reflect currency fluctuations and is IFRS compliant. Accrual and reversal entries can be automatically generated for unrealized gains/losses.

10.17. Specimen Risk Map: Accounts Receivable

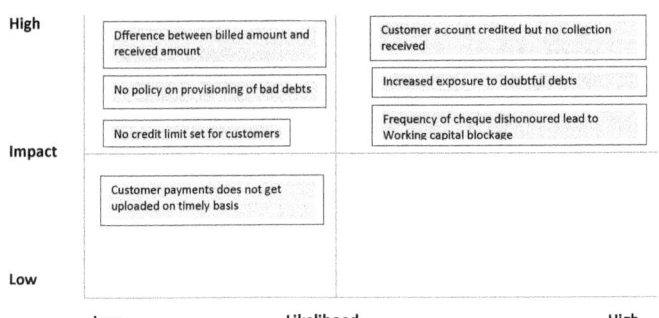

High	
Difference between billed amount and received amount	Customer account credited but no collection received
No policy on provisioning of bad debts	Increased exposure to doubtful debts
No credit limit set for customers	Frequency of cheque dishonoured lead to Working capital blockage

Impact

Customer payments does not get uploaded on timely basis

Low

| Low | Likelihood | High |

10.18: Receivables: Audit check list

Accounts Receivable Controls	Yes	No	N/A	Comments
1. Sales orders prenumbered				
2. Credit approval				
3. Credit and sales departments independent				
4. Control of back orders				
5. Sales order and sales invoice comparison				
6. Shipping invoices prenumbered				
7. Names and addresses on shipping invoice				
8. Review of sales invoices				
9. Control over returned merchandise				
10. Credit memoranda prenumbered				
11. Matching of credit memoranda and receiving reports				
12. Control over credit memoranda				
13. Control over scrap sales				
14. Control over sales to employees				
15. Control over C.O.D. sales				
16. Sales reconciled with cash receipts and A/R				
17. Sales reconciled with inventory change				
18. A/R statement to all customers				
19. Periodic preparation of aging schedule				
20. Control over collections of written-off receivables				
21. Control over A/R write off, e.g., proper authorization				
22. Control over A/R written off, i.e., review for possible collection				
23. Independence of sales, A/R, receipts, billing and shipping personnel				

Notes Receivable Controls	Yes	No	N/A	Comments
1. Proper authorization of notes				
2. Detailed records of notes				
3. Periodic detail to control comparison				
4. Periodic confirmation with makers				
5. Control over notes discounted				
6. Control over delinquent notes				
7. Physical safety of notes				
8. Periodic count of notes				
9. Control over collateral				
10. Control over revenue from notes				
11. Custodian of notes independent from cash and recordkeeping				

10.19. Risk Control Matrix summary: Accounts Receivable (specimen format)

Item	1	2
Mega process	Sales	Accounts Receivable
Process	Revenue	Accounts Receivable
Activity	Recognition of Revenue as per agreement	Statutory compliance of Accounts Receivable
Risk description	Inaccurate/unauthorized creation of Invoice	Statutory matters not complied
Control objective	To ensure that invoice is created as per agreement	To ensure statutory compliance is done for recovery of accounts receivables
Control environment – to be certified by the process owner	Invoicing is done based on the agreement on monthly basis considering a mark-up of 20% on total cost for the month by the Accountant- Finance and the same is reviewed by Manager finance.	Accountant prepares AR ageing for outstanding trade receivables and manager reviews to same to ensure the time limit for recovery of foreign currency invoices prescribed under statutory guidelines
Risk category		
Fraud risk – yes / no	Yes	No
Risk category – high / medium / low	High	Medium
Internal financial control over financial reporting –	Yes	No
IFC/IFCR Component	Prevention and detection of frauds and errors	Policies and procedures
Prevention / detection of frauds – yes / no	Yes	No
Key Control – yes / no	Yes	Yes
Control category		
Completeness		
Existence	xx	xx
Accuracy	xx	xx
Valuation		
Rights / obligation		xx
Presentation		
Manual / Automatic	Manual	Manual
Preventive / detective	Preventive	Preventive
Frequency of measurement	Monthly	Event based
Document if any	Invoice	AR Ageing
Prepared by (maker)	Accounts Executive	Account Executive
Checked by (checker)	Manager - Finance	Director/ Country head
System solution – ERP – Yes/no	No	No
Whether covered under SOP – Yes / no	Yes	Yes
Process design gap – Yes / no	No	No

Chapter 11: Cash & bank

11.1. Cash: Control Environment

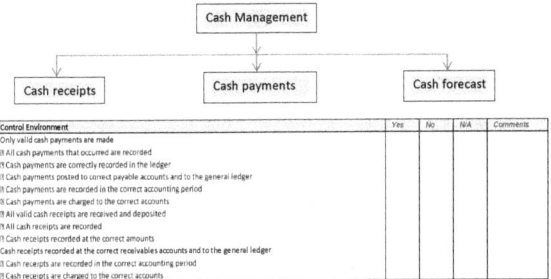

Control Environment	Yes	No	N/A	Comments
Only valid cash payments are made				
All cash payments that occurred are recorded				
Cash payments are correctly recorded in the ledger				
Cash payments posted to correct payable accounts and to the general ledger				
Cash payments are recorded in the correct accounting period				
Cash payments are charged to the correct accounts				
All valid cash receipts are received and deposited				
All cash receipts are recorded				
Cash receipts recorded at the correct amounts				
Cash receipts recorded at the correct receivables accounts and to the general ledger				
Cash receipts are recorded in the correct accounting period				
Cash receipts are charged to the correct accounts				

11.1.1. Control Environment: Delegation of Authority

Delegation of Authority					
Nature of transaction	Indenting authority	Processing authority	Checking authority	Approving Authority < Rs.2 lakhs	Approving authority >Rs.2 lakhs
Purchase orders & contracts	Production-GM Operations Office – Sr Manager HR	Purchase executive	Accounts Manager	Gen.Manager Operations	CMD
Projects – P&M	GM Operations	Purchase executive	Accounts Manager	Gen. Manager Operations	CMD
Projects – Construction	GM Operations	Purchase executive	Accounts Manager	Sr. Manager HR	CMD
Work orders	GM Operations	Purchase executive	Accounts Manager	Gen.Manager Operations	CMD
New appointments	Dept Head	Sr.Manager HR	Accounts Manager	Gen.Manager Operations < Rs.10k per month	CMD
Other approvals	Dept Head	Function heads	Accounts Manager	CMD	CMD
Write-offs related to assets, inventories, receivables	Dept Head	Function Heads	Accounts Manager	CMD	CMD
Petty cash - Prodn Petty cash - Others	GM Operations Sr. Manger HR	Function Heads	Accounts Manage	GM Operations < Rs.20 k	> Rs.20 k CMD

Delegation of Authority (Contd)

Nature of payment	Sanctioning authority	Paying authority	Cheque/NEFT/RTGS signing authority
Vendor payments	Gen. Manager Operations	Accounts Manager	CMD
Marketing expenses	GM Marketing	Accounts Manager	CMD
Statutory payments	Sr Manager HR	Accounts Manager	CMD
Employee payments	Sr. Manager HR	Accounts Manager	CMD
Other payments – cheque	GM Operations / Sr. Manager HR	Accounts Manager	CMD
Other payments – Cash (not more than Rs.20000)	GM Operations / Sr. Manager HR	Accounts Manager	CMD

11.2. Cash Payments

11.2.1. Vendor payments

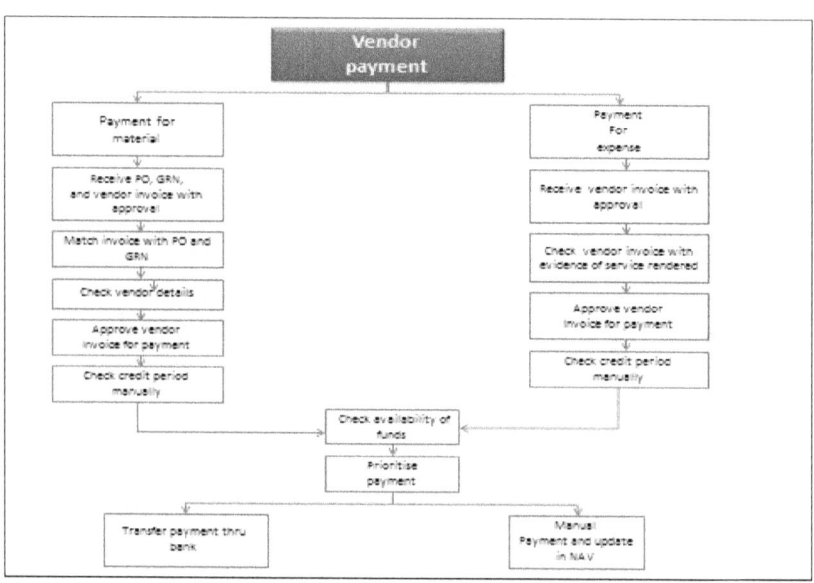

11.2.2. Statutory payments

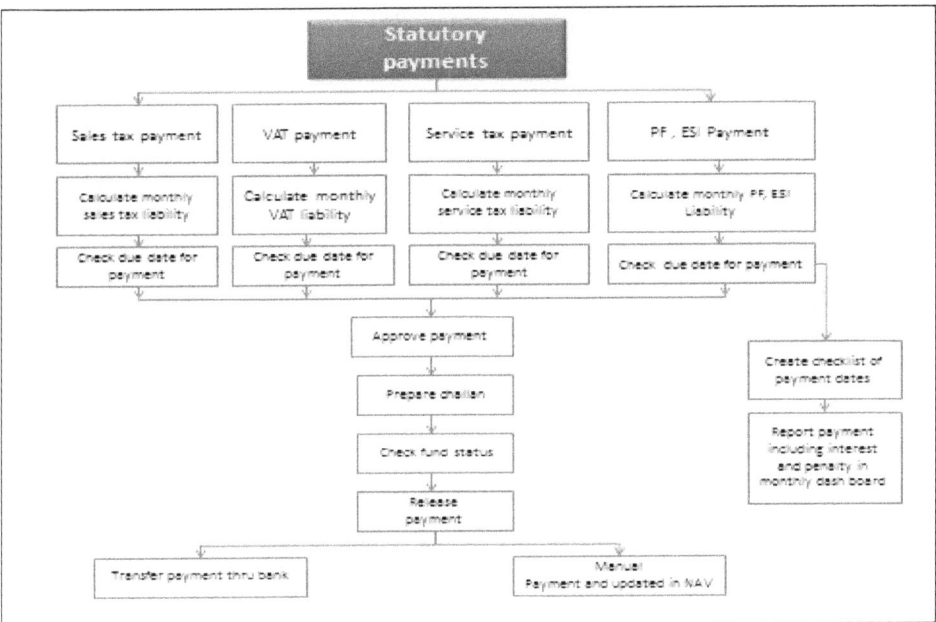

Statutory Payments

- ❑ PF , ESI, Professional tax
- ❑ Sales Tax (VAT / CST),
- ❑ Service Tax/work contract tax/cess
- ❑ TDS Payments

Section-193	: TDS on Interest on Securities
Section-194	: TDS on Dividends
Section-194A	: TDS on Interest other than Interest on securities
Section-194C	: TDS on payment to Contractors and sub - contractors
Section-194H	: TDS on Commission and Brokerage
Section-194I	: TDS on Rent
Section-194J	: TDS for Professional and Technical services

11.2.3. Employee payments

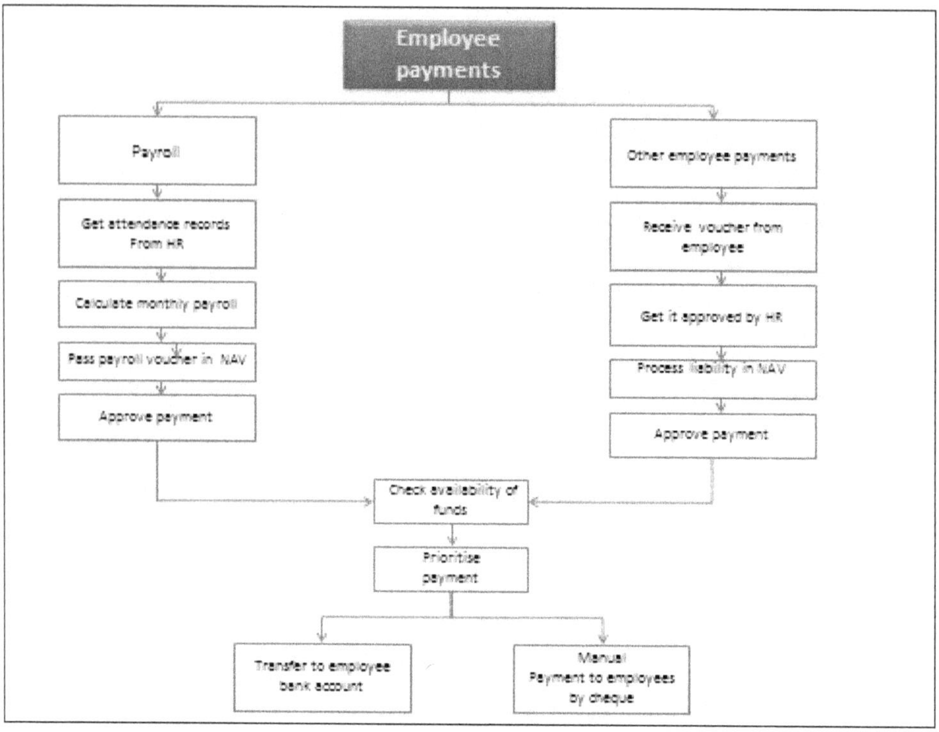

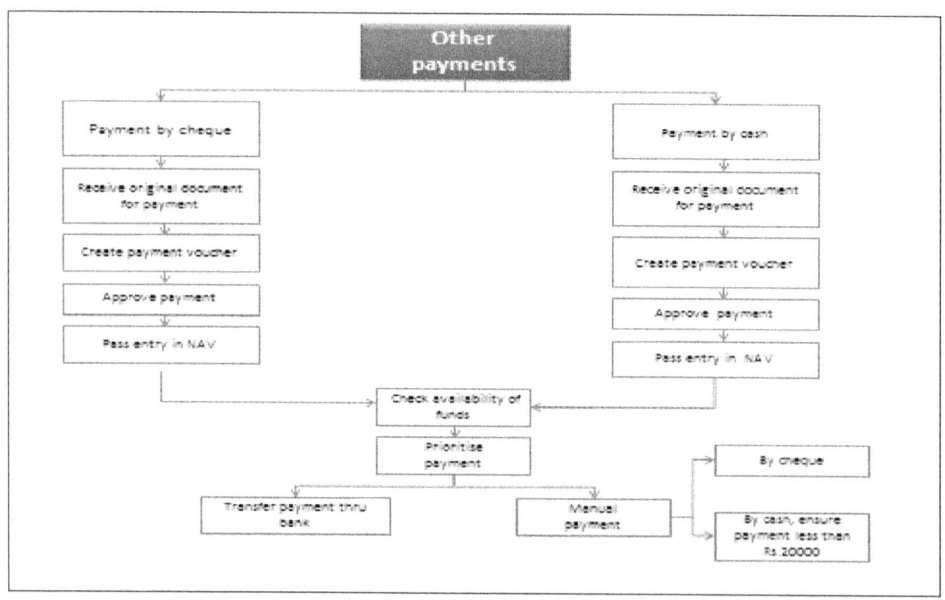

11.2.4. Other payments

11.2.5. Branch payments

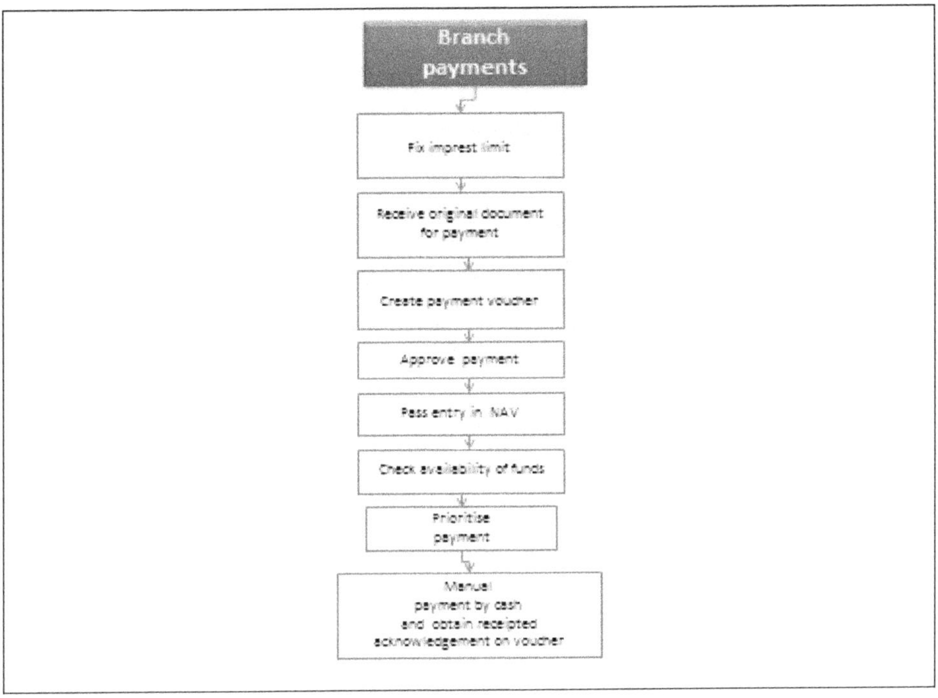

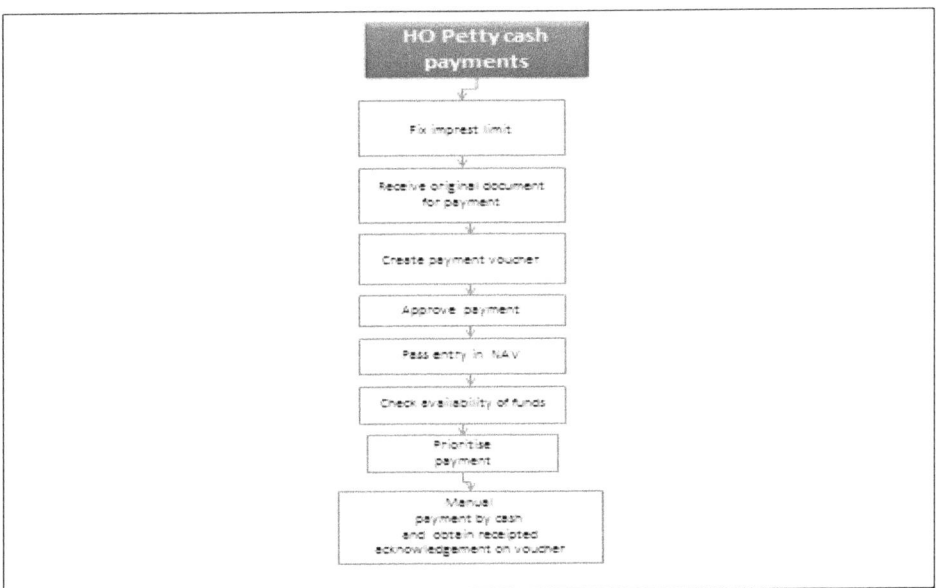

11.2.6. Petty cash payments

11.2.7. Suggested Payment procedure

Suggested Payment procedure

- All payments to be approved once a week, say every Friday of the week.
- Finance department to receive all documents related to payment by Friday of the previous week
- Finance department would need two working days to process the payments
- Finance department to check the availability of funds for payment during the week
- Finance department to finalise the list of vendors to be paid during the week
- Finance department to prepare a control sheet of payment (specimen format attached) and submit to CMD on Thursday
- Once the priority of payment is decided, Finance department to go ahead and process cheques.
- Finance department to get the cheques and attached documents in original and present to Outgrow personnel for pre-audit and vetting the documents
- Outgrow personnel will initial on the counterfoil of the cheque as a sign of pre-audit and also sign on the control sheet
- On the strength of the above, the cheques will be signed by CMD.

Payment control sheet

Sl no.	Description of vendor	Amount	Payment priority	Cheque no And date	Vetting by Finance	Initial by CMD

The above control sheet would be filled once a week for tracking of payment and submitted to CMD every Thursday

11.2.8. Financial Control over Financial Reporting

Activities	Risk environment	Preventive control	Detective control	Monitoring control Y/N/NA
Cash & bank Recording of Cash	*Core Risks and Controls* Cash receipts: • Have been recorded (when there are non-existent cash receipts), or have been improperly recorded • Have not been recorded/applied • Are not accurately recorded.	On a daily basis, cash receipts recorded to the general ledger are agreed to bank deposit slips by accounting personnel. Discrepancies are investigated and resolved	Bank statements are reconciled to the general ledger regularly and differences are investigated and resolved on a timely basis.	
Recording of Cash	Cash exists in bank accounts that have not been recorded in the general ledger.	Accounts personnel record bank account transactions to the general ledger on a daily basis; Accounts Manager (Management) reviews recorded transactions and cash position regularly for unusual activity and investigates and resolves issues on a timely basis	Bank statements are reconciled to the general ledger regularly and differences are investigated and resolved on a timely basis.	
Recording of Cash	Not all bank accounts have been recorded in the general ledger	New bank accounts are only opened through the direction and approval of Board of Directors. When new bank accounts are approved and opened, finance personnel create the general ledger account and prepare the journal entry to record the initial balance in the account. Management reviews and approves the new general ledger account and journal entry, including	Finance Manager with knowledge of existing and terminated bank accounts reviews the listing of bank accounts recorded in the general ledger and the related account transactions. Any unusual or omitted accounts are investigated and resolved on a timely basis	

		supporting documentation, before the journal entry is recorded.		
Recording of Cash	Cash stated in the general ledger does not reconcile to the cash records/bank statement, and/or the reconciliation contains invalid items.	Finance personnel analyse amounts recorded to cash suspense accounts and prepare journal entries to correct any unusual items. Management reviews and approves the journal entries and supporting analysis before the journal entry is recorded.	Bank statements are reconciled to the general ledger regularly and differences are investigated and resolved on a timely basis.	
Cash Disbursements	Acquisitions of fixed assets are not recorded	A 3-way match process is performed for fixed assets purchases that utilise the purchase order, receiving document, and vendor invoice. Once the 3-way match process is performed and the key terms of the purchase are agreed to supporting documentation, a transaction is posted in the fixed assets sub-ledger and general ledger to record the addition.	Bank statements are reconciled to the general ledger regularly and differences are investigated and resolved on a timely basis. Periodic counts of fixed assets are performed. Selections are made from the floor and reconciled to the fixed assets register, and any differences are investigated and resolved.	
Cash Disbursements	Cash/Bank payments are: • Not recorded • Recorded in the general ledger when no cash disbursement has been made • Recorded at the incorrect amount.	Cash/bank payments are generated through the ERP system. The ERP system automatically records the journal entry for cash/bank payments to the trade payables and cash/bank sub-ledgers. All manually generated cheques, including supporting documentation and the related journal entry, are reviewed	Bank statements are reconciled to the general ledger regularly and differences are investigated and resolved on a timely basis.	

		and approved by finance manager before the journal entry is recorded	
Cash Disbursements	Loan re- payments have been: • Made but are not recorded • Recorded but have not been paid • Recorded at an amount that differs from the actual amount paid.		Finance Manager with knowledge of loan obligation, payment schedules, and other terms and conditions, periodically reviews the transactions within the loan register. Discrepancies are investigated and resolved on a timely basis Bank statements are reconciled to the general ledger regularly and differences are investigated and resolved on a timely basis.
	Other Possible Risks and Controls		
Recording of Cash	Cash/bank balance denominated in foreign currencies is translated at the incorrect foreign exchange rate.	Cash/bank balance foreign currency translations are prepared by finance personnel and reviewed and approved by finance manager, who also reviews supporting documentation for the translation rate calculation ERP system calculates the cash/bank balance foreign currency translation rate, which is independently verified by finance manager	
Recording of Cash	Non-existent cash on hand has been recorded.	Daily bank deposits are made for additional cash on hand (i.e., cash on hand that exceeds the pre-determined limit).	On a periodic basis (and without forewarning) an employee independent of the employee(s) who handle cash performs a count of

			cash on hand.	
Recording of Cash	Cash on hand is not accurately recorded.		On a periodic basis (and without forewarning) an employee independent of the employee(s) who handle cash performs a count of cash on hand.	
Cash Disbursements	Electronic fund transfers and bank charges incurred are not recorded in the general ledger.	Finance personnel record bank account transactions to the general ledger on a daily basis; finance manager reviews recorded entries and cash position regularly for unusual activity and investigates and resolves issues on a timely basis	Bank statements are reconciled to the general ledger regularly and differences are investigated and resolved on a timely basis.	
Cash Disbursements	Loan re- payments are auto-deducted from the entity's bank account (or otherwise made) and not recorded in the general ledger.		Bank statements are reconciled to the general ledger regularly and differences are investigated and resolved on a timely basis. On a periodic basis, finance personnel perform a reconciliation of the loan register to the general ledger. Finance Manager reviews and approves the reconciliation and any reconciling items are reviewed and addressed on a timely basis	

11.2.9. Specimen Risk Map: Cash and bank

High

Incidence of unauthorised cash payments	Absence of proper Delegation of Authority on making payments
Absence of on-line real time Bank reconciliation statement	Exposure related to duplicate payments
	Exposure related to high incidence of cash payments to vendors beyond Rs.20000

Impact

Customer payments do not get uploaded on timely basis	

Low

| **Low** | **Likelihood** | **High** |

11.2.10. Audit Check-list

Cash Funds Controls	Yes	No	N/A	Comments
1. Imprest system				
2. Reasonable amount				
3. Completeness of vouchers				
4. Custodian responsible for fund				
5. Reimbursement checks to order of custodian				
6. Surprise audits				
7. No employee check cashing				
8. Physically secure				
9. Custodian has no access to cash receipts				
10. Custodian has no access to accounting records				

Cash Receipts Controls	Yes	No	N/A	Comments
1. Detail listing of mail receipts				
2. Restrictive endorsement of checks				
3. Special handling of postdated checks				
4. Daily deposit				
5. Cash custodians bonded				
6. Cash custodians apart from negotiable instruments				
7. Bank accounts properly authorized				
8. Handling of returned NSF items				
9. Comparison of duplicate deposit slips with cash book				
10. Comparison of duplicate deposit slips with detail A/R				
11. Banks instructed not to cash checks to company				
12. Control over cash from other sources				
13. Separation of cashier personnel from accounting duties				
14. Separation of cashier personnel from credit duties				
15. Use of cash registers				
16. Cash register tapes				
17. Numbered cash receipt tickets				
18. Outside salesmen cash control				
19. Daily reconciliation of cash collections				

Cash Disbursement Controls	Yes	No	N/A	Comments
1. Numbered checks				
2. Sufficient support for checks				
3. Limited authorization to sign checks				
4. No signing of blank checks				
5. All checks accounted for				
6. Detailed listing of checks				
7. Mutilation of voided checks				
8. Specific approval of unusually large checks				
9. Proper authorization of persons signing checks				
10. Control over signature machines				
11. Check listing compared to cash book				
12. Control over interbank transfers				
13. Prompt accounting for interbank transfers				
14. Checks not payable to cash				
15. Physical control of unused checks				
16. Cancellation of supporting documents				
17. Control over long outstanding checks				
18. Reconciliation of bank account				
19. Independence of person reconciling bank statement				
20. Bank statement direct to person reconciling				
21. No access to cash records or receipts by check signers				

11.3. Risk Control Matrix summary: Cash & Bank (specimen format)

Item	1	2	3	4
Mega process	Treasury	Treasury	Treasury	Treasury
Process	Cash & bank	Cash & bank	Cash & bank	Fund management
Activity	Bank Account Management	Bank Account Management	Bank Account Management	Raising of Funds

Risk description	Incorrect bank reconciliation statements	Unapproved opening/closing of bank accounts	Unauthorized changes in bank account signatories	Funds being raised without approval
Control objective	To provide assurance that bank balances are correctly reconciled on a timely basis.	To ensure approval is taken before opening/closing of bank accounts.	To ensure that authorized changes are made	To ensure that the fund has been raised as per our requirement and no excess fund has been kept.
Control environment – to be certified by the process owner	Bank reconciliation statement is prepared on a Daily basis by Accountant-Finance and same is reviewed by Manager Accounts.	1. Country head approval is taken by the company before opening/closing of any bank account. 2. Board resolution is also required before opening /closing of any bank account.	The change in bank signatories is carried out through resolution passed by the Board of Directors and communicating the same to the banks.	1. Accountant prepares the working capital requirement (i.e. fund requirement) basis the vendor payments to be made and same is reviewed by Manager Accounts. After review Manger Accounts shares this information Country Head and Global CEO.
Risk category				
Fraud risk – yes / no	Yes	No	Yes	No
Risk category – high / medium / low	Low	Low	Low	Medium
Internal financial control over financial reporting – yes / no	Yes	Yes	Yes	No
IFC/IFCR Component	Prevention and detection of frauds and errors	Policies and procedures	Accuracy and completeness of the accounting records	Policies and procedures
Prevention / detection of frauds – yes / no	Yes	No	No	No
Key Control – yes / no	Yes	Yes	Yes	Yes
Control category				
Completeness	xx		xx	
Existence	xx	xx	xx	xx
Accuracy	xx			
Valuation				
Rights / obligation				xx
Presentation				
Manual / Automatic	Manual	Manual	Manual	Manual
Preventive / detective	Detective	Preventive	Preventive	Preventive
Frequency of measurement	Monthly	Event based	Event based	Event based

Document if any	Cash Sheet, Bank reconciliation statements & Bank Statement	Board Resolution	Board Resolution	Board Resolution
Prepared by (maker)	Accounts Executive	Accounts Executive	Account Executive	Accounts Executive
Checked by (checker)	Manger – Finance	Board	Board	Manager - Finance
System solution – ERP – Yes/no	Yes	Yes	Yes	Yes
Whether covered under SOP – Yes / no	Yes	Yes	Yes	Yes
Process design gap – Yes / no	No	No	No	No

Chapter 12: Prepaid expenses, loans and advances

12.1. Control Environment

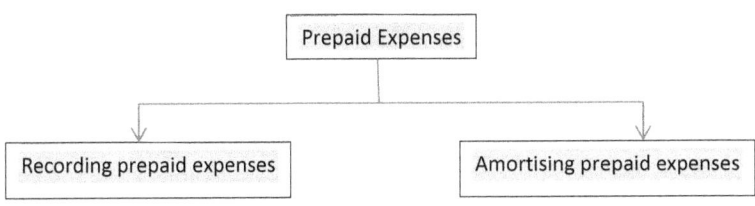

12.2. Financial Control over Financial Reporting

Activities	Risk environment	Preventive control	Detective control	Monitoring control Y/N/NA
Prepaid expenses Recording prepaid expenses	*Core Risks and Controls* Prepaid expenses are recorded for which no payment has been made.	Finance personnel prepare journal entries to record prepaid expenses, including supporting documentation. Management reviews the journal entry and supporting documentation to record prepayments prior to accounting personnel recording to the general ledger	Management with knowledge of prepaid expense activity reviews recorded prepaid expenses for proper recording, including verifying cash payment. Unusual items are investigated and corrected on a timely basis	
Recording Prepaid expenses	Expenditures where no future benefit exists to the entity are recorded as prepayments and deferred on the balance sheet.	Finance personnel prepare journal entries to record prepaid expenses, including supporting documentation. Management reviews the journal entries and supporting documentation to record prepayments prior to accounting personnel recording to the general ledger	Prepaid expenses and related other expense accounts are analysed on a monthly basis and compared to budget. Explanations are obtained for any significant variances and differences. The analysis is reviewed by senior management.	
Recording Prepaid expenses	Prepaid expenses are recorded at the incorrect amount.	Finance personnel prepare journal entries to record prepaid expenses, including supporting documentation. Management reviews the journal	Prepaid expenses and related other expense accounts are analysed on a monthly basis and compared to budget. Explanations are obtained for any significant variances	

		entries and supporting documentation to record prepayments prior to accounting personnel recording to the general ledger.	and differences. The analysis is reviewed by senior management.	
Recording Prepaid expenses	Expenditures where future benefits exist for the entity are incorrectly recorded as expenses instead of deferred.	Invoices for goods or services received are authorised and accompanied by appropriate supporting documentation. Management reviews supporting documentation and journal entries to record prepayments prior to accounting personnel recording to the general ledger. Finance personnel review the nature and type of expenses incurred, and codes the expense to the appropriate account. Management reviews the coding, supporting documentation, and journal entry before the journal entry is recorded.	Prepaid expenses and related other expense accounts are analysed on a monthly basis and compared to budget. Explanations are obtained for any significant variances and differences. The analysis is reviewed by senior management.	
Recording Prepaid Expenses	Prepaid expenses are not removed from the general ledger when a prepaid asset no longer exists.		Prepaid expenses and related other expense accounts are analysed on a monthly basis and compared to budget. Explanations are obtained for any significant variances and differences. The analysis is reviewed by senior management.	
Recording Prepaid Expenses	Prepaid expenses are incorrectly removed from the general ledger when a prepaid asset still exists.		Prepaid expenses and related other expense accounts are analysed on a monthly basis and compared to budget. Explanations	

			are obtained for any significant variances and differences. The analysis is reviewed by senior management Management with knowledge of service providers' transaction terms reviews prepaid expense general ledger activity for unusual adjusting entries. Discrepancies are investigated and resolved on a timely basis	
Recording Prepaid Expenses	Prepaid expenses stated in the general ledger do not reconcile to the prepaid expense records, and/or the reconciliation contains invalid items.		On a periodic basis, finance personnel reconcile prepaid expenses to the general ledger; management reviews the reconciliation, including supporting documentation. Unusual reconciling items are investigated and resolved on a timely basis	
Amortising Prepaid Expenses	Amortisation is recorded in advance of the time period associated with the prepaid expense.	Finance personnel prepare amortisation schedules for all recorded prepaid expenses, including preparing supporting documentation for the amortisation period and methodology. Management reviews and approves amortisation schedules for completeness and accuracy and supporting documentation before recording amortisation journal entries.	Management with knowledge of service providers' transaction terms reviews recorded prepaid expenses for proper recording, classification, and amortisation, including review of supporting documentation and analyses. Discrepancies are investigated and resolved on a timely basis	
Amortising Prepaid Expenses	Amortisation recorded does not include all prepaid items.	Finance personnel prepare amortisation		

		schedules for all recorded prepaid expenses, including preparing supporting documentation for the amortisation period and methodology. Management reviews and approves amortisation schedules for completeness and accuracy and supporting documentation before recording amortisation journal entries. Finance personnel prepare journal entries to record prepaid expenses, including supporting documentation. Management reviews the journal entries and supporting documentation to record prepayments prior to accounting personnel recording to the general ledger.		
Amortising Prepaid Expenses	Amortisation recorded includes prepaid items that do not exist.	Finance personnel prepare amortisation schedules for all recorded prepaid expenses, including preparing supporting documentation for the amortisation period and methodology. Management reviews and approves amortisation schedules for completeness and accuracy and supporting		

		documentation before recording amortisation journal entries. Finance personnel review the nature and type of expenses incurred and code the expense to the appropriate account. Management reviews the coding, supporting documentation, and journal entry before the journal entry is recorded		
Amortising Prepaid Expenses	Useful life assigned or amortisation methodology applied is inappropriate.	Finance personnel prepare amortisation schedules for all recorded prepaid expenses, including preparing supporting documentation for the amortisation period and methodology. Management reviews and approves amortisation schedules for completeness and accuracy and supporting documentation before recording amortisation journal entries		
	Other Possible Risks and Controls			
Amortising Prepaid Expenses	Amortisation of prepaid expenses is recorded in excess of the prepaid amount.		Management with knowledge of prepaid expense activity reviews the activity within the prepaid expense accounts. Discrepancies or unusual activity are investigated and resolved on a timely basis. Prepaid expenses and related other expense	

		accounts are analysed on a monthly basis and compared to budget. Explanations are obtained for any significant variances and differences. The analysis is reviewed by senior management.	
Recording Prepaid Expenses	Insurance recoveries receivable may be incorrect due to inappropriate recovery assumptions [specify assumptions] used by management.	On a periodic basis, management assesses the current insurance claims receivable based on the terms of the insurance contract and the current financial position of insurance companies in determining the insurance companies' creditworthiness and ability to pay on insurance claims	

12.3. Specimen Risk Map: Prepaid expenses

High

Prepaid expenses are recorded for which no payment has been made.	Expenditures where no future benefit exists to the entity are recorded as prepayments and deferred on the balance sheet.
Amortisation is recorded in advance of the time period associated with the prepaid expense.	Expenditures where future benefits exist for the entity are incorrectly recorded as expenses instead of being deferred

Impact

Prepaid expenses are recorded at the incorrect amount.	Prepaid expenses stated in the general ledger do not reconcile to the prepaid expense records, and/or the reconciliation contains invalid items.
Amortisation recorded includes prepaid items that do not exist.	

Low

Low   **Likelihood**   **High**

12.4. Audit check-list

Prepaid Expenses and Deferred Charges	Yes	No	N/A	Comments
1. Proper authorization to incur				
2. Authorization and support of amortization				
3. Detailed records				
4. Periodic review of amortization policy				
5. Control over insurance policies				
6. Periodic review of insurance needs				
7. Control over premium refunds				
8. Beneficiaries of company policies				
9. Physical control of policies				

Chapter 13: Revenue from Operations

13.1. Revenue from operations: Control Environment

Control Environment	Yes	No	N/A	Comments
One person is not responsible for taking orders, recording sales and receiving payment				
☑ Recorded sales transactions represent goods shipped				
☑ Goods and services are only supplied to customers with good credit rating				
☑ Goods and services are provided at authorised prices and on authorised terms				
☑ Customers are encouraged to pay promptly				
☑ All revenue relating to goods dispatch is recorded				
☑ All goods and services sold are correctly invoiced				
☑ All sales and adjustments are correctly journalised summarised and posted to the correct accounts				
☑ Transactions have been recorded in the correct period				
☑ All transactions are properly classified in accounts				

13.2. Sales process: Control environment

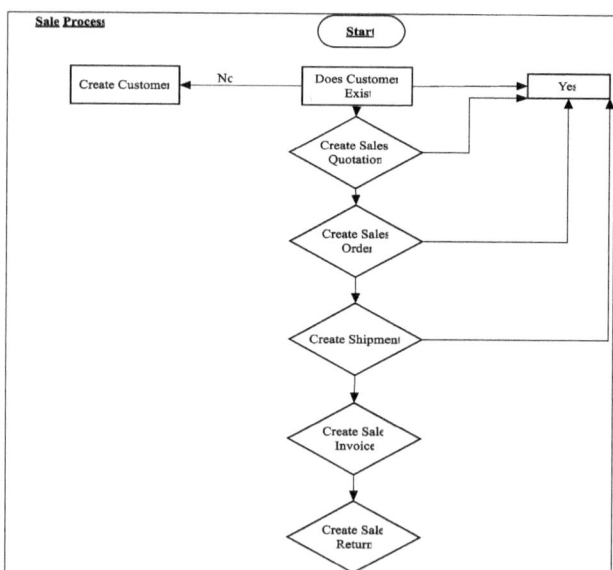

13.2.1. Business Process cycle

S/L No.	Nature of business processes Cycles
1	Inquiry & Quotation Processing
2	Route Sales Processing
3	Product Sales Processing
4	Consignment Sales Processing
5	Sample Sales Processing
6	Free of Charge / Replacement Order Processing
7	Sales Returns Processing
8	Deemed Export Sales Process
9	Export Sales Process
10	Stock Transfers
11	Scrap Sales

13.2.2. Enquiry, quotation and Sales order processing (SIPOC)

Supplier	Input	Process	Output	Customer
Prospect	Prospect enquiry	Customer communicates need for a product or service		
		Record enquiry in system		
		Create Sales enquiry and send to customer	Sales Enquiry	Prospect
	Email approval of Customer of sales enquiry and request RFQ	Customer approves sales enquiry and send Request for Quotation		
		Processing Sales		

		Quotation		
		Send quotation to customer	Sales quotation	Prospect
	Customer PO	Prospect approved quotation and sends PO		
		Raise Sales Order	Sales Order	Customer

13.2.3. Route sales processing

- Lot of Organisations specially in Fast Moving Consumer Goods (FMCG) segment e.g. Coke, Pepsi, Amul etc depend on Route sales in a significant way. They sell their products through various routes which involve distributors, institutions like modern trade (e.g. Big Bazaar) and resellers.

  The process followed for route sales are as under:

- Automation of complete order entry process right from the updating of delivery documents to the creation of deliveries for the next day requirements

- Document flow of order entry to billing can be tracked to check the process chain

- Real-time updating of stock availability, reservations and planning system to monitor the sales orders

- Accurate estimation of the order fulfillment to the customer, which will enhance customer satisfaction in future

- Price determination in the sales orders based on the masters maintained in the system and with reverse calculation

Please refer to Process flow diagram below.

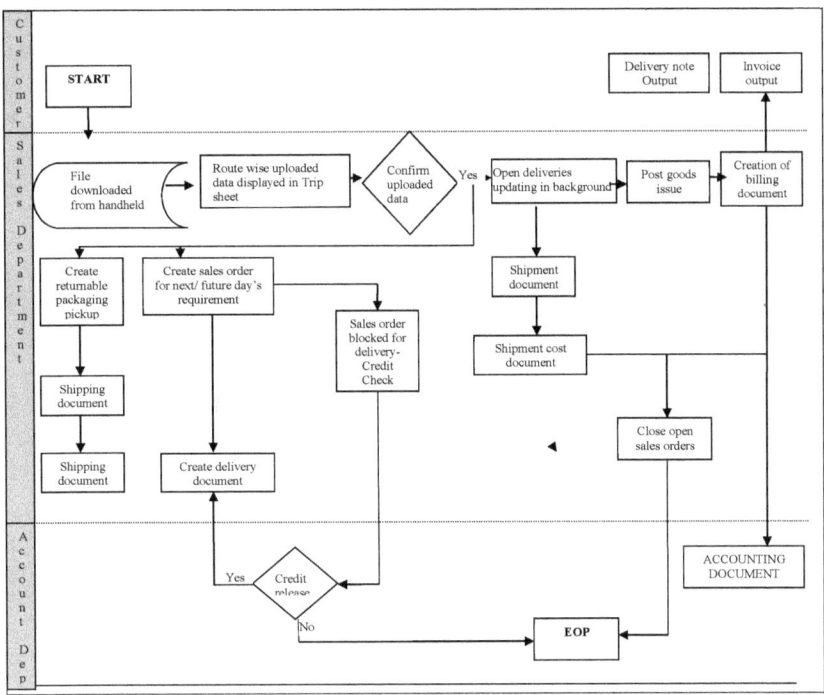

13.2.4. Product sales processing

13.2.4.1. Sales order processing

The sales order is a contractual agreement between a sales organization and a sold-to party about delivering products or providing a service for defined prices, quantities and times.

13.2.4.2. Process Deliveries

As soon as the material availability date or the transportation scheduling date for a schedule line is reached, the schedule line becomes due for shipping. When an outbound delivery is created by the user, shipping activities such as packing and transportation scheduling are initiated. A delivery is processed through one shipping point. This relief of inventory is the actual recording of the physical quantity that is being shipped to the customer. This result in the recording of the cost of goods sold in financial accounting.

13.2.4.3. Process Shipment Documents

As soon as the deliveries are scheduled for transportation planning, shipment cost documents are processed with the details of the route, transport / service vendors, vehicle types; shipment

timings etc and details of the stages with in a route are maintained. Shipment cost documents are processed for the calculation of shipment costs against each service vendor / cost and the cost settlement to respective cost elements. Transport costs will be distributed / calculate based on the gross weight of products in the delivery / shipment documents. A service purchase order, service entry sheet and goods receipt (services) are processed in the background against each service vendor.

13.2.4.4. Process Billing

Once the inventory has been relieved, the delivery can be invoiced and the revenue, together with the cost of goods sold, is recorded in management accounting. This step signifies the end of the business transaction in Sales and Distribution.

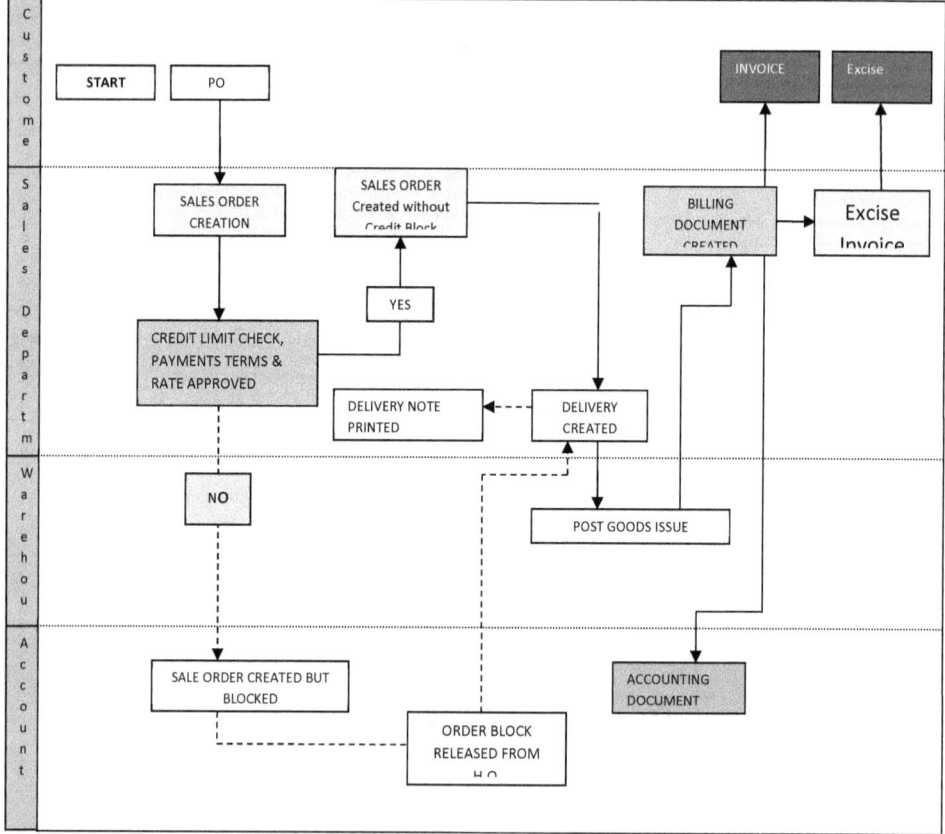

13.2.5. Export sales

Indents are received from overseas customer. The customer category is similar to any other local product distributor. The whole export sales transaction is routed through a bank, which acts as a channel for all communications for the trade. Upon receiving the indent and later the LC

(Irrevocable letter of credit) from the customer through the bank, the company prepares for the production. The LC specifies the terms and conditions for the sale transaction. Quantity and types of products required, period of delivery, required documents to be attached along with are some of the key specifications of the LC. Documents required for export sales are subjected to customers' requirements and products shipped. The entire transaction is supposed to adhere to the rules and regulations laid down in the LC. Any violation of which from either party would lead to penal charges. Within the confined time period as specified in the LC, the stock is dispatched to a location from where it can be shipped to the customer abroad. The local freight and other charges are borne by either party as per terms agreed initially; beyond which the customer takes up all applicable charges and the stock is received.

Bill of lading forms the confirmation for stock dispatched, which is sent to the customer through the bank. Invoice is raised after LC is received; the payable amount is realized through the bank, which is deposited into company's account. Insurance coverage if any will be borne by the customer. Taxes as applicable for internal transfers are borne by the company. C-Form / Stock Transfer depending upon the type of transfer transaction are generated.

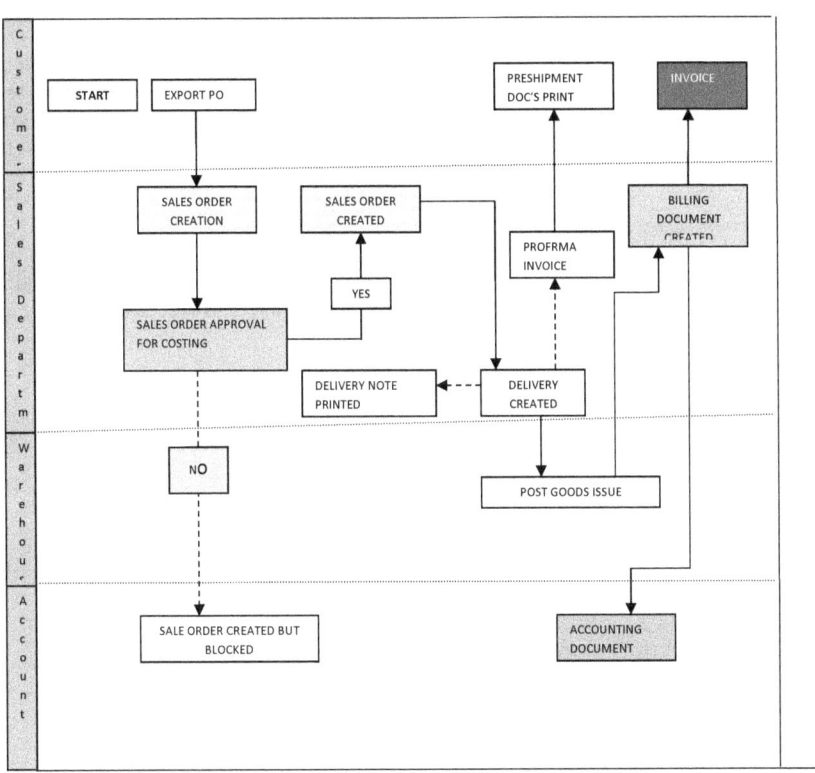

13.2.6. Stock transfer

13.2.6.1. Stock Transport order processing

Purchase order will be raised by receiving plant on supplying / delivery plant with delivery dates. The delivery of goods is created from the supplying plant.

13.2.6.2. Process Deliveries

As soon as the material availability date or the transportation scheduling date for a schedule line is reached, the schedule line becomes due for shipping. When an outbound delivery is created by the user, shipping activities such as packing and transportation scheduling are initiated. A delivery is processed through one shipping point. This relief of inventory is the actual recording of the physical quantity that is being shipped to the customer. This result in the recording of the cost of goods sold in financial accounting.

13.2.6.3. Process Shipment Documents

As soon as the deliveries are scheduled for transportation planning, shipment cost documents are processed with the details of the route, transport / service vendors, vehicle types; shipment timings etc and details of the stages with in a route are maintained. Shipment cost documents are processed for the calculation of shipment costs against each service vendor / cost and the cost settlement to respective cost elements. Transport costs will be distributed / calculate based on the gross weight of products in the delivery / shipment documents. A service purchase order, service entry sheet and goods receipt (services) are processed in the background against each service vendor.

13.2.6.4. Process Billing

Once the inventory has been relieved, the delivery can be invoiced and the revenue, together with the cost of goods sold, is recorded in management accounting. This step signifies the end of the business transaction in Sales and Distribution.

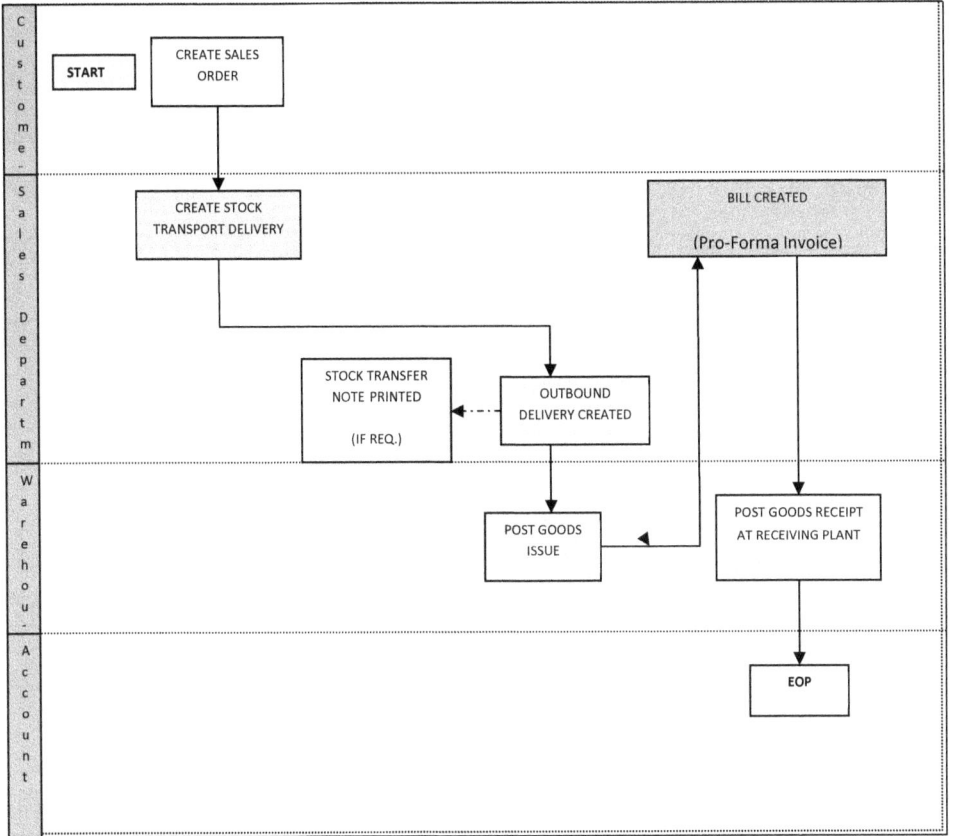

13.2.7. Sale of scrap

13.2.7.1. Sales Contract processing

The sales contract document is an agreement that the customer will order a certain quantity of a product from the company during a specified period. The contract contains basic quantity and price information, but does not specify delivery dates or quantities. The customer fulfills a contract by placing sales orders against it.

13.2.7.2. Sales order processing

The sales order is a contractual agreement between a sales organization and a sold-to party about delivering products or providing a service for defined prices, quantities and times

13.2.7.3. Process Deliveries

As soon as the material availability date or the transportation scheduling date for a schedule line is reached, the schedule line becomes due for shipping. When an outbound delivery is created by the user, shipping activities such as packing and transportation scheduling are initiated. A delivery is processed through one shipping point. This relief of inventory is the actual recording of the physical quantity that is being shipped to the customer. This result in the recording of the cost of goods sold in financial accounting.

13.2.7.4. Process Billing

Once the inventory has been relieved, the delivery can be invoiced and the revenue, together with the cost of goods sold, is recorded in management accounting. This step signifies the end of the business transaction in Sales and Distribution.

13.3. Financial Control over Financial Reporting

Activities	Risk environment	Preventive control	Detective control	Monitoring control Y/N/NA
Revenue from operations Recording of Sales	*Core Risks and Controls* Sales and trade receivables are recorded: • That do not relate to valid sales/dispatches • At the incorrect amount • In the incorrect period.	Invoices are generated only upon matching the purchase order and shipping documents, completing a 3-way match. The 3-way match process is performed within an ERP system that identifies the purchase order and dispatch note and generates an invoice within established tolerances. Proof of delivery is provided by third-party carriers for all dispatches/deliveries made. The proof of delivery is required in order for the invoice to be generated		
Recording of Sales	Supplementary agreements or credit memos exist that are not known to accounting		Representations are received on a quarterly basis from sales personnel and management regarding the existence of customer side agreements or credit memos not yet communicated to accounting. Credit notes issued after period-end are scrutinised by management for association with supplementary agreements and	

		proper accounting.	
Recording of Sales	Sales are recorded prior to all necessary revenue recognition criteria being met.	Sales agreements are reviewed by personnel with requisite experience to determine if the revenue recognition criteria are met.	
Recording of Sales	Goods are dispatched to customers and no invoice is generated and recorded.	Invoices are generated only upon matching the purchase order and dispatch documents, completing a 3-way match. The 3-way match process is performed within an ERP system that identifies the purchase order and dispatch note and generates an invoice within established tolerances.	**Dispatches** of goods to customers are logged. The log is used to determine that all shipments dispatches are invoiced and that all invoices are recorded Management reviews relevant sales, trade receivables, costs of sales, and inventory reports related to order entry, dispatch, and invoicing; significant, unusual relationships are monitored and acted upon	
Recording of Sales	Sales are not classified appropriately as per Schedule III to the Companies Act, 2013	Finance personnel review the nature and type of sale transaction and appropriate account. Management reviews the supporting documentation, and journal entry before the journal entry is recorded		
Sales Returns and Credit Memos	Credit notes are not issued and recorded for goods returned by customers.	All returned goods are logged when received and the returned goods log automatically generates the credit notes	All returned goods are logged when received. Return details per the log are compared to credit notes issued to determine that credit notes are issued in accordance with company policy.	
Sales Returns and Credit Memos	Credit notes are issued or committed to the customer but not recorded.		All returned goods are logged when received. Return details per the log are compared to credit notes issued and recorded to	

			determine that credit notes are issued in accordance with company policy Representations from operations and sales personnel are obtained indicating that no verbal or unrecorded credit memos exist that have not been reported to finance management.	
Sales Returns and Credit Memos	Credit notes are issued to customers without the receipt of returned goods.	All returned goods are logged when received and the returned goods log automatically generates the credit notes	All returned goods are logged when received. Credit notes issued are compared to the return log to determine that credits issued are for valid returns.	
Sales Returns and Credit Memos	Credit notes are issued for the incorrect amount	Credit notes are generated by the ERP system. Credit pricing information is obtained from the original sales invoice ERP system validates the amount of the issued credit note against the original invoice. Credit memos issued in excess of the original invoice are flagged and must be reviewed and approved by management Policy requires that credit notes are not issued in amounts in excess of the original invoice amount; compliance with this policy is monitored by management		
Sales Returns and Credit Memos	Sales returns reserves are not accurately estimated as a result of: • An inappropriate	Sales return methodology, significant assumptions, and supporting	Management performs a retrospective review supporting the appropriateness of the	

	methodology • Significant assumptions [*specify assumptions*] being inappropriate, lacking sufficient basis, or lacking sufficient support.	documentation are reviewed by management prior to recording the journal entry	methodology and significant assumptions Sales returns are analysed on a monthly basis and compared to budget. Explanations are obtained for any significant variances and differences. The analysis is reviewed by senior management and taken into consideration when estimating the sales return reserve	
Sales Returns and Credit Memos	Sales return transactions occurring around period-end are not recorded in the correct period.		Returned goods received and credit memos issued at, before, or after the end of an accounting period are scrutinised and/or reconciled to make certain the sales return is recorded in the appropriate accounting period. Manual sales return entries made to the general ledger are reviewed and approved by management for proper inclusion in the correct accounting period	
	Other Possible Risks and Controls			
Recording of Sales	Invoices are generated and sales recorded for dispatches to fictitious customers.	Invoices can only be generated for customers that exist in the customer master file. Access to add, change, or delete information in the customer master file is limited to approved personnel	The customer master file generates an exception report listing new and deleted customers, shipping address changes, etc., and the report is reviewed by the credit manager and controller. Customer master file data is periodically reviewed by management for accuracy and ongoing pertinence	

Recording of Sales	Invoices are issued and recorded for dispatches to non-customer offsite locations.	The ERP system only permits invoices to be issued for dispatches to valid customer locations based on information contained in the customer master file.	The customer master file is reviewed for ongoing relevance.	
Recording of Sales	Invoices are generated and recorded for sales of consigned inventory based on incorrect data provided to the entity by the consignee.		Consigned inventory is confirmed and confirmations are reconciled to inventory records and the general ledger. Randomly, consigned inventory is physically verified by company personnel. Customers who receive consigned goods are specifically identified as consignment customers in the ERP customer master file. The ERP system generates a report of invoices to consignment customers that are scrutinised by management for proper revenue recognition	
Recording of Sales	Inventory held on consignment and subsequently sold has not been invoiced and recorded as a sale and receivable.		Consigned inventory is confirmed and confirmations are reconciled to inventory records and the general ledger. Randomly, consigned inventory is physically verified by company personnel. Inventory consignee (third party) provides periodic reporting of consigned inventory held. These reports are reviewed and reconciled to internal records, and	

			differences are investigated.	
Recording of Sales	Sales transactions are recorded without being appropriately adjusted for unearned (or deferred) revenue, or they are adjusted at the incorrect amount.	Management (1) analyses significant sales contracts for revenue recognition considerations such as customer approval, delivery terms (e.g., FOB destination), and (2) references the applicable accounting framework and principles to support the amount recorded as revenue and unearned revenue for significant sales transactions	Sales transactions, volumes, and values are analysed on a monthly basis and compared to budget. Explanations are obtained for any variances above X% and differences are analysed. The analysis is reviewed by senior management	Accuracy; Occurrence
Recording of Sales	Sales are made to customers with poor credit, which may affect revenue recognition criteria being met and the ultimate write-off of uncollectible accounts	Credit limits are established by the credit manager based on the customer's ability to pay and past collection results, and are reviewed on a regular basis		
Recording of Sales	Invoices are generated in excess, individually or in the aggregate, of customer credit limits, which may affect revenue recognition criteria being met and the ultimate write-off of uncollectible accounts.	ERP system suspends purchase orders that individually or aggregately exceed customer credit limits. Approval by the credit manager is required prior to the ERP system recording the purchase order		
Sales Returns and Credit Memos	Credit notes are issued at an amount in excess of the original invoice.	Policy requires that credit notes are not issued in amounts in excess of the original invoice amount; compliance with this policy is monitored by management via review of credit memos prior to issuance.	ERP system validates the amount of the issued credit note against the original invoice and creates an exception report for credit notes in excess of the original invoices. Management reviews, then approves or corrects, items on the	

			exception report based on documentation and support provided.	
Sales Returns and Credit Memos	For sales transactions that trigger promotional allowances or volume discounts, the promotional allowance or volume discount is not appropriately recorded.	For sales transactions that trigger promotional allowances or volume discounts, the calculation for promotional allowances and volume discounts and supporting documentation are reviewed by management prior to recording the journal entry	For customers receiving promotional allowances or volume discounts, management periodically analyses goods returned that may indicate inappropriate recording of promotional allowances or volume discounts.\n\nPromotional allowances and volume discounts are analysed on a monthly basis and compared to budget. Explanations are obtained for any significant variances and differences. The analysis is reviewed by senior management	
Sales Returns and Credit Memos	Provisions for promotional allowances or volume discounts are not accurately estimated as a result of:\n• An inappropriate methodology\n• Significant assumptions [specify assumptions] being inappropriate, lacking sufficient basis, or lacking sufficient support.	The methodology for accruing for promotional allowances/volume discounts, significant assumptions used, and supporting documentation are reviewed by management prior to recording the journal entry.	Management performs a retrospective review supporting the appropriateness of the methodology and significant assumptions\n\nPromotional allowances and volume discounts are analysed on a monthly basis and compared to budget. Explanations are obtained for any significant variances and differences. The analysis is reviewed by senior management and taken into consideration when estimating the reserve for promotional allowances and rebates	
Recording of	Foreign sales and	Foreign sales and		

Sales	trade receivables are translated at the incorrect foreign exchange rate.	trade receivables translation is prepared by staff personnel and reviewed/approved by management. Analysis reviewed/approved by management includes supporting documentation for the translation rate calculation. ERP system calculates the foreign sales and trade receivables translation, which is independently verified by management		

13.4. Specimen Risk Map: Revenue from operations

High	Sales and trade receivables are recorded that do not relate to valid sales /dispatches	Sales are recorded prior to all necessary revenue recognition criteria being met.	
	Inventory held on consignment and subsequently sold has not been invoiced and recorded as a sale and receivable.	Goods are dispatched to customers and no invoice is generated and recorded.	
		Sales return transactions occurring around period-end are not recorded in the correct period.	
Impact	Sales are not classified appropriately as per Schedule III to the Companies Act, 2013	Invoices are generated in excess, individually or in the aggregate, of customer credit limits	
	Credit notes are issued at an amount in excess of the original invoice.		
Low	Foreign sales and trade receivables are translated at the incorrect foreign exchange rate.		

Low   **Likelihood**   **High**

13.5. Revenue from operations: Audit check-list

Control tests	Yes	No	N/A	Comments
Observe and evaluate whether proper segregation of duties is operating				
☐ Test a sample of sales invoices for authorised sales order form and shipping documentation				
☐ Examine application controls for authorisation				
☐ Review and test entity's procedures for accounting for numerical sequences of invoices				
☐ Review entity's procedures for sending out monthly statements and dealing with customer queries and complaints				
☐ Review entity's procedures for granting credit to customers				
☐ Examine a sample of sales orders for evidence of proper credit approval by the appropriate senior staff member				
☐ Examine application controls for credit limits				
☐ Review all new customer files to ensure satisfactory credit references have been obtained				
☐ Compare prices and terms on a sample of sales invoices to the authorised price list and terms of trade				
☐ Examine application controls for authorised prices and terms				
☐ Review and test entity's procedures for accounting for numerical sequences of invoices				
☐ Trace a sample of shipping documents to the sales invoices and ledger				
☐ Review a sample of reconciliations performed				
☐ Inspect the open-order file for unfilled orders				
Vouch recorded sales to supporting documents				
☐ Compare dates on sales invoices with dates of corresponding shipping documentation				
☐ Compare dates on sales invoices with dates recorded in the sales ledger				
☐ Review sales ledger for proper classification				
☐ Examine a sample of sales invoices for proper classification				
☐ Test application controls for proper codes				

Chapter 14: Material consumption / cost of sales

14.1. Cost of sales: Control Environment

Item	Yes	No	N/A
Existence of robust procure to pay cycle			
A strong ERP in place			
Item code masters are regularly cross checked to ensure these are free from errors			
Consumption accounting is properly in place to reconcile opening stock add purchases less closing stock for all items for which revenue is recognised			
Excise duty is properly accounted			

14.2. Cost of sales: Process

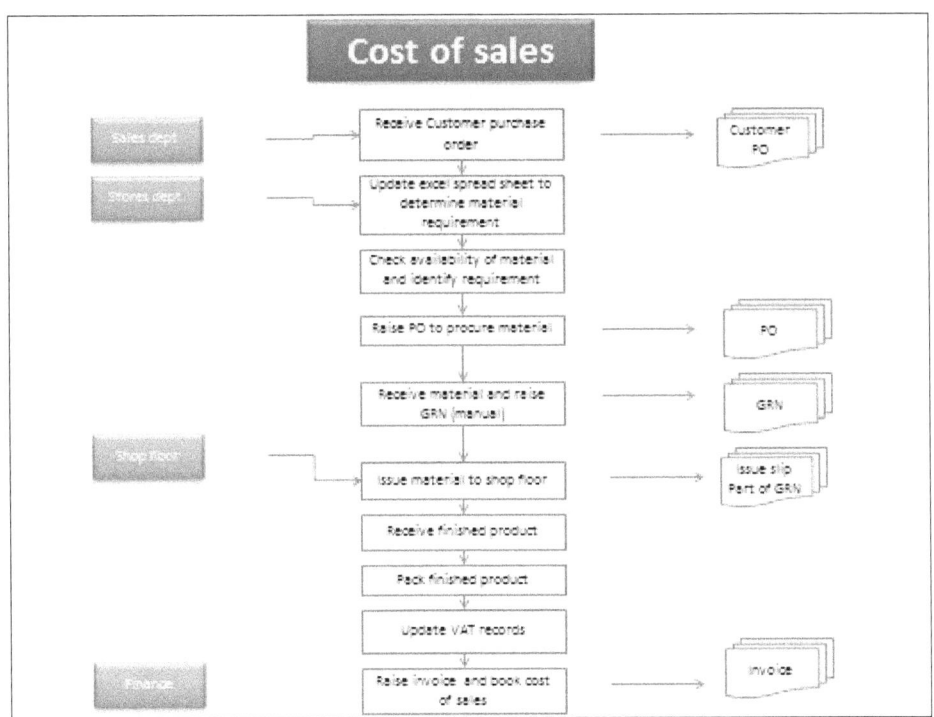

14.3. Financial Control over Financial Reporting

Activities	Risk environment	Preventive control	Detective control	Monitoring control Y/N/NA
Cost of sales Recording Cost	Core Risks and Controls	Finance personnel review the nature	Management periodically reviews	

of Sales	Costs of sales are: • Recorded when no sale exists • Not recorded when sales exist • Recorded at the incorrect amount • Recorded in the incorrect period • Incorrectly classified.	and type of costs incurred, and code the cost to the appropriate account. Management reviews the coding, supporting documentation, and journal entry before the journal entry is recorded.	actual inventory, cost of sales, gross profit, and other expense amounts in comparison to budget, historical amounts, or current-year trends, and investigates and resolves any significant variances. This review is performed at a sufficient level of detail and disaggregation (e.g., by type of product line, type of services).	
Recording Cost of Sales	Inventory may be removed from inventory records and recorded as a cost of sales when it has not actually been sold.	Cost of sales is recorded and inventory is relieved automatically by the ERP system upon matching the customer sales order, shipping documents, and the invoice generated, completing a 3-way match	Physical inventory is counted periodically and discrepancies are investigated and corrected within the inventory records. Inventory records based on the physical inventory are reconciled to the general ledger with any differences being recorded as a book-to-physical inventory adjustment.	
Recording Cost of Sales	Inventory records include inventory that was sold to customers and not recorded as a component of cost of sales.	Cost of sales is recorded and inventory is relieved automatically by the ERP system upon matching the customer sales order, shipping documents, and the invoice generated, completing a 3-way match.	Physical inventory is counted periodically and discrepancies are investigated and corrected within the inventory records. Inventory records based on the physical inventory are reconciled to the general ledger with any differences being recorded as a book-to-physical inventory adjustment	
Recording Cost of Sales	Inventory has been sold that is removed from the accounts at incorrect amounts.	On a periodic basis, accounting personnel calculate the inventory cost under the costing method utilised by the entity. Prior to recording the journal entry, management		

		reviews the calculation, methodology, significant assumptions used, supporting documentation, and the journal entry for accuracy and proper account classification Cost of sales is recorded and inventory is relieved automatically by the ERP system upon matching the customer sales order, dispatch documents, and the invoice generated, completing a 3-way match.		
Recording Cost of Sales	The entity uses inappropriate standard costs in valuing its inventory, including incorrectly calculating the allocation of labour and overhead.	Management reviews the new standard cost analysis and supporting documentation and approves changes to standard costs, including labour and overhead allocation assumptions, before the changes are made to the inventory ERP system Management compares the revised standard cost master file to the approved standard cost per the New Standard Cost Report		
Recording Cost of Sales	Inventory may be recorded at the incorrect cost under the entity's costing method.	On a periodic basis, accounting personnel calculate the inventory cost under the costing method utilised by the entity. Prior to recording the journal entry, management	On a quarterly basis, accounting personnel compare the costs automatically calculated by the ERP system to manually calculated inventory costs using the selected costing	

		reviews the calculation, methodology, significant assumptions used, supporting documentation, and the journal entry for accuracy and proper account classification Changes made to inventory costing methods are approved by management before becoming effective	method for a sample of inventory items. Management meets monthly in product cost review meeting to discuss results of operations, specifically focused on production cost evaluation including a comparison of current-period productions cost to the current-year budget and prior-period benchmarks	
Recording Cost of Sales	Inventory that was sold to customers and recorded as cost of sales are recorded in the incorrect period.	Cost of sales is recorded and inventory is reduced automatically by the ERP system upon matching the customer sales order, shipping documents, and the invoice generated, completing a 3-way match.	Physical inventory is counted periodically and discrepancies are investigated and corrected within the inventory records. Inventory records based on the physical inventory are reconciled to the general ledger with any differences being recorded as a book-to-physical inventory adjustment	
Recording Cost of Sales	Inventory stated in the general ledger does not reconcile to the inventory records and/or the reconciliation contains invalid items.		Management reviews and approves the reconciliation of the inventory records to the general ledger and any reconciling items are reviewed and addressed on a timely basis	
Recording Cost of Sales	Inventory may be recorded at an amount that exceeds the lower of cost or NRV as the significant assumptions [specify assumptions] utilised in the lower of cost or NRV analysis are inappropriate, do not have a sufficient basis, or do not have sufficient support.	Management reviews and approves the cost v/s NSR evaluation prepared by finance personnel and the resulting journal entry		

Recording Cost of Sales	The grouping of inventory for purposes of applying the COST V/S NSR evaluation is inappropriate for one or more of the following reasons: a)The grouping does not reflect the nature of inventory b)The grouping does not reflect how income and losses impact the Statement of Profit and Loss in the normal course of business, and c)The grouping is not applied consistently from one period to the next.	Management reviews and approves the cost v/s NSR evaluation prepared by finance personnel and the resulting journal entry		
Recording Cost of Sales	The adjustment for lower of cost or NRV is recorded in the incorrect accounting period.	Management reviews and approves the cost v/s NSR evaluation prepared by finance personnel and the resulting journal entry.		
Recording Cost of Sales	The adjustment for lower of cost or NRV stated in the general ledger does not reconcile to the calculation and/or contains mathematical errors.	Management reviews and approves the cost v/s NSR evaluation prepared by finance personnel and the resulting journal entry.		
Recording Cost of Sales	Obsolete, slow moving, or excess inventory does not exist but an adjustment is recorded against inventory and as a component of cost of sales.	Management reviews and approves the excess and obsolete adjustment calculation prepared by finance personnel and resulting journal entry.	Management periodically reviews actual inventory, cost of sales, gross profit, and other expense amounts in comparison to budget, historical amounts, or current-year trends, and investigates and resolves any significant variances. This review is performed at a sufficient level of detail and disaggregation (e.g., by type of product	

			line, type of services).	
Recording Cost of Sales	Obsolete, slow moving, or excess inventory exists but no adjustment is recorded against inventory and as a component of cost of sales.	Management reviews and approves the excess and obsolete adjustment calculation prepared by finance personnel and resulting journal entry.	Physical inventory is counted periodically and discrepancies are investigated and corrected within the inventory records. Inventory records based on the physical inventory are reconciled to the general ledger with any differences being recorded as a book to physical inventory adjustment	
Recording Cost of Sales	In evaluating the adjustments for obsolete, slow moving, or excess inventory: • Management's method for determining the E&O adjustments is inappropriate or has not been applied consistently. • The estimates are based on assumptions that are unreasonable, lack sufficient basis, or lack sufficient support. Assumptions used in estimating E&O adjustments include: [specify assumptions]	Management reviews and approves the excess and obsolete adjustment calculation prepared by finance personnel and resulting journal entry.		
Recording Cost of Sales	The calculations for obsolete, slow-moving, or excess inventory and related adjustments are based on inaccurate inventory usage/movement data.	The inventory management system generates the Inventory Usage/Movement Report based on parameters in the inventory management system		
Recording Cost of Sales	The adjustment for obsolete, slow moving, or excess inventory is recorded at the incorrect amount, in the	Management reviews and approves the excess and obsolete adjustment calculation prepared		

	incorrect general ledger account, or in the incorrect accounting period.	by finance personnel and resulting journal entry.		
Recording Cost of Sales	The adjustment for obsolete, slow-moving, or excess inventory stated in the general ledger does not reconcile to the calculation and/or contains mathematical errors.	Management reviews and approves the excess and obsolete adjustment calculation prepared by finance personnel and resulting journal entry.		
Recording Cost of Sales	Physical inventory counts are not performed on a periodic basis, potentially resulting in inaccurate inventory records.		Physical inventory is counted periodically and discrepancies are investigated and corrected within the inventory records. Inventory records based on the physical inventory are reconciled to the general ledger with any differences being recorded as a book-to-physical inventory adjustment	
Recording Cost of Sales	Physical inventory counts: • Count inventory that does not exist • Do not include counts of all inventory • Do not include consideration of movement of inventory during the physical inventory • Are not valued at the appropriate cost • Book to physical adjustments that are not recorded or recorded at the incorrect amount.		Physical inventory is counted periodically and discrepancies are investigated and corrected within the inventory records. Inventory records based on the physical inventory are reconciled to the general ledger with any differences being recorded as a book-to-physical inventory adjustment	
Sales returns	Inventory returns from customers are recorded: • Prior to receipt • At the incorrect amount	Manual journal entries to record inventory purchases or returns and related payable adjustments are	Physical inventory is counted periodically and discrepancies are investigated and corrected within the inventory records.	

	• In the incorrect period.	prepared by finance personnel and supported by documentation that the inventory has been received or title has transferred to the entity prior to recording the entry. Management reviews and approves the journal entry and underlying supporting documentation.	Inventory records based on the physical inventory are reconciled to the general ledger with any differences being recorded as a book-to-physical inventory adjustment.	
Sales returns	Goods returned by customers are: a)Not recorded b)Recorded at the incorrect amount c)Recorded in the incorrect period.	Warehouse personnel enter all goods received into the ERP system on the date of receipt, and the ERP system automatically records an adjustment to the inventory subsidiary ledger and to cost of sales in the general ledger.	All returned goods are logged when received. On a periodic basis, return details per the log are compared to the inventory records to verify the returned inventory is properly recorded in the inventory sub-ledger, and to verify cost of sales has been reduced in the general ledger	
Recording Cost of Sales	Inventory may be removed from inventory records and recorded as a cost of sales upon dispatch prior to transfer of ownership.	Management reviews and approves the journal entry and supporting documentation for inventory and cost of goods sold for goods that have been dispatched prior to transfer of ownership.		
Recording Cost of Sales	Inventory held by a third party that has been sold to a final customer has not been reduced from inventory or recorded as a cost of sales.	On a periodic basis, the reports provided by the third party to the entity, either directly or by confirmation, are reviewed and reconciled to internal records and used by the entity to reduce inventory and record cost of sales.		
Recording Cost of Sales	Inventory held by a third party and not yet sold is improperly	On a periodic basis, the reports provided by the third party to		

	reduced from inventory and recorded as cost of sales.	the entity, either directly or by confirmation, are reviewed and reconciled to internal records and used by the entity to reduce inventory and record cost of sales.		
Recording Cost of Sales	Inventory records include inventory that is not in a saleable condition.		Physical inventory is counted periodically and discrepancies are investigated and corrected within the inventory records. Inventory records based on the physical inventory are reconciled to the general ledger with any differences being recorded as a book-to-physical inventory adjustment	
	Other Possible Risks and Controls			
Recording Cost of Sales	Intercompany profits are: • Not eliminated from inventory • Eliminated at the incorrect amount.	Intercompany sales are analysed at period-end to calculate the amount of intercompany profit in inventory to be eliminated. Finance personnel prepare the journal entry, supporting documentation, and account analysis for intercompany profit in inventory to be eliminated. Management reviews and approves the journal entry, supporting documentation, and account analysis before the journal entry is recorded.		
Recording Cost of Sales	Inventory issued on consignment and not yet sold is improperly reduced from inventory and		Consigned inventory is confirmed and confirmations are reconciled to inventory records and	

	recorded as cost of sales.		the general ledger. On a periodic basis, consigned inventory is physically verified by company personnel and reconciled to the inventory records. Inventory consignee provides periodic reporting of consigned inventory sold to third parties, and consigned inventory held. These reports are reviewed and reconciled to internal records, and used by the entity to record cost of sales and relieve inventory	
Recording Cost of Sales	Inventory held on consignment and subsequently sold has not been invoiced and recorded as a sale and receivable.		Consigned inventory is confirmed and confirmations are reconciled to inventory records and the general ledger. Randomly, consigned inventory is physically verified by company personnel Inventory consignee (third party) provides periodic reporting of consigned inventory held. These reports are reviewed and reconciled to internal records and differences are investigated	
Recording Cost of Sales	Inventory held at offsite locations is improperly reduced from inventory and recorded as cost of sales.		Physical inventory, including inventory held at offsite locations, is counted periodically and discrepancies are investigated and corrected within the inventory records. Inventory records are reconciled to the general ledger.	
Recording Cost of Sales	Inventory records include inventory that does not exist due to		Physical inventory is counted periodically and discrepancies are	

	shrinkage, which has not been recorded as a component of cost of sales.		investigated and corrected within the inventory records. Inventory records are reconciled to the general ledger
Recording Cost of Sales	Inventory previously issued on consignment that has been sold to a third party has not been relieved from inventory or recorded as a cost of sale.		On a periodic basis, consigned inventory is physically verified by company personnel and reconciled to the inventory records. On a periodic basis, the inventory consignee provides the entity reporting of consigned inventory sold to third parties and consigned inventory still held, or the entity confirms consigned inventory with the consignee. These reports or confirmations are reviewed and reconciled to internal records, and used by the entity to record cost of sales and relieve inventory

Chapter 15: Employee Benefits

15.1. Payroll
15.1.1. Payroll: Control Environment

Control Environment	Yes	No	N/A	Comments
Payment is made only to bona fide employees of the entity				
⊡ All payroll costs are recorded for work done by employees				
⊡ All benefits and deductions are computed correctly				
⊡ Payroll transactions correctly recorded in the accounting system				
⊡ Payroll transactions are recorded in the correct accounting period				
⊡ Payroll transactions are properly classified in the financial statements				

15.1.2. Payroll: Financial Control over Financial Reporting

Preventive controls	Yes	No	N/A	Comments
Segregation of duties between HR and payroll function				
⊡ Personnel files held for all employees				
⊡ Authorisation procedures for hiring, terminating, time worked, wage rates, overtime, benefits etc.				
⊡ Any changes in employment status of employees informed to HR department (maternity or special leave)				
⊡ Use of time clocks to record time worked				
⊡ Clock cards approved by supervisor				
⊡ Only employees with valid employee numbers are paid				
⊡ Payroll budgets in place and reviewed by management				
Pre-number clock cards in use				
⊡ Authorisation of wage cheque cashed				
⊡ Security and prompt banking of unclaimed wages				
⊡ Security of pay packets				
⊡ Security of cash transit				
⊡ Verification of identity				
⊡ Recording of distributions				
⊡ Preparation and authorisation of cheques and bank transfer list				
⊡ Comparison of cheques and bank transfer list with payroll				
⊡ Maintenance and reconciliation of wages and salaries bank account				
⊡ Verification of payroll amounts and benefits calculations				
⊡ Payroll budgets in place and reviewed by management				
⊡ Agreement of gross earnings and total tax deducted with taxation returns				
⊡ Changes to master payroll file verified through before and after reports				
⊡ Payroll master file reconciled to general ledger				
⊡ All starters, leavers, changes to salaries and deductions are reported promptly to payroll department and changes are updated to the payroll master file promptly				
⊡ Chart of accounts				
⊡ Independent approval and review of accounts charged to payroll				
Payroll budgets in place and reviewed by management				

15.1.3. Payroll: Audit check list

Test of controls	Yes	No	N/A	Comments
Observe and evaluate proper segregation of duties				
☑ Review a sample of starters and leavers in the year to ensure correct documentation is in place				
☑ Review and test authorisation procedures in place				
☑ Review policies and procedures in place for changing status and consider whether adequate				
☑ Review personnel files for a sample of employees whose status changed in the year				
☑ Observe employees' use of time clocks				
☑ Inspect a sample of clock cards for evidence of approval by appropriate level of management				
☑ Review and test procedures for entering and removing employee numbers from the payroll master file				
☑ Review budgeting procedures				
☑ Review numerical sequence of clock cards				
☑ Attend the cash pay-out of wages to confirm that the official procedures are being followed				
☑ Before the cash wages are paid compare payroll with wage packets to ensure all employees have a wage packet				
☑ Examine receipts given by employees				
☑ Check unclaimed wages are recorded in unclaimed wages book				
☑ Observe whether any employee receives more than one wage packet				
☑ Inspect the unclaimed wages book entries on the pay roll to ensure they agree				
☑ Check that unclaimed wages are banked regularly by inspection of bank statements and supporting documentation				
☑ Inspect that unclaimed wages books to check it shows reasons why wages are unclaimed				
☑ Review pattern of unclaimed wages in unclaimed wages book for variations				
☑ Check the calculation of the holiday payments by recalculation				
☑ Make comparisons on holiday pay between payment records				
☑ Recalculate benefits and deduction for a sample of employees				
☑ Review budgeting procedures				
☑ Inspect documentation for evidence of management's review				
☑ Review reconciliation before and after reports to payroll master file				
☑ Review reconciliation of payroll master file to general ledger				
☑ Confirm whether discrepancies are followed-up promptly and resolved				

15.1.4. Employee benefits

Activities	Risk environment	Preventive control	Detective control	Monitoring control Y/N/NA
Employee benefits Measurement of Benefit Obligation	Core Risks and Controls The entity modifies or terminates existing plans or creates new plans and the changes are unknown to management and the actuary.	On a periodic basis, finance and human resource personnel meet to evaluate changes to the entity's employee benefit plan structure. Changes made to existing plans or creations of new plans are provided to the actuary. Finance personnel evaluate that changes to the plan were contemplated by the actuary when	Management reviews minutes from executive, board, audit committee, and other operational meetings to identify actions that may affect the benefit plan structure or significant assumptions underlying actuarial analysis. Matters identified are reviewed and analysed on a timely basis as to the effect on the benefit obligation.	

319

		preparing the actuarial report by reviewing the key plan information disclosed in the actuarial report and utilised by the actuary in making the actuarial calculations.		
Measurement of Benefit Obligation	Payroll and employee demographic data provided to the third-party actuary is inaccurate, incomplete, or includes ineligible employees.	On a periodic basis, finance personnel analyse the demographic data files and trace information back to source data on a test basis. Management reviews the analysis and testing results before the information is provided to the actuary	Demographic data maintained in the ERP system is monitored for integrity through user access controls and change management procedures. Information technology management reviews and approves changes to user access. Changes to employee data are reviewed and approved by human resource personnel independent of those who processed the change	
Measurement of Benefit Obligation	The third-party actuary does not utilise the employee and other data provided by the entity or inappropriately makes changes to the employee and other data when performing the actuarial measurement.		Finance personnel review the final actuarial report and reconcile the key data listed in the report to the data relating to employees and others provided to the actuary. Unusual items or errors are investigated and corrected on a timely basis

Recorded employee benefit obligation adjustments are regularly compared to budget, current-year trends, and historical amounts for unusual relationships; management investigates and resolves significant variances | |

Measurement of Benefit Obligation	In determining the employee benefit obligation: • The methodology used to calculate the employee benefit obligation is inappropriate under the circumstances. • The underlying significant assumptions [*specify assumptions*] are inappropriate, lack sufficient basis, or lack sufficient support.	The calculation of the employee benefit obligation is performed by a qualified actuary. The methodology, significant assumptions, and underlying data used are reviewed, evaluated, and approved by management with appropriate knowledge of benefit plan accounting and the actuarial calculation. Finance management reviews the results of the actuarial analysis with the actuary and investigates unusual items or relationships. Management approves the analysis before the journal entry is recorded.		
Measurement of Benefit Obligation	The entity inappropriately relies upon the findings of the third-party actuary who is not adequately competent or objective.	On a periodic basis, finance personnel obtain credentials, references, external data, etc., and assess and conclude upon the professional competency and objectivity of the actuary. Management reviews this assessment and supporting documentation and approves the engagement of the actuary before services are performed. Finance personnel analyse the actuary's professional service		

		engagements in process and pending (i.e., open proposals) with the entity. Management reviews the analysis and concludes on the independence and/or objectivity of the actuary before services are performed		
Recording benefit costs	Employee Benefit obligation adjustments, including unrecognised service cost or actuarial gains and losses, are: • Inaccurately recorded • Not recorded for all benefit plans • Recorded for benefit plans that are not the obligation of the entity.	Finance personnel prepare journal entries to record benefit obligation adjustments, including obtaining supporting documentation (e.g., the actuarial report). Management reviews and approves the journal entry and supporting documentation before the entry is recorded.	Management with knowledge of benefit obligation adjustments reviews the transactions in the benefit obligation-related general ledger accounts for unusual transactions. Unusual transactions or errors are investigated and resolved on a timely basis	
Transaction of plan assets	Contributions, benefit payments, and other transactions (as applicable) are made but are not recorded through the benefit obligation account.	Cash disbursements are generated through the ERP system. The ERP system automatically records the journal entry for cash disbursements to the benefit obligation account and cash sub-ledgers. All manually generated cheques, including the related journal entry and supporting documentation, are reviewed and approved by management before the journal entry is recorded	Bank statements are reconciled to the general ledger regularly and differences are investigated and resolved on a timely basis.	
Activity of Plan Assets	Contributions, benefit payments, and other transactions (as	Cash disbursements are generated through the ERP	Bank statements are reconciled to the general ledger	

	applicable) are recorded through the benefit obligation account that did not occur.	system. The ERP system automatically records the journal entry for cash disbursements to the benefit obligation account and cash sub-ledgers All manually generated cheques, including the related journal entry and supporting documentation, are reviewed and approved by management before the journal entry is recorded.	regularly and differences are investigated and resolved on a timely basis.	
Activity of Plan Assets	Contributions, benefit payments and other transactions (as applicable) made to the benefit plan are recorded at an amount that differs from the actual amount paid.	Cash disbursements are generated through the ERP system. The ERP system automatically records the journal entry for cash disbursements to the benefit obligation account and cash sub-ledgers All manually generated cheques, including the related journal entry and supporting documentation, are reviewed and approved by management before the journal entry is recorded.	Bank statements are reconciled to the general ledger regularly and differences are investigated and resolved on a timely basis.	Valuation and Allocation
	Other Possible Risks and Controls			
Termination benefits	For benefits given to employees that qualify as special termination benefits, the entity does not record an expense/liability as per the requirements of AS 15.	Operational changes (e.g., plant closures, voluntary lay-offs, terminations) and plan amendments are reviewed by finance personnel with the requisite expertise and knowledge of the		

		applicable accounting framework and principles. Finance personnel assess the effect of the operational changes or amendments on the entity's financial statements, including reference to the appropriate accounting framework and principles. The assessment and supporting documentation are reviewed and approved by management before the journal entry is recorded.		
Measurement of Benefit Obligation	An event occurs that significantly reduces the number of years of expected future service, or eliminates the accrual of benefits for a significant number of employees, but the event is not known to management or the actuary and the effect on the benefit obligation is not analysed.	Management (1) reviews minutes from executive, board, audit committee, and other operational meetings to identify operational changes or events that may have an effect on existing benefit plans and the entity's financial statements and (2) communicates the changes or events to the actuary		
Activity of Plan Assets	The entity makes lump sum payments to plan participants in exchange for their rights to receive future benefits and the effect on the benefit obligation is not recognised or accounted for by management.	On a periodic basis, finance personnel review minutes from executive, board, audit committee, and other operational meetings to identify actions and initiatives that may affect the benefit obligation, benefit plan structure, or significant assumptions underlying actuarial		

		analyses, etc. Matters identified are reviewed and analysed on a timely basis as to the effect on the benefit obligation		

Chapter 16: Depreciation/Amortisation and other expenses

16.1. Depreciation / Amortisation: Control Environment

Activities	Yes	No	N/A	Remarks
Evaluation of useful life of assets				
Apply depreciation methods				
Ensure consistency in applying depreciation policy				
Follow guidelines as per Schedule II of Companies Act 2013 and Accounting Standard AS 10 and Indian Accounting Standard Ind AS 16				

16.2. Depreciation / Amortisation and other expenses: Financial Control over Financial Reporting

Activities	Risk environment	Preventive control	Detective control	Monitoring control Y/N/NA
Depreciation / amortisation and Other expenses Recording Other Expenses	Other Expenses are: • Recorded for transactions that did not occur • Not recorded for transactions that did occur • Recorded at incorrect amounts	Trade payables and other expenses are recorded automatically by the ERP system upon matching the purchase order, completed service order, and the invoice received, completing a 3-way match.	Manual journal entries to trade payables, inventory, or Other Expenses, including period-end payable accruals, and supporting documentation, are reviewed and approved by management before the journal entry is recorded. On a periodic basis, management compares actual results with budgeted and prior-year amounts; significant and/or unusual differences are investigated and resolved	
Recording Other Expenses	Other Expenses are recorded in the incorrect accounting period.	Other Expenses at, or after, period-end are reviewed and scrutinised by management for proper accounting in the proper period prior to recording.	Management compares monthly financial statements, including financial metrics, to budget and prior-year amounts; significant unusual relationships are	

			monitored, investigated, and resolved	
Recording Other Expenses	Other Expenses are recorded in the incorrect general ledger account.	Manual journal entries are prepared by accounting personnel, and management, who examines the supporting documentation, makes certain the journal entry has been recorded correctly by the preparer	Management compares monthly financial statements, including financial metrics, to budget and prior year amounts; significant unusual relationships are monitored, investigated, and resolved	
Recording Other Expenses	Amounts recorded to trade payables and other expenses do not relate to goods or services received.	Trade payables and other expenses are recorded automatically by the ERP system upon matching the purchase order, completed vendor work order, or GRN Manual journal entries to trade payables, inventory, or other expenses, including period-end payable accruals, and supporting documentation, are reviewed and approved by management before the journal entry is recorded.		
Recording Other Expenses	Prepaid expenses are incorrectly removed from the general ledger when a prepaid asset still exists.		Prepaid expenses and related other expense accounts are analysed on a monthly basis and compared to budget. Explanations are obtained for any significant variances and differences. The analysis is reviewed by senior management. Management with knowledge of service providers' transaction	

			terms reviews prepaid expense general ledger activity for unusual adjusting entries. Discrepancies are investigated and resolved on a timely basis.	
Recording Other Expenses	Expenditures where future benefits exist for the entity are incorrectly recorded as expenses instead of prepaid.	Invoices for goods or services received are authorised and accompanied by appropriate supporting documentation. Management reviews supporting documentation and journal entries to record prepayments prior to accounting personnel recording to the general ledger Finance personnel review the nature and types of expenses incurred, and code the expense to the appropriate account. Management reviews the coding, supporting documentation, and journal entry before the journal entry is recorded	Prepaid expenses and related other expense accounts are analysed on a monthly basis and compared to budget. Explanations are obtained for any significant variances and differences. The analysis is reviewed by senior management.	
Recording Other Expenses	Expenditures where no future benefit exists to the entity are recorded as prepaid expenses and deferred on the balance sheet.	Finance personnel prepare journal entries to record prepaid expenses, including supporting documentation. Management reviews the journal entries and supporting documentation to record prepaid expenses prior to accounting personnel recording to the general ledger.	Prepaid expenses and related other expense accounts are analysed on a monthly basis and compared to budget. Explanations are obtained for any significant variances and differences. The analysis is reviewed by senior management.	
Recording	Amortisation of	Finance personnel	Management with	

Other Expenses	prepaid is recorded in advance of the time period associated with the prepaid expense.	prepare amortisation schedules for all recorded prepaid expenses, including preparing supporting documentation for the amortisation period and methodology. Management reviews and approves amortisation schedules and supporting documentation before recording amortisation journal entries	knowledge of service providers' transaction terms reviews recorded prepaid expenses for proper recording, classification, and amortisation, including review of supporting documentation and analyses. Discrepancies are investigated and resolved on a timely basis	
Recording Other Expenses	Amortisation recorded does not include all prepaid items.	Finance personnel prepare amortisation schedules for all recorded prepaid expenses, including preparing supporting documentation for the amortisation period and methodology. Management reviews and approves amortisation schedules for completeness and accuracy and supporting documentation before recording amortisation journal entries		
Recording Other Expenses	Amortisation recorded includes prepaid items that do not exist.	Finance personnel prepare amortisation schedules for all recorded prepaid expenses, including preparing supporting documentation for the amortisation period and methodology. Management reviews and approves		

		amortisation schedules for completeness and accuracy and supporting documentation before recording amortisation journal entries.		
Recording Other Expenses	Period assigned or amortisation methodology applied is inappropriate.	Finance personnel prepare amortisation schedules for all recorded prepaid expenses, including preparing supporting documentation for the amortisation period and methodology. Management reviews and approves amortisation schedules and supporting documentation before recording amortisation journal entries		
Recording Other Expenses	Inappropriate methodology for calculating the provision for doubtful trade receivables could result in misstated trade receivables and bad debt expense.		Management reviews the provision for doubtful trade receivables methodology, assumptions, and underlying calculation for appropriateness on a periodic basis	
Recording Other Expenses	Provision for doubtful trade receivables calculation is based on inaccurate receivables aging data.	The ERP system ages the trade receivables based on the parameters established within the ERP system and this computer-generated information is used in the calculation of the Provision for doubtful trade receivables.		
Recording Other Expenses	Improvements made to fixed assets (e.g., remodels, additions)	Improvement project plans are reviewed by finance	Recorded Other Expenses are compared to budget	

	are incorrectly expensed.	personnel with knowledge of the entity's capitalisation policy. The journal entry and supporting documentation for capital improvement expenditures are reviewed by management prior to the journal entry being posted	regularly; management investigates and resolves significant variances	
Recording Other Expenses	Expenditures of a non-capital nature (e.g., repairs and maintenance) have been incorrectly capitalised	Expenditures of a non-capital nature are reviewed and approved by finance personnel with knowledge of the entity's capitalisation policy. Journal entry and supporting documentation for expenditures of a non-capital nature are reviewed by management prior to the journal entry being posted.	Recorded capital expenditures and other expenses are compared to budget regularly; management investigates and resolves significant variances	
Recording Other Expenses	Depreciation expense is: • Calculated using an inappropriate rate or using an inappropriate methodology • Recorded at the incorrect amount • Not calculated for all fixed assets.	Management reviews fixed assets additions for appropriate assignment of depreciable lives and methodology, and performs a periodic review of useful lives and depreciation methodology for all fixed assets for ongoing appropriateness	On a periodic basis, management performs a retrospective analysis of fixed assets disposals to challenge the depreciable lives and methodology being applied to fixed assets	
Recording Other Expenses	Depreciation expense is recorded for assets of a non-capital nature or for assets that have been disposed.	Expenditures of a non-capital nature are reviewed and approved by finance personnel with knowledge of the entity's capitalisation policy. Journal entry and supporting documentation for expenditures of a	Management reviews fixed assets additions for appropriate assignment of useful lives and methodology, and performs a periodic review of useful lives and depreciation methodology for all fixed assets for ongoing	

		non-capital nature are reviewed by management prior to the journal entry being posted.	appropriateness On a periodic basis, management performs a retrospective analysis of fixed assets disposals to challenge the depreciable lives and methodology being applied to fixed assets	
Recording Other Expenses	Intangibles where no future economic benefit is expected are recorded or are recorded in excess of the asset amount rather than as an other expense.		Finance personnel periodically reconcile intangible asset balances to supporting documentation; management reviews and approves the reconciliations, including supporting documentation for account activity. Unusual activity or invalid reconciling items are investigated and resolved on a timely basis and adjusted to other expense Finance personnel maintain a listing of recorded intangible assets. The listing is reviewed by operational management, including in-house legal counsel, as appropriate, for completeness. Discrepancies are investigated and resolved on a timely basis and adjusted to other expense	
Recording Other Expenses	Impairment indicators may exist for recorded fixed assets, but are not known to or identified by management.	On a periodic basis, accounting and operations management meet to assess internal or external factors that may be indicators of impairment	Management periodically reviews budgeted versus actual results for the entity, including its product lines and segments. The results of this review are utilised by management in	

			assessing whether impairment indicators may be present.	
Recording Other Expenses	Management's impairment assessment uses business and valuation assumptions that are not based on its best and most supportable estimates.	Finance management reviews the business assumptions (including the reporting unit carrying amounts and assessment date) for appropriateness prior to being provided to management's valuation expert Management from different areas of the entity meet to review the forecast for appropriateness using historical performance, their knowledge of the entity's strategic plans, industry projections, and peer company data Management reviews the calculations performed and assumptions used within the goodwill impairment assessment for consistency with commonly accepted valuation practices, prior-year assumptions, and publicly available peer company and industry information		
Recording Other Expenses	Amortisation is not calculated for all recorded intangible assets.		Management reviews intangible asset additions for appropriate assignment of useful lives and methodology, and performs a periodic review of useful lives and amortisation	

			methodology for all intangible assets for ongoing appropriateness	
Recording Other Expenses	Amortisation is recorded for intangible assets that have been disposed, fully amortised, or for which the entity does not have legal ownership.		Finance personnel periodically reconcile intangible asset balances, and related amortisation, to supporting documentation; management reviews and approves the reconciliations, including supporting documentation for account activity. Unusual transactions or invalid reconciling items are investigated and resolved on a timely basis and adjusted to other expense.	
Recording Other Expenses	Intangible assets are amortised using an inappropriate useful life or method that is inappropriate under the circumstances.	On a periodic basis, finance personnel analyse intangible assets for the best estimate of useful lives, and an amortisation method that reflects the pattern in which economic benefits of the intangible asset are consumed or otherwise used up. Management reviews and approves the analysis and supporting documentation.	On a periodic basis, management performs a retrospective analysis of intangible assets that have been fully amortised in prior periods to challenge the useful lives and methodology being applied to intangible assets	
Recording Other Expenses	Goods received by, or services rendered to, the entity are: • Not recorded in trade payables or Other Expenses • Recorded at the incorrect amount	Trade payables and other expenses are recorded automatically by the ERP system upon matching the purchase order, completed vendor work order, or GRN On a periodic basis, finance personnel review open	On a periodic basis, management compares actual results with budgeted and prior-year amounts; significant and/or unusual differences are investigated and resolved.	

		purchase orders and record Other Expenses and accrued payables for goods or services rendered for which a completed service order or vendor invoice has not been received. The journal entry and supporting documentation are reviewed and approved by management before the journal entry is recorded.		
Recording Other Expenses	Accruals and other expenses are initially recorded when no liability exists.	Finance personnel prepare the journal entry, supporting documentation, and account analysis to record provision for expenses. Management reviews and approves the journal entry, supporting documentation, and account analysis before the journal entry is recorded	On a periodic basis, finance personnel reconcile provision for expenses to supporting detail. Management reviews the reconciliation and supporting documentation, and unusual activity or invalid reconciling items are investigated and resolved on a timely basis	
Recording Other Expenses	Provision for expenses exist but are not recorded.	On a periodic basis, finance personnel meet with members of management (e.g., sales, operational, human resources, legal counsel) to discuss developments and/or changes in the business that may affect recorded provision for expenses, or may affect the need to record an provision for expense. Finance personnel prepare a journal entry and supporting documentation, which are reviewed by management before the journal entry is recorded		

Recording Other Expenses	The entity uses an inappropriate methodology or incorrect significant assumptions or underlying data to calculate and record provision for expenses.	On a periodic basis, provision for expenses is recorded based on an analysis performed by qualified personnel at the entity or by a qualified third-party specialist. The methodology, significant assumptions, and underlying data used, as well as the journal entry, are reviewed, evaluated, and approved by management with appropriate knowledge before the journal entry is recorded.	On a periodic basis, management retrospectively reviews prior-year provision for expenses; including the methodology used, significant assumptions utilised, and the underlying data relied upon in developing such estimates. Revisions are made to the methodology or significant assumptions and underlying data used in the current-period estimation process, as necessary.	
Recording Other Expenses	Costs are incorrectly classified (e.g., costs of another expense nature are incorrectly classified as inventory costs, costs of an inventory nature are incorrectly classified as another expense).	Finance personnel review the nature and type of costs incurred, and codes the cost to the appropriate account. Management reviews the coding, supporting documentation, and journal entry before the journal entry is recorded	Management periodically reviews actual inventory, cost of sales, gross profit, and other expense amounts in comparison to budget, historical amounts, or current-year trends, and investigates and resolves any significant variances. This review is performed at a sufficient level of detail and disaggregation (e.g., by type of product line, type of services).	
	Other Possible Risks and Controls			
Recording Other Expenses	Operating leases for fixed assets are incorrectly accounted for as finance leases.	New lease contracts and lease modifications are reviewed by finance personnel to determine whether they meet the criteria for finance or operating lease treatment, including reference to the appropriate accounting framework and	New lease contracts and lease modifications recorded in the lease register are periodically reviewed by management to verify that the lease has been properly accounted for as a finance or operating lease.	

		principle. The journal entry and supporting documentation are reviewed by management prior to the journal entry being posted.		
Recording Other Expenses	Finance leases for fixed assets are incorrectly accounted for as operating leases.	New lease contracts and lease modifications are reviewed by finance personnel to determine whether they meet the criteria for finance or operating lease treatment, including reference to the appropriate accounting framework and principle. The journal entry and supporting documentation are reviewed by management prior to the journal entry being posted.	New lease contracts and lease modifications recorded in the lease register are periodically reviewed by management to verify that the lease has been properly accounted for as a finance or operating lease.	
Recording Other Expenses	Provision for doubtful trade receivables is insufficient in reserving for both unknown but historically predictable bad debt and specific known bad debt.		Management reviews the Provision for doubtful trade receivables methodology, assumptions, and underlying calculation for appropriateness on a periodic basis	
Recording Other Expenses	Management does not appropriately consider economic, industry, or customer financial considerations in the calculation of Provision for doubtful trade receivables.	Management reviews the assumptions utilised in calculating the provision to assess and conclude whether the assumptions take into consideration the current economic environment, specific customer financial conditions, regulatory changes, industry issues, etc. Based on their		

		review, management approves the Provision for doubtful trade receivables.		
Recording Other Expenses	Provision for doubtful trade receivables is overstated due to possible management bias concerning specific customer reserves.	Credit manager reviews aged trade receivables and documentation of collection activities performed by the credit personnel supporting the specific reserve and approves the recorded specific reserves.		
Recording Other Expenses	Receivables write-offs using the direct write-off method are not authorised in accordance with the established policy and, as a result, may be invalid.		Trade receivables write-offs are performed by accounting personnel in accordance with the write-off policy. Management reviews trade receivables write-offs for compliance with the established policy	
Recoveries of other expenses	Customer-specific reserves do not take into consideration information regarding pending losses or recoveries.	Management responsible for developing the provision for doubtful trade receivables obtains and reviews credit department documentation regarding collection efforts on aged receivables for information indicating a pending loss or recovery		
Recording Other Expenses	Trade receivable are incorrectly written off.		Management reviews and approves write-offs of trade receivables.	
Recording Other Expenses	Recoveries of trade receivables previously written off are improperly recorded in the Statement of Profit and Loss.		Management reviews recoveries of trade receivables previously written off. Journal entries made to record trade receivables recoveries	

			are reviewed and approved by management prior to recording.	
Recording Other Expenses	Capital work-in-progress (CWIP) is not transferred to fixed assets when the asset is placed into service and therefore not depreciated.		Operations management periodically reviews the listing of CWIP assets and communicates to accounting management any CWIP assets that have been put into service	
Recording Other Expenses	Internally developed intangible assets (e.g., copyrights, trademarks, patents) are inappropriately recorded as expenses.	Finance personnel with the requisite expertise and knowledge of the applicable accounting framework, review costs incurred related to intangible assets. Supporting documentation and the journal entry are prepared by finance personnel, and reviewed and approved by management before the journal entry is recorded		
Recording Other Expenses	The entity inappropriately capitalises costs related to internally developed intangible assets rather than expense such costs.	Finance personnel with the requisite expertise and knowledge of the applicable accounting framework, review costs incurred related to intangible assets. Supporting documentation and the journal entry are prepared by finance personnel and reviewed and approved by management before the journal entry is recorded	Finance personnel periodically reconcile intangible asset balances to supporting documentation. Management reviews and approves the reconciliations, including supporting documentation for account activity. Unusual activity or invalid reconciling items are investigated and resolved on a timely basis.	
Recording Other Expenses	Provision for payroll, taxes, and other costs are recorded at incorrect amounts.	Finance personnel prepare the journal entry, supporting documentation, and	Management periodically reviews actual inventory, cost of sales, gross profit,	

		account analysis to record provision for expenses. Management reviews and approves the journal entry, supporting documentation, and account analysis before the journal entry is recorded	and other expense amounts in comparison to budget, historical amounts, or current-year trends, and investigates and resolves any significant variances. This review is performed at a sufficient level of detail and disaggregation (e.g., by type of product line, type of services). Spreadsheets utilised to analyse and calculate significant provision for expenses are locked from formula editing. On a test basis, finance personnel test the calculations within the spreadsheet for ongoing accuracy	
Recording Other Expenses	Provision for bonuses are incorrectly calculated and recorded due to misapplication of the bonus criteria.	Finance personnel calculate accrued bonuses based on the provisions of the bonus program. Management reviews and approves the bonus calculation and journal entry before the journal entry is recorded. Management bonuses are reviewed and approved by the CEO and/or a board of governance (e.g., Board of Directors, Remuneration Committee of the Board of Directors) before the management bonuses are recorded	On a periodic basis, management compares actual results with budgeted and prior-year amounts; significant and/or unusual differences are investigated and resolved	
Recording Other Expenses	Compensated absences are incorrectly calculated and recorded (i.e., not	On a periodic basis, finance personnel calculate compensated	On a periodic basis, management compares actual results with budgeted	

consistent with the stated human resource policy).	absence and prepare the supporting documentation and related journal entry. Management, including human resource management, reviews the calculation and journal entry for consistency with the stated policy and approves the journal entry before it is recorded	and prior-year amounts; significant and/or unusual differences are investigated and resolved.		

16.3. Finance cost: Financial Control over Financial Reporting

Activities	Risk environment	Preventive control	Detective control	Monitoring control Y/N/NA
Finance cost Recording Finance Cost	*Core risks and controls* Finance cost is recorded but does not exist.	Finance personnel prepare the journal entry, supporting documentation, and account analysis to record finance cost. Management reviews and approves the journal entry, supporting documentation, and account analysis before the journal entry is recorded.	On a periodic basis, finance personnel reconcile accrued interest to supporting detail. Management reviews the reconciliation and supporting documentation, and unusual activity or invalid reconciling items are investigated and resolved on a timely basis.	
Recording Finance Cost	Finance Cost exists but is not recorded	On a periodic basis, finance personnel meet with members of management (e.g., sales, operational, human resources, legal counsel) to discuss developments and/or changes in the business that may affect recorded finance cost, or may affect the need to record additional finance cost. Finance personnel prepare a journal entry and supporting documentation,		

		which are reviewed by management before the journal entry is recorded.		
Recording Finance Cost	Finance Cost is recorded at incorrect amounts.	Finance personnel prepare the journal entry, supporting documentation, and account analysis to record accrued finance cost. Management reviews and approves the journal entry, supporting documentation, and account analysis before the journal entry is recorded.	Spreadsheets utilised to analyse and calculate significant accrued finance costs are locked from formula editing. On a test basis, finance personnel test the calculations within the spreadsheet for ongoing accuracy.	
Recording Finance Cost	Finance Costs are recorded in the incorrect accounting period.	Finance Costs at, or after, period-end are reviewed and scrutinised by management for proper accounting in the proper period prior to recording.	Management compares monthly financial statements, including financial metrics, to budget and prior-year amounts; significant unusual relationships are monitored, investigated, and resolved.	
Recording Finance Cost	Finance Costs are recorded in the incorrect general ledger account.	Manual journal entries are prepared by accounting personnel, and management, who examines the supporting documentation, makes certain the journal entry has been recorded correctly by the preparer.	Management compares monthly financial statements, including financial metrics, to budget and prior-year amounts; significant unusual relationships are monitored, investigated, and resolved.	
	Other Possible Risks and Controls			
Recording Finance Cost	Capitalised interest is: • Inappropriately recorded for assets directly purchased and put into service • Not recorded for assets constructed • Recorded at the incorrect amount.	CWIP is reviewed by finance personnel with knowledge of the entity's capitalisation policy. Finance personnel consider whether the assets constructed qualify for capitalised interest based on the nature of the		

		asset and the amount of interest incurred in the period, and calculate the amount of interest to be capitalised. The journal entry and supporting documentation for capitalised interest are reviewed by management prior to the journal entry being posted.		

16.4. Foreign currency: Financial Control over Financial Reporting

Activities	Risk environment	Preventive control	Detective control	Monitoring control Y/N/NA
Foreign currency	Foreign Currency Translation Adjustments	The ERP system automatically calculates the foreign currency translation adjustment for accounts denominated in foreign currencies. The proposed translation adjustment is independently reviewed and approved by management prior to recording.	Management with knowledge of the entity's share capital transactions reviews the share capital for unrecorded or inaccurately recorded transactions. Unusual activity or errors are investigated and resolved on a timely basis.	

16.5. Risk Control Matrix summary: Depreciation (specimen format)

Item	1
Mega process	Fixed Assets
Process	Depreciation
Activity	Depreciation on Fixed Assets
Risk description	Wrong entries and Calculation
Control objective	To ensure that depreciation expense is correctly levied on assets of capital nature, accurately reflected in the financial statements

	To ensure that amortization expense is correctly levied on intangible assets and accurately reflected in the financial statements
Control environment – to be certified by the process owner	Depreciation/Amortization on Fixed Assets is computed by accountant on monthly basis and the same is reviewed by Manager.
Risk category	
Fraud risk – yes / no	No
Risk category – high / medium / low	Low
Internal financial control over financial reporting – yes / no	Yes
IFC/IFCR Component	Prevention and detection of frauds and errors
Prevention / detection of frauds – yes / no	Yes
Key Control – yes / no	Yes
Control category	
Completeness	xx
Existence	xx
Accuracy	xx
Valuation	
Rights / obligation	
Presentation	
Manual / Automatic	Manual
Preventive / detective	Preventive
Frequency of measurement	Event based
Document if any	Fixed Asset Register, Depreciation calculation report through ERP
Prepared by (maker)	Accounts Executive
Checked by (checker)	Finance Manager
System solution – ERP – Yes/no	Yes
Whether covered under SOP – Yes / no	Yes
Process design gap – Yes / no	No

Chapter 17: Recording to reporting process

17.1. Recording to reporting: Control environment

Financial Reporting: Control Environment	Yes	No	N/A	Comments
1. Chart of accounts				
2. Accounting procedures manual				
3. Organizational chart to define responsibilities				
4. Absence of entries direct to ledgers				
5. Posting references in ledgers				
6. Review of journal entries				
7. Use of standard journal entries				
8. Use of prenumbered forms				
9. Support for all journal entries				
10. Access to records limited to authorized persons				
11. Rotation of accounting personnel				
12. Required vacations				
13. Review of system at every level				
14. Appropriate revision of chart of accounts				
15. Appropriate revision of procedures				
16. Separation of recordkeeping from operations				
17. Separation of recordkeeping from custodianship				
18. Record retention policy				
19. Bonding of employees				
20. A conflict of interest policy				

17.2. Recording to reporting: Process

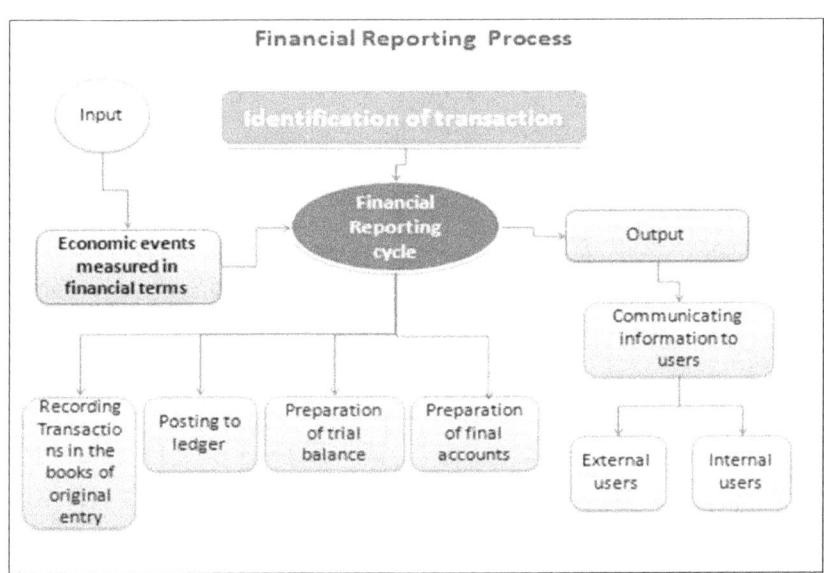

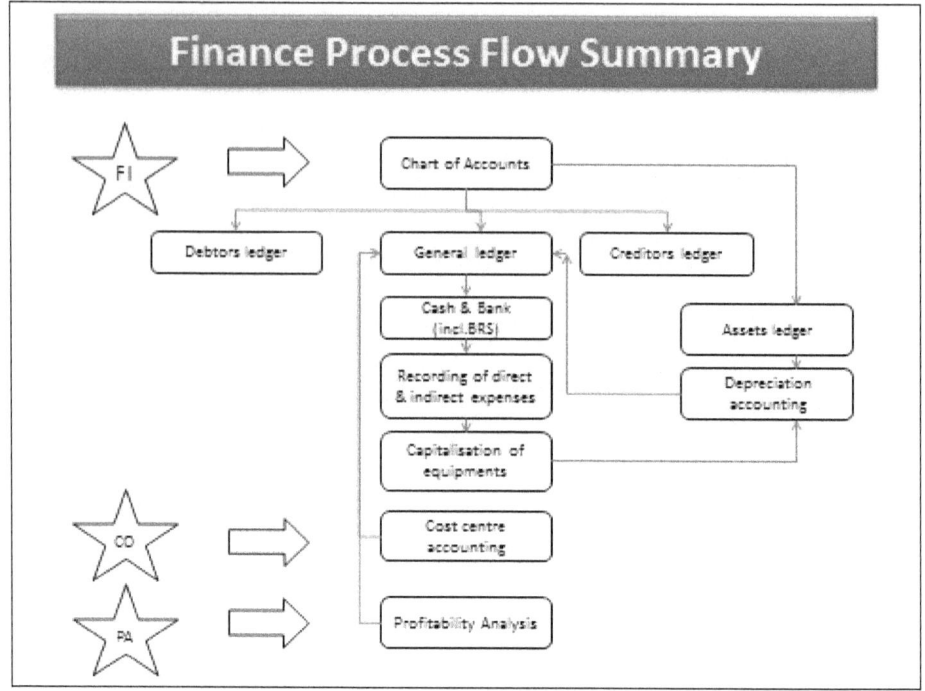

17.2.1. Enterprise hierarchy matrix: Control environment

Enterprise structure	Business Area Profit centre	Plant code Corp office Processing Plant Marketing office Region Depot	Sales office / Depots	
Operating concern (COPA)	Profit centre	Product group	Customer group	Distribution channel Direct Sales Route Sales Distributors Consignment Institutional Deemed Export STO Direct Sales
Controlling Area	Cost centre groups	Cost centres		
Sales organisation	Sales Org. category Domestic Export	Distribution channel Direct Sales Route Sales	Division Product group	Sales Area

		Distributors Consignment Institutional Deemed Export STO Direct Sales		
Purchasing organisation	**Categories** -Central Purchase Organization -Processing / Manufacturing Plants Purchase Organisation -Branch Purchase org -Depot purchase org	**Purchasing groups** Purchase of RM General Consumables Lab Purchases Packing Materials Sundry. Materials Capital Items Project Items Services Subcontracting Trading Stock Transfer		
Credit control areas	**Profit centres**	**Customer group**		

17.2.2. Chart of Accounts: Control Environment

General Ledger would be numbered in the following sequence:

1. Liabilities

2. Assets

3. Revenues

4. Material Consumption & Manufacturing Expenses

5. Employee Benefits & Administrative Expenses

6. Selling Expenses & Interest and other charges

7. Depreciation, Deferred Expenses & Appropriations

8. Noted Items

A model Chart of Accounts hierarchy would be as under:

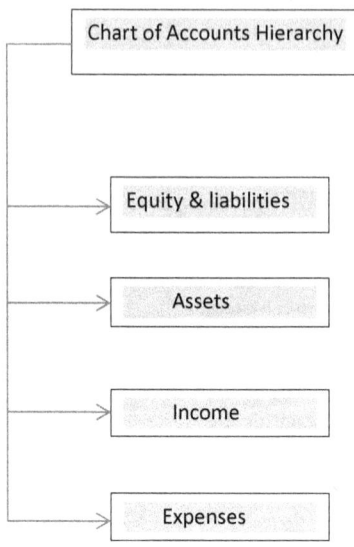

17.2.3. Five level CoA will be maintained for all drawer whether assets, equity, liabilities, revenue and expenditure.

Five levels will be as follows:

S. No.	GL Name	COA Level	Accounts Type
1	Assets	1st Level	Title Account
2	Non-current Assets	2nd Level	Title Account
3	Tangible Fixed Assets	3rd Level	Title Account
4	Plant & Machineries	4th Level	Title Account
5	Office Equipments	5th Level	Posting/Title Accounts

17.2.4. An illustrative Equity & liabilities hierarchy would be as under:

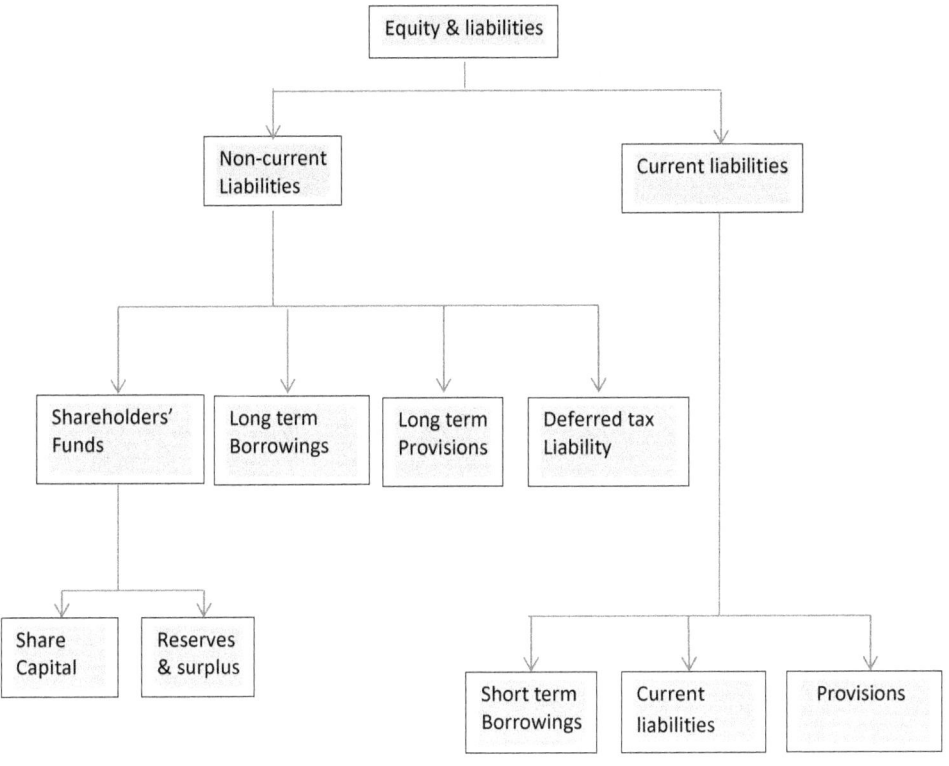

17.2.5. An illustrative Assets hierarchy would be as under:

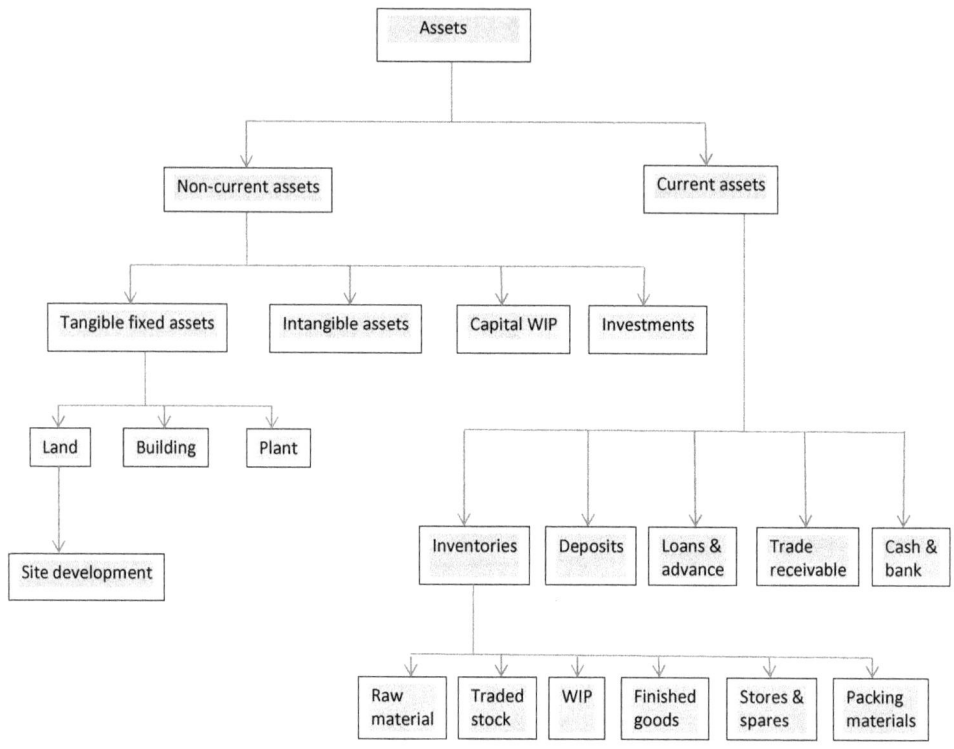

17.2.6. An illustrative Income hierarchy is as under:

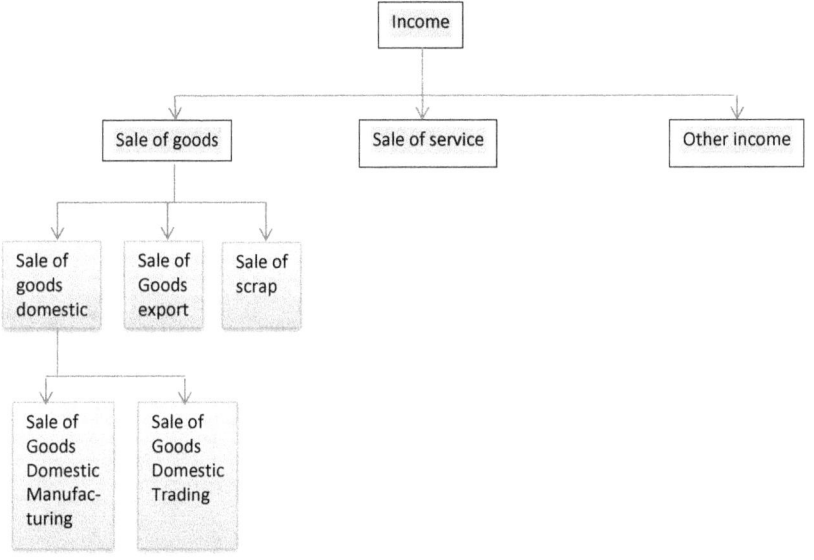

17.2.7. An illustrative expense hierarchy is as under:

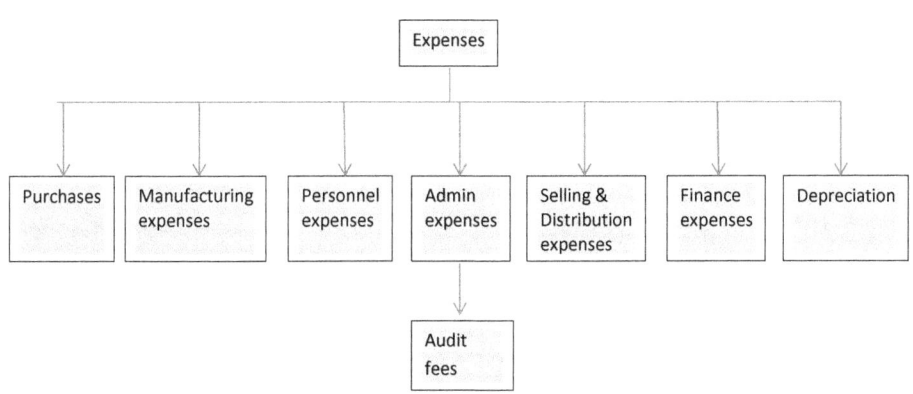

17.2.8. Specimen Chart of Accounts covering all the elements of accounting is as under:

Chart of Accounts	Group	Sub-group	Ledger
Balance Sheet account heads			
11000	Shareholders' funds		
11100		Share Capital	
11110			*Authorised*
11120			*Issued and subscribed*
11130			*Partners capital*
11140			*Proprietors capital*
11150			*Share capital*
11200		Reserves & Surplus	
11210			*Profit & Loss Account*
11220			*Share Premium Account*
11230			*Capital reserve*
11240			*General reserve*
11250			*Revaluation Reserve*
11260			*Share capital pending allotment*
12000	Long term borrowings		
12100		Term Loan from bank	
12110			*Banks*
12120			*Interest accrued and due*
12200		Term loan from financial institutions	
12210			*Financial institutions*

12220			*Interest accrued and due*
12300		**Loan from Directors, Partners & Relatives**	
12310			*Directors*
12320			*Partners*
12330			*Relative*
12400		**Loan from Related Parties**	
12401			*Related party*
12500		**Vehicle Loans**	
12510			*BANK-CAR LOAN*
12520			*Interest accrued and due*
13000	**Deferred tax**		
13100		**Deferred tax liability / assets**	
13110			*Deferred tax liability - revaluation of assets*
13120			*Deferred tax liability - depreciation*
13130			*Deferred tax liability - others*
13140			*Deferred tax assets*
14000	**Long term provisions**		
14100		**Long term provisions**	
14110			*Provision for employee benefits*
14120			*Provision for others*
15000	**Current liabilities**		
15100		**Secured loans**	
15101			*WORKING CAPITAL TERM LOAN-WCTL*

15102			Bank OD A/c
15103			Bank CC A/c
15104			Interest accrued and due
15200		**Unsecured loans**	
15201			WORKING CAPITAL TERM LOAN -WCTL
15202			Bank OD A/c
15203			Bank CC A/c
15204			Interest accrued and due
15300		**Trade Payables**	
15310			Trade creditors for goods
15320			Trade creditors for expenses
15330			Trade creditors - related parties
15400		**Current liabilities others**	
15401			Audit Fee Payable
15402			ESIC payable
15403			Provident Fund payable
15404			Salary payable
15405			Wages payable
15406			Interest accrued but not due
15407			Advance from customers
15500		**Duties and taxes**	
15510			CGST
15520			SGST
15530			IGST
15540			TDS
15550			TCS

16000	Short term provisions		
16100		Short term provisions	
16110			*Provision for gratuity*
16120			*Provision for leave encashment*
16130			*Provision - others*
21000	Non-current Assets		
21100		Tangible (fixed)Assets	
21110			*Land*
21120			*Building*
21130			*Plant & Machinery*
21140			*Electrical Installations*
21150			*Electronic & Office equipment*
21151			*Computer hardware*
21160			*Furniture & fittings*
21170			*Vehicle*
21180			*Capital Work in Progress*
21200		Intangible Assets	
21210			*Computer software*
21220			*Patents and copyrights*
21230			*Intangible assets - others*
21300		Investments	
21310			*Investment in securities*
22000	Current Assets		
22100		Inventories	
22110			*Raw materials*

22120			*Traded stock*
22130			*Work-in-progress*
22140			*Finished goods*
22150			*Stores & spares*
22160			*Packing materials*
22200		**Trade Receivables (Sundry Debtors)**	
22210			*Trade Debtors*
22220			*Trade Debtors - over six months*
22230			*Trade Debtors - related parties*
22300		**Cash & bank balances**	
22310			*Cash in hand*
22320			*Bank Accounts*
22330			*Imprest Account*
22400		**Loans & Advances (Asset)**	
22410			*Advance tax & TDS*
22420			*Earnest Money Deposit*
22430			*Advance to suppliers*
22440			*STAFF ADVANCE*
22450			*Advance to others*
22500		**Deposits (Asset)**	
22510			*Security Deposit*
22600		**Branch / Divisions**	
22610			*Location 1*
22620			*Location 2*
22630			*Location 3*
22700		**Misc. Expenses (ASSET)**	
22710			*Preliminary Exp*

Statement of Profit & Loss - Account heads			
31000	**Sales and other income**		
31100		**Sales of goods**	
31110			*Sales of goods - Manufacturing*
31120			*Sales of goods - Trading*
31130			*Sales of goods - export*
31140			*Sales of scrap*
31200		**Sales of service**	
31210			*Technical support services*
31220			*Consulting services*
31230			*Training services*
31240			*Other services*
31300		**Other income**	
31301			*Misc. Income*
31302			*Profit on Disposal of Fixed Assets*
31303			*Claims /Refunds Received*
31304			*Discounts Received*
31305			*Interest Income on Bank Deposit*
31306			*Interest Income on Loans Given*
31307			*Interest Income from Investments*
31308			*Interest Income Others*

31309			*Realised Foreign Exchange Gains*
31310			*Unrealised Foreign Exchange Gains*
31311			*Bad debt recovery*
41000	**Direct Expenses**		
41100		**Purchase of goods / services**	
41101			*Purchase of Goods (Domestic) Raw material*
41102			*Purchase of Goods (Domestic) Packing material*
41103			*Purchase of Goods (Domestic) Consumables*
41104			*Purchase of Goods (Domestic) Trading*
41105			*Purchase of Goods(import)*
41106			*Stock Revaluation Losses*
41107			*Purchase services*
41108			*Stock write off*
41109			*Raw Materials - write off*
41110			*Finished Goods - Write-off*
41111			*Trading Goods - Write-off*
41112			*Packing Materials - Write-off*
41113			*Components - Write-off*
41200		**Manufacturing expenses**	
41201			*Repairs & maintenance - building*
41202			*Repairs & maintenance - Plant & Machinery*

41203			Repair & Maintenance - Others
41204			Electricity Charges
41205			Consumable Expenses
41206			Loading & unloading charges
41207			Factory Watch & ward
41208			Job work expenses
41209			Technical knowhow
41210			Packing expenses - Production
41211			Inspection fees - Production
41212			Quality Control - Production
41213			Testing fees/Certification charges - Production
41214			Other Factory Expenses - Production
41215			Freight & Carriage Inbound
41216			Custom Clearing Charges
41217			Demurrage
41218			Clearing & Forwarding Expenses
41219			Warehouse charges
41220			Factory license fees
41221			R & D Expenses
41222			Laboratories expenses
41300		Opening Stock A/c	
41310			Raw materials
41320			Traded stock
41330			Work-in-progress
41340			Finished goods

41350			Stores & spares
41400		**Cost of goods / services sold**	
41410			Cost of goods sold
41420			Cost of service
42000	**Indirect Expenses**		
42100		**Personnel Expenses**	
42101			*Staff salaries*
42102			*Wages*
42103			*Director Salaries*
42104			*Director Commission*
42105			*Partners remuneration*
42106			*Partners commission*
42107			*Casual labour*
42108			*Employers contribution to PF*
42109			*Employers contribution to ESI*
42110			*Recruitment and hiring expenses*
42111			*Employee acquisition expenses*
42112			*Employees relocation expenses*
42113			*Employees joining expenses*
42114			*Training charges*
42115			*Employee incentives*
42116			*Staff Welfare Expenses*
42117			*Leave travel assistance*

42118			*Medical benefits*
42119			*Bonus*
42120			*Gratuity*
42121			*Leave encashment – unavailed leave with wages*
42122			*Staff bus / cab services*
42123			*Motivation allowance*
42124			*Uniform, shoes allowance*
42125			*Attire allowance (international)*
42126			*Canteen / Pantry expenses*
42127			*Meals expenses*
42200		**Administration Expenses**	
42201			*Office repairs and maintenance*
42202			*Computer & printer repairing expenses*
42203			*Repairs & Maintenance - Other office equipments*
42204			*Office Supplies*
42205			*Postage and courier charges*
42206			*Car parking expenses*
42207			*Cartage & porterage*
42208			*Vehicle Expenses*
42209			*Overseas travelling*
42210			*Domestic travelling*
42211			*Local conveyance*
42212			*Visa charges*
42213			*Ticket booking & cancellation charges*

42214			Printing & Stationary
42215			Audit fees
42216			Legal and professional charges
42217			ROC Charges
42218			Provision for bad and doubtful debts
42219			Office rent
42220			Municipal taxes
42221			License fees
42222			Penalties
42223			Court fees and stamps expenses
42224			Commission & brokerage on rent
42225			Insurance charges
42226			Consultancy charges
42227			Rounding off charges
42228			Loss on sale of assets
42229			Newspapers, books & periodicals
42230			Computer AMC Charges
42231			Office security expenses
42232			Donation
42233			Subscription & membership
42234			Fees to chamber of commerce / business associations
42235			Townhall / communication expenses
42236			Telephone expenses
42237			Mobile expenses
42238			Internet expenses

42239			*Website expenses*
42240			*Telecalling expenses*
42241			*Liasioning expenses*
42242			*Meetings & conferences*
42243			*Seminar expenses*
42244			*Sponsorship expenses*
42245			*Tender fees*
42246			*Miscellaneous expenses*
42300		**Selling & Distribution expenses**	
42301			*Freight Outward & Cartage A/c*
42302			*Business Promotion Exp.*
42303			*Advertisement & publicity expenses*
42304			*Export clearance charges*
42305			*Export license charges*
42306			*Marketing & selling expenses*
42307			*Exhibition expenses*
42308			*Rebates & discounts*
42309			*Campaign expenses*
42400		**Financial Expenses**	
42401			*Bank Charges*
42402			*Interest charges*
42403			*Inward remittance charges*
42404			*Exchange difference*
42500		**Depreciation**	
42510			Depreciation on assets
50000	**Profit & Loss**		

	A/c		
50010		**Profit & Loss A/c**	Profit & Loss A/c

17.2.9. Document Types

- Document Number
- Document header details (Reference / Header Text)
- Classification of nature of business transactions e.g. customer invoice, Customer Incoming Payment, Customer Credit Memo, Vendor payments / Invoice, etc.
- Area of Posting (Customers, Vendors, Assets, GL Accounts)

17.2.9.1. Specimen document types

Doc Type	Description
AA	Asset Posting
AB	Accounting Document
AF	Dep. Posting
AN	Net asset posting
C0	Cash voucher
C1	Cash Receipt
C2	Cash Payment
DA	Customer Document
DG	Customer credit memo
DR	Customer Invoice
DZ	Customer Payment
DN	Customer Debit Memos
KA	Vendor Document
KG	Vendor credit memo

Doc Type	Description
KR	Vendor Invoice
KN	Net vendors
KP	Account maintenance
KZ	Vendor Payment
PR	Price change
RE	Invoice – gross
RN	Invoice – net
RV	Billing document transfer
SA	G/L account document
WA	Goods issue
WE	Goods receipt
WI	Inventory document
WL	Goods issue/delivery
WN	Net goods receipt
ZP	Bank Payment posting
ZR	Bank reconciliation
ZS	Bank Payment by check
ZV	Bank Payment clearing
X1	Recurring Entries
X2	Sample Documents
ED	Excise Document

Doc Type	Description
TD	TDS Document

17.3. General Ledger Master Maintenance

GL account master records	<ul><li>Create a new account at Chart of Account Level</li><li>Extend the new account at Company Code Level</li><li>Create a new account centrally (both COA and Company Code level)</li><li>Create a new account with template</li><li>Change an account</li><li>Display an account</li><li>Block/unblock an account for creation, posting</li><li>Mark an account for deletion</li></ul>

17.4. General ledger: Control Environment

Activity	Yes	No	N/A	Remarks
❑ Integrate sales journal with invoicing in system ❑ Update all receipt and payment entries in cash book ❑ Complete Bank Reconciliation statement in the system ❑ Post payroll journal on a monthly basis ❑ Create functionality of Copy journal ❑ Document nos to be generated by system ❑ Parking and posting of vouchers ❑ Implement workflow on approvals ❑ Post all other provision related entries ❑ Automatic reversal of journal entries ❑ Creation of budget and comparison with actuals month and YTD ❑ Multi currency posting ❑ Drill down from financial statements to voucher level ❑ Import and export of data to and from the system ❑ System should carry an audit trail				

17.5. General Ledger: process steps

Main process	Description	Process in ERP
1. General	Creating a New GL and Posting of	Creation of new account

Main process	Description	Process in ERP
	documents	Posting an entry
		Viewing a document
		Viewing an Account
2. Parking of the document:	Parking of documents where authorization is required before posting.	Parking of the document
		Releasing parked document
1. Sample Document	When there is a transaction which will be posted every month whose date is fixed but amount is not fixed, this technique will be utilized.	Creation of sample document
		Posting with reference
2. Recurring Document	When there is a transaction which will be posted every month and whose date and amount are fixed, this technique will be used.	Creation of recurring document
		Recurring document display
		Recurring document posting
3. Accrual / deferral documents	Whenever there is a provision to be made for accrual / deferral documents, SAP provides a screen to make it and later reverse the transaction.	Posting of accrual / deferral document
		Reversing the accrual / deferral document
4. Reversal of documents	Whenever there is an error while posting SAP offers a methodology to make a reverse posting. A reversal reason is configured and different number ranges were given for reversal documents from FI as per the requirement.	Individual reversal
		Mass reversal
		Cleared item reversal
		Accrual / deferral document reversal

Main process	Description	Process in ERP
		Reversal of reversal
5. General Ledger account analysis	By using SAP we can see the line items / balances of GL accounts and also change the layout of display by adding any necessary things like cost center etc.,	GL Line Item Analysis
		GL Balance Analysis
6. Account clearing	Open items in GL accounts ex. Like outstanding expenses can be cleared one by one and can be arranged in ascending / descending order and can be cleared.	Without Specification of Clearing Currency
		With Specification of Clearing Currency
7. Foreign currency revaluation	In closing, foreign currency loans or items related to foreign currency can be revaluated using the transaction FAGL_FC_VAL and represented in the balance sheet. Based on either loss or profit different GL accounts can be mentioned and the values can be automatically sent to those GL accounts to maintain the balances.	Posting of loan
		Repayment (outgoing payment)
		Revaluation of FC Transaction
8. GR/IR Clearing and material valuation	At the time of closing GR/IR account has to be cleared from SAP transaction F.19. Revaluation of materials has to be done t o represent the new values (market value or realization value whichever is less) in the balance sheet.	GR/IR Clearing
9. Interest	Whenever it is required to	Define GL accounts and attach the

Main process	Description	Process in ERP
calculation:	calculate interest on GL accounts an interest indicator is set and attached with the GL account master record, it is also possible to see interest accrued based on number of days.	Repayment by posting
		Viewing and posting the interest accumulated

17.5.1. Internal control on parking and posting of documents

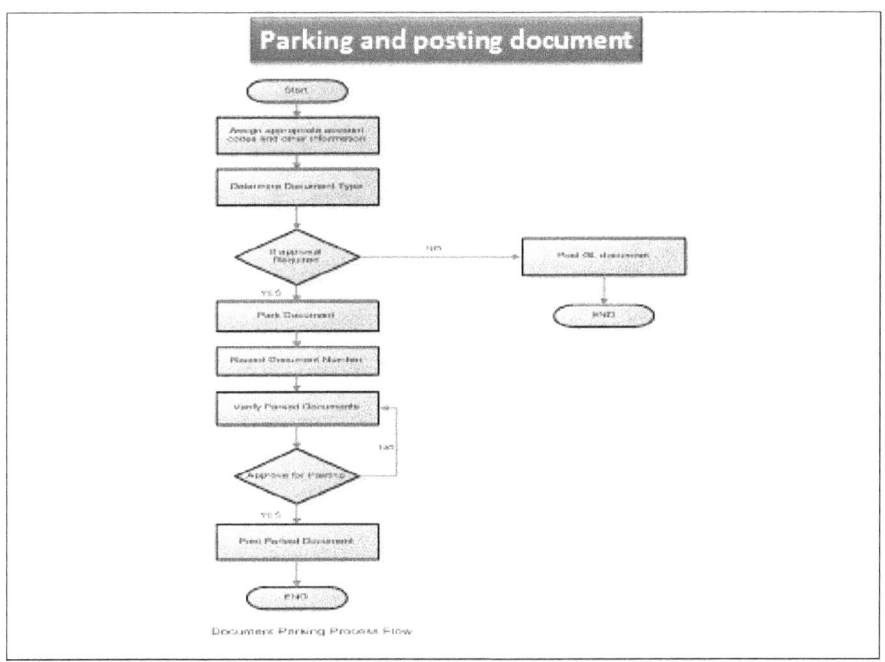

17.6. Period-end process flow

Month-end process

Item	-4	-3	-2	-1	0	+1	+2	+3	+4	+5
Post all invoices, receipts and vouchers up to 25th in books of accounts	x									
Complete bank reconciliation up to 25th		x								
Complete reconciliation of customer accounts with receipts up to 25th		X								
Complete reconciliation of all vendor accounts with payments up to 25th		X								
Complete reconciliation of all stock and consumption accounts up to 25th		x								
Take first cut ledger printout up to 25th		X								
Post all adjustment entries / rectification entries up to 25th			x							

Month-end process (Contd)

Item	-4	-3	-2	-1	0	+1	+2	+3	+4	+5
Post payroll voucher for the month				x						
Post all sales invoices from 26th till 30th of the month						x				
Post all receipts and vouchers from 26th till 30th						x				
Complete bank reconciliation till month-end							x			
Complete customer account reconciliation with invoices and receipts							x			
Complete vendor account reconciliation with purchase invoices and payments							x			
Post all GRN entries against which vendor invoices not received							x			

Month-end process (Contd)

Item	-4	-3	-2	-1	0	+1	+2	+3	+4	+5
Complete raw material stock and consumption reconciliation with GRNs and Production report							x			
Complete finished stock reconciliation with despatches and invoices and production records							x			
Complete posting of all excise records including RG 23 Part I and Part II							x			
Complete updation of all provisions related to statutory liabilities							x			
Print final customer and vendor ledger and check for errors								x		
Print final trial balance and check for errors								x		
Reconcile stock ledger with general ledger								x		

Month-end process (Contd)

Item	-4	-3	-2	-1	0	+1	+2	+3	+4	+5
Finalise Profit & Loss Accounts									x	
Finalise Balance Sheet and Cash flows									x	
Circulate draft financial statement to CMD for review and approval									x	
Release approved monthly financial statements									x	
Release month-wise and YTD customer wise sales report							x			
Release month-wise and YTD production report							x			
Release month-wise manpower utilisation report							x			
Release month-wise and YTD Financial Dash Board and present to CEC meeting										x

17.7. Journal Vouchers: Financial Control over Financial Reporting

Activities	Risk environment	Preventive control	Detective control	Monitoring control Y/N/NA
Journal Vouchers Capturing and processing routine information	There is a mismatch between sub- ledger and General Ledger		Sub-ledgers are reconciled to the general ledger on a regular basis. All reconciling items are identified, investigated, and cleared on a timely basis. Management reviews reconciliations and follows up on unusual matters on a timely basis.	
Capturing and processing non-routine information	The appropriate accounting treatment is not specified for each non-routine event, transaction, and account balance.	Accounting treatment for significant non-routine events and transactions (including those requiring the use of accounting estimates and judgment in the selection and application of accounting principles) is researched, analysed, documented, updated, and communicated to responsible parties on a regular basis. Such communication also includes the timeframes and appropriate methods for computing estimates and the framework for judgments involved.		
Capturing and processing non-routine information	There is no evaluation of each non-routine event or transaction	Accounting policies and procedures specify correct treatment for major types of non-routine events and		

		transactions. Proper application to facts and circumstances is monitored independently across business units and across accounting periods.		
Capturing and processing non-routine information	There is no relevant, sufficient, and reliable data to record, process, and report each non-routine event.	Data and other information used in preparing the analysis for each non-routine event or transaction are relevant. Appropriate controls or procedures are in place and operating effectively to ensure the validity, accuracy, and completeness of the data and other information used in preparing the analysis. This includes controls over any process used to extract, summarise, and accumulate data and information that is obtained directly from the general ledger (e.g., the data is reconciled to the underlying supporting documentation).		
Capturing and processing non-routine information	Application of the entity's accounting policies to each non-routine event or transaction is not performed on a timely basis and appropriately documented.	Accounting policies and procedures specify correct treatment for major types of non-routine events and transactions. Proper application to facts and circumstances is monitored independently across business units and across accounting periods.		
Capturing and processing non-routine	Application of the entity's accounting policies to each non-	For each non-routine event or transaction, a supporting analysis		

information	routine event or transaction is not performed on a timely basis and appropriately documented.	is prepared and documented by knowledgeable personnel in accordance with relevant generally accepted accounting principles (including relevant regulatory rules) and the entity's accounting policies. An entity-specific checklist of the entity's policies and procedures, a generally accepted accounting principles checklist, or other suitable mechanism is used to ensure each non-routine event or transaction is valid, complete, and appropriately recorded in the appropriate accounting period.		
Capturing and processing non-routine information	There is no independent review of application of the entity's accounting policies to each non-routine event or transaction for appropriateness and absence of bias by an individual with the appropriate level of authority and experience.	Management reviews details of significant non-routine events and transactions for completeness and validity on a regular basis. Information about each significant non-routine event and transaction is analysed and documented in a timely manner. Management reviews all documentation and analysis supporting significant non-routine transactions prior to recording amounts in the general ledger.		
Capturing and processing non-routine information	Application of the entity's accounting policies to each non-routine event or transaction is not	An independent review of significant judgments and estimates included in the financial		

	performed on a timely basis and appropriately documented.	records is performed at the end of every accounting period by knowledgeable personnel. The independent review includes a comparison with subsequent outcomes and an evaluation to determine degree of accuracy, fairness of information, and evidence of bias		
Capturing and processing non-routine information	Journal entries for non-routine event or transaction are not approved by management.	Journal entries have adequate supporting documentation and are reviewed and approved independently prior to posting		
Capturing and processing non-routine information	There are no appropriate basis for non-routine transactions involving significant estimates and judgements	Significant estimates and judgments and changes thereto are reported to the audit committee on a regular basis.		
Capturing and processing non-routine information	There are no appropriate basis for non-routine transactions involving significant estimates and judgements		An independent review of significant judgments and estimates included in the financial records is performed at the end of every accounting period by knowledgeable personnel. The independent review includes a comparison with subsequent outcomes and an evaluation to determine degree of accuracy, fairness of information, and evidence of bias.	

17.8. Recording to Reporting: Financial Control over Financial Reporting

Activities	Risk environment	Preventive control	Detective control	Monitoring control Y/N/NA
Financial Reporting	There is no appropriate	Management establishes a well-		

Defining the Financial Closing and Reporting Process	documented process with respect to financial closing and reporting, including the identification and updating of internal and external financial reporting requirements and deadlines.	defined process for financial reporting based on the specific characteristics of the entity. The process and its overall timing, methodology, format and frequency of analysis are formally documented, approved, and reviewed on a regular basis.		
Defining the Financial Closing and Reporting Process	There is no appropriate documented process with respect to financial closing and reporting, including the identification and updating of internal and external financial reporting requirements and deadlines.	Corporate accounting policies and procedures, standard charts of accounts and related guidance are appropriately created and updated on a regular basis and distributed to subsidiaries. Knowledgeable personnel monitor changes in authoritative guidance and regulations (e.g.: Companies Act, Accounting Standards, Income Tax Act etc.) that affect the entity and make the appropriate changes to the entity's corporate accounting policies and procedures on a timely basis. Management and personnel involved in the financial closing identify all applicable generally accepted accounting principles affecting the entity and ensure that entity's accounting policies reflect the most		

		recent, applicable authoritative guidance (e.g.: Companies Act, Accounting Standards, Income Tax Act etc.) which are properly documented and communicated to achieve consistency across business units and accounting periods.		
Defining the Financial Closing and Reporting Process	There are no procedures and timetables for communicating relevant information affecting the financial closing and reporting process within the entity and these are not sufficiently documented, and updated on a timely basis.	Processes and policies are established and documented regarding the requirements for entity personnel to timely communicate to the financial reporting department, information related to events and transactions affecting financial reporting, including significant contracts and agreements. The compliance with communication processes and policies is monitored on a regular basis.		
Defining the Financial Closing and Reporting Process	Changes made to the financial closing and reporting process are not valid and properly authorised.		Changes to the entity's financial closing and reporting process (e.g., changes to the chart of accounts, including addition and deletion of general ledger accounts) are monitored; any significant change is independently reviewed and approved.	
Defining the Financial	Roles and responsibilities in the	Management defines, documents,		

Closing and Reporting Process	financial closing and reporting process are not clearly defined, documented, updated, and not communicated to appropriate departments and individuals on a timely basis. Individuals in financial reporting roles do not have the necessary understanding of the organisation's operations and appropriate accounting knowledge to properly perform their assigned responsibilities.	communicates and periodically reviews roles and responsibilities in the financial closing and reporting process in order to have adequate personnel with the appropriate skills and experience managing all accounting aspects. Knowledgeable personnel are hired into financial reporting roles and provided with adequate training, in line with Corporate guidelines		
Defining the Financial Closing and Reporting Process	When alternative accounting treatments are available for a significant event or transaction, the decisions on which treatments to select are not documented, approved by management, and are not communicated to the audit committee.		Evaluations of alternative accounting treatments for significant events and transactions are documented and approved by management. Alternative accounting treatments selected (including those related to critical accounting policies) for significant events and transactions are communicated to the Audit Committee on a timely basis in accordance with applicable laws and regulations.	
Defining the Financial Closing and Reporting Process	General policies are not established and documented regarding permissible overrides of existing policies and procedures for the financial closing and reporting process.		All overrides require proper authorisation and are documented for subsequent independent review and monitoring.	
Defining the Financial Closing and	User profiles (on G/L system) are not monitored /	System-access profiles are set up by management. A		

Reporting Process	maintained to ensure that appropriate individuals have access to financial reporting process.	form establishing the specific access to be granted is completed by the manager.		
Capturing and processing NON routine information	The appropriate accounting treatment is not specified for each non-routine event, transaction, and account balance, including those requiring the use of accounting estimates and judgment in the selection and application of accounting principles.		Accounting policies and procedures specify correct treatment for major types of non-routine events and transactions. Proper application to facts and circumstances is monitored independently across business units and across accounting periods.	
Capturing and processing NON routine information	Relevant, sufficient, and reliable data necessary to record, process, and report each non-routine event or transaction is not captured.	Data and other information used in preparing the analysis for each non-routine event or transaction are relevant. Appropriate controls or procedures are in place and operating effectively to ensure the validity, accuracy, and completeness of the data and other information used in preparing the analysis. This includes controls over any process used to extract, summarise, and accumulate data and information that is obtained directly from the general ledger (e.g., the data is reconciled to the underlying supporting documentation).		
Capturing and processing NON routine	There are no procedures to ensure all postings have	When using computerised systems, the access		

information	occurred in the correct period.	rights to open and close financial periods is adequately restricted to prevent late entries from posting without appropriate management review after the books are closed.	
Capturing and processing NON routine information	Significant estimates and judgments are not well determined and have sufficient supporting documentation.		Formulas used for accruals, write-offs and reserves are periodically reviewed by the appropriate responsible and consistently followed. Appropriate management approves changes to formulas.
Capturing and processing NON routine information	The application of the entity's accounting policies to each non-routine event or transaction is not performed on a timely basis and appropriately documented by knowledgeable and qualified personnel using approved methods and formats.		For each non-routine event or transaction, a supporting analysis is prepared and documented by knowledgeable personnel in accordance with relevant generally accepted accounting principles (including relevant regulatory rules) and the entity's accounting policies. An entity-specific checklist of the entity's policies and procedures, a generally accepted accounting principles checklist, or other suitable mechanism is used to ensure each non-routine event or transaction is valid, complete, and appropriately recorded in the appropriate accounting period.
Capturing and	There is no		Management reviews

processing NON routine information	independent review of application of the entity's accounting policies to each non-routine event or transaction for appropriateness and absence of bias by an individual with the appropriate level of authority and experience. All non-routine events and transactions are not accurately processed in the appropriate accounting period. Non-routine events and transactions are not valid and properly recorded in the appropriate accounting period.		details of significant non-routine events and transactions for completeness and validity on a regular basis. Information about each significant non-routine event and transaction is analysed and documented in a timely manner. Management reviews all documentation and analysis supporting significant non-routine transactions prior to recording amounts in the general ledger.	
Performing the Accounting Period Close	There is no independent review of application of the entity's accounting policies to each non-routine event or transaction for appropriateness and absence of bias by an individual with the appropriate level of authority and experience. There is no basis for significant estimates and judgments associated with each non-routine event or transaction.		An independent review of significant judgments and estimates included in the financial records is performed at the end of every accounting period by knowledgeable personnel. The independent review includes a comparison with subsequent outcomes and an evaluation to determine degree of accuracy, fairness of information, and evidence of bias. Significant estimates and judgments and changes thereto are reported to the audit committee on a regular basis.	
Performing the Accounting Period Close	No analysis is prepared accurately and consistently in accordance with the entity's defined		Required analysis (including the format, timeline, preparers, and reviewers) are prepared, updated,	

	financial closing process and in the appropriate accounting period.		and distributed on a regular basis. Management has processes in place at the end of the accounting period to ensure that all analysis are appropriately performed and independently reviewed.	
Performing the Accounting Period Close	All sources of information for routine and non-routine events and transactions are not identified and analysed.		Routine and non-routine events and transactions occurring near the period-end are analysed and reviewed to determine whether they are accounted for in the appropriate accounting period.	
Performing the Accounting Period Close	There are no reconciliations for all significant accounts and no independent review of such reconciliation. All required analysis are not prepared accurately and consistently in accordance with the entity's defined financial closing process.		All significant analysis and reconciliations are independently reviewed in comparison with established guidelines by knowledgeable personnel. All issues identified through the analysis and reconciliations are resolved.	
Performing the Accounting Period Close	There are no reconciliations for all significant accounts and no independent review of such reconciliation. All required analysis are not prepared accurately and consistently in accordance with the entity's defined financial closing process.		Unusual items and exceptions in analysis and reconciliations are documented upon identification. Resolution and treatment of unusual items identified are documented and reviewed independently for appropriateness on a timely basis. Management reviews resolution of items on a regular basis.	
Performing the Accounting	All intercompany transactions and balances are not	Knowledgeable personnel prepares and updates a list of		

Period Close	identified, reconciled, and appropriately eliminated in consolidation in the appropriate accounting period.	recurring journal entries, including adjusting, self-reversing, consolidating, and eliminating journal entries, and compare journal entries proposed during the closing process to such list to determine completeness and validity.	
Performing the Accounting Period Close	All required analysis are not prepared accurately and consistently in accordance with the entity's defined financial closing process.		Monthly exception and aging reports are generated highlighting unusual items. Significant items are investigated and resolved on a timely basis and in the appropriate accounting period.
Performing the Accounting Period Close	All suspense accounts are not identified and monitored.		All suspense accounts are identified and significant accounts / items are reviewed by management or other supervisory personnel on a timely basis. Appropriate journal entries to reclassify amounts into the appropriate general ledger account are prepared and reviewed as part of this process.
Performing the Accounting Period Close	All suspense accounts are not identified and monitored.		The underlying cause for significant suspense items is investigated, assessed, and appropriately resolved. Appropriate changes to the financial-reporting process are made to address the underlying cause for significant suspense items.
Performing	The trial balance(s)	Management has a	

the Accounting Period Close	used to prepare the financial statements are not generated from the final general ledger(s).	process in place to ensure that the trial balance(s) used in the financial-statement-preparation process are final, contain all valid journal entries made, and net to zero.		
Performing the Accounting Period Close	All trial-balance accounts are not appropriately and consistently grouped for presentation in the financial statements for accounting periods presented.	A financial statement accounts grouping schedule is prepared, updated, and used in the drafting of the financial statements.		
Performing the Accounting Period Close	All trial-balance accounts are not appropriately and consistently grouped for presentation in the financial statements for accounting periods presented.		Financial statement account groupings are independently reviewed for (1) compliance with presentation in conformity with the entity's accounting policies and generally accepted accounting principles, (2) accuracy and consistency, and (3) comparability between the current and previous accounting period(s).	
Performing the Accounting Period Close	There are no restrictions to access and to run transactions in the automated consolidation software which may compromise the integrity of financial data	Only employees involved in the reporting package process have access to such automated applications, with specific user-profiles.		
Performing the Accounting Period Close	All related-party events and transactions are not identified and authorised, appropriately accounted for, and disclosed in the appropriate		All related-party events and transactions are identified and a schedule of such related-party events and transactions is prepared. For purposes of financial-	

	accounting period.		statement presentation and disclosure, an independent review of such schedule is performed by the disclosure committee (or other suitably qualified personnel) and the legal department. Any issues identified are addressed on a timely	
Performing the Accounting Period Close	There are no procedures to ensure all postings have occurred in the correct period.	When using computerised systems, the access rights to open and close financial periods is adequately restricted to prevent late entries posting without appropriate management review after the books are closed.		
Performing the Accounting Period Close	All related-party events and transactions are not identified and authorised, appropriately accounted for, and disclosed in the appropriate accounting period.		Audit committees must approve all related-party transactions Board approval is required for specified types of related-party transactions and this approval is appropriately documented.	
Performing the Accounting Period Close - Consolidation & Reporting	All subsidiaries and other entities are not identified and appropriately included in the consolidation process.		Management reviews the consolidation for the proper inclusion of the results of all subsidiaries and other entities for which consolidation is appropriate. A list of subsidiaries and other entities is prepared, updated for new acquisitions and stake disposals. Newly promulgated generally accepted accounting principles, if any should also be	

			evaluated for any inclusions/exclusions to be made to the subsidiary listing Subsidiaries and other entities included in the consolidation during the consolidation process are compared to this master list of subsidiaries.	
Performing the Accounting Period Close - Consolidation & Reporting	Consolidation packages received from subsidiaries do not accurately reflect the underlying financial records at each subsidiary.		Internal audit (or other suitably qualified individuals) on a test basis, verifies the accuracy of financial reporting package contents by comparing reporting package amounts with the subsidiary records.	
Performing the Accounting Period Close - Consolidation & Reporting	Consolidation packages received from subsidiaries do not accurately reflect the underlying financial records at each subsidiary.	Subsidiary's reporting package is reconciled with the trial balance (prepared directly from the subsidiary's GL). Supporting information for significant items included in the package is tested for reasonableness.		
Performing the Accounting Period Close - Consolidation & Reporting	All trial-balance accounts are not appropriately and consistently grouped for presentation in the financial statements for all accounting periods presented. Entries recorded directly to the financial statements are not valid.		Internal financial statement packages are reconciled to the trial balance and the general ledger. Any post-close adjusting journal entries are posted to the final financial package.	
Performing the Accounting Period Close - Consolidation & Reporting	Entries recorded directly to the financial statements are not valid.		Entries recorded directly to the financial statements require direct approval of the entity's principal	

			accounting officer and such recording and approval follow a predetermined process. Entries recorded directly to the financial statements are (1) tracked and recorded in the general ledger on a timely basis and (2) properly included in subsequent accounting periods.	
Preparing and reviewing financial-statement disclosures	All necessary disclosures in draft financial-statement are not made.	The entity uses up-to-date disclosure checklists (or other suitable mechanisms) to ensure that all relevant financial information is disclosed (1) appropriately in accordance with generally accepted accounting principles and the entity's accounting and disclosure policies and (2) in the appropriate accounting period. Management ensures that all personnel preparing and reviewing disclosures receive the relevant checklists and instructions to perform their assigned duties in accordance with the entity's disclosure policies.		
Preparing and reviewing financial-statement disclosures	All necessary disclosures in draft financial-statement are not made.		An independent review of the financial statements and all related disclosures using a generally accepted accounting principles financial statement presentation and	

			disclosure checklist (or other suitable mechanisms) is performed by management, the disclosure committee, or other suitably qualified personnel to review the draft financial statements and related disclosures as a whole for completeness, consistency across accounting periods, and compliance with generally accepted accounting principles and the entity's accounting and disclosure policies.	
Preparing and reviewing financial-statement disclosures	All necessary disclosures in draft financial-statement are not made.		Management establishes processes to ensure that all required disclosure analysis are prepared and reviewed on a timely basis. Such review consists of whether disclosures are prepared using the appropriate assumptions and methodology, and whether disclosures are properly presented in accordance with generally accepted accounting principles and the entity's accounting and disclosure policies. Management receives the appropriate reporting packages, sign-offs, and representations from business units to ensure all relevant information has been disclosed.	
Preparing and reviewing financial-	All necessary disclosures in draft financial-statement	A list of all sources of event and transaction		

statement disclosures	are not made.	information or other suitable mechanism is used and communicated to appropriate personnel to ensure the completeness of disclosed information. Management, the disclosure committee, or other suitably qualified personnel are involved, as considered necessary, in analysing the effect of event and transaction information on the financial-statement disclosures.		
Preparing and reviewing financial-statement disclosures	Each financial-statement disclosure is not prepared in accordance with generally accepted accounting principles (including relevant regulatory rules) and the entity's accounting and disclosure policies.	For each financial-statement disclosure, a supporting analysis is prepared and documented by knowledgeable personnel in accordance with relevant generally accepted accounting principles (including relevant regulatory rules) and the entity's accounting and disclosure policies. An entity-specific checklist, a generally accepted accounting principles disclosure checklist, or other suitable mechanism is used to ensure each disclosure is valid, complete, and appropriately presented in the appropriate accounting period.		
Preparing and	Each financial-		If third parties assist in	

reviewing financial-statement disclosures	statement disclosure is not prepared in accordance with generally accepted accounting principles (including relevant regulatory rules) and the entity's accounting and disclosure policies.		the preparation of financial-statement disclosure information, knowledgeable personnel reviews the information prepared by the third party for reasonableness and consistency with the entity's business and prior-period information. All issues identified through the review are resolved prior to the disclosure information being included in the reports released to the public and filed with regulatory agencies.	
Reviewing and approving the financial statements	Each financial-statement disclosure is not prepared in accordance with generally accepted accounting principles (including relevant regulatory rules) and the entity's accounting and disclosure policies.		Management and those responsible for oversight of the financial closing and reporting process review the draft financial statements and related disclosures to be included in external reports prior to their release to the public. The review consists of analysing the draft financial statements and related disclosures and raising challenging questions. After any issues or questions raised have been resolved, the financial statements and related disclosures are approved by the board of directors or audit committee; such approval is documented.	
Reviewing and approving the financial statements	Each financial-statement disclosure is not prepared in accordance with generally accepted accounting principles		Management and the audit committee or board of directors are briefed by senior financial reporting personnel on a regular	

	(including relevant regulatory rules) and the entity's accounting and disclosure policies.		basis and at each period end for which financial statements are released to the public. Such briefing includes a discussion of key estimates and judgments, significant non-routine events and transactions, selection and application of critical accounting policies, areas with unusual fluctuations, and other relevant significant issues.	
Reviewing and approving the financial statements	Each financial-statement disclosure is not prepared in accordance with generally accepted accounting principles (including relevant regulatory rules) and the entity's accounting and disclosure policies.		Management accumulates and tracks issues and concerns identified as part of the review of the external reports for each period-end financial closing and reporting process and follows up on a timely basis to verify that items have been properly resolved in the appropriate accounting period and prior to the release of the reports to the public.	
Reviewing and approving the financial statements	The published financial statements (in print and electronic form) are not free from publishing, printing, or electronic-conversion errors.		The financial statements and related disclosures, in print and electronic form, are reconciled to the approved financial statements, trial balance, and supporting information prior to final publishing, printing, or electronic submission.	
Reviewing and approving the financial statements	All related party transactions and balances are not identified and appropriately		Knowledgeable personnel prepare and update a listing of all related-party transactions and	

disclosed in consolidation in the appropriate accounting period.		review appropriate disclosures in the financial statements for completeness and accuracy.	

17.9. Risks and System controls

Risks	System controls
1. All authorized journals are not posted to the general ledger.	• **General Ledger**. Run a transaction report to identify any journals that have been recorded but not yet posted. The posting process produces the "Batch/Transaction Bypassed List". This lists any transactions that were skipped and provides an explanation. • **Job Scheduler**. Use SBDC sessions to schedule posting to run automatically based on date or other criteria. Only approved transactions are posted.
2. An unauthorized journal is posted to the general ledger.	• **General Ledger**. Use menu security to restrict access to the posting function to authorized persons. In addition, you can place a journal code on "hold" to prevent posting of any transactions recorded for that journal until these have been reviewed and approved. You can also place specific transactions or batches of transactions on hold. • **Journal Cycle Management**. Use JCM to automatically route journals for approval to authorized persons. Flexible business rules control routing and determine when a transaction is released for posting.
3. Journals posted to the general ledger do not balance	• **General Ledger**. The system does not permit this. When a journal transaction is entered for the actuals data class, the system requires that debits and credits balance within company. It is also possible to enforce balancing at a lower organizational level – for example, within department (this is known as the "fixed break level" feature). • **General Ledger**. The system may be set up to force balancing of intercompany transactions. Intercompany balancing may be enforced during direct entry or balancing entries may be generated automatically as part of the posting process.
4. Journals are posted to the wrong account or for the wrong amount.	• **General Ledger**. The system requires a valid posting account. Use "combo identifiers" or "forced identifiers" to ensure that only valid combinations of posting account segments (for example, organization and natural account) are used. • **General Ledger**. The system enforces balancing of individual transactions within company. In addition, the "fixed break level" feature may be used to force balancing at a lower organization level. After the first transaction line item is entered, the "fixed" portion of the posting account defaults to subsequent lines and is non-modifiable. • **General Ledger**. Use batch and/or transaction control totals to verify amounts.
5. Journals are not adequately supported with source documents	• **General Ledger**. Use reference fields or extended text to record supporting information justifying the entries. • **Journal Cycle Management**. Users can attach to each journal supporting documents and notes justifying the entries.

6. Accounts for some entities (for example, acquired subsidiaries) are not properly classified on consolidated financial statements.	• **General Ledger.** Consider reorganizing the chart of accounts. In General Ledger, a common chart of account structure may be created for use in consolidated reporting, even though individual companies may have different structures. Make use of Attributes and Alternate Paths.
7. Intercompany accounts do not balance.	• **General Ledger.** The system may be set up to force balancing of Inter-company transactions. Intercompany balancing may be enforced during direct entry or balancing entries may be generated automatically as part of the posting process.
8. Accounts are not properly eliminated on the consolidated financial statements.	• **General Ledger.** Use the Automatic Journal (set-off) facility to automatically perform the necessary account eliminations and update a separate data class in General Ledger. This journal is then used to produce the consolidated financial statements.
9. Amounts used in the consolidation for subsidiaries or other business entities do not agree to the amounts reported by these entities.	• **Consolidation module.** Use the Consolidation module of all the holding and subsidiaries and set-off intercompany balances. Take the help of excel embedded into the program where required
10. Financial statements do not agree to the general ledger.	• **General Ledger.** Errors can occur when data is sent from GL to another system that produces financial statements or when data is rekeyed into Excel. Use the reporting facilities that are included with General Ledger to produce financial statements. Alternatively, use **Excel embedded into the system** to extract information from GL into predefined Excel report templates. • **General Ledger.** Report definitions created should be reviewed periodically (for example, if new account ranges have been added to the chart of accounts). It is imperative to make sure that personnel are properly trained to create or revise these reports. Use Profile Security to ensure that only authorized persons can modify the report definitions.
11. Financial statements are not clerically accurate.	• **General Ledger.** Errors can occur when data is rekeyed into Excel or other documents. Use the reporting facilities that are included with GL – Power Report Writer (Pro or Basic & Extended) to produce financial statements. Alternatively, use GL Excel to extract information from GL into predefined Excel report templates.
12. Management is not alerted about discrepancies between account balances and amounts that have been budgeted or forecast.	• **General Ledger.** Budgets and forecasts can be entered in the General Ledger using a variety of methods. Use standard GL reporting facilities to create "actual vs. budget variance" reports and distribute to responsible managers. • **Budget Cycle Management.** BCM can be used to create Excel based budgets for organizational units and route the budgets for revision and approval prior to updating GL. • **GL Excel.** Use GL Excel to create Excel-based "actual versus budget

	variance" reports and route automatically to managers for review.
13. Account balances in general ledger cannot be reconciled to amounts in sub-ledger systems.	• **Financial Statements**. Run reports to identify transactions that have not yet been posted (for AP and AR). Use Standard reports are available to assist with reconciling AP and AR with GL, including the aged as of requirements reports.
14. There is no audit trail of transactions or changes to General Ledger master files.	• **General Ledger**. The system can be set up to automatically maintain audit trails for changes to transactions prior to posting as well as additions or changes to master files, such as the posting accounts file. Information tracked includes the User ID, date and time. • **General Ledger**. The ledger detail file in GL contains detail information for all posted transactions. The End of Year function allows historic ledger detail data to be archived for future reference. • **Journal Cycle Management**. The Workflow Activity Log tracks all the steps (who, what, when) in the journal entry/approval process.

17.10. Specimen Risk Map: Recording to reporting

High

There is no audit trail of transactions or changes to General Ledger master

Financial statements do not agree to the general ledger.

All authorized journals are not posted to the general ledger.

There is a mismatch between sub- ledger and General Ledger

Account balances in general ledger cannot be reconciled to amounts in sub-ledger systems.

Journal entries are not supported by source documents

Impact

Financial statements are not clerically accurate.

Intercompany accounts do not balance

There are no reconciliations for all significant accounts and no independent review of such reconciliation.

Accounts are not properly eliminated on the consolidated financial statements.

Low

Journals are posted to the wrong account or for the wrong amount

Low   **Likelihood**   **High**

17.11. Risk Control Matrix summary: Financial closure (specimen format)

Item	1	2	3	4
Mega process	Financial closure	Financial closure	Financial closure	Financial closure
Process	Financial closure	Financial closure	Financial closure	Financial closure
Activity	Closure of Books of Accounts	Re-opening of books	Reporting	Approval and adoption of Financial Statements

Risk description	Delayed closure of monthly books of Account	Unauthorized re-opening of books of account and Unauthorized posting of entries during period re-open period	Financial statements are not prepared and presented in line with Company's Accounting Policies and applicable accounting guidelines and relevant prevailing law.	Prior approval from Board of Directors and Statutory Auditor is not obtained before statutory disclosures/ filling of financial statements
Control objective	To ensure that the books of account closed on timely basis.	To ensure that no back dated entries are posted in system without approval.	To ensure that Compliance with Laws and Standards	To ensure financial statements are approved.
Control environment – to be certified by the process owner	Books of account are finalized on a monthly basis and financial information is compiled by the 6th working day and reported to promoters / parent. The promoters / parent company raises queries, if any, which are subsequently addressed by the Finance team.	The system is locked for any back dated entry after the monthly report is sent. The right to reopen books of account is restricted and approval of Finance head is required. The entries then passed after re-opening of earlier period are reviewed and tracked by Internal Audit team.	To ensure the compliance with Company law, accounting standards, and disclosure requirements in Financial statements, Finance discusses the updates with the auditors. In case of any changes which has an impact on the Company, the same is discussed and recorded.	The Board of Directors of the Company pass a resolution for acceptance/ approval of financial statements, evidenced by the minutes of board meeting, prepared by Company Secretary. Statutory auditors sign off annually on the company's financial statements. Audited financial statements are adopted in the following Annual General Meeting.
Risk category				
Fraud risk – yes / no	No	No	No	No
Risk category – high / medium / low	Medium	High	Medium	Low
Internal financial control over financial reporting – yes / no	Yes	Yes	Yes	Yes

IFC/IFCR Component	Accuracy and completeness of the accounting records	Accuracy and completeness of the accounting records	Accuracy and completeness of the accounting records	Accuracy and completeness of the accounting records
Prevention / detection of frauds – yes / no	No	No	No	No
Key Control – yes / no	Yes	Yes	Yes	Yes
Control category				
Completeness	xx	**xx**	xx	**xx**
Existence	xx	xx	xx	xx
Accuracy	xx	xx	xx	xx
Valuation				
Rights / obligation				
Presentation	xx			xx
Manual / Automatic	Manual	Automatic	Manual	Manual
Preventive / detective	Detective	Preventive	Preventive	Preventive
Frequency of measurement	Monthly	Monthly	As and when	Annual
Document if any	Financial statements	System related controls		
Prepared by (maker)	Accounts Executive	Accounts Executive	Account Executive	Accounts Executive
Checked by (checker)	Financial controller	Financial controller	Financial controller	Financial controller
System solution – ERP – Yes/no	Yes	Yes	Yes	Yes
Whether covered under SOP – Yes / no	Yes	Yes	Yes	Yes
Process design gap – Yes / no	No	No	No	No

Chapter 18: Internal Financial Control of Branches

18.1. Branch operations: Control Environment

Activities	Yes	No	N/A	Remarks
Segregation of duties implemented in the branch				
Proper attendance records maintained in the branch				
Expenses are based on replenishment of petty cash				
Cash and bank transactions are up-to-date and bank reconciliation system is handled on-line without any back-log				
Proper records of inventories are maintained in the branch				
Regular and up-to-date transaction entries are made in ERP in order that there is no back-log				
Robust internal audit carried out from HO at the branches on periodic basis				
Exception reporting on operations is regularly made available to HO to people charged with governance related to the functioning of the branch				
Regular meetings of branch managers are conducted at HO to ensure governance issues and deficiency in systems are discussed.				

18.2. Branch operations: Financial Control over Financial Reporting: Audit checklist

S/L No	Audit check list	Yes	No	Remarks
1	What is the delegation of authority in the branch?			
2	What are the powers the branch manager has?			
3	Does the branch manager have cheque signing authority? If yes how much			
4	Cash management Physical cash count Compare with cash book / petty cash statement Reconcile cash with book balance Scutinise bank statement of the last six months and review large payments Go through the latest Bank reconciliation statement Are there material cash receipts? If so what nature? Identify transactions which are made in cash and see whether payments are made greater than Rs.20000/-			

	Whether recipient's acknowledgement recorded. Are there unbooked vouchers against cash disbursed?			
5	**Purchase process**			
	Review local purchase process			
	Is there any indent from branch manager on purchases ?			
	What is the basis of authorisation for payment?			
	Are there local Purchase Orders generated? If so what is the limit?			
	Is there a list of approved vendors from whom purchases are made?			
	Are there any comparative quotes where there are multiple vendors?			
	Are all purchases booked in Navision on-line real time?			
	Is there a back-log of purchases booked?			
	Are there cash purchases? If yes up to what threshold ?			
6	**Receiving process**			
	Are Receipt Notes generated against each Purchase Order?			
	Is quality of materials purchased checked			
	On receipt of yarns from Bikaner / Jaipur what documentation is maintained?			
	Can quantity received at branch be cross checked with quantities despatched from the sending location?			
	Is there transit insurance in stock transfers?			
	Are materials tracked through sku / item number created in ERP?			
	Are receipts tracked to PO raised in system and entered in system			
	Is there a back-log of receipts booked in the ERP?			
7	**Issuing process**			
	Are issue slips created for each issue of material?			
	When yarn is sent for dying is there a Returnable Gate Pass created?			
	Is it immediately updated in the ERP?			
	When yarn comes back after dying is there a receipt entry?			
	Again is it immediately updated in the ERP?			
	On receipt of yarns from Bikaner / Jaipur what documentation is maintained?			
	Can quantity received at branch be cross checked with quantities despatched from the sending location?			
	Is there transit insurance in stock transfers?			
	What is the process of materials issued to weavers? Can these materials be tracked to a issuing document?			
	Is there a process to track material lying with job workers for more than six months?			
	Are materials tracked through SKU / item number created in ERP?			

	Are receipts tracked to PO raised in system and entered in system?			
	Is there a back-log of receipts booked in the ERP?			
8	Material storage			
	How are the materials stored in the branch?			
	Are there SKU wise item list available in branch?			
	Are branch wise book stocks updated in ERP ?			
	How frequently are they reconciled with physical stocks?			
	Are there minimum level, maximum level and reorder level built in for each item of inventories?			
	Is there a procedure of inventory ageing?			
	What is the valuation - FIFO / LIFO / Weighted average?			
	Are the inventories covered under insurance?			
	What is the process of recording of RMR in the system? Are these materials taken back in stores in the ERP system?			
	Please carry out physical verification of some test items and track them to inventory records as per ERP			
9	Assets			
	How many assets are controlled from the branch?			
	What is the useful life of assets? Is there a record kept for these assets?			
	What is the process of charging depreciation?			
10	Job work			
	What is the process of job cards issued?			
	Does it have date, pre-numbering and a system serial number?			
	Is there a signature of materials released on this job card by the weavers?			
	Are these job cards regularly inspected and updated?			
	Are these job cards tracked in the system?			
11	Repairs and maintenance			
	What is the process of repairs and maintenance?			
	What are the documents based on which materials are sent on repairs?			
	Are the materials returned on repairs matched with pre-numbered Returnable Gate Pass?			
	What is the process of custody, recording and accounting of these materials which are returned?			
12	Attendance records			
	How many people are there in the branch?			
	Is there a process of maintaining attendance records in the branch?			
	Are these records sent to Corp of processing of salaries?			
	Who do the branch managers report into in HO?			
	Are leave records maintained in the branch?			

13	**Sales orders**			
	Who creates sales orders in the branch?			
	Are these sales orders serially pre-numbered?			
	Is there a process of tracking sales orders?			
	Is there a control check to assess number of sales orders not delivered?			
	Are these sales order uploaded in the system?			
14	**Application of ERP**			
	How many licences are issued in the branch?			
	Is the ERP used continuously by the users?			
	Are there any transaction entered without entering into ERP?			
	What is the speed of ERP?			
	What are the functionalities used in the ERP by the branch?			
	Do the users have secrecy of log in and password?			
	Is there an audit trail on the transaction in the system?			

Chapter 19: Specimen Audit Reports on Internal Financial Control

19.1 Appendix III to Internal Financial Control over Financial Reporting

Specimen audit reports related to Internal Financial Control over Financial Reporting are illustrated below.

Illustration 19.1: Separate reports

The following is an **example of separate unmodified audit report for an audit of internal financial controls over financial reporting in the case of standalone financial statements.**

ANNEXURE TO THE INDEPENDENT AUDITOR'S REPORT OF EVEN DATE ON THE STANDALONE FINANCIAL STATEMENTS OF ABC COMPANY LIMITED

Report on the Internal Financial Controls under Clause (i) of Sub-section 3 of Section 143 of the Companies Act, 2013 ("the Act")

I / We have audited the internal financial controls over financial reporting of ABC Company Limited ("the Company") as of March 31, 20X1 in conjunction with my / our audit of the standalone financial statements of the Company for the year ended on that date.

Management's Responsibility for Internal Financial Controls

The Company's management is responsible for establishing and maintaining internal financial controls based on _____ [for example, "the internal control over financial reporting criteria established by the Company considering the essential components of internal control stated in the Guidance Note on Audit of Internal Financial Controls Over Financial Reporting issued by the Institute of Chartered Accountants of India".] These responsibilities include the design, implementation and maintenance of adequate internal financial controls that were operating effectively for ensuring the orderly and efficient conduct of its business, including adherence to company's policies, the safeguarding of its assets, the prevention and detection of frauds and errors, the accuracy and completeness of the accounting records, and the timely preparation of reliable financial information, as required under the Companies Act, 2013.

Auditors' Responsibility

My / Our responsibility is to express an opinion on the Company's internal financial controls over financial reporting based on my / our audit. I / We conducted my / our audit in accordance with the Guidance Note on Audit of Internal Financial Controls Over Financial Reporting (the "Guidance Note") and the Standards on Auditing, issued by ICAI and deemed to be prescribed under section 143(10) of the Companies Act, 2013, to the extent applicable to an audit of internal financial controls, both applicable to an audit of Internal Financial Controls and, both issued by the Institute of Chartered Accountants of India. Those Standards and the Guidance Note require that I / we comply with ethical requirements and plan and perform the audit to obtain reasonable assurance about whether adequate internal financial controls over financial reporting was established and maintained and if such controls operated effectively in all material respects.

My / Our audit involves performing procedures to obtain audit evidence about the adequacy of the internal financial controls system over financial reporting and their operating effectiveness.

My / Our audit of internal financial controls over financial reporting included obtaining an understanding of internal financial controls over financial reporting, assessing the risk that a material weakness exists, and testing and evaluating the design and operating effectiveness of internal control based on the assessed risk. The procedures selected depend on the auditor's judgement, including the assessment of the risks of material misstatement of the financial statements, whether due to fraud or error.

I / We believe that the audit evidence I/we have obtained is sufficient and appropriate to provide a basis for my /our audit opinion on the Company's internal financial controls system over financial reporting.

Meaning of Internal Financial Controls over Financial Reporting

A company's internal financial control over financial reporting is a process designed to provide reasonable assurance regarding the reliability of financial reporting and the preparation of financial statements for external purposes in accordance with generally accepted accounting principles. A company's internal financial control over financial reporting includes those policies and procedures that (1) pertain to the maintenance of records that, in reasonable detail, accurately and fairly reflect the transactions and dispositions of the assets of the company; (2) provide reasonable assurance that transactions are recorded as necessary to permit preparation of financial statements in accordance with generally accepted accounting principles, and that receipts and expenditures of the company are being made only in accordance with authorisations of management and directors of the company; and (3) provide reasonable assurance regarding prevention or timely detection of unauthorised acquisition, use, or disposition of the company's assets that could have a material effect on the financial statements.

Inherent Limitations of Internal Financial Controls over Financial Reporting

Because of the inherent limitations of internal financial controls over financial reporting, including the possibility of collusion or improper management override of controls, material misstatements due to error or fraud may occur and not be detected. Also, projections of any evaluation of the internal financial controls over financial reporting to future periods are subject to the risk that the internal financial control over financial reporting may become inadequate because of changes in conditions, or that the degree of compliance with the policies or procedures may deteriorate.

Opinion

In my / our opinion, the Company has, in all material respects, an adequate internal financial controls system over financial reporting and such internal financial controls over financial reporting were operating effectively as at March 31, 20X1, based on _____ [for example, "the internal control over financial reporting criteria established by the Company considering the essential components of internal control stated in the Guidance Note on Audit of Internal Financial Controls Over Financial Reporting issued by the Institute of Chartered Accountants of India"].

For XYZ & ASSOCIATES
Chartered Accountants
(Firm's Registration No._____)
Signature
(Name of the Member Signing the Audit Report)
(Designation)
(Membership No. XXXXX)

Place:
Date:

Illustration 19.2: Separate reports

The following is an example of separate modified (qualified / adverse) audit report for an audit of internal financial controls over financial reporting and not impacting the audit opinion on the standalone financial statements of the company.

ANNEXURE TO THE INDEPENDENT AUDITOR'S REPORT OF EVEN DATE ON THE STANDALONE FINANCIAL STATEMENTS OF ABC COMPANY LIMITED

Report on the Internal Financial Controls under Clause (i) of Sub-section 3 of Section 143 of the Companies Act, 2013 ("the Act")

I / We have audited the internal financial controls over financial reporting of ABC Company Limited ("the Company") as of March 31, 20X1 in conjunction with my / our audit of the standalone financial statements of the Company for the year ended on that date.

Management's Responsibility for Internal Financial Controls

The Company's management is responsible for establishing and maintaining internal financial controls based on _____ [for example, "the internal control over financial reporting criteria established by the Company considering the essential components of internal control stated in the Guidance Note on Audit of Internal Financial Controls over Financial Reporting issued by the Institute of Chartered Accountants of India"]. These responsibilities include the design, implementation and maintenance of adequate internal financial controls that were operating effectively for ensuring the orderly and efficient conduct of its business, including adherence to company's policies, the safeguarding of its assets, the prevention and detection of frauds and errors, the accuracy and completeness of the accounting records, and the timely preparation of reliable financial information, as required under the Companies Act, 2013.

Auditors' Responsibility

My / Our responsibility is to express an opinion on the Company's internal financial controls over financial reporting based on my/our audit. I/We conducted our audit in accordance with the Guidance Note on Audit of Internal Financial Controls Over Financial Reporting (the "Guidance Note") and the Standards on Auditing, to the extent applicable to an audit of internal financial controls, both issued by the Institute of Chartered Accountants of India. Those Standards and the Guidance Note require that I / we comply with ethical requirements and plan and perform the audit to obtain reasonable assurance about whether adequate internal financial controls over financial reporting was established and maintained and if such controls operated effectively in all material respects.

My / Our audit involves performing procedures to obtain audit evidence about the adequacy of the internal financial controls system over financial reporting and their operating effectiveness. My / Our audit of internal financial controls over financial reporting included obtaining an understanding of internal financial controls over financial reporting, assessing the risk that a material weakness exists, and testing and evaluating the design and operating effectiveness of internal control based on the assessed risk. The procedures selected depend on the auditor's judgement, including the assessment of the risks of material misstatement of the financial statements, whether due to fraud or error.

I / We believe that the audit evidence I / we have obtained is sufficient and appropriate to provide a basis for my / our qualified / adverse audit opinion on the Company's internal financial controls system over financial reporting.

Meaning of Internal Financial Controls over Financial Reporting

A company's internal financial control over financial reporting is a process designed to provide reasonable assurance regarding the reliability of financial reporting and the preparation of financial statements for external purposes in accordance with generally accepted accounting principles. A company's internal financial control over financial reporting includes those policies and procedures that (1) pertain to the maintenance of records that, in reasonable detail, accurately and fairly reflect the transactions and dispositions of the assets of the company; (2) provide reasonable assurance that transactions are recorded as necessary to permit preparation of financial statements in accordance with generally accepted accounting principles, and that receipts and expenditures of the company are being made only in accordance with authorisations of management and directors of the company; and (3) provide reasonable assurance regarding prevention or timely detection of unauthorised acquisition, use, or disposition of the company's assets that could have a material effect on the financial statements.

Inherent Limitations of Internal Financial Controls over Financial Reporting

Because of the inherent limitations of internal financial controls over financial reporting, including the possibility of collusion or improper management override of controls, material misstatements due to error or fraud may occur and not be detected. Also, projections of any evaluation of the

internal financial controls over financial reporting to future periods are subject to the risk that the internal financial control over financial reporting may become inadequate because of changes in conditions, or that the degree of compliance with the policies or procedures may deteriorate.

Scenario 1 - Qualified Opinion on adequacy (and therefore operating effectiveness) of Internal Financial Controls over Financial Reporting

Qualified opinion

According to the information and explanations given to me / us and based on my / our audit, the following material weakness/es has / have been identified as at March 31, 20X1:

a) The Company did not have an appropriate internal control system for customer acceptance, credit evaluation and establishing customer credit limits for sales, which could potentially result in the Company recognising revenue without establishing reasonable certainty of ultimate collection.

b) [list other deficiencies identified]

A 'material weakness' is a deficiency, or a combination of deficiencies, in internal financial control over financial reporting, such that there is a reasonable possibility that a material misstatement of the company's annual or interim financial statements will not be prevented or detected on a timely basis.

In my / our opinion, except for the effects/possible effects of the material weakness/es described above on the achievement of the objectives of the control criteria, the Company has maintained, in all material respects, adequate internal financial controls over financial reporting and such internal financial controls over financial reporting were operating effectively as of March 31, 20X1, based on _____ [for example "the internal control over financial reporting criteria established by the Company considering the essential components of internal control stated in the Guidance Note on Audit of Internal Financial Controls Over Financial Reporting issued by the Institute of Chartered Accountants of India"].

I / We have considered the material weakness/es identified and reported above in determining the nature, timing, and extent of audit tests applied in my / our audit of the March 31, 20X1 standalone financial statements of the Company, and the / these material weakness/es does not / do not affect my / our opinion on the standalone financial statements of the Company.

Scenario 2 - Adverse Opinion on adequacy (and therefore operating effectiveness) of Internal Financial Controls over Financial Reporting

Adverse opinion

According to the information and explanations given to me / us and based on my / our audit, the following material weakness/es has / have been identified as at March 31, 20X1:

a) The Company did not have an appropriate internal control system for customer acceptance, credit evaluation and establishing customer credit limits for sales, which could potentially result in the Company recognising revenue without establishing reasonable certainty of ultimate collection.

b) The Company did not have an appropriate internal control system for inventory with regard to receipts, issue for production and physical verification. Further, the internal control system for identification and allocation of overheads to inventory was also not adequate. These could potentially result in material misstatements in the Company's trade payables, consumption, inventory and expense account balances.

c) [list other deficiencies identified]

A 'material weakness' is a deficiency, or a combination of deficiencies, in internal financial control over financial reporting, such that there is a reasonable possibility that a material misstatement of the company's annual or interim financial statements will not be prevented or detected on a timely basis.

In my / our opinion, because of the effects/possible effects of the material weakness/es described above on the achievement of the objectives of the control criteria, the Company has not maintained

adequate internal financial controls over financial reporting and such internal financial controls over financial reporting were not operating effectively as of March 31, 20X1, based on _____ [for example "the internal control over financial reporting criteria established by the Company considering the essential components of internal control stated in Guidance Note on Audit of Internal Financial Controls Over Financial Reporting issued by the Institute of Chartered Accountants of India"].

I / We have considered the material weakness/es identified and reported above in determining the nature, timing, and extent of audit tests applied in my / our audit of the March 31, 20X1 standalone financial statements of the Company, and the / these material weakness/es does not / do not affect my / our opinion on the financial statements of the Company.

Scenario 3 - Qualified Opinion on operating effectiveness of Internal Financial Controls over Financial Reporting and unmodified opinion on adequacy of such controls

Qualified opinion
According to the information and explanations given to me / us and based on my / our audit, the following material weakness/es has / have been identified in the operating effectiveness of the Company's internal financial controls over financial reporting as at March 31, 20X1:

a) The Company's internal financial controls over customer acceptance, credit evaluation and establishing customer credit limits for sales, were not operating effectively which could potentially result in the Company recognising revenue without establishing reasonable certainty of ultimate collection.

b) [list other deficiencies identified]

A 'material weakness' is a deficiency, or a combination of deficiencies, in internal financial control over financial reporting, such that there is a reasonable possibility that a material misstatement of the company's annual or interim financial statements will not be prevented or detected on a timely basis.

In my / our opinion, the Company has, in all material respects, maintained adequate internal financial controls over financial reporting as of March 31, 20X1, based on _____ [for example, "the internal control over financial reporting criteria established by the Company considering the essential components of internal control stated in the Guidance Note on Audit of Internal Financial Controls Over Financial Reporting issued by the Institute of Chartered Accountants of India"], and except for the effects/possible effects of the material weakness/es described above on the achievement of the objectives of the control criteria, the Company's internal financial controls over financial reporting were operating effectively as of March 31, 20X1.

I / We have considered the material weakness/es identified and reported above in determining the nature, timing, and extent of audit tests applied in my / our audit of the March 31, 20X1 financial statements of the Company, and the / these material weakness/es does not / do not affect my / our opinion on the standalone financial statements of the Company.

Scenario 4 - Adverse Opinion on operating effectiveness of Internal Financial Controls over Financial Reporting and unmodified opinion on adequacy of such controls

Adverse opinion
According to the information and explanations given to me / us and based on my / our audit, the following material weakness/es has / have been identified in the operating effectiveness of the Company's internal financial controls over financial reporting as at March 31, 20X1:

a) The Company's internal control system for customer acceptance, credit evaluation and establishing customer credit limits for sales, were not operating effectively which could potentially result in the Company recognising revenue without establishing reasonable certainty of ultimate collection.

b) The Company's internal control system for inventory with regard to receipts, issue for production and physical verification were not operating effectively. Further, the internal control system for identification and allocation of overheads to inventory was also not operating effectively. These could potentially result in material misstatements in the Company's trade payables, consumption, inventory and expense account balances.

c) [list other deficiencies identified]

A 'material weakness' is a deficiency, or a combination of deficiencies, in internal financial control over financial reporting, such that there is a reasonable possibility that a material misstatement of the company's annual or interim financial statements will not be prevented or detected on a timely basis.

In my / our opinion, the Company has, in all material respects, maintained adequate internal financial controls over financial reporting as of March 31, 20X1, based on _____ [for example, "the internal control over financial reporting criteria established by the Company considering the essential components of internal control stated in the Guidance Note on Audit of Internal Financial Controls Over Financial Reporting issued by the Institute of Chartered Accountants of India"], and because of the effects/possible effects of the material weakness/es described above on the achievement of the objectives of the control criteria, the Company's internal financial controls over financial reporting were not operating effectively as of March 31, 20X1.

I / We have considered the material weakness/es identified and reported above in determining the nature, timing, and extent of audit tests applied in my / our audit of the March 31, 20X1 standalone financial statements of the Company, and the / these material weakness/es does not / do not affect my / our opinion on the financial statements of the Company.

Scenario 5 - Adverse Opinion on Internal Financial Controls Over Financial Reporting – essential components of internal controls not adequately considered in the internal financial controls established by the company

Adverse opinion

According to the information and explanations given to me / us and based on my / our audit, the following material weakness/es has / have been identified as at March 31, 20X1:

a) The Company did not have an appropriate internal financial control system over financial reporting since the internal controls adopted by the Company did not adequately consider risk assessment, which is one of the essential components of internal control, with regard to the potential for fraud when performing risk assessment,

b) [list other deficiencies identified]

A 'material weakness' is a deficiency, or a combination of deficiencies, in internal financial control over financial reporting, such that there is a reasonable possibility that a material misstatement of the company's annual or interim financial statements will not be prevented or detected on a timely basis.

In my / our opinion, because of the effects/possible effects of the material weakness/es described above on the achievement of the objectives of the control criteria, the Company has not maintained adequate and effective internal financial controls over financial reporting as of March 31, 20X1, based on _____ [for example, "the internal control over financial reporting criteria established by the Company considering the essential components of internal control stated in the Guidance Note on Audit of Internal Financial Controls Over Financial Reporting issued by the Institute of Chartered Accountants of India"].

I / We have considered the material weakness/es identified and reported above in determining the nature, timing, and extent of audit tests applied in my / our audit of the March 31, 20X1 standalone financial statements of the Company, and the / these material weakness/es does not / do not affect my / our opinion on the standalone financial statements of the Company.

For XYZ & ASSOCIATES

Chartered Accountants
(Firm's Registration No._____)
Signature
(Name of the Member Signing the Audit Report)
(Designation)
(Membership No. XXXXX)

Place:
Date:

Illustration 19.3: Separate reports

The following is an example of separate modified (disclaimer) audit report for an audit of internal financial controls over financial reporting with / without impact on audit opinion on the standalone financial statements.

ANNEXURE TO THE INDEPENDENT AUDITOR'S REPORT OF EVEN DATE ON THE STANDALONE FINANCIAL STATEMENTS OF ABC COMPANY LIMITED

Report on the Internal Financial Controls under Clause (i) of Sub-section 3 of Section 143 of the Companies Act, 2013 ("the Act")

I / We were engaged to audit the internal financial controls over financial reporting of ABC Company Limited ("the Company") as of March 31, 20X1 in conjunction with my / our audit of the financial statements of the Company for the year ended on that date.

Management's Responsibility for Internal Financial Controls

The Company's management is responsible for establishing and maintaining internal financial controls based on [..................for example, "the internal control over financial reporting criteria established by the Company considering the essential components of internal control stated in the Guidance Note on Audit of Internal Financial Controls Over Financial Reporting issued by the Institute of Chartered Accountants of India"]. These responsibilities include the design, implementation and maintenance of adequate internal financial controls that were operating effectively for ensuring the orderly and efficient conduct of its business, including adherence to company's policies, the safeguarding of its assets, the prevention and detection of frauds and errors, the accuracy and completeness of the accounting records, and the timely preparation of reliable financial information, as required under the Companies Act, 2013.

Auditors' Responsibility

My / Our responsibility is to express an opinion on the Company's internal financial controls over financial reporting based on my/our audit conducted in accordance with the Guidance Note on Audit of Internal Financial Controls Over Financial Reporting (the "Guidance Note") and the Standards on Auditing, to the extent applicable to an audit of internal financial controls, both issued by the Institute of Chartered Accountants of India.

Because of the matter described in Disclaimer of Opinion paragraph below, I / we was / were not able to obtain sufficient appropriate audit evidence to provide a basis for an audit opinion on internal financial controls system over financial reporting of the Company.

Meaning of Internal Financial Controls over Financial Reporting

A company's internal financial control over financial reporting is a process designed to provide reasonable assurance regarding the reliability of financial reporting and the preparation of financial statements for external purposes in accordance with generally accepted accounting principles. A company's internal financial control over financial reporting includes those policies and procedures that (1) pertain to the maintenance of records that, in reasonable detail, accurately and fairly reflect the transactions and dispositions of the assets of the company; (2) provide reasonable assurance that transactions are recorded as necessary to permit preparation of financial statements in accordance with generally accepted accounting principles, and that receipts and expenditures of the

company are being made only in accordance with authorisations of management and directors of the company; and (3) provide reasonable assurance regarding prevention or timely detection of unauthorised acquisition, use, or disposition of the company's assets that could have a material effect on the financial statements.

Disclaimer of Opinion

Scenario 1 – Framework for internal financial control over financial reporting not established but does not impact the audit opinion on financial statements

According to the information and explanation given to us, the Company has not established its internal financial control over financial reporting on criteria based on or considering the essential components of internal control stated in the Guidance Note on Audit of Internal Financial Controls over Financial Reporting issued by the Institute of Chartered Accountants of India.

Because of this reason, we are unable to obtain sufficient appropriate audit evidence to provide a basis for my / our opinion whether the Company had adequate internal financial controls over financial reporting and whether such internal financial controls were operating effectively as at March 31, 20X1.

I / We have considered the disclaimer reported above in determining the nature, timing, and extent of audit tests applied in my / our audit of the standalone financial statements of the Company, and the disclaimer does not affect my / our opinion on the standalone financial statements of the Company.

Scenario 2 – Auditor unable to obtain sufficient appropriate audit evidence on internal financial controls over financial reporting but does not impact audit opinion on the financial statements

The system of internal financial controls over financial reporting with regard to one of the significant branches of the Company at _____ were not made available to me / us to enable me / us to determine if the Company has established adequate internal financial control over financial reporting at the aforesaid branch and whether such internal financial controls were operating effectively as at March 31, 20X1.

I / We have considered the disclaimer reported above in determining the nature, timing, and extent of audit tests applied in my / our audit of the financial statements of the Company, and the disclaimer does not affect my / our opinion on the financial statements of the Company.

Scenario 3 – Auditor unable to obtain sufficient appropriate audit evidence on internal financial controls over financial reporting and impacting audit opinion on the financial statements

The system of internal financial controls over financial reporting with regard to the Company were not made available to me / us to enable me / us to determine if the Company has established adequate internal financial control over financial reporting and whether such internal financial controls were operating effectively as at March 31, 20X1.

I / We have considered the disclaimer reported above in determining the nature, timing, and extent of audit tests applied in my / our audit of the standalone financial statements of the Company, and the disclaimer has affected my / our opinion on the financial statements of the standalone Company and I / we have issued a qualified (/ adverse / disclaimer of) opinion on the financial statements.

For XYZ & ASSOCIATES
Chartered Accountants
(Firm Registration No._____)
Signature
(Name of the Member Signing the Audit Report)
(Designation)
(Membership No. XXXXX)

Place:
Date:

Illustration 19.4: Separate reports

The following is an example of separate modified (adverse) audit report for an audit of internal financial controls over financial reporting causing a modified report on the standalone financial statements.

ANNEXURE TO THE INDEPENDENT AUDITOR'S REPORT OF EVEN DATE ON THE STANDALONE FINANCIAL STATEMENTS OF ABC COMPANY LIMITED

Report on the Internal Financial Controls under Clause (i) of Sub-section 3 of Section 143 of the Companies Act, 2013 ("the Act")

I / We have audited the internal financial controls over financial reporting of ABC Company Limited ("the Company") as of March 31, 20X1 in conjunction with my / our audit of the financial statements of the Company for the year ended on that date

Management's Responsibility for Internal Financial Controls

The Company's management is responsible for establishing and maintaining internal financial controls based on _____ [for example "the internal control over financial reporting criteria established by the Company considering the essential components of internal control stated in the Guidance Note on Audit of Internal Financial Controls Over Financial Reporting issued by the Institute of Chartered Accountants of India"]. These responsibilities include the design, implementation and maintenance of adequate internal financial controls that were operating effectively for ensuring the orderly and efficient conduct of its business, including adherence to company's policies, the safeguarding of its assets, the prevention and detection of frauds and errors, the accuracy and completeness of the accounting records, and the timely preparation of reliable financial information, as required under the Companies Act, 2013.

Auditors' Responsibility

My / Our responsibility is to express an opinion on the Company's internal financial controls over financial reporting based on my/our audit. I/We conducted our audit in accordance with the Guidance Note on Audit of Internal Financial Controls Over Financial Reporting (the "Guidance Note") and the Standards on Auditing, to the extent applicable to an audit of internal financial controls, both issued by the Institute of Chartered Accountants of India. Those Standards and the Guidance Note require that I / we comply with ethical requirements and plan and perform the audit to obtain reasonable assurance about whether adequate internal financial controls over financial reporting was established and maintained and if such controls operated effectively in all material respects.

My / Our audit involves performing procedures to obtain audit evidence about the adequacy of the internal financial controls system over financial reporting and their operating effectiveness.

My / Our audit of internal financial controls over financial reporting included obtaining an understanding of internal financial controls over financial reporting, assessing the risk that a material weakness exists, and testing and evaluating the design and operating effectiveness of internal control based on the assessed risk. The procedures selected depend on the auditor's judgement, including the assessment of the risks of material misstatement of the financial statements, whether due to fraud or error.

I / We believe that the audit evidence I / we have obtained is sufficient and appropriate to provide a basis for my / our adverse audit opinion on the Company's internal financial controls system over financial reporting.

Meaning of Internal Financial Controls over Financial Reporting

A company's internal financial control over financial reporting is a process designed to provide reasonable assurance regarding the reliability of financial reporting and the preparation of financial statements for external purposes in accordance with generally accepted accounting principles. A company's internal financial control over financial reporting includes those policies and procedures that (1) pertain to the maintenance of records that, in reasonable detail, accurately and fairly reflect

the transactions and dispositions of the assets of the company; (2) provide reasonable assurance that transactions are recorded as necessary to permit preparation of financial statements in accordance with generally accepted accounting principles, and that receipts and expenditures of the company are being made only in accordance with authorisations of management and directors of the company; and (3) provide reasonable assurance regarding prevention or timely detection of unauthorised acquisition, use, or disposition of the company's assets that could have a material effect on the financial statements.

Inherent Limitations of Internal Financial Controls Over Financial Reporting

Because of the inherent limitations of internal financial controls over financial reporting, including the possibility of collusion or improper management override of controls, material misstatements due to error or fraud may occur and not be detected. Also, projections of any evaluation of the internal financial controls over financial reporting to future periods are subject to the risk that the internal financial control over financial reporting may become inadequate because of changes in conditions, or that the degree of compliance with the policies or procedures may deteriorate.

Adverse Opinion

According to the information and explanations given to me / us and based on my / our audit, the following material weakness/es has / have been identified as at March 31, 20X1:

(a) The Company did not have appropriate internal controls for reconciliation of physically inventory with the inventory records, which has resulted in misstatement of inventory values in the books of account.

(b) [list other deficiencies identified]

A 'material weakness' is a deficiency, or a combination of deficiencies, in internal financial control over financial reporting, such that there is a reasonable possibility that a material misstatement of the company's annual or interim financial statements will not be prevented or detected on a timely basis.

In my / our opinion, because of the effect of the material weakness/es described above on the achievement of the objectives of the control criteria, the Company has not maintained adequate and effective internal financial controls over financial reporting as of March 31, 20X1, based on _____

[for example, "the internal control over financial reporting criteria established by the Company considering the essential components of internal control stated in the Guidance Note on Audit of Internal Financial Controls Over Financial Reporting issued by the Institute of Chartered Accountants of India".

I / We have considered the material weakness/es identified and reported above in determining the nature, timing, and extent of audit tests applied in my / our audit of the March 31, 20X1 standalone financial statements of the Company, and the / these material weakness/es has / have affected my / our opinion on the standalone financial statements of the Company and I / we have issued a qualified (/ adverse / disclaimer of) opinion on the standalone financial statements.

For XYZ & ASSOCIATES
Chartered Accountants
(Firm Registration No._____)
Signature
(Name of the Member Signing the Audit Report)
(Designation)
(Membership No. XXXXX)

Place:
Date:

Illustration 19.5: Separate reports in case of consolidated financial statements
Assumption:

The Group has:

- Certain components which have been audited by auditor/s other than the Principal Auditor and such component/s is/ are material to the consolidated financial statements of the Group. The auditors of such components which are Indian companies, have submitted report on section 143(3)(i) of the Companies Act, 2013.
- Certain components which are unaudited and such component/s is/ are not material to the consolidated financial statements of the Group.

The independent auditor of Consolidated Financial Statements

- Gives a clean opinion in respect of section 143(3)(i) of the Companies Act, 2013
- Discloses the aforementioned facts about the Components in the "Other Matters" Paragraph in accordance with the Announcement issued by the Auditing and Assurance Standards Board under the authority of the Council of ICAI in February 2014.

ANNEXURE TO THE INDEPENDENT AUDITOR'S REPORT OF EVEN DATE ON THE CONSOLIDATED FINANCIAL STATEMENTS OF ABC COMPANY LIMITED

Report on the Internal Financial Controls under Clause (i) of Sub-section 3 of Section 143 of the Companies Act, 2013 ("the Act")

In conjunction with my / our audit of the consolidated financial statements of the Company as of and for the year ended March 31, 20X1, I / We have audited the internal financial controls over financial reporting of ABC Company Limited (hereinafter referred to as "the Holding Company") and its subsidiary companies, its associate companies and jointly controlled companies, which are companies incorporated in India, as of that date.

Management's Responsibility for Internal Financial Controls

The respective Board of Directors of the of the Holding company, its subsidiary companies, its associate companies and jointly controlled companies, which are companies incorporated in India, are responsible for establishing and maintaining internal financial controls based on _____ [for example, "the internal control over financial reporting criteria established by the Company considering the essential components of internal control stated in the Guidance Note on Audit of Internal Financial Controls Over Financial Reporting issued by the Institute of Chartered Accountants of India (ICAI)".] These responsibilities include the design, implementation and maintenance of adequate internal financial controls that were operating effectively for ensuring the orderly and efficient conduct of its business, including adherence to the respective company's policies, the safeguarding of its assets, the prevention and detection of frauds and errors, the accuracy and completeness of the accounting records, and the timely preparation of reliable financial information, as required under the Companies Act, 2013.

Auditor's Responsibility

My / Our responsibility is to express an opinion on the Company's internal financial controls over financial reporting based on my / our audit. I / We conducted my / our audit in accordance with the Guidance Note on Audit of Internal Financial Controls Over Financial Reporting (the "Guidance Note") issued by the ICAI and the Standards on Auditing, issued by ICAI and deemed to be prescribed under section 143(10) of the Companies Act, 2013, to the extent applicable to an audit of internal financial controls, both issued by the Institute of Chartered Accountants of India. Those Standards and the Guidance Note require that I/we comply with ethical requirements and plan and perform the audit to obtain reasonable assurance about whether adequate internal financial controls over financial reporting was established and maintained and if such controls operated effectively in all material respects.

My / Our audit involves performing procedures to obtain audit evidence about the adequacy of the internal financial controls system over financial reporting and their operating effectiveness. My / Our

audit of internal financial controls over financial reporting included obtaining an understanding of internal financial controls over financial reporting, assessing the risk that a material weakness exists, and testing and evaluating the design and operating effectiveness of internal control based on the assessed risk. The procedures selected depend on the auditor's judgement, including the assessment of the risks of material misstatement of the financial statements, whether due to fraud or error.

I / We believe that the audit evidence I / we have obtained and the audit evidence obtained by the other auditors in terms of their reports referred to in the Other Matters paragraph below, is sufficient and appropriate to provide a basis for my /our audit opinion on the Company's internal financial controls system over financial reporting.

Meaning of Internal Financial Controls over Financial Reporting

A company's internal financial control over financial reporting is a process designed to provide reasonable assurance regarding the reliability of financial reporting and the preparation of financial statements for external purposes in accordance with generally accepted accounting principles. A company's internal financial control over financial reporting includes those policies and procedures that (1) pertain to the maintenance of records that, in reasonable detail, accurately and fairly reflect the transactions and dispositions of the assets of the company; (2) provide reasonable assurance that transactions are recorded as necessary to permit preparation of financial statements in accordance with generally accepted accounting principles, and that receipts and expenditures of the company are being made only in accordance with authorisations of management and directors of the company; and (3) provide reasonable assurance regarding prevention or timely detection of unauthorised acquisition, use, or disposition of the company's assets that could have a material effect on the financial statements.

Inherent Limitations of Internal Financial Controls over Financial Reporting

Because of the inherent limitations of internal financial controls over financial reporting, including the possibility of collusion or improper management override of controls, material misstatements due to error or fraud may occur and not be detected. Also, projections of any evaluation of the internal financial controls over financial reporting to future periods are subject to the risk that the internal financial control over financial reporting may become inadequate because of changes in conditions, or that the degree of compliance with the policies or procedures may deteriorate.

Opinion

In my / our opinion, the Holding Company, its subsidiary companies, its associate companies and jointly controlled companies, which are companies incorporated in India, have, in all material respects, an adequate internal financial controls system over financial reporting and such internal financial controls over financial reporting were operating effectively as at March 31, 20X1, based on _____ [for example, "the internal control over financial reporting criteria established by the Company considering the essential components of internal control stated in the Guidance Note on Audit of Internal Financial Controls Over Financial Reporting issued by the Institute of Chartered Accountants of India"].

Other Matters

Our aforesaid reports under Section 143(3)(i) of the Act on the adequacy and operating effectiveness of the internal financial controls over financial reporting insofar as it relates to __(number) subsidiary companies, __(number) associate companies and __(number) jointly controlled companies, which are companies incorporated in India, is based on the corresponding reports of the auditors of such companies incorporated in India.

For XYZ & ASSOCIATES
Chartered Accountants
(Firm's Registration No._____)
Signature
(Name of the Member Signing the Audit Report)
(Designation)
(Membership No. XXXXX)

Place:
Date:

19.2. Appendix IV: Illustrative Risks of Material Misstatement, Related Control Objectives and Control Activities (Referred to in paragraphs 77 and 100 of ICAI Guidance Note)

The Guidance Note provides illustrative work paper templates for testing controls in a CD for the following account balances and processes:

1. Cash/Bank Balances
2. Prepaid Expenses
3. Trade Receivables
4. Inventory
5. Fixed Assets
6. Goodwill and Intangible Assets
7. Trade payables
8. Provision for expenses
9. Loans/Borrowings
10. Employee Benefits
11. Income Taxes
12. Deferred Taxes
13. Provision for Income taxes/Advance Income taxes
14. Share Capital
15. Revenue from Operations
16. Cost of Sales
17. Depreciation/ Amortisation and Other Expenses
18. Finance Cost
19. Journal Entries
20. Financial Reporting

19.3. Appendix V: Examples of Control deficiencies

Examples of Deficiencies in the Design of Controls	• Inadequate design of internal control over the preparation of the financial statements being audited.
	• Inadequate design of internal control over a significant account or process.
	• Inadequate documentation of the components of internal control.
	• Insufficient control consciousness within the organization, for example, the tone at the top and the control environment.
	• Absent or inadequate segregation of duties within a significant account or process.
	• Absent or inadequate controls over the safeguarding of assets (this applies to controls that the auditor determines would be necessary for effective internal control over financial reporting).
	• Inadequate design of information technology (IT) general and application controls that prevent the information system from providing complete and accurate information consistent with financial reporting objectives and current needs.
	• Employees or management who lack the qualifications and training to fulfill their assigned functions. For example, in an

	entity that prepares financial statements in accordance with generally accepted accounting principles, the person responsible for the accounting and reporting function lacks the skills and knowledge to apply generally accepted accounting principles in recording the entity's financial transactions or preparing its financial statements. • Inadequate design of monitoring controls used to assess the design and operating effectiveness of the entity's internal control over time. • The absence of an internal process to report deficiencies in internal control to management on a timely basis.
Examples of Failures in the Operation of Internal Control	• Failure in the operation of effectively designed controls over a significant account or process, for example, the failure of a control such as dual authorization for significant disbursements within the purchasing process. • Failure of the information and communication component of internal control to provide complete and accurate output because of deficiencies in timeliness, completeness, or accuracy, for example, the failure to obtain timely and accurate consolidating information from remote locations that is needed to prepare the financial statements. • Failure of controls designed to safeguard assets from loss, damage, or misappropriation. This circumstance may need careful consideration before it is evaluated as a significant deficiency or material weakness. • Failure to perform reconciliations of significant accounts. For example, accounts receivable subsidiary ledgers are not reconciled to the general ledger account in a timely or accurate manner. • Undue bias or lack of objectivity by those responsible for accounting decisions, for example, consistent understatement of expenses or overstatement of allowances at the direction of management. • Misrepresentation by client personnel to the auditor (an indicator of fraud). • Management override of controls. • Failure of an application control caused by a deficiency in the design or operation of an IT general control.
Examples of Significant Deficiencies	• Controls over the selection and application of accounting principles that are in conformity with generally accepted accounting principles. Having sufficient expertise in selecting and applying accounting principles is an aspect of such controls. • Antifraud programs and controls. • Controls over non-routine and non-systematic transactions. • Controls over the period end financial reporting process, including controls over procedures used to enter transaction totals into the general ledger; initiate, authorize, record, and process journal entries into the general ledger; and record recurring and non-recurring adjustments to the financial statements.

Examples of Material Weaknesses	• Ineffective oversight of the entity's financial reporting and internal control by those charged with governance
	• Restatement of previously issued financial statements to reflect the correction of a material misstatement. (The correction of a misstatement includes misstatements due to error or fraud; it does not include restatements to reflect a change in accounting principle to comply with a new accounting principle or a voluntary change from one generally accepted accounting principle to another generally accepted accounting principle.)
	• Identification by the auditor of a material misstatement in the financial statements for the period under audit that was not initially identified by the entity's internal control.
	• This includes misstatements involving estimation and judgment for which the auditor identifies likely material adjustments and corrections of the recorded amounts. (This is a strong indicator of a material weakness even if management subsequently corrects the misstatement.)
	• An ineffective internal audit function or risk assessment function at an entity for which such functions are important to the monitoring or risk assessment component of internal control, such as for very large or highly complex entities.
	• For complex entities in highly regulated industries, an ineffective regulatory compliance function. This relates solely to those aspects of the ineffective regulatory compliance function for which associated violations of laws and regulations could have a material effect on the reliability of financial reporting.
	• Identification of fraud of any magnitude on the part of senior management. (The auditor has a responsibility to plan and perform procedures to obtain reasonable assurance about whether the financial statements are free of material misstatement caused by error or fraud. However, for the purposes of evaluating and communicating deficiencies in internal control, the auditor should evaluate fraud of any magnitude including fraud resulting in immaterial misstatements on the part of senior management, of which he or she is aware.)
	• Failure by management or those charged with governance to assess the effect of a significant deficiency previously communicated to them and either correct it or conclude that it will not be corrected.
	• An ineffective control environment. Control deficiencies in various other components of internal control could lead the auditor to conclude that a significant deficiency or material weakness exists in the control environment.

www.ingramcontent.com/pod-product-compliance
Lightning Source LLC
Chambersburg PA
CBHW071409180526
45170CB00001B/32